The Powers of War and Peace

JOHN YOO

The Powers
of War and Peace

THE CONSTITUTION
AND FOREIGN AFFAIRS
AFTER 9/11

THE UNIVERSITY OF CHICAGO PRESS

CHICAGO AND LONDON

John Yoo is professor of law at the University of California at Berkeley School of Law and a visiting scholar at the American Enterprise Institute. From 2001 to 2003 he served as a deputy assistant attorney general in the Office of Legal Counsel of the U.S. Department of Justice, where he worked on issues involving foreign affairs, national security, and the separation of powers.

The University of Chicago Press, Chicago 60637
The University of Chicago Press, Ltd., London
© 2005 by The University of Chicago
All rights reserved. Published 2005
Printed in the United States of America

14 13 12 11 10 09 08 07 06 05   2 3 4 5

ISBN: 0-226-96031-5 (cloth)

Library of Congress Cataloging-in-Publication Data

Yoo, John.
The powers of war and peace : the constitution
and foreign affairs after 9/11 / John Yoo.
p. cm.
Includes bibliographical references and index.
ISBN 0-226-96031-5 (cloth : alk. paper)
1. War and emergency powers—United States.   2. United
States—Foreign relations—Law and legislation.   I. Title.
KF5060.Y66 2005
343.73'01—dc22
2005004222

♾ The paper used in this publication meets the minimum requirements of the American National Standard for Information Sciences—Permanence of Paper for Printed Library Materials, ANSI Z39.48-1992.

CONTENTS

PREFACE

As I was finishing the manuscript for this book, controversy arose over the Bush administration's legal approach to the September 11, 2001, attacks. The legal issues raised by the war on terrorism are novel, complex, and unprecedented. They range from the use of force, to targeting, to the detention and interrogation of enemy combatants who do not fight on behalf of a nation; this is a conflict that knows no borders. As a deputy assistant attorney general in the Office of Legal Counsel at the Department of Justice from 2001 to 2003, I participated in developing the Bush administration's legal policies in the war on terrorism. This book, however, does not attempt to mount a specific defense of those policies; in fact, I conceived of the book and began work on it well before I left for Washington, D.C. Rather, my purpose here is to explore the constitutional framework that gave rise to the policies. This is an important step of analysis that must occur before undertaking discussion of the substance of the war on terrorism. We cannot begin to evaluate the Bush administration's legal approach to that war without first understanding the Constitution's distribution of the foreign affairs power among the branches of government.

Nor can we discuss the legality of the Afghanistan or Iraq invasions without first identifying the scope of the president's commander-in-chief power to use force unilaterally and the tools at Congress's disposal to restrain him. Similarly, arguing over whether the Geneva Conventions apply to terrorists may prove fruitless without first unpacking the Constitution's allocation of the power to interpret treaties among the president, Senate, Congress, and the courts. To debate these issues without understanding their constitutional context would be akin to arguing about government policy toward speech without knowing the standards established by the First Amendment.

This book proposes a constitutional theory of the foreign affairs power that differs, at times sharply, from the conventional academic wisdom but that describes more accurately the actual practice of the three branches of government. More than a decade has passed since major legal works about the war and treaty powers appeared: John Hart Ely's *War and Responsibility* (1993), Thomas Franck's *Political Questions/Judicial Answers* (1992), Michael Glennon's *Constitutional Diplomacy* (1990), and Harold Koh's *National Security Constitution* (1990). They adopted similar constitutional frameworks and responded to the same geopolitical environment. Arguing that all uses of force abroad, except those in self-defense, must be pre-approved by Congress, these scholars, some of the leading lights of the American legal academy, criticized U.S. military interventions during and in the immediate aftermath of the Cold War. They posited a similar partnership of equals between the president and Congress with regard to most other foreign affairs functions, such as making, breaking, and interpreting treaties. They also argued for an intrusive judicial role in overseeing this legalistic arrangement to keep the presidency within its restricted bounds.

I argue that the constitutional text, structure, and history lead to a different approach. Chapters 2–4 reconstruct the historical understanding of the constitutional text and structure held by the Framers by exploring the Constitution's eighteenth-century British roots, the first state constitutions and the Articles of Confederation, and the drafting and ratification of the Constitution in 1787 and 1788. These chapters conclude that the Constitution depends less on fixed legal processes for decisionmaking and more on the political interaction of the executive and legislative branches. It allocates different powers to the president, Senate, and Congress that allow them to shape different processes depending on the contemporary demands of the international system and their relative political position. The Constitution does not require a single, correct method for making war or peace, for making international agreements or breaking them, or for interpreting and enforcing international law. Rather, it allows the branches to cooperate or compete in the foreign affairs field by relying on their unique constitutional powers. Chapter 5 develops this approach in the context of

the war power, while chapters 6 and 7 apply it to the making and breaking of peace through the Constitution's handling of treaties. Chapter 8
explores the relationship between lawmaking and treatymaking. Chapter
9 concludes with some thoughts about the future. These latter chapters
show in more specific contexts how a flexible decisionmaking system allows the political branches of government to shape more flexible policies
for the international political system of their time.

At the time such leading scholarly works as those mentioned above
were written, the nature of war continued to be thought of as occurring
solely between nation-states. The Persian Gulf War had just witnessed an
American-led coalition's defeat of Iraq's grab for Kuwait—a traditional
war over territory fought by the regular armed forces of nation-states.
Nation-states were presumed to be both rational and susceptible to various levels of coercion, with force often being used only as a last resort.
Warfare, if it were to come, would take predictable forms with clearly
identified armed forces seeking to take control over territory and civilian populations. In 1993, the military strength and economic size of the
United States had begun to so outdistance its nearest competitors that
American thinkers may well have assumed that there were no significant
military threats on the horizon. The Soviet Union's dissolution seemed
to render hypothetical what had been the most compelling case against a
requirement of ex ante congressional approval for military hostilities: the
need for swift presidential action to respond to a Soviet nuclear first strike.
The disappearance of the threat of a war that could directly harm American national security allowed policymakers and intellectuals the luxury to
envision a future in which they could reduce the overall level of international armed conflict. In such an environment, a constitutional model that
required the approval of multiple institutions before the United States
could use force may have made some sense.

The world after September 11, 2001, however, is very different. It is
no longer clear that the United States must seek to reduce the amount
of warfare, and it certainly is no longer clear that the constitutional system ought to be fixed so as to make it difficult to use force. Rather than
disappearing from the world, the threat of war may well be increasing.
Threats now come from at least three primary sources: the easy availability
of the knowledge and technology to create weapons of mass destruction
(WMD); the emergence of rogue nations; and the rise of international

terrorism of the kind represented by the al Qaeda terrorist organization. Because of these developments, the United States may no longer have the luxury of assuming that military conflict is a thing of the past, and the need to use force may actually be dramatically higher than before. In particular, the emergence of direct threats to the United States that are more difficult to detect and prevent may demand that the United States undertake preemptive military action to prevent these threats from coming to fruition. The costs of inaction, for example, by allowing the vetoes of multiple decisionmakers to block warmaking, could entail much higher costs than scholars in the 1990s had envisioned. At the time of the Cold War, the costs to American national security of refraining from the use of force in places like Haiti, Somalia, or Kosovo would have appeared negligible. The September 11, 2001, terrorist attacks, however, demonstrate that the costs of inaction can be extremely high—the possibility of a direct attack on the United States and the deaths of thousands of civilians.

These new threats to American national security, driven by changes in the international environment, should change the way we think about the relationship between the process and substance of the warmaking system. The scholarly consensus of the 1990s might have been more appropriate at the end of the Cold War, when conventional warfare between nation-states remained the chief focus of concern and few threats seemed to challenge American national security. The international system allowed the United States to choose a warmaking system that placed a premium on consensus, time for deliberation, and the approval of multiple institutions.

If, however, the nature and the level of threats are increasing, and military force unfortunately remains the most effective means for responding to those threats, then it makes little sense to commit our political system to a single method for making war. At the very least it seems clear that we should not adopt a warmaking process that contains a built-in presumption against using force abroad. Earlier scholarly approaches assumed that in the absence of government action peace would generally be the default state. The events of September 11 strongly suggest that this assumption is no longer realistic. The United States must have the option to use force earlier and more quickly than in the past. This book proposes that we understand our Constitution's allocation of the foreign affairs power to permit a flexible decisionmaking system that can respond to such sweeping changes in the international system and in America's national security posture.

I have accumulated a number of debts over the years in completing this project. Akhil Amar first taught me constitutional history, Harold Koh sparked my interest in foreign affairs and the Constitution, and Peter Schuck showed me the importance of understanding politics for understanding law. Laurence Silberman showed me how the worlds of law and national security work in practice. My colleagues David Caron, Jesse Choper, Andrew Guzman, Sandy Kadish, Laurent Mayali, Paul Mishkin, and Howard Shelanski have been tireless readers and advisers on different ideas and portions of the manuscript. A wide group of colleagues and friends at other institutions have commented on different chapters in the guise of drafts of articles. In particular, I would like to thank Curt Bradley, Brad Clark, Viet Dinh, Bill Eskridge, Jack Goldsmith, John Manning, Sai Prakash, and Adrian Vermeule for all their suggestions and criticisms. My colleagues near and far may not have all agreed with me, but they all helped make this work better.

I have been lucky to have had the research assistance of some fine students at Boalt Hall: Jason Beutler, Nick Ganjei, David Kaye, Jin Kim, Eric Lai, Will Trachman, and Michael Zara. I also thank the editors of the following law reviews, which gave me the chance to try out some ideas in a tentative form: the *California Law Review* (chapters 4 and 6),[1] the *Chicago Law Review* (chapter 5),[2] the *Columbia Law Review* (chapter 7),[3] the *Michigan Law Review* (chapter 8),[4] and the *Pennsylvania Law Review* (chapter 9).[5] I have also learned a great deal from other foreign affairs scholars who have written comments or responses to these articles, including Lou Fisher, Marty Flaherty, Mike Ramsey, Bill Treanor, Michael Van Alstine, and Carlos Vázquez.

I also owe important debts to the institutions that contributed time and place for the book's writing. The law school at the George Washington University and the John M. Olin Foundation provided a sabbatical to start this book. The American Enterprise Institute and its president, Chris De-Muth, and the Rockefeller Foundation and its wonderful research center at Bellagio, Italy, provided me a place to finish it. My two years working with the outstanding attorneys of the Office of Legal Counsel at the Department of Justice helped me think through the practical implications of my theories. The Boalt Hall School of Law of the University of California, Berkeley, its students and faculty, and its four recent deans—Herma Hill Kay, John Dwyer, Bob Berring, and Chris Edley—provided my intellectual home for the last ten years during which time the initial ideas for this book grew. I cannot imagine having better editors than John Tryneski, Leslie Keros, and David Bemelmans of the University of Chicago Press, who made a number of critical suggestions that greatly improved the book's content and organization.

My greatest debts remain personal ones: to my parents, John Hyun Soo Yoo and Sook Hee Lee Yoo, from whom I first began to learn; to my brother Christopher Yoo, with whom I learned; and to my wonderful wife, Elsa Arnett, from whom I am grateful to learn something new every day.

1

INTRODUCTION

The end of the millennium neither brought a halt to history nor ushered in millennial peace. Terrorism, genocide, major human rights violations, and the proliferation of weapons of mass destruction (WMD) are among the urgent new threats that have arisen over the past ten years. The United States has become militarily assertive, using force in Kuwait and the Persian Gulf, Somalia, Haiti, Bosnia, Serbia—and in Afghanistan and Iraq, where even "regime change" has been imposed.

Apart from the making of war, the United States has also actively re-aligned its international commitments. Once the cornerstone of international arms control, the Anti-Ballistic Missile (ABM) Treaty has been terminated. The U.S. signature, proffered by the Clinton administration, was recently withdrawn from the Statute of Rome that established the International Criminal Court, as well as from the Kyoto Accords on global warming. In 1999, the Senate rejected the Comprehensive Test Ban Treaty—the first rejection of a treaty by the Senate since the failed Treaty of Versailles in 1919. America has also avoided multilateralism by staying out of new entangling alliances, such as our 1997 refusal to join the convention banning the use of anti-personnel land mines, and by giving other countries notice that we will not participate in a new protocol to regulate biological weapons and small arms.

Complaints that we have gone completely unilateral in our approach to international affairs, however, are not quite true. The United States has formed ad hoc coalitions of allies for its most significant conflicts. It has worked with its North American Treaty Organization (NATO) allies in Kosovo, and with a broad international alliance to remove the

Taliban militia in Afghanistan; a smaller "coalition of the willing" has fought alongside U.S. forces in Iraq. The United States has invoked the Non-Proliferation Treaty and asked the International Atomic Energy Agency to address Iran's and North Korea's suspected development of nuclear weapons. In 2002, we ratified international conventions to suppress terrorist bombings and terrorist financing, instruments that created uniform international criminal standards and obligations for cooperation with other nations. In matters of trade, moreover, the United States entered into the World Trade Organization (WTO) in 1993 and led the current Doha round of negotiations to expand free trade in agriculture, intellectual property, and services. It also negotiated bilateral free trade agreements with Chile, Singapore, and Jordan.

In short, we are living through a time of remarkable change in the international system, characterized by globalization, the disappearance of the Soviet Union, the emergence of international regulation, the appearance of terrorism and rogue states, and the proliferation of technology. This has placed new focus, interest, and energy in the area of American law that directly touches on these developments—namely, foreign relations law. Indeed, many of these developments in America's relationship with the world have been questioned not just on policy grounds, but on claims that they are inconsistent with the U.S. Constitution. Leading constitutional scholars, for example, have contended that several recent wars with other nations were illegal under the Constitution, under international law, or both. John Hart Ely asserts that the post–World War II era has witnessed nothing less than "the disappearance of the separation of powers, the system of checks and balances, as it applies to decisions to go to war."[1] Thomas Franck, perhaps the leading American scholar of international law, has also accused presidents of waging unconstitutional wars. Congress has shirked its constitutional responsibilities, he says, and the courts' refusal to intervene carries a "powerful whiff of hypocrisy."[2] Members of Congress have attempted to stop recent wars in Kosovo and Iraq, and when their legislative efforts have failed have even gone to federal court claiming that the wars were unconstitutional.[3]

War is not the only bone of contention. Legal questions dog the heels of American activity in foreign affairs, including President George W. Bush's decision to terminate the ABM Treaty and President Clinton's decision, with Congress's approval, to join the WTO. Lawsuits seeking to overturn the judgment of the executive branch and/or Congress were filed against both. Two of our leading constitutional scholars, Laurence Tribe and Bruce Ackerman, sparred in a sharp debate before the Senate Committee on Foreign Relations over the constitutionality of the American entry into the North American Free Trade Agreement (NAFTA) and the WTO.[4] The ongoing war on terrorism, spurred by the September 11, 2001 attacks on the World Trade Center and the Pentagon, has raised further questions. In January 2002, for example, President Bush interpreted the Geneva Conventions as not applying to members of the al Qaeda terrorist network, a decision that some claim exceeds the president's power to interpret treaties.[5]

The questions raised by these events, however, are not new ones but in fact have been unresolved since the birth of the Republic. Struggle between executives and legislatures over the means of making war had been a persistent feature of British history leading up to the framing of the Constitution. Indeed, one can understand the break between Great Britain and the colonies as a dispute over whether the colonies could exercise a check over military affairs through its control over funding. Presidents and Congress have long since quarreled over the authority to initiate military hostilities, and several have argued in the past that only a congressional declaration of war may begin military conflict. Yet, as shown by the 1798 Quasi-War with France (no declaration of war) and the War of 1812 with Great Britain (declaration of war), the federal government from its very beginnings has used different constitutional methods for going to war.

President, Senate, and Congress similarly have never settled on the nature of treaties within our domestic constitutional system. A requirement that Congress implement treaties, rather than allowing the executive branch as composed by the president and the Senate for the purpose of making treaties, has been heatedly debated ever since the United States entered its first treaty under the Constitution—the 1796 Jay Treaty with Great Britain.[6] Chief Justice John Marshall found in 1829 that some types of treaties could not take legal effect within the United States without the approval of Congress.[7] Ever since, treaties at times have been thought to take direct effect in American domestic law, even though they are made by the president and two-thirds of the Senate, without the participation of the House of Representatives.[8] At other times, however, courts have considered treaties to only represent obligations between nations under international law, and have refused to give them effect in suits brought by individuals.[9] Can the President and Senate, acting alone, create obligations that have a direct effect on domestic affairs without requiring the consent of the full Congress? If they cannot, what is the point of the Treaty Clause and that part of the Supremacy Clause that makes treaties the "supreme law of the land"? And what are we to make of treaties, typically human rights agreements, to which the president and Senate attach declarations specifically denying that the treaties have any legal effect?[10]

A related long-standing question concerns the relationship between treaties and statutes. The Constitution appears to contain only one method, the Treaty Clause, for making international agreements, which creates a supermajority process requiring approval by two-thirds of the Senate. Yet, at least since the late nineteenth century, the nation has regularly entered into international agreements without going through the treaty process, and since World War II, the use of statutes to make international agreements has far outpaced the use of the Treaty Clause. The United States entered into two of its most significant international agreements, the NAFTA and WTO agreements, through this process rather than making a treaty. At the same time, however, statutes have not simply replaced treaties. Treaties still remain in use in other areas, such as reaching arms control pacts and making political or military alliances, where they are virtually exclusive. Perhaps statutes are necessary to implement the domestic aspects of our international agreements, as when Congress enacts a criminal law that fulfills an obligation established by treaty to punish certain conduct. Statutes have also been used in the past to supercede the obligations created by international agreements or have been used to terminate treaties. But it is unclear whether statutes can simply replace treaties as a form of making international agreements. The question of the self-executing nature of treaties and that of congressional-executive agreements are really different aspects of the same problematic relationship between treaties and statutes.

A third area of recurring controversy is the president's authority to interpret treaties. While the president has a limited authority to interpret domestic statutes, particularly those that delegate rulemaking authority to administrative agencies, we are accustomed to thinking that the predominant role in defining the meaning of a law rests with the other branches.

Congress gives meaning to a statute both by the words it chooses to use and the legislative history it creates in committee reports and floor debates. The federal courts interpret law in the context of deciding cases or controversies that arise within their jurisdiction over the meaning of a federal regulation, statute, or constitutional provision. With regard to treaties, however, presidents have exercised in practice much greater sway over interpretation, with often significant results. President Bush's interpretation of the Geneva Conventions, for example, determined whether al Qaeda and Taliban fighters would receive prisoner of war status, while President Clinton's reading of the ABM Treaty governed the U.S. research and development into a national missile defense.[11]

Again, however, this was not a new issue, but one that has its origins in the earliest years of the Republic. The very first international agreement signed by the independent colonies was the 1778 Treaty of Alliance with France, without which the new nation would likely not have prevailed in the war with Great Britain. When revolutionary France declared war on Great Britain and Holland in February 1793, the Washington administration had to decide whether the treaty's mutual defense clause required it to come to France's aid.[12] After heated debate between Treasury Secretary Alexander Hamilton and Secretary of State Thomas Jefferson, Washington issued the Neutrality Proclamation, which interpreted the treaty as not requiring American entry into the Napoleonic Wars. Washington's interpretation, and its implications for U.S.-French relations, sparked vigorous resistance from Jefferson and Madison and contributed to the beginning of partisan politics in the United States by encouraging the formation of the Democratic Party.[13] Our constitutional system has yet to settle the question of the allocation of power over the interpretation of treaties, now more than two hundred years old.

This book seeks to answer these long-running questions by carefully examining the text, structure, and ratification history of the Constitution. For the past fifteen years, American foreign relations law has been dominated by a paradigm developed in three books: Louis Henkin's 1975 *Foreign Affairs and the U.S. Constitution* (updated in 1996), Harold Koh's 1990 *National Security Constitution,* and Michael Glennon's 1990 *Constitutional Diplomacy.*[14] Their approach argues in favor of national power against any role for the states in foreign affairs and maintains that the Constitution requires the equal participation of Congress and the federal judiciary in national security decisionmaking. They draw support primarily from precedent, particularly the 1952 *Steel Seizure Case*, in which the Supreme Court blocked President Truman's order to take over striking steel mills during the Korean War.[15] In particular, they draw on the three-part framework set forth by Justice Robert Jackson's concurrence in that case, which argued that: (i) In cases where the president acted pursuant to congressional authorization, "his authority is at its maximum." (ii) When the president acts in the absence of any authorization in an area concurrently regulated by Congress, "there is a zone of twilight" where the outcome is uncertain. In the zone of twilight, where there is no explicit congressional authorization, the "actual test of power is likely to depend on the imperatives of events and contemporary imponderables rather than on abstract theories of law." (iii) When the president acts contrary to congressional wishes, "his power is at its lowest ebb."[16] Jackson's *Youngstown* concurrence hinged the legality of presidential power on explicit congressional authorization.

Following this approach, authors such as Henkin, Koh, and Glennon generally criticize unilateral presidential actions in foreign affairs that do not meet with legislative approval. They disapprove, for example, of executive branch warmaking that does not at least receive legislative authorization if not a declaration of war. They believe that Congress should grant approval of presidential actions such as interpreting or terminating treaties, but they also counsel deference when the executive and legislative branches agree, such as with the congressional-executive agreement. These authors generally reject the idea that judges should stay out of foreign affairs, and instead believe that issues involving war and peace are no more difficult than other constitutional questions addressed by the Supreme Court. Other important works, such as John Hart Ely's 1993 *War and Responsibility* and Thomas Franck's 1992 *Political Questions/Judicial Answers* agree on the basic framework: that the Constitution requires that the president and Congress share authority in foreign affairs and that the federal courts adjudicate disputes between the branches to enforce that principle.[17] Importantly, they share the assumption that the Constitution establishes defined processes for the regulation of foreign relations that makes them capable of judicial enforcement, much as the Constitution does for domestic affairs.

No prominent monographs in foreign relations law have appeared since the publication of these foundational works. In the intervening period, dramatic changes have swept the international system. While the end of the Cold War produced a decline in superpower tensions and the possibility of nuclear war, new threats emerged, including destabilizing humanitarian disasters, rogue nations, the proliferation of WMD, and now international terrorism. At the same time, new opportunities for international cooperation presented themselves, perhaps most notably the expansion of free trade via NAFTA and the WTO and the renewed relevance of international human rights. It should come as no surprise that this same period witnessed profound change in the field of foreign relations law. A new generation of scholars, including Curtis Bradley, Jack Goldsmith, Sai Prakash, and Michael Ramsey, among others, has questioned the dominant intellectual paradigm established earlier.[18] Sometimes labeled "revisionists," they generally seek to subject foreign relations questions to the same methodological approaches and arguments that apply in other areas of constitutional law, are reluctant to provide special constitutional treatment to foreign affairs, and are more amicable to analysis based in constitutional text, structure, and original understanding. They have been engaged by yet another group of young scholars, including Sarah Cleveland, Martin Flaherty, David Golove, Peter Spiro, William Treanor, and Carlos Vázquez, among others, who have defended, modified, and refined the arguments of the earlier generation of foreign affairs scholars.[19]

This book, which no doubt will be counted as a contribution to the revisionist side, cannot do justice to the many interesting arguments and nuances raised in these different debates. It can, however, propose answers to what might be considered the most important questions in foreign relations law—those involving war and peace. First, it will address war powers, and in particular the question whether the Constitution requires congressional approval of war or whether the president has the discretion to initiate military hostilities. Second, it will examine the methods by which the United States engages in peaceful relations with other nations, in particular the different methods for making international agreements. Third, it will discuss the enforcement of international agreements, with particular attention to their interpretation and termination.

Two distinguishing features, I believe, account for this book's different examination of these issues compared with earlier efforts. First, it argues that the Constitution generally does not establish a fixed process for foreign relations decisionmaking. Rather, it allocates different powers to the president, Senate, and Congress, which allows them to shape different processes depending on the contemporary demands of the international system at the time and the relative political position of the different branches. This stands in sharp contrast to the process for enacting legislation, which must be approved by both Houses of Congress and signed by the president as required by Article I, Section 7 of the Constitution, and whose subjects are carefully limited to those enumerated in Article I, Section 8. The Constitution draws a sharp distinction between the executive and legislative powers, which can be used by the president and Congress to cooperate, but which can also be used to pursue independent and conflicting foreign policies. This approach, I argue, makes better sense of the constitutional text and structure, which provide the political branches with far more flexibility in managing foreign relations than is commonly assumed.

Second, this book concentrates less on judicial precedent and more on constitutional text, structure, and history. It begins by telling the story of the place of foreign affairs in the development of the American constitutional system during the late eighteenth century. It describes how the founding generation understood the foreign affairs power, both as subjects of the British Empire and revolutionaries, and then as writers and ratifiers of a new Constitution. They conceived of the executive and legislative branches of government as distinct functions occupying different spheres in foreign affairs. While the bulk of the foreign affairs power was vested in the executive, the legislature retained control over the domestic effects of these decisions through its control over legislation and funding. Courts did not play a significant role. This was a flexible system for making foreign policy in which the political branches could opt to cooperate or compete. The Constitution did not intend to institute a fixed, legalistic process for the making of war or treaties.

On the question of war, flexibility means there is no one constitutionally correct method for waging war. The president need not receive a declaration of war before engaging the U.S. armed forces in hostilities. Rather, the Constitution provides Congress with enough tools through its control over funding to promote or block presidential war initiatives. As to treaties, the president, not Congress or the courts, has the primary initiative to make, interpret, and terminate international agreements under the Constitution. Nonetheless, Congress's authority over funding and law-making is a powerful tool that can easily frustrate unilateral executive policies. Should it so choose, Congress can force the United States to comply with international agreements that the president no longer wishes to obey. Similarly, Congress has ample power to check the making of treaties by the president and the Senate. Treaties may not automatically regulate matters within the authority of the Congress or the states under our constitutional framework. New forms of international agreements have arisen to resolve this problem and to give the missing legislative sanction to treaties. Such tools as the congressional-executive agreement, as applied to subjects under Congress's exclusive constitutional authority, tend to preserve Congress's role in regulating those areas, rather than ceding them to the executive branch.

It is the project of the remainder of this book to explain why our constitutional system does not dictate a single process for developing foreign policy. Rather, the Constitution allocates different powers to the president and Congress and allows their interaction to determine the framework for reaching foreign affairs decisions. Practice as it has developed over the last few decades generally falls within the range of permissible outcomes allowed by the Constitution. While the central focus of the book concerns the original understanding of the foreign affairs power and its application to questions of war and peace, it may be helpful here to make a few points about methodology.

First, it is important to be clear about the place of the framing history in the evaluation of practice. By "practice," I mean the existing processes and relationships developed by the three branches of government for reaching decisions on foreign policy. Practice is important for several reasons. Its role in understanding the constitutional text is heightened in the foreign affairs and national security areas, where there is an absence of judicial precedent.[20] As the Supreme Court itself has noted in a case concerning presidential power in foreign affairs, "the decisions of the Court in this area have been rare, episodic, and afford little precedential value for subsequent cases."[21] Without much judicial guidance, we should look for authority to the long history of interbranch interpretation and interaction. "Practice" also represents the reading that government leaders throughout American history have given to the constitutional text and structure in the foreign affairs area. It shows the ways that the political branches have adapted some of the Constitution's vague provision to real-world demands. Justice Frankfurter may have made this point best in the *Steel Seizure Case:* "The Constitution is a framework for government. Therefore the way the framework has consistently operated fairly establishes that it has operated according to its true nature. Deeply embedded traditional ways of conducting government cannot supplant the Constitution or legislation, but they give meaning to the words of a text or supply them."[22] Both the Supreme Court and the political branches have often recognized that governmental practice represents a significant factor in establishing the contours of the constitutional separation of powers.[23]

Several prominent scholars argue that government practice in foreign affairs departs from the original understanding of the Constitution. Thus, on the question of war powers, both critics and defenders of the current system, in which the president has often waged war without congressional authorization, maintain that the Framers intended Congress to approve all wars with a declaration or authorization of war first. Critics such as Henkin, Koh, and Glennon argue that the presidents must obey the original understanding, while executive branch defenders such as Eugene Rostow respond that the Constitution's original design cannot govern in the world of modern warfare.[24] As we will see, critics of practice usually base their arguments in the original understanding of the war or treaty power.

It is true, as we will see, that modern practice has established a working system of the foreign affairs power in such areas as war and the making, interpretation, and termination of treaties that runs inconsistent with prevailing academic theories that demand congressional approval and consent. In all of these areas, initiative has been concentrated in the presidency, with Congress usually playing an *ex post* role of approval through the power of funding or implementing legislation. Part of this book describes the framework established by government practice. My approach, however, is not to immediately challenge this framework as inconsistent with the Framers' original understanding of the Constitution. Rather, the book first asks whether modern practice falls within the bounds set by the constitutional text and structure. Generally, it finds that the constitutional text and structure provide far more flexibility to the president and Congress than has been commonly understood.

This book then turns to the constitutional history to determine whether it so clearly dictates a certain result that overrides ambiguity in the constitutional text or flexibility in the constitutional structure. I expand the scope of investigation to include not only the standard sources such as the *Federalist Papers* or the reports of the Philadelphia Convention, but also British, colonial, and early state practice, eighteenth-century constitutional thought, and the overall development of attitudes toward the executive power during the ratification of the Constitution. Following that methodology leads to the conclusion that the constitutional history often does not yield a clear and decisive command as to how the government must operate in foreign affairs. Rather, the original understanding suggests that the Constitution provides both president and Congress with sufficient tools of their own to check the actions of the other. This book views the historical evidence from the original understanding as important and perhaps decisive, but not as the sole avenue of analysis. It responds to those who have concluded that current government practices violate the original intent of the Framers by arguing that the history suggests that the Constitution is far more open-ended in the structure required for foreign affairs.

The Lessons of Practice

The approach just outlined helps explain several dilemmas that have plagued the study of the law of American foreign relations. It clarifies why the basic questions of American foreign relations law have remained open. As noted before, there has been no definitive settlement of the power to make war or the place of treaties in our constitutional system. In essence, previous scholars have sought to articulate a legal order of fixed rules to rectify the disorder of foreign affairs, usually by adopting the template set by our domestic lawmaking system—that is, Congress legislating, the president executing, and the judiciary adjudicating. According to this book's theory, however, the unsettled nature of foreign affairs does not arise from a systematic defect in the constitutional regime. The conflict among the branches of government over foreign affairs, I contend, is not a flaw in the constitutional design, but is instead its conscious product. In the area of foreign affairs, the Constitution does not establish a strict, legalized process for decisionmaking. Instead, it establishes a flexible system permitting a variety of procedures. This not only gives the nation more flexibility in reaching foreign affairs decisions, it gives each of the three branches of government the ability to check the initiatives of the others in foreign affairs. The deepest questions of American foreign relations law remain open because the Constitution wants it that way.

This approach helps explain practice better than competing theories, which have generally criticized practice as inconsistent with the Constitution. Variations in the different institutional arrangements over time, or between issues, can be explained by the wide discretion provided to the political branches, under my approach, to shape decisionmaking in foreign affairs as they wish. Take war powers, for example. World Wars I and II might have lead to the assumption that a congressional declaration of war is needed to trigger the president's powers as commander in chief. Formal declarations of war, however, have constituted the exception rather than the rule. The United States has declared war only five times: during the War of 1812, the Mexican-American War of 1848, the Spanish-American War of 1898, and the two World Wars. Yet, the United States has committed military forces into hostilities abroad at least 125 times in the Constitution's 207-year history, although many of these were small-scale actions to protect American property, citizens, or honor abroad that had little risk of significant combat.[25] In some cases, such as the Quasi-War with France in 1798, the Vietnam War, the Persian Gulf War, and most recently the conflicts in Afghanistan and Iraq, Congress has "authorized" the president to engage in military operations, but more often it has not. When President Truman sent American troops into Korea in 1950, he did not seek congressional approval, relying instead on his inherent executive and commander-in-chief powers.[26] In the Vietnam conflict, President Johnson never obtained a declaration of war nor unambiguous congressional authorization, although the Gulf of Tonkin Resolution expressed some level of congressional support for military intervention.[27] American actions in Grenada, Panama, Somalia, and Kosovo, to name a few, received no express congressional authorization.

Statutory efforts to control presidential warmaking have met with little success. In 1973, Congress enacted the War Powers Resolution (WPR), which prohibits the president from introducing the American military into hostilities, whether actual or imminent, without either a declaration of war, specific statutory authorization, or an attack on the United States or its forces.[28] The WPR requires that the president "consult with Congress" before sending the armed forces into hostilities and to report to Congress within forty-eight hours of sending the military into hostilities. Sixty days after the report, the president must terminate the intervention. Presidents have never acknowledged the WPR's constitutionality, and their recent actions have ignored its terms.[29] Congress could have stopped these wars, had it possessed the political will to do so, merely by *refusing* to appropriate the funds to keep the military operations going. In these conflicts, Congress chose instead to allow the president to take the initiative in warmaking but also to suffer the political consequences alone.

These examples suggest that the branches of government have established a stable, working system of war powers. The president has taken the primary role in deciding when and how to initiate hostilities. Congress has allowed the executive branch to assume the leadership and initiative in war, and has chosen for itself the role of approving military actions after the fact by declarations of support and by appropriations. At the same time, courts have invoked the political question doctrine to avoid interfering in war powers questions. Put less charitably, we have a system that Harold Koh describes as one of "executive initiative, congressional acquiescence, and judicial tolerance."[30]

In contrast to the single, straightforward struggle between the president and Congress over the initiation of military hostilities, practice with regard to the treaty power has emerged in several different dimensions. First, there is the question of the relative roles of the president and Senate in the treatymaking process, and whether the Senate's advice and consent function is reduced only to a limited review of treaties that have already been negotiated and signed by the executive branch. Second, there is the question whether treaties are "self-executing," and third, the issue of "interchangeability": are treaties the sole constitutional mechanism to make international agreements, or can the political branches use a statutory method instead? In each of these areas, practice has permitted the president to capture a large measure of independent initiative in setting and carrying out American foreign policy, while reserving to Congress significant ability to constrain the executive using its plenary powers over legislation and funding.

The first question arises when presidents argue that senators ought to defer to executive branch judgments on the value of entering an international agreement. Presidents, for example, make similar claims with regard to the appointment of executive branch officials and judges, which are regulated in the same clause of the Constitution. This deference argument, it seems, has never held much sway. From as early as the Jay Treaty to important agreements such as the Treaty of Versailles, which ended World War I, to the more recent Comprehensive Test Ban Treaty (CTBT), which seeks to ban the testing of nuclear weapons, the Senate has exercised its own judgment on important international agreements. Thus in 1794 the Senate made its consent to the Jay Treaty conditional on changes in the treaty's text, a practice now known as "attaching reservations," because it did not adequately favor American commerce in the Caribbean.[31] In 1919, the Senate went farther in rejecting the Treaty of Versailles, which President Wilson had negotiated with the leaders of the other great powers, because of suspicions toward fully joining the League of Nations. In 1999, the Senate rejected the CTBT because it believed that the United States, as the sole world superpower, ought to have the option to test and improve the effectiveness of its nuclear stockpile.[32] Questions about whether the Senate can exercise its own independent judgment on treaties seem to have been long settled by the political system.

The issue of the relative roles of the president and Senate with regard to treaties arises with more frequency, but with the same significance, in the interpretation and termination of international agreements. If the Constitution requires that the Senate be present for the birth of a treaty, it does not speak directly to its role during the course of the treaty's life and death. The latter issue, that of treaty termination, has long been the subject of interbranch dispute, but appears to have been settled in favor of unilateral presidential authority. Treaty termination has been fairly rare in U.S. diplomatic history, and no single method of termination has been consistently used. Nonetheless, at least as early as the Lincoln administration, the executive branch has terminated treaties without the consent of the Senate or Congress. President Carter terminated the Mutual Defense Treaty with Taiwan, and more recently President George W. Bush terminated the ABM Treaty and withdrew the signature of the United States from the Statute of Rome, which established the International Criminal Court.[33] Two studies have found that of the few treaties the United States has terminated, ranging in number from eighteen to twenty-six depending on who is counting, half were terminated by the president acting alone.[34] In the other half of cases, Congress has sometimes forced the termination by enacting legislation inconsistent with the international obligation, and on a few occasions the president and Senate acting together have terminated treaties.[35] Nonetheless, Congress does not appear to have ever prevented a president from terminating a treaty, and the courts have never intervened to reverse a presidential decision to withdraw from an international agreement.[36]

With regard to the power of interpretation, presidential control has proven controversial, but enduring. I already alluded to President Washington's interpretation of the 1778 Treaty of Alliance in the Neutrality Proclamation.[37] More recent examples include the Senate's efforts from 1985 to 1988 to prevent reinterpretation of the ABM Treaty to permit research and deployment of new, "exotic" forms of antimissile defense, and President Clinton's decision to continue U.S. compliance with the agreement, even after the other state party, the Soviet Union, had ceased to exist.[38] Aside from such high-profile conflicts, executive dominance of treaty interpretation has become a fact of life. Whether by constitutional intention or by its functional superiority in acting swiftly, secretly, and with unity, the executive branch controls the day-to-day operation of American foreign policy. The president and his subordinate officers develop the nation's foreign policy, communicate with foreign nations, negotiate international agreements of all kinds, and command U.S. officers abroad to take action. In the course of managing relations with the world, the executive branch must interpret treaties, and international law for that matter, on a daily basis.[39] Congress cannot monitor or participate in the many ways that the executive branch interprets treaties in forming and executing foreign policy, and it does not have any formal constitutional authority to issue binding interpretations on its own. It can, however, make its cooperation in foreign policy contingent on the executive's agreement with its views on treaties, such as by withholding funding from executive foreign policy.

Even on the difficult question of the domestic legal effect of treaties, the branches have developed a settled practice that emphasizes flexibility. Sometimes treaties are thought to take direct effect in American domestic law, even though they are created by the president and two-thirds of the Senate without the participation of the House.[40] At other times, however, courts consider treaties to be obligations between nations under international law, and refuse to give them effect in suits brought by individuals.[41] The political branches also pursue a course of non-self-execution, particularly when it comes to human rights treaties such as the International Covenant on Civil and Political Rights, the Genocide Convention, or the Torture Convention, by rendering them nullities as a matter of domestic law. In ratifying a treaty, for example, the president and Senate often attach reservations, understandings, or declarations that preclude treaty provisions from taking effect as domestic law and prevent the courts from enforcing them. The political branches attach such reservations to prevent treaty provisions from intruding into areas that are subject to congressional regulation or the reserved powers of the states.[42] Non-self-execution, however, is not so much a denial of the Supremacy Clause as a vital means whereby the Congress can check the executive branch.[43] By preventing the nation from carrying out the legislative elements of its international obligations, Congress can check efforts by the executive branch to achieve a certain treaty-based foreign policy.

The exclusivity of the treaty power itself is a last area where practice has given the political branches more discretion than that initially suggested by the constitutional text. In the early period of the nation's history, the treaty process held a virtual monopoly on the making of agreements.[44] In recent years, however, the federal government has used simple statutes—known as congressional-executive agreements—to enter into some of our most significant international obligations. Several recent agreements of significance, such as the U.S.-Canada Free Trade Agreement, NAFTA, and the WTO agreement, have undergone this statutory process, as have America's earlier entry into important elements of the global financial system, such as the International Monetary Fund and the World Bank. While in its first fifty years the nation concluded twice as many treaties as nontreaty agreements, since World War II the United States has concluded more than 90 percent of its international agreements through a nontreaty mechanism.[45] Under international law, either mechanism is sufficient to enter into an international agreement, but under domestic constitutional law this practice seems to run counter to the Treaty Clause. While some prominent scholars, such as Laurence Tribe,[46] suggest this represents an end-around the Treaty Clause, congressional-executive agreements also preserve Congress's control over the subjects that fall within its domestic competence. Hence, congressional-executive agreements, as we will see, usually are used in areas where implementing legislation would normally be necessary to execute the international obligation.

CONSTITUTIONAL TEXT, STRUCTURE, AND HISTORY

These results might initially appear inconsistent with the plain meaning of the constitutional text. Congress, for example, has the power to declare war. Shouldn't that provision require Congress's pre-approval for military hostilities? The Senate gives its advice and consent to the making of treaties. Should that not give the Senate an equal say with the president as to making, interpreting, and terminating treaties? The Supremacy Clause makes treaties the laws of the land. Why shouldn't all treaties take immediate effect as domestic law? The Treaty Clause provides the only explicit means for making international agreements. Should it not be the exclusive method for entering into binding obligations with foreign nations? Doesn't practice, in other words, run directly counter to the Constitution?

In the chapters that follow, I explore in detail the textual and structural provisions related to these issues. At this point, it is worth making some broader observations about the general allocation of the foreign affairs power among the president, Senate, and Congress. My argument is that the Constitution, in particular the dynamic manner in which it balances the executive against the legislative branches, can be read to permit existing practice. Subsequent chapters are devoted to reconstructing the framing history of the foreign affairs power, with special attention paid to the original understanding of the distribution of the war and treaty powers. They show that rather than foreclose the reading of the constitutional text and structure proposed here, historical evidence tends to support a more dynamic and open struggle between the executive and legislative powers over foreign affairs.

As Saikrishna Prakash and Michael Ramsey have observed, many of the leading theories about foreign affairs assume that the Constitution's text is incomplete.[47] Many significant foreign affairs powers, such as the authority to develop foreign policy, to communicate with foreign nations, to make nontreaty international agreements, and to break international agreements, are not specifically enumerated in the constitutional text. The Constitution "seems a strange, laconic document," says Professor Henkin, characterized by "troubling lacunae" that leaves "many powers of government . . . not mentioned."[48] The Constitution's silence has led many commentators to fall back on extraconstitutional sources, practice, or inferences from the Constitution's structure to support their preferred system for managing foreign affairs. Because of the "astonishing brevity regarding the allocation of foreign affairs authority," Professor Koh concludes that a "normative vision of the foreign policy making process," implicit in the constitutional structure, must govern. Analogizing to the constitutional structure governing domestic affairs, he argues that Congress must authorize policy and that the president simply implements it.[49] Professor Henkin believes that due to the Constitution's gaps, the management of foreign affairs should be determined in accordance with "the facts of national life [and] the realities and exigencies of international relations."[50]

Rather than reading the Constitution to suffer from such significant oversights, it is more fruitful to take a closer look at the text and structure to discern its deeper patterns. As many have observed since the time of Hamilton's *Pacificus* essays, the Constitution provides a general grant of executive power to the president. Article II, Section 1 provides that "[t]he executive power shall be vested in a President of the United States." As Justice Scalia has written, this "does not mean *some of* the executive power, but *all of* the executive power."[51] By contrast, Article I, Section 1 gives to Congress only those legislative powers "herein granted." In order to give every word in the Constitution meaning, we must construe "herein granted" as limiting Congress only to those powers enumerated in Article I, Section 8. Article II's Vesting Clause, by contrast, grants to the president an unenumerated executive authority. By analogy, Article III vests an unspecified "judicial power" of the United States in the Supreme Court and inferior federal courts, which some have read to give the judiciary certain core judicial powers.[52]

If we assume that the foreign affairs power is an executive one, Article II effectively grants to the president any unenumerated foreign affairs powers not given elsewhere to the other branches. This understanding is further reinforced by the structure of Article II, which in Section 2 grants the president the power of commander in chief as well as the power to make treaties with the Senate's advice and consent. These powers were specifically included in Article II, rather than subsumed into the general Vesting Clause, because parts of these once plenary executive powers have been transferred to other branches or have been altered by participation of the Senate. While the Constitution does not embody a pure separation of powers in which each branch solely exercises all functions peculiar to it, the Senate's participation in treatymaking and appointments reflects an effort to dilute the unitary nature of the executive branch, rather than to transform these functions into legislative powers. When the Constitution, for example, grants the executive a power that is legislative in nature, such as the veto power, it does so in Article I, not in Article II. Participation of the Senate in treatymaking does not transform treaties into legislative acts, just as its role in appointments does not make the appointment of officers legislative in nature.

There are two sources of support for reading Article II as vesting the bulk of the foreign affairs power in the President. First, as we will see in subsequent chapters, the executive power was understood at the time of the Constitution's framing to include the war, treaty, and other general foreign affairs powers. Both political theory, as primarily developed by thinkers such as Locke, Montesquieu, and Blackstone, and shared Anglo-American constitutional history from the seventeenth century to the time of the framing, established that foreign affairs was the province of the executive branch of government. Thus, when the Framers ratified the Constitution, they would have understood that Article II, Section 1 continued the Anglo-American constitutional tradition of locating the foreign affairs power generally in the executive branch.

Second, we might classify the conduct and control of foreign policy as inherently "executive" in nature due to practice and function. In terms of early practice, presidents from the very beginning of the Republic have exercised a general foreign affairs power, and the executive power has been understood to grant the president control over the conduct of foreign relations. As Thomas Jefferson, then the secretary of state, observed during the first Washington administration, "[t]he constitution has divided the powers of government into three branches [and] has declared that 'the executive powers shall be vested in the president,' submitting only special articles of it to a negative by the senate." Due to this structure, Jefferson continued, "[t]he transaction of business with foreign nations is executive altogether; it belongs, then, to the head of that department, except as to such portions of it as are specially submitted to the senate. Exceptions are to be construed strictly."[53] In defending President Washington's authority to issue the Neutrality Proclamation of 1793, Alexander Hamilton came to the same conclusion regarding the president's foreign affairs powers. As

Pacificus, Hamilton argued that Article II "ought . . . to be considered as intended . . . to specify and regulate the principal articles implied in the definition of Executive Power; leaving the rest to flow from the general grant of that power . . . ." Hamilton further contended that the president was "[t]he constitutional organ of intercourse between the UStates [*sic*] & foreign Nations . . . ."[54] As future Chief Justice John Marshall famously declared a few years later: "The President is the sole organ of the nation in its external relations, and its sole representative with foreign nations. . . . The [executive] department . . . is entrusted with the whole foreign intercourse of the nation . . . ."[55] Rather than a congressional ministry of foreign affairs, the president and his subordinates have exercised primary responsibility for the direction of foreign policy. A general glance through any standard diplomatic history text will show that presidents have historically played the leading role in setting foreign policy, while congressional influence has waxed and waned.

A functional analysis of the conduct of foreign affairs should also lead to the classification of foreign affairs as an executive power. If we assume, as many scholars do, that the international system is governed by anarchy in which nations seek to maximize their security and power (realism), or even that nations can cooperate in various ways to escape a prisoner's dilemma (institutionalism), then the demands of the international system promote vesting the management of foreign affairs in a unitary, rational actor. The rational actor can identify threats, develop responses, evaluate costs and benefits, and seek to achieve national strategic goals through value-maximizing policies and actions. Only a limited set of institutional designs will lead to the most effective exercise of national power necessary to achieve these foreign policy objectives. As Thomas Schelling has written, a nation-state would want "to have a communications system in good order, to have complete information, or to be in full command of one's own actions or of one's own assets."[56] While bureaucratic or political imperatives may distort policy, or domestic interest groups may at times overcome the national interest, a unitary rational actor remains an ideal to guide foreign policy. It seems obvious that the presidency best meets the requirements for taking rational action on behalf of the nation in the modern world. As Edward Corwin observed, the executive's advantage in foreign affairs include "the unity of office, its capacity for secrecy and dispatch, and its superior sources of information, to which should be added the fact that it is always on hand and ready for action, whereas the houses of Congress are in adjournment much of the time."[57]

One can see the influence of this ideal in the American legal system even before its formal expression in modern political science. Federalists defended the centralization of the executive power in the president precisely in order to enable the federal government to respond to the unknowable threats of a dangerous world. As Hamilton noted in *The Federalist* No. 70, "Energy in the executive is a leading character in the definition of good government. It is essential to the protection of the community against foreign attacks."[58] This point applies perhaps most directly in war than in any other context. "Of all the cares or concerns of government, the direction of war most peculiarly demands those qualities which distinguish the exercise of power by a single hand," Hamilton wrote in *The Federalist* No. 74.[59] "The direction of war implies the direction of the common strength," wrote Hamilton, "and the power of directing and employing the common strength forms a usual and essential part in the definition of the executive authority." It was for this reason, Hamilton argued, that the Constitution vested executive authority in one person, rather than the multimember executives of the Continental Congress and the states. Again, in *The Federalist* No. 70, he wrote: "Decision, activity, secrecy, and dispatch will generally characterize the proceedings of one man in a much more eminent degree than the proceedings of any greater number."[60]

Supreme Court opinions have followed this line of thought beyond the context of war. In *Curtiss-Wright,* for example, the Supreme Court famously observed: "In this vast external realm, with its important, complicated, delicate and manifold problems, the President alone has the power to speak or listen as a representative of the nation."[61] Quoting from a Senate report, Justice Sutherland further explained that "[t]he nature of transactions with foreign nations . . . requires caution and unity of design, and their success frequently depends on secrecy and dispatch."[62] Because of the unitary executive's perceived superiority to other approaches for addressing the dangers of the international world, the Framers maintained the executive's commander-in-chief power, its power to make (with the advice and consent of the Senate) treaties, and its power to conduct diplomatic relations. As Professor Koh describes it, "[h]is decision-making processes can take on degrees of speed, secrecy, flexibility, and efficiency that no other governmental institution can match."[63] As a result, both the structural advantages of the executive branch and the functional exigencies of international politics have led to the centralization of foreign affairs power in the president. The history of American foreign relations has been the story of the expansion of the executive's power thanks to its structural abilities to wield power quickly, effectively, and in a unitary manner.[64]

All of this is not to say that the president controls all aspects of foreign affairs. Clearly the Constitution rejected the British constitutional system of a complete monopoly for the executive branch over the conduct of international relations. Of course, the Constitution grants to the Congress and the Senate significant powers in respect to war, treaties, and international commerce. Some of these powers, most significantly the power to declare war, the Constitution reclassifies as legislative and transfers to Congress in Article I. Others, such as the treaty power, remain executive, but the unity of the executive branch is disrupted by the inclusion of the Senate as an advisory council of state. Still others, like the power to regulate international commerce, the Constitution gives to Congress alone for the first time and preempts state activity in the field. Thus, the executive branch cannot wage a total war without Congress's declaration of war, it cannot make treaties without the Senate, and it cannot regulate international trade without Congress. In these fields, the president cannot conduct a complete foreign policy without the approval and cooperation of other branches of government.

Congress's other constitutional powers, those that are not specific to foreign affairs, generate even more meaningful checks on the president. The Constitution clearly vests in Congress plenary control over all funding and the enactment of legislation. *Simply by refusing to do anything,* by not affirmatively acting to vote funds or to enact legislation, Congress may block presidential initiatives in our international relations. Without funding for the armed forces, for example, presidents will lack the weapons for war. Thus, the appropriations power and the power to raise the military give Congress a sufficient check on presidential warmaking. Even with today's modern conflicts, waged by America's large standing militaries, the great expense in conducting war requires the president to seek supplemental appropriations from Congress. In the course of approving these measures, Congress can consider fully the merits of war, and it can easily forestall hostilities simply by refusing to appropriate a single dollar.[65]

Congressional control over legislation also gives it a significant check on the treatymaking power. While Article II grants all of the executive power to the president, it grants him no legislative powers. Aside from the president's conditional veto, granted in Article I, the Constitution reserves the legislative power delegated by the people to the federal government to Congress alone. As Henry Monaghan has concluded, the constitutional text resists the notion that an "independent, free-standing presidential law-making authority exists insofar as the rights of American citizens are concerned."[66] Congress can refuse to grant the funding or enact the legislation necessary to live up to a treaty commitment made by the executive branch. It can effectively terminate a treaty by enacting legislation that causes the United States to violate its international obligations. This division of authority also indicates that the president and Senate cannot use their treatymaking authority, an Article II executive authority, to engage in domestic regulation that falls within the preserve of Congress's Article I, Section 8 authority. Just as the president could not issue an order under his inherent executive authority seizing steel mills during World War II,[67] which the Supreme Court concluded was a federal action that could only be undertaken by Congress's legislative authority, so too the executive branch cannot use the treaty power to issue domestic regulation on subjects within Article I, Section 8. As the Court said in blocking President Truman's order during the height of the Korean War, "[t]he Constitution limits [the president's] functions in the lawmaking process to the recommending of laws he thinks wise and the vetoing of laws he thinks bad."[68] Maintaining a separation between treaties and lawmaking preserves not just the executive branch's role in foreign affairs, but that of Congress as well.

Funding and legislation further combine to potentially restrict the president's other, unenumerated powers in foreign affairs. The president may wish to exercise the nation's vote in the United Nations or its interests in the World Bank or the International Monetary Fund, but Congress can respond by refusing to appropriate funds to any of those international institutions. The president may decide to terminate the ABM Treaty and begin construction of a national missile defense system, but Congress can refuse to fund research and development and prohibit further work on the project. The president may wish to expand free trade by lowering tariffs or agreeing to international standards for intellectual property, but Congress can refuse to change American laws to bring them into harmony with the executive's commitments. The president may be empowered to set foreign policy, to communicate with foreign nations, and to marshal the resources of the administrative state to meet his goals. But he has no immediate right to funds necessary to carry out his policies or legislation to directly regulate private people and their property within the United States, which can only be provided by Congress.

HISTORY: THE WHY AND HOW

The history of the framing of the Constitution provides the context for exploring the mix of practice, constitutional text, and structure. It may seem odd to study the most cutting-edge questions in constitutional law by turning the clock back two hundred years. What can framing-era debates reveal about peacekeeping missions and preemptive war, the global economy, and multilateral treaties? Americans drafted and ratified their Constitution at a time when it took several days for written letters to travel from Boston to Charleston and several weeks for news from Europe to reach America, when people and goods moved by horse and by sail, and when the most dangerous weapons were the front-loaded cannon and the musket.

While the political branches over time have developed a system to regulate foreign affairs, practice alone cannot provide the answer to its own constitutional legitimacy. And judicial precedent has been noticeably absent in the foreign affairs area. This is precisely why the history surrounding the drafting and ratification of the Constitution is of critical importance. At the same time, foreign affairs cannot be characterized as one of those areas that the Constitution's drafters and ratifiers had never thought about. America's relations with the outside world were the driving force behind efforts to reform the Articles of Confederation and replace it with a new federal government. According to historian Walter LaFeber, "nothing contributed more directly to the calling of the 1787 Constitutional Convention than did the spreading belief that under the Articles of Confederation Congress could not effectively and safely conduct foreign policy."[69] At the same time, the exact operation of important aspects of the foreign affairs power was left undefined by the Constitution. Consulting the historical materials allows us to better understand how, for example, the commander in chief and the power to declare war were expected to interact. History may provide a clue as to whether treaties were expected to take effect immediately as federal law or were to await subsequent implementation by Congress.

There are several other reasons why, as G. Edward White has observed, we have witnessed a "turn to history" in foreign affairs scholarship and constitutional studies generally.[70] The Supreme Court has turned to the original understanding of the Constitution in a line of recent separation of powers cases.[71] Cases on the balance of authority between the national government and the states have also drawn from the thinking of those who drafted and ratified the Constitution.[72] Other decisions by the Court indicate that a majority at least believe history to be relevant, if not decisive, on questions of constitutional structure and constitutional rights.[73] Some justices of the Supreme Court, such as Justices Scalia and Thomas, would make historical evidence dispositive on questions of constitutional interpretation.[74] Of course, other justices, most famously Justice Brennan, rejected historical investigation in favor of a "living Constitution" whose meaning changed as it adapted to new circumstances. This difference of opinion is mirrored in academia, particularly in the scholarship on the structure of the Constitution. Nonetheless, the debate over the nature of the unitary executive continues to rely heavily on the original understanding.[75] Most recent scholarship about renascent federalism has focused on the original intent of the Commerce Clause and the Tenth Amendment.[76] Both the Supreme Court and leading academics have come to accept that evidence of the original understanding of the Constitution is relevant to any discussion of the document's meaning. The difference among academics, for the most part, has been over how much deference to provide the Framers, not whether to provide any deference at all.

More importantly, many prominent scholars of foreign relations law anchor their arguments on the original understanding. On the question of war powers, for example, Professor Ely has written that "the 'original understanding' of the document's framers and ratifiers can be obscure to the point of inscrutability"; but "in this case," Ely says bluntly, "it isn't." He goes on to say that the inescapable conclusion is that "all wars, big or small, 'declared' in so many words or not . . . had to be legislatively authorized."[77] Professor Glennon, too, turns to history to show that the Framers intended the president's warmaking power to be "narrowly circumscribed" and that the Commander in Chief Clause conferred "minimal policy-making authority" except in the case of sudden attacks.[78] Professor Koh also believes that practice is inconsistent with the original understanding. "Although the Constitution's drafters had assigned Congress the dominant role in foreign affairs, the president's functional superiority in responding to external events enabled him to seize the preeminent role in the foreign policy process, while Congress accepted a reactive, consultative role."[79]

Regardless of the conclusions reached by these and other scholars, then, all rely heavily on the Framers' intent. Non-self-execution of treaties, Professor Henkin concludes, is "not what the Constitution provides or what the Framers intended."[80] The most thorough writer on the subject, Carlos Vázquez, says that the reason all treaties must be judicially enforceable is because the Framers thought so. "The Convention and ratification debates, and contemporaneous statements, show clearly that the Framers were concerned about treaty violations," he argues. "To prevent or remedy treaty violations before they produced these consequences, they declared treaties to be the 'supreme Law of the Land.' By so doing," he concludes, "the Framers intended to make treaties operative on individuals and enforceable in the courts in cases between individuals."[81] Recently, lawyer-historians such as William Treanor and Martin Flaherty have brought more sophisticated historical methodology to the study of foreign affairs questions while continuing to agree with these outcomes.[82]

Critics of historical approaches to constitutional interpretation, such as Jesse Choper or Paul Brest, argue that historical intent is impossible to determine, that one can always counter the quoted words of some of the Framers on a given issue with quotations from those on the other side.[83] This might be true, for example, in cases where the Framers simply did not think about a certain issue or engaged in a confusing and inconclusive debate about a constitutional provision. Foreign affairs, however, did not suffer from such neglect. Federalists and Anti-Federalists conducted an extensive, sophisticated debate (of which *The Federalist* is the most famous example) over the organization of the federal government, the separation of powers, and foreign affairs. Indeed, it may not be an overstatement to say that the Constitutional Convention was called not just to form a nation out of a collection of autonomous states, but to organize a government to respond to foreign affairs crises urgently besetting the new nation.

How did the Framers actually see the foreign affairs power? The three chapters that follow pursue a comprehensive approach to historical sources. I review legal texts and set them in the political and institutional context of their times. Of course, the Constitution is a legal document, and the phrases and clauses in its precursors, which were proposed but discarded or extended, can provide vital clues for interpreting the final phrasing of the document. An example may illustrate this approach. In interpreting the meaning of the Declare War Clause, we should not look exclusively at what a particularly influential Framer said about the provision at the Federal Convention. To better understand the historical context, we should look to the British constitution in the seventeenth and eighteenth centuries, state constitutions, and the Articles of Confederation. We should attempt to reconstruct what the British believed a declaration of war to be, and how this power was to be exercised; the Framers, after all, had been citizens of the British Empire for most of their lives. Examples of British warmaking suggest the processes, institutional relationships, and patterns of activity that the Framers understood would be created by adopting—or rejecting—British constitutional models. State constitutions can provide similar context concerning the meaning of constitutional texts and the governmental conduct that these phrases were expected to permit. Finally, the ratification debates record the formal expression of approval for the Constitution.

Approaching constitutional interpretation in this way has several benefits. First, focusing on the text employs history at an effective level of generality. It avoids the dangers of allowing pure intellectual history to scatter our analysis. Although we can use historical works about systems of belief widely held by Americans at the time of the Constitution's framing, such views are relevant only to the extent that they appear in the constitutional text. The Constitution distilled the abstract political theories and beliefs of the time into a workable system of government, but it was these concrete texts, and the political institutions and relationships to which they gave rise, that defined the foreign affairs power.

Second, this book focuses on the Framers' beliefs and actions in the ratification process because the Constitution was the result of a democratic political process. Ratification by popularly elected conventions gave the Constitution its political legitimacy.[84] What those who ratified the Constitution believed the meaning of the text to mean is therefore more important than the intentions of those who drafted it. It is the original *understanding* of the document held by its ratifiers that matters, not the original *intentions* of its drafters. On this point, I am following the distinction made by several scholars of the framing, among them Leonard Levy, Jack Rakove, and Charles Lofgren.[85] These scholars distinguish between "original intent," which refers to the purposes and decisions of the Constitution's authors, and "original understanding," which includes the impressions and interpretations of the Constitution held by its "original readers—the citizens, polemicists, and convention delegates who participated in one way or another in ratification."[86] If we are looking at history from the ratification simply to inform a contemporary decision regarding the Constitution's meaning, then all sorts of material, including the Philadelphia Convention debates and postratification interpretations of the Constitution, are relevant. For that matter, history well after the ratification could prove just as useful as a sign of consistent practice. If we begin, however, at the normative starting point that the Constitution's legitimacy derives from its popular ratification, a narrower set of sources becomes authoritative. Because the approval of the state ratifying conventions gave the Constitution its life, the understanding of those who participated in the ratification should guide our interpretation of the text. Speeches, pamphlets, and debates during the ratification will indicate what those convention delegates believed the text and structure of the Constitution to mean. My effort is to reconstruct the understandings of the delegates who participated in the ratification process of the state conventions and the leaders who debated the proposed Constitution in the press, rather than the intentions of those who drafted the Constitution but were not politically authorized to adopt it.

Conventional foreign affairs scholarship has not brought a systematic methodology to the study of the framing. Focusing on the views of famous Framers at the Philadelphia Convention cannot fully recreate the legal and political world of the ratifiers. In fact, such an approach may yield a decidedly distorted view of the Constitution. To understand the political, legal, and constitutional world of the late-eighteenth-century American, we can benefit from the outpouring of excellent primary and secondary sources on the American Revolution and founding periods that make such historical reconstruction possible and worthy of effort. The *Documentary History of the Ratification of the Constitution* collects, and continues to collect, into one place almost all of the extant speeches, debates, and pamphlets of the ratification period.[87] Over the last fifty years, historians have produced a rich trove of works on the intellectual origins of the Revolution and the Constitution, including Bernard Bailyn's *Ideological Origins of the American Revolution*, Gordon Wood's *The Creation of the American Republic, 1776–1787*, Forrest McDonald's *Novus Ordo Seclorum: The Intellectual Origins of the Constitution*, and Jack Rakove's *Original Meanings*.[88] In this respect, this book seeks to be sensitive to the broader intellectual context of the founding generation and the secondary works that attempt to recreate it.[89]

My exploration focuses on important historical factors that have hitherto been virtually ignored. Among these are British constitutional theory and practice in foreign affairs; the experiences of the states; changes made by the Articles of Confederation; and the arguments put forward in state ratifying conventions. I use sources that have not been systematically examined, such as the wider body of Federalist and Anti-Federalist writing, and attempt to show how the foreign affairs power fit into the larger intellectual and constitutional world of the Framers. This analysis finds that the Framers were part of a political world that viewed the power to fund (or defund) and to legislate as a critical check on executive powers in foreign affairs, a power that had been won after decades of struggle, first between the king and Parliament, and then between Parliament and the colonial assemblies. Failed state experiments in legislative supremacy led to a Thermidorean reaction that restored power to the unitary executive.[90] This yields a picture of the foreign affairs power very different than the image of a legalistic process in which both president and Congress must participate in certain constitutionally established ways at constitutionally required times. Rather, in foreign affairs the Constitution gave birth to a dynamic process in which each branch was given certain powers and was expected to use those powers, either in cooperation or in competition, to shape foreign policy.

2

THE EIGHTEENTH-CENTURY ANGLO-AMERICAN CONSTITUTION AND FOREIGN AFFAIRS

This chapter begins the work of locating the Constitution's textual allocation of the foreign affairs power within the legal and political context of
Anglo-American government in the eighteenth century. It sets the stage
for a more complete discussion of the framing period by examining the
treatment of the war and treaty powers in eighteenth-century political
thought and in Anglo-American political practice. I then proceed to explore the relationship between foreign affairs and legislation during the
revolutionary and early national periods. The following chapter traces
the evolution and definition of the foreign affairs power in the period of
the drafting and ratification of the Constitution.

These historical chapters begin the reconstruction of the original understanding according to the standards set out by historians. That reconstruction focuses on important factors that have often been overlooked in
previous foreign affairs works, such as the British approach to war powers and treaties and the discussion of the Constitution in the state ratifying conventions. In the process, I turn to sources that have not been
systematically examined in the scholarly literature, such as the great mass
of Federalist and Anti-Federalist writing, and attempt to show how questions of war and peace fit into the larger intellectual and constitutional
world of the Framers. This analysis finds that the Framers were part of
a political world that saw a sharp distinction between the exercise of executive and legislative powers in foreign affairs. Certain powers, such as
the war and treaty powers, were understood to rest with the executive
branch. Nonetheless, the framing generation saw the legislature's power
over funding and legislation as a critical check on executive powers in for-

eign affairs, one that had been won after decades of struggle, first between the king and Parliament, and then between Parliament and the colonial assemblies. Rather than establishing a strict legal process, the Constitution was understood to draw on the existing framework for the management of foreign relations, one that was dynamic and looked to the political interaction of the executive and legislative branches.

FOREIGN AFFAIRS AND THE THEORY OF THE BRITISH CONSTITUTION

To begin, we examine the legal, constitutional, and political background of the Anglo-American world during the eighteenth century. The Framers were former citizens of the British Empire; the constitutional and political history of Great Britain had been, until 1776, their shared history.[1] How legal authorities described the relationship between wars and funding, treaties and laws, and the history of constitutional and political struggle between Crown and Parliament, formed the context within which the Framers would have understood the new Constitution. Events during the Revolution and the Critical Period that followed also shaped the views of the framing generation on foreign affairs. This part of my analysis shows that the Anglo-American legal, constitutional, and political world recognized a sharp distinction between the power over war and treaties and the power over funding and legislation, with the former seen as an executive power and the latter vested solely in the hands of the people's most direct representatives. War and peace dealt with matters involving foreign affairs, while the funding of the military and the regulation of private conduct remained the province of domestic legislation.

The effort to determine the original understanding of the treaty power starts with the British constitution. In the area of foreign affairs, the Framers borrowed from English legal concepts such as "declare War," "commander in chief," and "Letters of Marque and Reprisal." Understanding what those terms meant in the British context, and how they worked in practice, will create the constitutional context for the Framers' work. The eighteenth-century British constitution was composed of a series of unwritten principles, expressed in practice, statutes, and understandings that had developed over the course of centuries. These principles, which defined the relationship between the government and its people, and between the Crown and Parliament, had undergone significant change during the seventeenth and eighteenth centuries. The meaning and significance of these constitutional developments would have been familiar to the ratifiers of the American Constitution. Also of intellectual importance was the political philosophy of the period, which often served as legal and constitutional authority in the British world. To reconstruct the mindset of the Framers, then, I first examine the thinking of seventeenth- and eighteenth-century political theorists on foreign affairs and law, and then turn to the political and constitutional struggle between Crown and Parliament and its impact on the foreign affairs power.

The British constitution provided two important precedents and models for the Framers. First, it set out the formal roles that the Crown and Parliament were to play in war and treatymaking. In short, the English system gave the executive leadership in the initiation and conduct of war and the making of treaties, while the legislature primarily played a role by funding the wars, enacting implementing legislation, and impeaching ministers. Second, within these boundaries, the British constitution provided the two branches with substantial leeway to shape a dense network of "subconstitutional" understandings, relationships, and practices governing foreign affairs. This network provided Parliament with a way to gain a substantial role in decisions on war and treaties, even though its formal powers extended only to appropriations and legislation. Both of these elements—formal power and real-life practice—would make a substantial impression on England's colonists in North America.

On questions concerning international law, the Framers first would have turned to the well-known publicists Hugo Grotius and Emmerich Vattel. Their treatises were a regular resource both for the Framers and for English legal authorities, such as William Blackstone, to whom the revolutionary generation looked for guidance. Of course, these writers could not anticipate the growth in the breadth and depth of international law that is now taking place. Indeed, they laid but the barest of foundations for the structure of modern international law, which at this time remained the preserve of relations between nation-states concerning basic issues of war, peace, and security.[2] Nonetheless, their views independently held importance for the framing generation and, filtered through Blackstone, took a place in their understanding of the workings of the British constitution.

Well known to the Framers, Grotius's *De Jure Belli ac Pacis* contained extensive discussion of both war and treaties. As treaties were used generally to end wars, Grotius linked the power to enter into treaties to the authority to make war. "Those who have the right of initiative in conducting a war have the right to enter into treaties for the purpose of ending it."[3] Distilling Roman practice, Grotius believed that wars and treaties were made by the "highest authority" in a nation, meaning the domestic power that exercised sovereign authority. In democracies, this power would be lodged with the people; in aristocracies, it would rest with a state council. According to Grotius, "in a war which is public on both sides the right to end it belongs to those who have the right to exercise supreme power."[4] Vattel, whose *The Law of Nations or the Principles of Natural Law* was well received in Britain and early America following its publication in English in 1758, followed Grotius's lead in viewing the war and treaty powers as unified in the sovereign authority of the nation in its foreign affairs.[5]

Significantly, neither Grotius nor Vattel discussed declarations of war as necessary to the initiation of hostilities. They agreed that a declaration of war was not needed either to begin or to wage a war, but rather served as a courtesy to the enemy and a definition of the status of their relations under international law. Declarations derived from the ancient practice of sending heralds to the enemy capital to announce that a state of war existed between the two nations.[6] According to Grotius and Vattel, a declaration of war played a dual legal purpose. First, it notified the enemy that a state of war existed between them. If a nation warned its enemy of future hostilities, its later actions would receive the protection of international law.[7] A declaration announced that hostile actions by its soldiers were taken under national aegis, and thus did not constitute piracy or robbery. Grotius commented: "[A] more satisfactory reason [for requiring declarations] may be found in the necessity that it should be known for certain, that a war is not the private undertaking of bold adventurers, but made and sanctioned by the public and sovereign authority on both sides; so that it is attended with the effects of binding all the subjects of the respective states . . . ."[8] Given this purpose, a declaration would have little use unless the warring nation announced the inauguration of hostilities to the other state and to its own citizens. According to Vattel, "[t]he declaration of war must be known to the state against whom it is made. This is all which the natural law of nations requires." Once the declaration is issued, the warring nations lawfully could attack the other's citizens and territory and seize the contraband goods of neutrals. Vattel remarked: "Without such a public declaration of war, it would be difficult to settle in a treaty of peace, those acts which are to be accounted the effects of the war, and those which each nation may consider as wrongs, for obtaining reparations."[9]

Second, declarations played a domestic legal role by informing citizens of an alteration in their legal rights and status. Vattel wrote: "It is necessary for a nation to publish the declaration of war for the instruction and direction of its own subjects, in order to fix the date of the rights belonging to them from the moment of this declaration, and relatively to certain effects which the voluntary law of nations attributes to a war in form."[10] Declarations instructed citizens of their new relationship with the enemy state, and informed them that they could take hostile actions against the enemy without fear of sanction. With a declaration of war in hand, citizens of the contending nations could "annoy" the persons or property of the enemy and lawfully keep captured vessels. Grotius, for example, devoted one of the chapters of *De Jure Belli ac Pacis* to "On the Right of Killing an Enemy in Lawful War and Committing Other Acts of Hostility." According to Grotius, a citizen of a nation formally at war if captured "cannot be treated as a robber, malefactor, or murderer . . . for being found in arms."[11]

Thus, a declaration of war served the purpose of notifying the enemy, allies, neutrals, and one's own citizens of a change in the state of relations between one nation and another. In none of these situations did a declaration of war serve as a vehicle for domestically authorizing war. The seventeenth- and eighteenth-century writers on international law never implied that a nation had to issue a declaration of war before waging hostilities.

With regard to treaties, Grotius argued that the symmetry between the warmaking and the treatymaking powers sometimes ought to be broken. In the case of treaties that called for the transfer of sovereignty, such as ceding territory, population, or possessions, the approval of more than just a nation's representative in foreign affairs was required. Due to the transfer of territory or citizens, Grotius considered such agreements to be an alienation of sovereignty that required the approval of the people of a nation through its legislature. "In order, therefore, that the undivided sovereignty may be transferred in a valid manner, the consent of the whole people is necessary." This "may be effected," Grotius observed, "by the representatives of the parts which are called the estates," or, in modern terms, the legislature. Even if the nation were a monarchy, it still must seek the approval of the people for changes in sovereignty, because the Crown held its power "as if in usufruct."[12]

Although both thinkers had sought to derive rules of international law and politics from natural law, Vattel pursued a more extreme position on sovereignty. Grotius, for example, believed that sovereignty sometimes could be vested in a king by its people, just as an individual could sell himself into slavery. Vattel, however, argued for a background principle that "true sovereignty is essentially inalienable."[13] According to Vattel, this rule was necessary because of the nature of civil society: people form into a society in order to live according to their own laws; a public authority is formed solely to administer those laws; government power cannot be transferred to another entity without the approval of the people who created the society. Therefore, even if a nation authorizes its leader to represent it abroad, it still cannot delegate to that person the authority to transfer sovereignty unless it has given its express approval. In the absence of an express delegation or a history of executive practice, "the concurrence of the Nation or of its representatives" is necessary in order to transfer sovereign powers.[14]

Vattel's and Grotius's early discussions of delegated powers in the context of treaties provide a useful analogy for our inquiry. Their conceptualization of an "alienation" of sovereignty is roughly similar to the rise of lawmaking authority in today's regulatory treaties. While modern agreements do not require the alienation of land or people to another government, they do call for something similar—a sovereign nation's transfer of control over conduct or individuals within its jurisdiction. To the extent that the works of Vattel and Grotius bear on this question, they suggest that international agreements that transfer sovereignty cannot be made by the unilateral actions of the executive; international agreements require the consent of the legislative power, which represents the people. As Grotius described it, "[I]n order to validly alienate any part of the sovereignty there is need of a twofold consent, that of the whole body, and in particular the consent of that part of which the sovereignty is at stake . . . . " Approval by the people of such a treaty is necessary, he believed, "since without its consent [sovereignty] cannot be separated from the body to which it has belonged."[15] If a nation is ceding part of its sovereign powers over a certain subject matter, then popular sovereignty, as articulated by Grotius and Vattel, would seem to require a majoritarian process to approve the treaty.

In addition to these authorities on international law, the Framers consulted theorists on constitutional structure. As warmaking and treatymaking involved domestic as well as international law, the Framers' thinking looked to authorities such as Locke, Montesquieu, and Blackstone.[16] As Professors Bailyn and Wood have shown, the ideas of these thinkers, combined with radical eighteenth-century English opposition ideology, provided the intellectual foundations for the American Revolution.[17] Together, these ideas describe the abstract forms of government that the Framers sought to emulate in part, and to reject in part. They also provide conceptions of the separation of powers against which we can measure current arrangements and arguments about the war and treaty powers.

Examining these sources indicates that eighteenth-century Anglo-American constitutional thought distinguished between the foreign affairs power on the one hand, and domestic legislation on the other, and that this distinction was integral to the development of the separation of powers. As historians have observed, the birth of the modern concept of the separation of powers occurred in Great Britain during the time of its civil war and Protectorate.[18] At this time, British political thinking began to move away from the model of mixed government—the ancient idea that government should represent different classes of society (monarch, nobility, and the people) that could check and balance one another. In its place, English writers articulated a rudimentary constitutional theory that sought to divide government by function, rather than by class. In his *Second Treatise of Government,* John Locke distinguished between the legislative power and the executive power, and then differentiated the functions of the executive power itself. Both powers derived, according to Locke, from human capabilities in the state of nature. The legislative power traced its roots to the individual's power to do as he pleased. The executive power found its origins in the individual's right to punish crimes against natural law. In a modern commonwealth, the legislative power included the authority to establish rules of conduct, while the executive power, a "power always in being," bore responsibility to "see to the execution of the laws that are made and remain in force."[19]

On foreign affairs, Locke identified yet another power, the "federative" power. Although individuals, when they form a society, are governed by its laws, they are still "in the state of nature with the rest of mankind."[20] Thus, a federative power was necessary to govern "the power of war and peace, leagues and alliances, and all the transactions with all persons and communities without the commonwealth."[21] While the federative and executive powers were usually vested together, Locke observed that they were "really distinct in themselves."[22] The executive power was concerned with "the execution of the municipal laws of the society within itself upon all that are parts of it," while the federative power focused on "the management of the security and interest of the public without, with all those that it may receive benefit or damage from." To separate the federative from the executive power would lead to "disorder and ruin," Locke predicted, because "the force of the public would be under different commands."[23]

Locke's reasons for differentiating the federative from the executive power, which no one had done so before, are important. He envisioned the executive power as providing an agency of government that, since it was always in being, could execute the laws that an intermittently sitting legislature would enact. Executives would be subject to the laws passed by the Parliament, which should establish rules to anticipate most domestic contingencies. Foreign affairs, by contrast, "are much less capable to be directed by antecedent, standing, positive laws" because "what is to be done in reference to foreigners," since it was dependent on their actions, "must be left in great part to the prudence of those who have this power committed to them."[24] Because foreign affairs are not easily controlled by prior legislation, when the executive acts abroad it is not actually executing the law. Instead, the executive is leading a united society in its relations with other societies, governed only by the law of nature.[25]

In this respect, the executive's performance of the federative function is similar to its use of the "prerogative." Locke argued that the executive employed the prerogative in cases of emergency "to act according to discretion for the public good, without the prescription of the law, and sometimes even against it." "Many things there are which the law can by no means provide for, and those must necessarily be left to the discretion of him that has the executive power in his hands, to be ordered by him as the public good and advantage shall require.[26] Such power rested in the hands of the executive, Locke believed, because the legislature was sometimes too numerous or slow to act or could not anticipate unforeseen situations. In Locke's eyes, the king must have the prerogative because he represented the interests of the community. Although potentially of great benefit, executive prerogative raised the "old question" of how to judge when the prerogative came into conflict with the legislative power. In such disputes, Locke wrote, "there can be no judge on earth." Thus, when the executive and legislature oppose one another, the branches must either work out a political compromise or "appeal to heaven."[27]

Locke's vision of the separation of powers suggests that the federative power, joined with the executive, would manage matters that were governed by the sudden flux of international relations. Because such activities could not be governed by legislation, they were given to the executive, which could act with discretion, flexibility, and quickness. At the same time, the legislative power would regulate domestic conduct, which could be governed by fixed, antecedent rules. This conclusion is consistent with Locke's broader goal of subjecting the executive to the rule of law, and of restricting the ability of the government to act in a manner "absolutely arbitrary over the lives and fortunes of the people."[28] Locke's separation of powers sought to subject the power to regulate individual conduct to general, "promulgated" laws, rather than "extemporary arbitrary decrees." Nor could the legislative power be exercised by anyone other than the people's representatives. "The legislative cannot transfer the power of making laws to any other hands; for it being but a delegated power from the people, they who have it cannot pass it over to others."[29] Use of the federative power to enact domestic regulations would have raised in Locke's mind the fear of uniting the executive and legislative powers.

Locke was not the only English political writer to influence the Framers. As Bailyn, Wood, and J. G. A. Pocock have shown, the revolutionary generation was steeped in the opposition "Country" mentality that challenged the "Court" policies of the Walpole administration.[30] Not quite the result of partisan conflict, Country ideology was a reaction to the Hanoverian establishment of a permanent executive ministry that oversaw the new financial and administrative system needed to manage Britain's expensive wars and its national debt. Polemicists such as John Trenchard and Thomas Gordon, the authors of the popular *Cato's Letters,* interpreted these developments as an effort by the Crown and its ministers to corrupt the mixed constitution, which had maintained the liberties of the people by balancing power against power.[31] A power-grabbing ministry used bribery, the sale of offices, costly wars, a standing army, and heavier taxes and public debts to sap the independence of Parliament, oppress the people, and enrich the upper classes. Such methods allowed the Crown to engage in an end-run around the checks and balances of the ancient constitution, and gave it the power to erode Parliament's ability to defend the rights of the people. In response, Country writers urged a return to simpler government, with less bureaucracy and war, in which Parliament recaptured its independence through control over funding and legislation.

Locke and English opposition thought reached the Framers both directly and through the writings of Charles Louis de Secondat, Baron Montesquieu. Montesquieu is the thinker most cited by Federalists and Anti-Federalists in the 1780s.[32] In the field of foreign affairs, Montesquieu closely followed Locke in maintaining a line between matters of war and peace, on the one hand, and domestic legislation on the other. His famous discussion of the English constitution in *Spirit of the Laws* begins with the declaration that "[i]n every government there are three sorts of powers: the legislative; the executive in respect to things dependant on the law of nations; and the executive in regard to matters that depend on the civil law."[33] Montesquieu adopted Locke's understanding of the executive power as composed of a foreign affairs power (Locke's federative power) and a domestic responsibility to execute the law. Under the foreign affairs power, Montesquieu observed, the executive "makes peace or war, sends or receives embassies, establishes the public security, and provides against invasions."[34]

Legislative power, in contrast, encompasses the authority to declare the "voice of the nation" and the rules of conduct that citizens owe one another. Apart from establishing the domestic regulations that bound society, the legislature also maintains a check on the executive through its funding power, particularly in the area of foreign affairs. While Montesquieu's major innovation in the separation of powers was an independent judiciary, which apparently was to have no role in foreign affairs, he wrote little that altered Locke's basic vision of a federative power—a power distinct from the legislature's regulation of domestic conduct.

While following Locke in classifying government functions, Montesquieu also sought to give the executive and legislature checks on each another. In military affairs, Montesquieu argued that the executive should possess exclusive control over the army. "Once an army is established, it ought not to depend immediately on the legislative, but on the executive power; and this from the very nature of the thing; its business consisting more in action than in deliberation."[35] The legislature, however, exercised two checks on executive authority. First, the legislature could terminate the funding for the military. Praising the British practice of annually voting military appropriations, Montesquieu wrote: "If the legislative power was to settle the subsidies, not from year to year, but for ever, it would run the risk of losing its liberty, because the executive power would no longer be dependent."[36] Second, the legislature could terminate authorization for the army: "The legislative power should have a right to disband [a standing army] as soon as it pleased."[37] In discussing foreign affairs, as in separation of powers theory generally, Montesquieu carried Locke further by joining functional separation with checks and balances.

As Locke had acknowledged, the federative power was fused often—if not always—with the executive power because both functions required quick, decisive action. In his *Commentaries on the Laws of England,* William Blackstone took Locke one more step by declaring that the conduct of foreign affairs was purely executive in nature. In fact, it became the quintessential executive function. Initially, Blackstone had followed Locke's emphasis on the functional superiority of the executive as the reason for vesting the war and treaty powers in the Crown. Because "[i]t is impossible that the individuals of state, in their collective capacity, can transact the affairs of that state with another community equally numerous as themselves," Blackstone observed, "[w]ith regard to foreign concerns, the sovereign is the delegate or representative of his people."[38] Hence, the people vested their foreign affairs power in the king because "[u]nanimity must be wanting to their measures, and strength to the execution of their counsels."[39]

Blackstone employed similar functional reasoning in explaining the Crown's sole control over the military, declaring war, and negotiating with foreign nations. He envisioned an absolute power for the executive in matters of war and peace. The English jurist defended the king's powers in matters of peace and war on international and natural law principles, rather than on just history and tradition:

> [T]he king has also the sole prerogative of making war and peace. For it is held by all the writers on the law of nature and nations, that the right of making war, which by nature subsisted in every individual, is given up by all private persons that enter into society, and is vested in the sovereign power: and this right is given up not only by individuals, but even by the [e]ntire body of people, that are under the dominion of a sovereign. It would indeed be extremely improper, that any number of subjects should have the power of binding the supreme magistrate, and putting him against his will in a state of war.[40]

Primacy in making war and peace required that the executive possess the lion's share of the war powers. Thus, Blackstone stated that the king is the "generalissimo, or the first in military command, within the kingdom." As with the treaty power, this aspect of the war power devolves to the king because of his role as the sovereign representative and protector of the people and because "united strength in the best and most effectual manner" is exercised by a monarch. His capacity as "general of the kingdom" also gives the king "the sole power of raising and regulating fleets and armies." Military command, Blackstone claimed, "ever was and is the undoubted right of his majesty, and his royal predecessors."[41]

In discussing the power to declare war, Blackstone borrowed extensively from Grotius and Vattel, but emphasized the legal significance of a declaration rather than its purpose as a form of notice. Under Blackstone's version of the British constitution, the monarch had no need to declare war before beginning hostilities against another nation. Such a requirement would have served little purpose, due to the Crown's other prerogatives in the field of war. Instead, a declaration of war plays two roles: it protects British citizens by notifying an enemy that their hostile actions have received state approval, and it serves to legally bind the people to the king's decision to wage war.

> Why according to the law of nations a denunciation of war ought always to precede the actual commencement of hostilities, is not so much that the enemy may be put upon his guard, (which is a matter rather of magnanimity than right) but that it may be certainly clear that the war is not

undertaken by private persons, but by the will of the whole community; whose right of willing is in this case transferred to the supreme magistrate by the fundamental laws of society. So that, in order to make a war completely effectual, it is necessary with us in England that it be publicly declared and duly proclaimed by the king's authority; and, then, all parts of both the contending nations, from the highest to the lowest, are bound by it. [42]

A declaration of war only perfected, or made "completely effectual," hostilities between two nations, which otherwise could take the form of "incomplete state of hostilities." When the British monarch exercised his sole authority on questions of war and peace, he could issue a declaration of war either before or after "the actual commencement of hostilities." Although part of the war power, the authority to declare war was not necessary to begin or to conduct hostilities.

From a legal perspective, the declaration performed an important function in distinguishing between limited hostilities and an all-out conflict. It was clearly understood in the eighteenth century that a "declared" war was only the ultimate state in a gradually ascending scale of hostilities between nations. For example, Blackstone described letters of marque and reprisal as creating "only an incomplete state of hostilities" that could eventually produce "a formal denunciation of war." Any unauthorized hostilities committed by private citizens, therefore, would not constitute war, but would be the actions of "pirates and robbers." [43]

Blackstone, however, recognized that a nation could authorize private citizens to wage war against another state. Hence he described the executive's authority to issue letters of marque and reprisal as "nearly related to, and plainly derived from, [the prerogative] of making war." [44] Recognized by the law of nations, such letters authorized their bearers to "seize the bodies or goods of the subjects of the offending state" in order to satisfy some oppression or injury received earlier. But the plaintiffs received formal protection from piracy or robbery laws because the letter of marque and reprisal gave their conduct the sanction of state approval. The Crown's power to issue letters of marque and reprisal were of a piece with the power to declare war: they did not form the power to initiate hostilities, but instead served to define the legal significance under international law of hostile acts.

Blackstone expanded the justification—from function to sovereignty—for locating the foreign affairs power in the Crown. With regard to treaties, he argued that treaties must be made "by the sovereign power" so that they would be "binding upon the whole community."[45] In the case of treaties, "in England the sovereign power, *quoad hoc,* is vested in the King." Because the Crown served as the representative of all the people in the area of treatymaking, Blackstone argued, "no other power in the kingdom can legally delay, resist, or annul" the king's treaties, which he referred to as "contracts." "What is done by the royal authority, with regard to foreign powers, is the act of the whole nation," Blackstone concluded.[46] His treatment of the treaty power in this respect was consistent with his overall approach to the executive, in which he collapsed Locke's distinctions in describing the power of the Crown. Thus, Blackstone described the treatymaking and warmaking powers as the "principal prerogatives of the sovereign," and subjected them to the control of the law, whereas Locke thought of the prerogative as an extraconstitutional authority.[47]

Again unlike Locke, Blackstone did not undertake a detailed consideration of the legislative power. He nonetheless recognized that Parliament played the dominant role in the regulation of domestic affairs. Parliament, Blackstone said, was "the place where that absolute despotic power, which must in all governments reside somewhere, is intrusted by the constitution of these kingdoms."[48] Parliament enjoys the "sovereign and uncontrollable authority" in all forms of legislation concerning matters "of all possible denominations, ecclesiastical or temporal, civil, military, maritime, or criminal." Only Parliament could approve the imposition of taxes, which are needed for funding and supplying the army. Parliamentary authority, Blackstone noted, had regulated the succession to the Crown, changed the national religion, and even altered the constitution. "[T]hat what the parliament does no authority upon earth can undo," Blackstone wrote.[49] While the Crown could issue proclamations interpreting and enforcing parliamentary laws, it could not "contradict the old laws or tend to establish new ones," because "the making of laws is entirely the work of a distinct part, the legislative branch, of the sovereign power."[50] Blackstone, however, does not seem to have considered the interaction between the Crown's monopoly over the war and treaty powers and Parliament's supremacy over funding and the regulation of domestic affairs.

For example, Blackstone did not discuss what would happen if Parliament refused to fund a war or implement a treaty. Yet his declaration of parliamentary supremacy over taxation and domestic legislation suggests that only the legislature could undertake the domestic actions needed to make the Crown's war or treaty decisions effective.

Blackstone's categorization of the warmaking and treatymaking powers as part of the royal prerogative suggests that he too thought of war and treaties as separate from domestic lawmaking. Modifying Locke, he conceived of the prerogative as acting in those situations in which the positive laws are silent, rather than as a power to act in the public interest against the standing laws. Repealing legislation would be of little use in reversing exercises of the prerogative, because any abuse would cease once the royal action had ended. Impeachment was the only remedy for misuse of the prerogative, because the prerogative was instant action, rather than ongoing regulation.[51] "Thus the sovereign may make a treaty with a foreign state, which shall irrevocably bind the nation; and yet when such treaties have been judged pernicious, impeachments have pursued those ministers, by whose agency or advice they were concluded."[52] Likewise, the Crown's ministers would be restrained in exercising the war power by "the same check of parliamentary impeachment, for improper or inglorious conduct, in beginning, conducting, or concluding a national war."[53] Blackstone envisioned impeachment as one of the chief parliamentary checks on the Crown's exclusive authority to make war, and as treaties usually accompanied the outbreak of war and the agreement for peace, it seems unsurprising that the constitution treated the two powers in the same manner.

The similar checks and balances on the war and treaty powers indicate the deep affinity between the two. Both powers involved the nation's state of relations with other countries under international law, rather than the regulation of domestic conduct and events. When the Crown decided to wage war, the declaration served to notify both the British people and other nations that Great Britain considered itself to be in a state of war under international law. So too, the king's authority over treatymaking defined the rights and obligations that Great Britain held toward other nations under international law, such as strategic alliances and neutrality pacts. Both powers involved the declaration of Great Britain's relationship with another nation under international law, rather than the domestic actions necessary to carry out those relationships. The latter would be the subject of legislation by Parliament.

Although Blackstone was not as clear in his thinking as perhaps Locke or Montesquieu, he implicitly shared their distinction between foreign affairs and lawmaking. This difference in approach, but similarity in outcome, may have resulted from Blackstone's thinking on the separation of powers. Locke and Montesquieu pursued a pure separation of powers scheme, one in which each governmental function was classified as either legislative, executive, or judicial, and then allocated to that branch. Blackstone, on the other hand, adapted the separation of powers to fit a more traditional checks and balances framework, in which different functions were distributed so that each organ of government could restrain the other. In the former, maintaining a line between war and treaties on the one hand, and domestic lawmaking and funding on the other, fits the distinction between executive power in foreign affairs and legislative control over domestic regulation. Limiting wars and treaties to matters of international affairs, however, and requiring parliamentary participation for any war or treaty undertakings of a domestic nature also provided Parliament with a check on the royal prerogative over international agreements. As we will see presently, these theories drew on the actual workings of British politics in the seventeenth and eighteenth centuries.

British Constitutional Practice
at the Time of the Framing

In considering the foreign affairs power, the Framers would have looked to recent British political history as much as to intellectual thought on the separation of powers. While drafting and discussing different constitutional provisions, the delegates to the Constitutional Convention and the Federalists and Anti-Federalists in the press and the state ratifying conventions often invoked British examples to predict how different governmental arrangements would work.[54] British political history was the Framers' shared history, at least until 1776, and the revolutionaries believed that they were defending the ancient constitution against the political corruption that appeared to take hold of the British government after the Seven Years' War.[55] Furthermore, while Locke, Montesquieu, and Blackstone certainly informed the Framers' thinking on the formal aspects of the British constitution, that constitution itself was not a fixed text. It was instead a series of unwritten principles that changed in response to significant political events and practices. To understand the British constitution, and the background principles it embodied for the Framers, we must retrace British political history of the seventeenth and eighteenth centuries as it related to the making of wars and treaties.[56]

Struggle over the powers of war and peace would have remained at the center of the Framers' memories of British political history. The contest between Crown and Parliament for primacy in foreign affairs was a critical element of the British civil war, the Interregnum, the Restoration, and the settlement. While the Crown entered the seventeenth century with absolute authority over war and treaties, this monopoly came under attack by Parliament, which primarily used its control over finances to win significant influence over the course of foreign policy. During the Interregnum, Parliament went farther and claimed ultimate control over issues of war and peace, but formal authority over foreign policy returned to the monarchy during the Restoration. Nonetheless, the political settlement of the eighteenth century provided Parliament with significant checks on the foreign affairs power through its monopoly over domestic lawmaking. After the struggles of the seventeenth and eighteenth centuries, the British constitution did not permit treaties to regulate domestic conduct, nor did it require Parliament to fund or implement wars or treaty obligations. Such a result would have subverted both the separation of powers principles and the checks and balances that two centuries of political struggle had wrought.

Under the Stuarts foreign affairs became the source of one of the central conflicts between the monarchy and Parliament.[57] When the first Stuart king, James I, assumed the throne in 1603, it had been the tradition that the monarch exercise the powers to make war and peace, to conclude treaties, and to control the army and navy. However, Parliament's power over the purse rendered the king's prerogative to raise armies and navies an empty one, unless the Crown could find other sources of funding. Parliament's "exclusive control over finance enabled it to criticize all the acts of the executive government, to stop projects of which it disapproved, to force the executive to adopt policies of which it approved, and to supervise the methods adopted to carry them out."[58]

James I, however, sought to follow an independent foreign policy without parliamentary interference. Initially, he attempted to rule England without calling Parliament into session—primarily by relying on revenues from Crown properties—because Parliament had provided a forum for the criticism of Stuart policies. But the beginning of the Thirty Years' War in 1618 led James I to undertake several military and diplomatic initiatives requiring the financial support of Parliament, which had the sole constitutional power to raise taxes and appropriate supplies.[59] Parliament distrusted James's motives and his foreign policy goals, which included the establishment of an alliance with Spain and France. Though it had no formal role in the processes of making war or treaties, Parliament used its powers over supply to force James to alter his diplomatic strategy to one of hostility toward the Catholic powers. In 1621, Parliament petitioned James, in return for a small subsidy, to terminate his alliance with Spain and attack that nation in order to slow the pace of Catholic victories in Germany. In response, the king rejected these efforts to alter his foreign policy, warned the Commons that "none therein shall presume henceforth to meddle with anything concerning our Government or deep matters of State," and claimed that Parliament's powers derived only from the monarchy's "grace and permission."[60]

Nonetheless, disputes over the Crown's peacetime revenues, and, more importantly, the onset of the costly Thirty Years' War on the Continent, forced James I to seek parliamentary support. In 1621 and again in 1624, Parliament effectively forestalled his plans to fight in the German wars by approving only meager funds for the army. Parliament instead encouraged James I to break England's treaties and initiate hostilities against Spain by voting funds contingent only for such a war.[61] By 1624 James had given in, called another Parliament, and even publicly sought its advice on foreign affairs.[62] He broke off relations with Spain and a naval war began in earnest in 1624. Parliament funded the conflict, even though Britain did not officially declare war until September of 1625.[63]

Charles I's ascension to the throne the following year led Parliament to push its powers even farther. In exchange for larger subsidies to pursue the new foreign policy, Parliament demanded that the Crown terminate its alliance with France and explain the conduct of military operations on the Continent.[64] Resisting what he saw as further encroachment on the prerogative, Charles ruled without Parliament for eleven years, during which time the Crown raised funds through forced loans, a tax on maritime communities to support the navy, and the sale of royal property.[65] By 1640, internal rebellion in Scotland forced Charles to turn to Parliament again for supplies, which set in motion another struggle over the prerogative and funding that eventually led to Cromwell, Charles's execution, and the Interregnum.[66] Even during this final struggle, Parliament recognized that the king retained the power to make war and treaties, although it sought to force the king to use that power to enter into alliances with other Protestant nations as one of the conditions for parliamentary cooperation. In his final answer as king, Charles admitted that the Commons exercised a check on his foreign affairs powers by its control over lawmaking, funding (which he called "the sinews as well of peace as of war"), and impeachment. Until his execution, Charles consistently refused to accept any proposals for further parliamentary controls over war and peace.[67]

Governing without a king produced several experiments concerning the allocation of the war and treaty powers, all of which maintained their distinction from funding and the authority to legislate. Some early proposals for a new constitution placed the conduct of foreign policy in the hands of a king with a Council of State, but with control over war and peace ultimately in the hands of Parliament, while others centralized all powers in the Parliament. Throughout these experiments, the victors continued to distinguish between "the enacting, altering and repealing of laws" that governed domestic conduct on the one hand, and "the making [of] war and peace" and the "treating with foreign states" on the other, even when both powers were given to the same body. In all of these proposals, the power to fund and legislate remained in the hands of Parliament, which was seen as the representative of the people, while the war and treaty powers were vested either in Parliament as a whole or in an executive with the participation of the Parliament or its representatives.[68]

Cromwell's efforts to legitimate his rule through written constitutions continued to recognize this distinction. In *The Instrument of Government,* which he issued in 1653 to a hand-picked Parliament, all the "supreme legislative authority" of the English Commonwealth was vested in the "Lord Protector" and the Parliament by the people.[69] The Instrument declared that "the laws shall not be altered, suspended, abrogated, or repealed, nor any new law made, nor any tax, charge or imposition laid upon the people" without the consent of Parliament. Not conceiving of war and treaties as part of that authority, the Instrument separately vested the powers to conduct foreign affairs and to make war and peace on the Lord Protector and his council of advisers. The Instrument required Cromwell to seek the "consent of the major part of the Council" on matters of war and peace. The Instrument also constrained the executive's control over the military forces by permitting the Lord Protector to "dispose and order" the militia, army, and navy only "by consent of Parliament," and when Parliament was not sitting, by a majority vote of the council. The Instrument made clear that the executive could not raise money to pay for "the present wars" without the approval of Parliament, except in emergency. Four years later, the instability of the political system gave rise to yet another constitution, *The Humble Petition and Advice,* which came even closer to reproducing the traditional constitution's division of powers by allocating war and treaty powers to the executive and reserving domestic lawmaking to Parliament.

Restoration of the monarchy soon renewed tension with Parliament over funding and legislation in support of foreign affairs. Charles II's assumption of the throne signaled the restoration of the Crown's prerogatives over war and peace, over the conduct of diplomatic relations, and over the making of treaties. Parliament passed a statute returning to the king "the sole supreme government, command and disposition of the militia and of all forces" and abjuring Parliament's right to the same.[70] If the civil wars had ended the debate over control over the armed forces, they also had locked into place Parliament's sole control over the funding of national policies.[71] Instead of voting lump sums to the Crown, Parliament began to appropriate funds specifically for the army and to forbid the transfer of money from other accounts for military purposes. Making war or treaties and pursuing a successful foreign policy would thenceforth require the cooperation of Parliament.[72] It was this balance between executive initiative and planning and legislative control of appropriations and legislation that would characterize British foreign relations for at least another century.

The Framers would have taken note of the ample opportunities available to Parliament to use its financial power to participate in the development of foreign policy. Consider that from 1660 to 1801 Britain seemed to be at war more often than not: 1665–67 (Second Anglo-Dutch War),

1672–74 (Third Anglo-Dutch War), 1689–97 (War of the Grand Alliance), 1702–13 (War of the Spanish Succession), 1718–20 (War of the Quadruple Alliance), 1739–48 (War of the Austrian Succession), 1754–63 (Seven Years' War), 1775–83 (American Revolution), and 1793–1801 (War with revolutionary France). Continual war demanded continual funding, and important members of Parliament used their voting power over military appropriations to seek a cooperative arrangement with the Crown in the setting of foreign policy.[73] In addition to funding the wars against the Dutch in 1665 and 1672, Parliament was called on to enact a series of Navigation Acts in order to wage economic warfare on the United Provinces. Although the Crown retained the initiative in foreign affairs throughout this period, Parliament at times sought to use its powers to persuade Charles II to adopt a more vigorous stance against France. Only when doubts arose about the Stuarts' flirtations with Catholicism at home and abroad did politicians "seek to use the opportunities that parliamentary control over war finance presented to curtail the Crown's power."[74] In 1677 and 1678, for example, the Commons voted funding for the military contingent on the formation of an alliance against Louis XIV, and in so doing declared that it would refuse to "grant supplies for maintenance of wars and alliances before they are signified in Parliament."[75] Although Charles protested this invasion of his prerogative over war and treaties, he eventually entered into an alliance with the Dutch against France, as Parliament desired.[76] Charles ended his reign by governing without Parliament, and funding his administration by subsidies from Louis XIV, which only demonstrated further that the Crown could not conduct a meaningful foreign policy without parliamentary support.

While the Glorious Revolution in 1688 produced no formal rearrangement of this constitutional balance between Crown and Parliament, the years of settlement witnessed the rise of Parliament, through the use of its constitutional powers, as a political counterweight in international affairs. The Bill of Rights removed from the royal prerogative the power to raise and keep a standing army in peacetime; thereafter, the decision to raise a standing army required statutory authorization through annual Mutiny Acts.[77] Blackstone was only partially correct when he wrote that the king had the prerogative to raise and regulate armies and navies; the king could do so only with Parliament's consent. The Act of Settlement barred the Crown from engaging in "any war for the defence of any dominions or territories which do not belong to the crown of England, without the consent of parliament."[78] In practice, Parliament used its authority in the areas of legislation and funding to encourage wars and to repudiate treaties with more regularity. In 1698 and 1700, for example, parliamentary opposition effectively prevented William III from living up to what were known as the Partition treaties, while in 1713 Parliament rejected outright an Anglo-French commercial treaty that was seen as crucial to the government's efforts to repair relations with France.[79] Parliament's funding powers gave it a formal veto over any treaties that required military expenditure, financial subsidies to other powers, or favorable commercial treatment. Just as parliamentary resistance could render wars empty and treaties stillborn, parliamentary support had the opposite effect. Parliament's financial and, perhaps more important, its political support allowed the Crown to act with a stronger hand abroad by signaling domestic stability and access to resources to carry out threats and promises. "As Parliament was the public forum in which the ministry formally presented and defended its policy and was criticised in a fashion that obliged it to reply," a British diplomatic historian of the period has observed, "it was Parliament where the public debate over foreign policy can be seen as most intense and effective."[80] Even if the funding check should fail, Parliament ultimately could use the power of impeachment to remove ministers for pursuing wars or treaties with which it disagreed. Parliament's constitutional role gave it the leverage to become a forum for the determination of foreign policy and the national interest.

British practice also underscored the irrelevance of the declaration of war to the balance of war powers between Crown and Parliament. In two of Britain's major military engagements in the seventeenth and eighteenth centuries—the entry into the Thirty Years' War against Spain in 1624 and the struggle with France during the Seven Years' War beginning in 1756—the king did not declare war until more than a year after offensive operations had begun.[81] In fact, in the many wars fought after the Restoration (the Second and Third Anglo-Dutch Wars, King William's War, the War of the Spanish Succession, the War of the Austrian Succession, and the Seven Years' War), England declared war only once before or at the commencement of hostilities.[82] This period also witnessed numerous minor conflicts in which England never declared war at all.[83] If the British of the seventeenth and eighteenth centuries (including the American colonists) believed a declaration of war played an authorizing function for hostilities, they certainly failed to practice what they preached.

The declarations of war published in the British colonies during this time confirm that the view of declarations as important for determining the status of legal relations, but not for initiating hostilities, was understood throughout the empire. Declarations usually catalogued the offenses committed by the other nation (usually France) in an effort to show that a state of war already existed, with Britain's own declaration playing the happy role of merely recognizing the ongoing state of hostilities. For example, William and Mary devoted most of their May 7, 1689 declaration of war against France to a recitation of French actions—seizing English possessions in the Americas, attacking English ships, persecuting English nationals in France, and seeking to foment rebellion against the new monarchy—that had the effect of commencing the war between the two nations. The March 29, 1744 declaration against France similarly narrated a litany of French provocations and attacks on British possessions— going so far as to describe in detail captured French documents ordering commanders to attack British settlements in a time of peace, and a French declaration of war against Britain and her allies—to show that war already existed. Britain's declaration of the Seven Years' War on May 17, 1756, while giving the pretexts for the king's decision, characterized previous hostile actions by both nations as already a "war." Underscoring their formal nature, all three declarations were devoted to describing the new legal status certain actions would gain during wartime: hostile attacks by British commanders were permitted; communications with the French king were illegal; French ships captured were lawfully prize ships; wartime materials were contraband; and French subjects helping the British cause would receive protection.[84] In these documents, the British king recognized the wrongs committed by the French, their impact in creating a state of war, and the domestic implications.

The usual British course toward war involved months, if not years, of direct armed conflict without a declaration of war. Many of these wars remained vivid in the minds of the Framers, whose fathers fought in them as subject of the British Empire. The colonies themselves were often a substantial part of the theater of war and, in any event, they were valuable wartime assets of the Crown. Thus, we can expect the Framers to have remembered the full year of British naval attacks against the French and Spanish that preceded Queen Anne's declaration of the War of the Spanish Succession on May 4, 1702. The War of the Austrian Succession, which England declared against Spain on October 13, 1739, and against France on March 29, 1744, would have remained even more vivid in their minds. Months before the 1739 declaration, British naval commanders in North America began offensive operations against Spanish forces and settlements. Almost a year before the 1744 declaration, the entire empire celebrated the battle of Dettingen, in which King George II himself led British troops to victory over the French.[85]

If any event impressed on the Framers the idea that declarations of war were unnecessary to the conduct of hostilities, it was the Seven Years' War. Not only was it the most recent war, and the one in which George Washington saw his first significant military action, it was also the first conflict between the great powers that began in America. Great Britain did not declare war on France until May 17, 1756. Nonetheless, American and British troops had engaged in direct conflict with French troops as early as July 3, 1754, when French troops defeated colonial forces under Major George Washington in the disputed Ohio Valley. One year later (but still eleven months before a declaration of war), the French scored a stunning victory at the battle of Fort Duquesne over two regiments of British regulars led by the unskilled commander in chief of British North America, General Braddock. Americans remembered the date of the battle well, for Washington had served as aide-de-camp to Braddock and, in revolutionary myth, had led the Virginia militia courageously in Indian-style fighting tactics while the British troops had died like cowards. Even in the early decades of the nineteenth century, American legal scholars such as Chancellor Kent still remembered that the Seven Years' War had broken out in America several years before England formally declared war.[86]

By the time of the framing, the British constitutional system had reached an accommodation concerning the royal prerogative over war and treaties that provided the legislature with a significant role. The eighteenth-century English monarch was commander in chief of the armed forces and possessed exclusive power to enter into treaties, to declare war, and to raise and regulate the army and navy. Although formal power was allocated to the monarch, Parliament exerted its influence in these areas through its sole control over the public fisc, implementing legislation, and impeachment. Parliament could end wars by threatening to eliminate supplies for the army. It could try to force the king into war by voting funds for wars it wanted the Crown to initiate. It could eviscerate treaties by refusing to enact necessary implementing legislation. It could hold the Crown accountable for decisions concerning treaties and war by impeaching the king's ministers for foreign policy failures. As one British diplomatic historian has written, Parliament's authority over implementing legislation and financial support allowed it to "exert[ ] a more direct influence over foreign policy" than the formal allocation of constitutional powers would suggest.[87] A foreign observer of the eighteenth-century British constitution summarized the system nicely:

> The king of England . . . has the prerogative of commanding armies, and equipping fleets; but without the concurrence of his parliament he cannot maintain them. He can bestow places and employments; but without his parliament he cannot pay the salaries attending on them. He can declare war; but without his parliament it is impossible for him to carry it on. In a word, the royal prerogative, destitute as it is of the power of imposing taxes, is like a vast body, which cannot of itself accomplish its motions; or, if you please, it is like a ship completely equipped, but from which the parliament can at pleasure draw off the water, and leave it a-ground—and also set it afloat again, by granting subsidies.[88]

The allocation of foreign affairs power under the British constitution was not some peculiar practice that developed more through happenstance than thoughtful intention. Rather, the distinction between the foreign affairs power and the power to fund and legislate was a core element of the separation of powers and the rise of parliamentary government. It provided Parliament with an important means to check the Crown's power in foreign affairs, one that it gradually used to seize an influential role in the setting of national policy. Not only did this shared history inform the Framers as they ratified the Constitution, it also suggests that any effort to reverse the British rule would have prompted significant protest and opposition, as it would have removed one of the legislature's crucial checks on the executive.

3

FOREIGN AFFAIRS AND THE PRELUDE
TO THE CONSTITUTION

Although the war and treaty powers may not have been as central to the Revolution as the issue of taxation, the relationship between the legislative power and foreign affairs was bound up in the dispute between colonies and mother country over the nature of sovereignty. We can understand the constitutional arguments of the revolutionaries as a defense of the rights of popularly elected assemblies to tax and enact internal legislation, rights they felt to be threatened by the foreign affairs power exercised by a central government. This chapter discusses the balance between the foreign affairs power and the legislative power as illuminated by the colonial charters, state constitutions, and the Articles of Confederation. Although Blackstone and the Articles of Confederation have been the primary focus of scholarly attention, colonial charters and state constitutions deserve a central place in the historical debate. The colonies, and later the states, provided the Framers with a shared system of reference with which to understand the workings of government. Colonial governments provided examples of legislative participation in foreign affairs through the appropriations power. State governments provided working examples of a separate executive branch. As the most significant governmental legal documents of their day, state constitutions provided the most relevant legal context for construing the meaning of the federal Constitution.

State experience prior to the drafting of the Constitution demonstrated both the dangers and the advantages of a strong executive. While the revolutionaries had rebelled against the power of the royal governors, they also bore witness to the excesses of the postrevolutionary state legislatures. By studying the evolution of the state constitutions, we can better understand the Constitution and foreign affairs as part of the Framers' attempt to cure legislative excess by establishing a unitary, independent executive. In this effort, the Framers borrowed from the examples of successful governors and rejected executives whose power remained subordinated to their assemblies.

Although the Framers would have understood the war and treaty powers in the context of a restoration of executive constitutional authority, they also would have remained mindful of the need for balance. As the colonies became independent states, bound to each other through the Articles of Confederation, they maintained the distinction between treaties and legislation, with the former vested in the central government and the latter in the hands of the state legislatures. This continuing separation of powers, divided between two levels of government rather than two branches of government, caused enormous foreign policy difficulties for the new nation. State refusal to implement treaty obligations not only justified Britain's military presence within American borders, it also undermined American diplomatic efforts to reach vital trade agreements with other great powers. The nature of treaties and their place in the legal system developed into one of the critical questions for American foreign policy and the future of the Union. We cannot analyze the decisions made during the ratification without understanding the foreign policy and political context of the Revolution and of the Articles of Confederation.

During the colonial and revolutionary periods, the development of the war and treaty powers began to diverge. Allocation of the war power became swept up in the story of the revolutionaries' hate-love relationship with executive power, which found its final constitutional expression in the institution of the American presidency. State constitutions served as a model and testing ground for approaches to war powers and to the executive. Treaties became entangled in the contentious relationship between the early national and state governments—what we today know as an issue of federalism. Implementation of treaties took on this character, however, because of fundamental defects in national authority, and so it is perhaps not surprising that the beginnings of reform began in the allocation of powers among the branches of a new national government.

REVOLUTIONARY IDEOLOGY AND
THE LEGISLATIVE POWER

A ratifier studying the proposed Constitution's treatment of foreign affairs would have drawn on not only British constitutional history, but also the revolutionary experience. Questions regarding war and peace, treaties and their implementation, and the role of the three branches of government would have raised analogies to the constitutional issues at stake in the break with Great Britain. As several historians of the revolutionary period have argued, Americans of 1776 believed that they were defending their customary constitutional rights from tyranny and corruption on the part of the king and Parliament.[1] Colonists argued that both had overstepped their constitutional boundaries by raising taxes to pay for the costs of the Seven Years' War and Britain's colonial military presence. While Americans agreed that the war and treaty powers were the province of the central government in London, they argued that these authorities remained distinct from powers over internal matters, such as taxation and supply, which rested within the province of the colonial assemblies. This distinction between foreign affairs and domestic law would continue throughout the early years of independence, creating difficulties that would lead to the Constitutional Convention in 1787.

While the constitutional relationship between the American colonies and Great Britain at the end of the Seven Years' War was uncertain, we can identify some broad outlines. Power was not centralized in London; rather, it was diversified at different levels on different issues. Until the early 1760s, the king and Parliament had almost entirely avoided any interference in internal colonial matters, while the colonies acknowledged the Crown's primacy over foreign policy.[2] Like their counterpart in the mother country, the colonial assemblies exercised full legislative powers within their jurisdictions, and were even able to enjoy substantial influence on the governor's control over foreign affairs through their control over the purse.[3] As Bernard Bailyn has observed, the king and Parliament "touched only the outer fringes of colonial life; they dealt with matters obviously beyond the competence of any lesser authority. . . . All other powers were enjoyed, in fact if not in constitutional theory, by local, colonial organs of government."[4] A series of political precedents and

constitutional custom had established the assemblies as the political representatives of the colonists on internal matters. "[T]he colonial assemblies by the middle of the eighteenth century," Professor Greene writes,

> managed through precedent and custom to establish their authority and
> status as local parliaments, as the most important institutions in the colo-
> nial constitutions and the primary guardians of the colonists' inherited
> rights as Englishmen, including especially the right not to be subjected to
> any taxes or laws relating to their internal affairs without the consent of
> their representatives in assembly.[5]

Beginning with the imposition of the Stamp Act in 1764, Parliament's
efforts to change this arrangement helped precipitate the American Revolution. In order to pay for the costs of the Seven Years' War and the continuing military protection of North America, Parliament sought to impose
taxes and internal regulations on the colonies. It based its actions on an
evolving theory of parliamentary supremacy.[6] London's actions sparked
such resistance because parliamentary supremacy encroached on at least
three firmly held beliefs held by colonial Americans. First, from an ideological perspective, the Crown's efforts to extend its monopoly from foreign affairs to internal legislation amounted to a plan to overturn the
balanced constitution. In its place would appear a centralized absolutist
state centered on government bureaucracy, standing armies, and the new
financial classes. Predictions of the eighteenth-century country, or oppositionist writers in Britain, whose works helped shape the Framers' world-
view, seemed to be coming true. More than a rationalization for revolution, this mindset gave meaning to the new taxes, the new declarations of
supremacy, the quartering of soldiers, and the closing of ports. The founding generation interpreted these events as a deliberate conspiracy by the
Crown and its ministers to establish a military-financial state, to corrupt
Parliament, and to use its legislative authority to steal individual liberty.

Second, as John Philip Reid has argued, the events leading to revolution took place in a rapidly evolving constitutional context in which the
views in the colonies and those in the mother country were moving apart.
British defenders of the Stamp Act and the Declaratory Act located in
the King-in-Parliament all sovereignty in the empire; its legislation had to
be supreme, therefore Parliament was supreme. Under this theory, Parliament was supreme over the Crown, and as the final sovereign voice

in the British government, Parliament was supreme over the colonies. Parliamentary sovereignty and supremacy could admit no place for the claims of colonial assemblies over taxes and internal regulation. American revolutionaries recalled an earlier vision of the British constitution, in which the colonists and their assemblies enjoyed a direct relationship with the English king, rather than with Parliament. From the founding of the colonies, these revolutionaries argued, the Crown had granted the colonists the right to regulate themselves on all internal matters.[7] In their minds, there was a clear distinction between the power to legislate—the essence of the Revolution was where this power lay, in the assemblies or the Parliament—and the executive monopoly over war and treaties. The Revolution came not because of the king's decision to fight the Seven Years' War or the stationing of troops and bureaucracy in British North America. Rather, the fight came when Parliament sought to pass legislation for the colonies without the consent of the assemblies. From the colonial perspective, the Revolution responded to Parliament's effort to seize the power of the colonial assemblies over domestic legislation, which served as a critical counterbalance to the Crown's control over foreign affairs.

Parliament's attempts to bring the colonies under tighter imperial control raised alarm bells on yet a third level, that of colonial institutional politics. As Professor Greene has observed, "[t]he rise of the representative assemblies was perhaps the most significant political and constitutional development in the history of Britain's overseas empire before the American Revolution."[8] Formal constitutional arrangements vested broad authority in the royal governors, who possessed the authority externally to wage war, make treaties (which they generally did with Indian tribes), and represent the colony in intercolony negotiations.[9] Internally, governors enjoyed the authority to veto laws, to prorogue the legislature, to appoint officers, and to sit as a court of equity.[10] Formal authority, however, did not yield actual power. During the period after the Glorious Revolution, the assemblies engaged in a campaign to win the rights to tax, to control funding, and to enact laws.[11] Because Parliament did not finance colonial governments, governors were dependent on the assemblies to fund their operations. Assemblies came to be identified closely with the individual rights of the colonists, particularly their right to representation and to govern their internal matters. After the Seven Years' War, the assemblies had pushed their powers even beyond those enjoyed by the House of Commons, and they had taken a strong hand in developing an independent role for themselves in the British imperial system.[12]

Measures like the Declaratory Act attempted to impose a centralized imperial government on a system that had allowed several independent power centers to develop. Parliament's metropolitan theory of empire threatened the political existence of the assemblies. It was no mistake that as events moved toward a break with the mother country, Parliament suspended the New York assembly and sought to alter the Massachusetts assembly. The Revolution became a fight not just for individual liberties, but for the rights of the assemblies to engage in self-government. Fusing control over foreign affairs and internal legislation in the same institution, even if it were King-in-Parliament, would have threatened the framework that had become central to American political identity.

From Colony to States

At the more detailed level of institutional colonial structure, the colonists had an intimate familiarity with executive government. Colonial government—whether royal, corporate, or proprietary—had come to mirror the formal arrangements of the British constitution. Each colony had an executive governor, appointed by the Crown for an indefinite term, a representative legislature, and some type of council or upper house.[13] In most cases, the formal powers of the colonial governors exceeded those of the monarchy back home. For example, colonial governors possessed the authority to veto colonial legislation, to dissolve the legislature, and to appoint and dismiss judges at will, all powers that the king had not exercised since before the turn of the eighteenth century.

As in these areas, so too it was in the arena of war. Colonial charters gave the governors full control over raising and deploying the military, which most often took the form of a militia. Royal commissions, for example, authorized colonial governors

> to arm, muster, and command all persons residing within his province; to transfer them from place to place; to resist all enemies, pirates, or rebels; if necessary, to transport troops to other provinces in order to defend such places against invasion; to pursue enemies out of the province; in short, to do anything properly belonging to the office of commander-in-chief.[14]

The Massachusetts Charter contained a typical colonial provision for making war. It vested in "the Governor of our said Province" the "full Power by himselfe" to "traine instruct Exercise and Govern the Militia," "to assemble in Martiall Array and put in Warlike posture" the inhabitants, and to lead the militia "to Encounter Expulse Repell Resist and pursue by force of Armes," and "to kill slay destroy and Conquer" any person or group that attempted to invade or annoy the colony.[15] The governor also had the sole power to impose and administer martial law, to fortify strongholds, and to stockpile weapons.

One of the few formal checks on the governor's military command came from the declaration of war. Governors could not impose martial law without a declaration of war from Great Britain. This again highlights the role of the declaration of war in eighteenth-century Anglo-American constitutional law as fundamentally one of defining legal relationships, especially at home. Only after a declaration of war could the governor take the domestic steps, such as infringing temporarily on colonists' liberties, needed to fight a war. These provisions also show that the governor's war powers encountered the limits of his subordinate position in the British governmental hierarchy. Governor Dinwiddie of Virginia, for example, could not very well declare war on France without the approval of the British king. It does not appear that the declaration had to precede military operations, for a historical study uncovers only three declarations of war in the colonies, even though the colonists engaged in almost constant hostilities with various Indian tribes (and other European settlers and troops) throughout the prerevolutionary period.[16] The declaration of war's main purpose lay not in authorizing military operations, but in triggering the governor's exercise of his domestic powers, such as the authority to impose martial law.

An absence of formal limits did not prevent the same type of political processes that checked the British monarch from constraining the colonial governors. Although this structure of government produced relative harmony in England by the mid-eighteenth century, it spawned the exact opposite in the colonies. According to Professor Bailyn, "[t]here was bitter, persistent strife within the provincial governments almost everywhere," particularly between the different branches of government.[17] As their brethren did in Great Britain, colonial legislators used their broad powers over the purse to inject themselves into all manner of policymaking, including military and diplomatic affairs. Assemblies passed legislation to man and equip the military, to define militiaman duties, and even to conduct military and diplomatic affairs with the Indians. Governors depended on the assemblies for "temporary acts for the enforcement of the simplest military obligations," such as legislation defining how long a militiaman had to serve and what weapons he should have.[18] The history of the southern colonies is replete with legislatures using their powers to man, equip, and maintain the military, and to specify how, when, and where the governor could exercise force.[19]

Virginia provides an example of the manner in which colonial legislatures followed Parliament's use of its funding powers to influence military affairs. In passing appropriations for the military, Virginia's House of Burgesses regularly specified the number of soldiers to be called up, their duty stations, their officers, their pay, and their quota of ammunition. The house even went so far as to direct the governor how to command the force. To keep checks on the governor's use of the army, the legislature established a special committee to advise the governor on military operations. By 1676, the Virginia legislature had assumed "a large part of the responsibility for all military operations within the colony."[20] As in Great Britain, the appropriations power bestowed on the representative assemblies the ability to participate in issues of war and peace even in a frontier environment that could have otherwise encouraged deference to the executive.

Despite these checks, the revolutionaries turned against executive authority. The new state constitutions sought to tame the executive by placing explicit restrictions on its power and by diluting its structural unity and independence. These frameworks of government were significant not because they served as models for the 1787 Constitution, but because they contained mistakes that the Framers sought to avoid. As such, they are valuable foils for interpreting the Constitution's allocation of the foreign affairs power.

The mechanisms chosen by the revolutionaries to control the executive contrast sharply with the Constitution of 1787. States began by eliminating the independence and unity of the governor's office. For example, in all but one state, the legislators elected the governor (often one of their own), which made the governor directly accountable to the assembly rather than to the people.[21] States also limited the term and eligibility of the governor in an effort to reduce his power and influence. Most states either provided for the annual election of the governor, restricted the number of terms a governor could serve, or both. As the Maryland constitution declared, "a long continuance, in the first executive departments of power or trust, is dangerous to liberty; a rotation, therefore, in these departments, is one of the best securities of permanent freedom."[22]

States also eliminated the structural unity of the executive branch in an attempt to undermine executive power. Pennsylvania undertook the most radical reform by replacing the single governor with a twelve-man executive council.[23] Other states reformed their executive branches by creating councils of state, which were appointed by the legislature for the purpose of advising the governor before he pursued a course of action. The councils often made the governors "little more than chairmen of their executive boards."[24]

Some students of the presidency have focused on these institutional changes to show that the revolutionaries planned to do away with a strong executive government.[25] These structural modifications, however, do not bear as much significance for our study because the Constitution rejected many of them. More revealing is the substantive power that the states vested in the executive. Despite the fragmentation of the executive as a unitary institution, the states left many of the executive's traditional powers in place, which suggests that the Framers did not wish to alter the allocation of constitutional authorities. As Willi Paul Adams has observed in his authoritative work on the revolutionary state constitutions,

> [t]he striking fact of historical dimension is that the reaction against the colonial governor was so weak that it did not lead to parliamentary government with an executive committee of members of the legislature, but rather that within a decade the American system of presidential government evolved with full clarity and permanence.[26]

As we will see, when political and economic chaos beset the new states, these experiments in structural dilution were rejected in favor of a unitary president who retained the executive's traditional powers.

To be sure, many of the revolutionaries did hope to restrict the substance as well as the structure of executive power. A noted scholar of the presidency found in the revolutionary constitutions "the common practice of expressly submitting the exercise of either certain enumerated powers, the field of enumerated powers, or even the whole of the executive power to the legislative will."[27] Perhaps Thomas Jefferson was the most ambitious in terms of strictly controlling the power of the executive. Jefferson's title for the executive in his draft of the Virginia constitution was merely the "Administrator."[28] Jefferson enumerated the powers that the executive could *not* exercise: the administrator could not dismiss the legislature, regulate the money supply, set weights and measures, establish courts or other public facilities, control exports, create offices, or issue pardons. When it came to war powers, Jefferson's draft stated that the administrator could not "declare war or peace, issue letters of marque or reprisal, raise or introduce armed forces, or build armed vessels . . . forts or strongholds." Although the draft left to the administrator any remaining "powers formerly held by the king," there would seem little left.

Most states rejected Jefferson's approach. Instead of declaring that the administrator could not wage war or make peace, the states either gave the governor the exclusive power to decide when to use the militia or required that he consult the council before calling forth the military. Even Jefferson's native state put aside his suggestions: the Virginia constitutional convention of 1776 adopted George Mason's proposal, which allowed the governor to "embody the militia with the advice of the privy council, and when embodied, let the gov[ernor] alone have the direction of the militia, under the laws of the country."[29] The convention also deleted Jefferson's enumeration of war powers forbidden to the executive. Undeterred, Jefferson offered his language as a constitutional amendment, but the other members of the convention rejected it in favor of a provision permitting the governor, with the advice of a council of state, to "exercise the Executive powers of Government."[30] Although Virginia's approach of introducing council approval, which resembled that of many other states, placed structural checks on the governor's power, it was not a substantive limitation on the executive branch's powers. The privy council itself was part of the executive branch. Although a dead end, Jefferson's scheme was widely circulated, and it provided an example of how the Framers could have created a legislature-first approach to war—had they chosen to do so.

In drafting their new constitutions, states generally rejected Jefferson in favor of John Adams, who for once had his day over his friend and future rival. In his *Thoughts on Government,* which became the blueprint for many of the state constitutions, Adams suggested that the states should adopt bicameral legislatures and create a governor "who, after being stripped of most of those badges of domination called prerogatives, should have a free and independent exercise of his judgment, and be made also an integral part of the legislature."[31] Adams considered warmaking authority and the control of the armed forces not as "badges of domination," but as legitimate elements of the executive power. He recommended to the states that the "Governor should have the command of the militia, and of all your armies." In the area of war powers, as in other respects, Adams advised the states to reproduce the forms and powers of the British constitution, after adjusting the branches of government to be more responsive to popular sovereignty. His plan called for a governor, a commons, and a mediating senate, but did not enumerate each body's powers.

If we think of the allocation of war powers among the British and colonial governments as the background on which the state constitutions were drawn, state silence suggests an acceptance of the British approach. In other words, if the states had wanted to reject the traditional model of Anglo-American warmaking, which was composed of executive initiative and legislative appropriations, their constitutions would have followed the lines suggested by Jefferson. Instead, the revolutionaries decided to mimic the British forms of government, as recommended by Adams. While the Revolution may have represented a rebellion against the presence of the Crown, it was not an assault on the traditional relationship between the executive and legislature. As under the royal governors, the common practice of the states either assumed that the governors had broad warmaking authority, or explicitly gave them such power in terms reminiscent of the British constitution and the colonial charters. Unlike the federal Constitution, the state constitutions chose not to enumerate the powers of their legislatures, and instead allowed them to exercise their traditional power to fund and supply war.[32]

Although the states experimented radically with the structure of the executive branch, they left relatively unchanged the traditional allocation of powers between the legislative and executive branches. The Framers of the state constitutions did not alter the existing arrangement in war powers, but rather retained the prerevolutionary system of independent executive warmaking. Like New York and New Jersey, for example, Georgia vested the "supreme executive power" in the governor and declared that he "shall be captain-general and Commander in Chief over all the militia, and other military and naval forces belonging to this State."[33] State constitutions represented a continuation, rather than a break, from the example of the British constitution and the practice of the royal colonial governors.

To be sure, the state constitutions were not exact duplicates of the British. Nonetheless, an examination of the manner in which the states addressed the allocation of warmaking powers bears out the intent to continue the general British patterns. Of the different modifications made by the states, the most common was a provision that explicitly called on the governor to consult with others before deciding to deploy the military. These clauses usually required that before calling forth the militia the governor had to receive approval from a council of state appointed by the legislature but part of the executive branch. In a typical example, Delaware declared that its "president, with the advice and consent of the privy council, may embody the militia, and act as captain-general and commander-in-chief of them, and the other military force of this State, under the laws of the same."[34] These consultation provisions illustrate the common understanding among the revolutionaries that the governor generally had no preexisting duty to consult with the legislature before sending the state into war. Correspondingly, if the Framers of the federal Constitution had wanted the president to consult either with the legislature or within the executive before embarking on a military venture, they easily could have borrowed from these state provisions and required the president to consult with the Senate (as some in the Constitutional Convention proposed) or some other body.

Checks on the executive also arose from citizen participation in the militia. Composed of armed, everyday citizens, the militia not only often served as a state's only military force, it also played an important role in revolutionary ideology as a locus of republican values. Framers of the state constitutions hoped that the militia both would bring the people together and would provide them with a means of resisting oppressive government actions.[35] As a result, they took steps to increase the voice of the people directly in military affairs. State constitutions either prohibited or warned against the raising of a standing army. Virginia's provision is representative: "That a well-regulated militia, composed of the body of the people, trained to arms, is the proper, natural, and safe defence of a free State; that standing armies, in time of peace, should be avoided, as dangerous to liberty . . . ."[36] Other state constitutions permitted the militia to elect many of their own officers, making them representatives of the people rather than appointees responsible to the governor.[37] Two states, Massachusetts and New Hampshire, required that the governor receive the militia's approval before leading them outside state limits.[38] These provisions furthered the revolutionaries' belief that a democratic check on war emanated from the people themselves by virtue of their relationship with the executive as citizen-soldiers. The army and militia acted as a republican institution that not only fought the wars, but also participated in executive decisionmaking. Such arrangements obviated the need for legislative input in military matters beyond questions of funding, for legislators could play only an imperfect role as representatives of the people.

In many ways, the early state constitutions could have served as the model for a federal Constitution with limited executive war powers. Early proposals sought to prohibit the executive branch from beginning wars or from introducing armed forces. These suggestions were rejected in favor of continuing the traditional allocation of warmaking authority. Instead of placing substantive limits on the executive's war power, the Framers decided to alter the structure of the executive itself. Later state constitutions discarded these structural experiments and reinstituted a unified, vigorous executive, thereby leaving executive war powers for the most part in the hands of the governor.

New York's powerful executive received wide praise among the Framers.[39] Adopted in the spring of 1777, that constitution embodied what had been learned from the errors of other states, and also perhaps from the British occupation of a large portion of New York. Rejecting the structural handcuffs placed on the executive by other states, New York vested "the supreme executive power and authority of this State" in a single, popularly elected governor. No privy council was created to look over his shoulder, nor did any limitation exist on the number of terms a governor could serve.[40] New York married structural independence to the same broad war powers enjoyed by the executive's colleagues in other states. The constitution vested him with the position of "general and commander-in-chief of all the militia, and admiral of the navy of this State," and enumerated no war authorities for the assembly, which left to the legislature its customary role in making funding decisions. During the Revolution, George Clinton, New York's first governor, sent the militia on his sole authority to

reinforce General Gates's campaign against British forces. He later notified the legislature of the move in his first inaugural address.[41] Throughout the war, Clinton (himself a military officer) worked closely with General Washington and his subordinates to coordinate operations against the
British. Although it expressed its views when appropriating funds for the
war effort, the legislature generally obeyed Clinton's wishes. He encountered such success in running the war and the state that the voters returned
him to office for eighteen consecutive years, even though for most of the
war New York City remained in the hands of the enemy.

New York's example was significant not because it granted the executive broader substantive war powers than the other states. New York's
allocation of powers remained fairly unexceptional. It was only when
these substantive powers were combined with a structurally independent
and unitary executive that vigorous government emerged. These lessons
did not go unnoticed by the Framers. New York's experience influenced
not only the later constitution-writing efforts of Massachusetts and New
Hampshire, but also the work of the Philadelphia Convention.[42] During
the struggle for ratification, Publius expressed the thoughts of many when
he declared that the New York constitution "has been justly celebrated
both in Europe and in America as one of the best of the forms of government established in this country."[43] As Charles Thach concluded, "[H]ere
was a strictly indigenous and entirely distinctive constitutional system,
and, of course, executive department, for the consideration of the Philadelphia delegates."[44] As we will see, the Framers took the example of New
York to heart and proceeded to grant to an independent, unitary president
the substantive war powers exercised by king, colonial governor, and state
executive.

The post-1777 state constitutions carried forward, rather than rejected,
the progress in New York. Massachusetts, which adopted its constitution
in 1780, and New Hampshire, which ratified a similar document in 1784,
both provided for strong executive power in war:

> The president of this state for the time being, shall be commander in
> chief of the army and navy, and all the military forces of the state, by
> sea and land; and shall have full power by himself . . . to train, instruct,
> exercise and govern the militia and navy; and for the special defence and
> safety of this state to assemble in martial array, and put in warlike posture,
> the inhabitants thereof, and to lead and conduct them, and with them to

encounter, expulse, repel, resist and pursue by force of arms, as well by sea as by land, within and without the limits of this state; and also to kill, slay, destroy, if necessary, and conquer by all fitting ways, enterprize and means, all and every such person and persons as shall, at any time here-after, in a hostile manner, attempt or enterprize the destruction, invasion, detriment, or annoyance of this state; and to use and exercise over the army and navy, and over the militia in actual service, the law-martial in time of war, invasion, and also in rebellion, declared by the legislature to exist . . . and in fine, the president hereby is entrusted with all other powers incident to the office of captain-general and commander in chief, and admiral . . . . [45]

These war powers provisions not only gave the governor the commander-in-chief power, they also assumed that the governor had authority to make war. These provisions do not just limit executive warmaking authority to defensive responses to attack, they also explicitly provide for offensive operations under the direct authority of the executive, who may use any means he sees fit ("kill, slay, destroy, if necessary, and conquer by all fitting ways, enterprize and means") to achieve his war aims. Given the governor's duty to secure the safety of the state, these military provisions placed in the executive's hands the responsibility and incentive to act first. The provisions of both Massachusetts and New Hampshire also indicate the role of a declaration of war as a judicial announcement, rather than a legislative authorization for executive action. The power to declare war is vested in the legislature, but only acts as a triggering device for the governor's authority to declare martial law.

The history behind Massachusetts's 1780 constitution demonstrates the shared understanding that the governor enjoyed traditional executive warmaking powers. In 1778, a convention had recommended a constitution for popular ratification that permitted the governor to exercise military power only "according to the laws . . . or the resolves of the General Court," and that prohibited him from marching the militia out of the state without Senate approval.[46] However, the people rejected the proposed document, supplied their reasons, and sent proposals for a new constitution.

These criticisms and concerns were best expressed by the townspeople of Essex in the "Essex Result." Written mainly by Theophilus Parsons, the Result had a profound effect on the Framers' thinking about the separation of powers and individual rights.[47] One historian of the period describes the document as "an essay in political theory and constitutional practice comparable to *The Federalist Papers* in the sophistication of its argument (and in its political outlook)."[48] The Essex Result rejected the weak executive of the proposed constitution and called instead for an executive branch composed of an independent, directly elected governor and a privy council chosen by the legislature, with the power to veto legislation. The Result sharply criticized the proposed constitution for undermining the governor's powers as "Captain-General" of the army and navy: "The executive power is to act as Captain-General, to marshal the militia and armies of the state, and, for her defence, to lead them on to battle."[49] Divided authority would be foolish: "Was one to propose a body of militia, over which two Generals, with equal authority, should have the command, he would be laughed at." "Let the Governor alone marshal the militia, and regulate the same, together with the navy," the Result concluded.[50] Although the writers of the Essex Result recognized that the executive might try to expand his overall authority through the exercise of his war power, they decided that the governor's ability to respond quickly to emergencies justified centralizing all military decisions in his hands: "Should Providence or Portsmouth towns outside of, but near, Massachusetts be attacked suddenly, a day's delay might be of most pernicious consequence. Was the consent of the legislative body, or a branch of it, necessary, a longer delay would be unavoidable." The Result recommended that the governor receive the approval of the privy council before marching the army outside the state, and that within ten days after doing so he "convene the legislative body, and take their opinion." Even if the legislature disapproved, however, the governor could still press on if "the general good requires it, and then he will be applauded."[51]

Most of the Essex Result proposals, including those for an independent executive with strong legislative and military powers, made their way into the Massachusetts constitution. It provided the intellectual bridge between the New York and Massachusetts constitutions, which itself provided the model for the New Hampshire constitution and for the federal Constitution.[52] In sending the 1780 constitution to the people of the state for ratification, the Massachusetts constitutional convention further underscored the executive's primacy in war. The authors of the draft linked

the governor's military authority to his veto powers as the twin underpin-
nings of the separation of powers and of the people's safety:

> The Legislative, the Judicial and Executive Powers naturally exist in ev-
> ery Government: And the History of the rise and fall of the Empires of
> the World affords us ample proof, that when the same Man or Body of
> Men enact, interpret and execute the Laws, property becomes too precar-
> ious to be valuable, and a People are finally borne down with the force
> of corruption resulting from the Union of those Powers. The Governor is
> emphatically the Representative of the whole People, being chosen not
> by one Town, or County, but by the People at large. We have therefore
> thought it safest to rest this Power in his hands; and as the Safety of the
> Commonwealth requires, that there should be one Commander in Chief
> over the Militia, we have given the Governor that Command for the same
> reason . . . . [53]

The Massachusetts constitution previewed several of the themes that
would become prominent in the federal Constitution. The president is
seen as the representative and protector of the people, and his sole command over the military without formal legislative control is crucial to the
separation of powers and the public safety. Following the ideals set forth
in the Essex Result, the influential Massachusetts constitution envisioned
a system in which the executive first took action in war, and then sought
approval after the fact from the legislature and the people. Of course, the
legislature also would retain the ability to participate before the fact by
using its appropriations power to refuse to fund the military.

To the reformers who would attend the Philadelphia Convention, as
Gordon Wood has observed, the Massachusetts document "came to stand
for the reconsidered ideal of a 'perfect constitution.' . . . [It] seemed to . . .
have recaptured the best elements of the British constitution that had
been forgotten in the excitement of 1776."[54] Its enumeration of the powers
vested in the commander in chief, combined with the explanatory sidebar
of the Essex Result, illustrates the contemporary understanding of the
proper and most effective relationship between the executive and legislature in matters of war. Massachusetts's example also is particularly
compelling because it responded to a proposal that the legislature approve all military operations. Rejecting such an approach, the writers of
the Essex Result and of the 1780 state constitution have given us a full

explication of, and explanation for, the customary system of executive initiative in war.

As states embarked on the modification of their new constitutions, only one, South Carolina, chose to impose substantive, rather than structural, limitations on the executive's war powers. In its 1776 constitution, South Carolina decided to rein in the warmaking powers of the executive branch, even though it designated the executive as the "the president and commander-in-chief." South Carolina declared "that the president and commander-in-chief shall have no power to make war or peace, or enter into any final treaty, without the consent of the general assembly and legislative council."[55] Two years later, South Carolina made the restriction even clearer by declaring "that the governor and commander-in-chief shall have no power to commence war, or conclude peace, or enter into any final treaty" without legislative approval.[56] Unlike her sister states, South Carolina required formal legislative approval of the executive's decisions on war and peace, and prohibited the executive from beginning hostilities without the assembly's consent.

Although the Framers did not follow South Carolina's example, it is helpful in two ways. First, it indicates that the common understanding of war powers did not require the executive to receive formal legislative approval to commence hostilities. In the absence of such an understanding, there would have been little need for South Carolina to include explicit language shifting power to the assembly.[57] In other words, if the revolutionary Americans commonly believed that a legislative endorsement was necessary for war, then South Carolina's constitution would simply have remained silent, or it would have adopted the boilerplate language of the state charters, and left it at that. Second, South Carolina's war clause provides yet another example of a path not taken by the Philadelphia delegates. If the Framers had wanted to prevent the president from commencing war without congressional approval, as many legal scholars believe today, they could have adopted a provision not unlike South Carolina's (or Jefferson's, for that matter). Article I, Section 8, or Article II, Section 2, could have included a provision stating that "the President shall have no power to commence war, or conclude peace, without the consent of Congress." It did not.

In sum, the state constitutions are a significant but overlooked part of the history of the foreign affairs power. The accepted scholarly conclusion that the states reduced the independence of the executive branch fails to capture the subtleties in the change in executive power. The change embodied in these state constitutions was one of structure rather than of substance. Despite the revolutionaries' turn toward the legislatures as representatives of the people, the states were nearly unanimous that war-making authority should remain in the hands of the executive, leaving the legislature to exercise its power through its traditional role as keeper of the treasury. Early efforts to rein in executive power took the form of structural, rather than substantive, alterations in the nature of the state governors. South Carolina's radically different constitution is the exception that proves the rule: it was the only state to restrain the executive's war powers by placing decisionmaking authority in war in another branch of government. If the Framers of 1787 had wanted to adopt either South Carolina's system, or a system requiring consultations with other bodies such as a council or Senate, they had a clear example to follow.

THE ARTICLES OF CONFEDERATION

After achieving independence, Americans maintained the separation between war and treaties on the one hand, and funding and internal legislation on the other. Drafted in 1777 and ratified in 1781, the Articles of Confederation created the only national government Americans would know until 1788. Understandably, the Articles have become a focal point for historical studies of foreign affairs because they supplied many of the antecedents for various powers found in the Constitution. Since the Articles vested all national powers in the Continental Congress, including those over war and peace, historians often assume that the Framers believed the war powers to be legislative in nature. Arthur Bestor, for example, found in the Articles evidence of a common belief that foreign policy decisions were "to be arrived at through legislative deliberation—the very antithesis of the idea of vesting the power of war and peace in executive hands."[58]

Contrary to these assertions, the constitutional power over foreign relations formally devolved to the Continental Congress precisely because it was the nation's executive branch. Historians have pointed out that Congress was more of a treaty organization than a representative government. As Chief Justice John Marshall later described it, "[t]he confederation was, essentially, a league; and congress was a corps of ambassadors, to be recalled at the will of their masters."[59] Legislative powers—even in the foreign affairs arena—remained with the state assemblies.[60] War and treaty powers under the Articles of Confederation did not metamorphose into a legislative function, but remained an executive function subject to the traditional legislative check of funding and implementing laws. While these checks were once in the hands of Parliament, however, the Revolution located them in the assemblies. Under the Articles system, the separation of powers existed vertically rather than horizontally.

The separation of powers between the Continental Congress and the states paralleled the division of authority between the Crown and Parliament. Just as the Crown required the cooperation of Parliament in funding wars and implementing treaties, so too the Continental Congress relied on the states for supplies and changes in their internal laws to execute the nation's international obligations. Congress could not pass laws that applied to individuals; it could not impose direct taxes or raise troops; it could not regulate interstate commerce. Congress could only requisition the states for supplies and recommend legislation to the assemblies for adoption. As historians Eugene Sheridan and John Murrin have observed, "the legislative powers of Parliament tended to devolve upon the states, while the executive powers of the Crown passed to Congress, which we should probably conceptualize as more of a plural executive than a legislature."[61] The revolutionary generation had rebelled against Parliament because it had imposed taxes and internal regulations without representation. As only the states (which had one vote each), and not the people, were represented in Congress, it would have made little sense under revolutionary ideology to grant Congress the power to legislate or appropriate.

Having created a vacuum in executive authority by breaking with the Crown, the drafters of the Articles transferred all foreign affairs powers to the Continental Congress. Article IX declared that Congress possessed "the sole and exclusive right and power of determining on peace and war." It also had the sole authority for

> entering into treaties and alliances . . . of establishing rules for deciding in all cases what captures on land or water shall be legal, and in what manner prizes taken by land or naval forces in the service of the United States shall be divided or appropriated; of granting letters of marque and reprisal in times of peace.[62]

Article IX also vested Congress with the authority to appoint and commission all military officers and the powers "to build and equip a navy; to agree upon the number of land forces, and to make requisitions from each State for its quota." Nine states had to assent before Congress could "engage in a war," grant letters of marque and reprisal in peacetime, enter into treaties, fund an army and navy, or appoint a commander in chief.

The Articles anticipated the Constitution in preempting virtually all state activity with foreign nations. Article VI declared that "no state shall engage in any war" without congressional consent, unless it was "actually invaded by enemies," or it knew of an Indian attack so imminent that seeking congressional approval would result in dangerous delay. No state could "grant commissions to any ships or vessels of war, or letters of marque or reprisal, except it be after a declaration of war by the United States," unless it "be infested by pirates." No state could maintain warships or standing armies without congressional permission during peacetime.

Article VI prohibited states from sending or receiving ambassadors or from "enter[ing] into any conference, agreement, alliance or treaty" with any foreign nation or king without the consent of Congress. States also could not enter into any "treaty, confederation or alliance" with each other without congressional approval. Finally, Article VI prohibited states from imposing any imposts or duties, "which may interfere with any stipulations in treaties," already made or proposed, at the time of the Articles' ratification, between the United States and France or Spain. Article VI's explicit bar on this narrow type of implementing legislation implies that states possessed a broader authority over domestic execution of treaty obligations, an implication further reinforced by Article II's general reservation of each state's "sovereignty, freedom, and independence, and every power, jurisdiction, and right" not "expressly delegated" to Congress.[63]

At first glance, it might appear that Article IX's catalogue of powers demonstrates an intention to vest all foreign affairs powers in a legislature. This reading might suggest an understanding of the war and treaty powers as legislative, or at least not executive, in nature. However, the Congress of 1783 was not the Congress of 1789. The Continental Congress did not play the role of a legislative body as we understand it today. Rather, the Congress exercised a mixture of judicial, legislative, and executive functions. Article IX, for example, begins by giving Congress traditional executive powers—such as the powers to decide on war and peace and appoint government officials. It then gives Congress judicial powers, declaring that it shall act as an appellate court of last resort for interstate disputes. Only after listing the executive and judicial powers does Article IX proceed to those legislative powers most analogous to the Constitution's Article I, Section 8, but which under the British constitution had rested with the king. Thus, the latter portion of Article IX gives Congress the authority to coin money, fix weights and measures, establish post offices, and appoint officers and make rules to regulate the military. Congress did not have powers that the revolutionaries normally associated with a legislature, such as the authority to regulate trade or to levy taxes—powers that remained with the individual states. As one historian has concluded, "the executive and administrative responsibilities that had been exercised by or under the aegis of the king's authority were confided to the successor to his authority, the Congress."[64]

Hence, the story of the Continental Congress is a tale of failed attempts to organize its executive, not legislative, power effectively. Problems arose not because of the weaknesses of Congress's substantive powers in foreign relations, but because of defects in its internal structure. At first, Congress conducted its war and foreign policies by committee, which led to haphazard and sometimes disastrous results.[65] Seeking reform in structural changes, Congress in 1781 created executive departments under the control of individual ministers for war, foreign affairs, navy, and finance. But even executive reorganization failed to cure matters, as Congress still lacked the legislative authority to tax and to fund armies directly. It was these defects that would lead to demands for a new Constitution.

The story of the Articles also sheds light on the meaning of "declaration of war." Although it did not expressly grant Congress the authority to declare war, the Articles apparently subsumed that authority in the general power to decide on questions of war and peace. Other parts of the Articles show that the revolutionaries viewed this power primarily as one that defined the legal status of, and relationships among, American citizens and those of hostile nations under international law. Nor did the Articles contain an explicit provision requiring a declaration of war before the federal government could begin military operations.

Consider, for example, the important role played by a declaration of war in restricting the military operations of the independent states. Article VI prohibited state military action without a declaration of war. This prohibition on state action without a declaration serves as an example of a path not taken by the Framers. If the delegates to the Constitutional Convention had wanted to prohibit the president from initiating hostilities with another nation, they could have borrowed Article VI and adjusted it to apply to the federal executive as well. Article VI further suggests that the revolutionaries understood the declaration of war's core purpose to be one relevant to international law. The declaration acted as a permission slip for the states to initiate hostile activities, but only against identified enemies. Without a declaration of war, international law would consider such naval attacks as acts of piracy rather than as legitimate combat under the laws of war. In short, the declaration of war clothed what would have been an illegal act by the states—sending warships against another nation—with a legal status in international law.

Article VI is also significant because it presents a neat contrast with Article IX's grant of war powers to Congress. Article IX gave Congress the authority to decide on war and peace as well as the power to raise an army and navy. However, Article IX's provision, unlike Article VI's restrictions on the states, did not require Congress to issue a declaration of war before it initiated hostilities. Nor did Article IX require a declaration of war before Congress raised a military force or authorized naval attacks. If the Articles' drafters had wanted to make a declaration of war an exclusive trigger for military operations, they certainly knew how to do it, for they included such a provision in Article VI's restrictions on the states.

With regard to treaties, the Continental Congress suffered from the defect that its representation bore no relationship to population, thereby creating a threat that sectional concerns could override the national interest. One congressional controversy over foreign policy is worth examining in detail because it would become an important touchstone for the ratification debates that would occur the following year on the treaty power. From 1785 to 1786, John Jay, as secretary for foreign affairs, negotiated with Spain concerning various boundary disputes with Spain's North American territories. Chief among these issues was the right of American settlers to navigate the southern reaches of the Mississippi River, which passed through Spanish territory on its way to the sea. Spain had closed its portion of the Mississippi to American commerce in 1784; Congress specifically instructed Jay that any treaty with Spain had to win back that right. Spain's ambassador, Don Diego de Gardoqui, refused to accede to this demand out of Spanish fears of America's westward expansion. Instead, de Gardoqui offered to enter into a commercial treaty that would benefit the northeastern port cities of Boston, New York, and Philadelphia. With negotiations at an impasse, Jay sent home for guidance.[66]

When Congress in the summer of 1786 considered whether to modify Jay's instructions, a sharp sectional divide appeared. Seven northern states from New Hampshire to Pennsylvania stood to gain from a liberal commercial treaty with Spain. For the southern states, however, closing the Mississippi would cut off their expansion into the West. Although two-thirds of the states were required to make a treaty, a simple majority could terminate negotiations altogether. This meant that the four southern states, joined by Maryland, could not terminate the negotiations, but they could successfully block the ratification of any treaty. Nonetheless, the northern states, by a vote of 8 to 5, defeated southern attempts to end the Jay-Gardoqui discussions, and by a simple majority allowed Jay to dispense with the Mississippi River demand. But since five states had declared their opposition to such a provision, any treaty without free navigation of the Mississippi would fail to receive the necessary two-thirds vote.[67]

Controversy over the Jay-Gardoqui negotiations threatened the dissolution of the Union. It forced the states into two hardened camps defined by economic and sectional self-interest. As an economic and foreign policy dispute that mutated into a constitutional one, it revealed structural shortcomings in the way that the Articles of Confederation distributed the treatymaking power. To southerners, even the two-thirds requirement failed to protect the national interest, especially in regard to treaties that raised sectional divisions. The Jay-Gardoqui controversy suggested that less than two-thirds of the states could pursue a foreign policy that was not in the national interest. Southern delegates emerged from this controversy questioning whether a two-thirds requirement for treaties, with each state possessing one vote, provided adequate protection for their economic and territorial interests. It would prompt southern leaders during the next two years to search for a better approach to treatymaking that would include a more democratic voice to represent the people. It also demonstrated to some, such as James Madison, that treaty disputes could threaten the dissolution of the Union unless contained by a broader, republican national government.[68]

TREATIES AND THE PROBLEM OF ENFORCEMENT

Until this point, the treatment of the two core elements of the foreign affairs power—the war and treaty powers—received similar treatment. Revolutionary Americans continued to view both as inseparable from the executive power, and continued to vest them in executives that had been structurally weakened. They continued to expect the assemblies' power over funding and legislation to provide a sufficient check on the executive's foreign affairs power, just as it had in Great Britain. During the so-called Critical Period between the Revolution and the Constitution's ratification, however, an additional issue developed with regard to the enforcement of treaties. Because the Articles of Confederation gave Congress no textual authority to compel states to enforce treaties, Congress could only request that states honor the treaty rights of foreign subjects.[69] When it came to the Treaty of Paris of 1783, which made peace with Great Britain, some states resisted congressional requests for implementation, leading to foreign policy setbacks and calls for constitutional reform. The problems raised by this resistance were addressed by three of the leaders of the ratification effort and the authors of the *Federalist Papers*—Alexander Hamilton, John Jay, and James Madison. Not only would their concerns about treaties become widely known, but their thinking would be representative of the pro-Constitution cause. Their views reveal two distinct themes running through the founding period: one that turned to judicial enforcement of treaties, and another that looked to a national legislature capable of implementing treaties directly.

Inability to command compliance with its foreign policy virtually ensured Congress's failure. Congress could not raise revenue, enforce a common commercial policy, or even promise that the states would observe its agreements. States would not cooperate to win trade concessions from foreign nations, Congress could not guarantee that states would change their laws to comply with trade treaties, and neither the states nor Congress could impose meaningful sanctions.[70] The Treaty of Paris highlighted the weakness in America's governmental structure. Overall, the newly independent states received highly favorable terms: Britain recognized American independence, acknowledged America's borders to reach as far west as the Mississippi River and as far north as the Great Lakes, evacuated its forces from New York City and the South, and promised to turn over a series of strategic forts in the Great Lakes area.[71] London received three concessions in return. Article IV declared that "creditors on either side shall meet with no lawful impediment to the recovery of the full value . . . of all bona fide debts heretofore contracted." In other words, British financiers would be able to recover on prewar debts. Article V stated that "Congress shall earnestly recommend . . . to the legislatures of the respective states" that they compensate Loyalists whose property had been confiscated during the war. Article VI prohibited any further confiscation, prosecution, or civil action against individuals based on their roles in the war. British negotiators did not, however, consider these articles to be much of a victory; in the words of one historian, they were "trifling concessions and empty formulas."[72]

Nonetheless, the treaty's compensation and debt provisions proved to be the source of constitutional breakdown. Massachusetts, New York, Pennsylvania, and all of the southern states either passed laws that confiscated debts owed to British citizens or prevented the collection of such debts after Congress's ratification of the treaty. British diplomats claimed that state courts were refusing to suspend the operation of these laws, despite Article IV of the treaty. Historians generally agree that "[t]here was no question that the United States had violated the peace treaty."[73] In response, the British refused to evacuate the northern frontier forts, which controlled access to the Great Lakes and nearby rivers. British refusal to relinquish the forts was not just a blow to American pride, but a significant military and economic setback, for the forts served as centers of commerce and as support areas for hostile Indian tribes and Loyalists. Leading American politicians throughout the states concluded that the national government needed the power to compel obedience to treaty obligations in order to solve the crisis.

One of the first to reach this conclusion was Alexander Hamilton, who encountered the issue in the 1784 case of *Rutgers v. Waddington*.[74] As feelings against Loyalists and the British ran high in New York, much of which had been occupied at some point during the war, the state assembly passed a series of harsh measures against Loyalists. In addition to a wartime Confiscation Act of Loyalist property, the legislature enacted the 1782 Citation Act, which stayed the execution of debts owed to Loyalists, and the 1783 Trespass Act, which allowed Americans who had fled New York City to recover damages from those who had occupied their property during the war. Not only did these statutes conflict with the international laws of war, which allowed a defense for civilians acting under the orders of an occupying army, but they violated the Treaty of Paris.

Hamilton decided to challenge the Trespass Act by representing an English businessman who had operated a brewery during the occupation of New York City. He made three arguments before the state court: first, that the Act violated the laws of war; second, that the Act violated the Treaty of Paris, which had legislative effect as part of Congress's treaty power; and third, that the court had the authority to invalidate the Act as contrary to the treaty, which had been ratified by Congress and was now part of the New York constitution. Plaintiffs forcefully responded that state courts, as creatures of the legislature, had no authority to invalidate the statute. In an ambiguous decision, the court avoided the question of the supremacy of the peace treaty by reading the Act narrowly, as Hamilton had urged in a secondary argument.

To the extent that it is still remembered, *Rutgers v. Waddington* usually appears in discussions of the early foundations for judicial review. It also stands, however, as one of the earliest—if not the first—American judicial encounter with arguments for treaty self-execution. Hamilton's arguments were more than the product of his representation of a paying client. Around the same time that he was filing briefs in *Rutgers,* Hamilton wrote two pamphlets under the pseudonym "Phocion" that provided a fuller exposition of his arguments.[75] Hamilton argued that the Treaty of Paris constituted higher law because it emanated from the Continental Congress, the repository of national sovereignty. "Does not the act of confederation place the exclusive right of war and peace in the United States in Congress?" Hamilton asked rhetorically. "Are not these among the first rights of sovereignty, and does not the delegation of them to the general confederacy, so far abridge the sovereignty of each particular state?" Allowing states to pass laws in conflict with a treaty would "involve the contradiction of *imperium in imperio,*" wrote Hamilton.

Hamilton was unwilling to place any bounds on the extent of the treaty power, so long as it was used to advance the national interest. "It follows that Congress and their Ministers acted wisely in making the treaty which has been made; and it follows from this, that these states are bound by it, and ought religiously to observe it." Prohibiting treaties from affecting "the internal police" of a state, Hamilton responded, would make "a mere nullity" of Congress's power to make treaties. "In short," Hamilton concluded, "if nothing was to be done by Congress that would affect our internal police, . . . would not all the powers of the confederation be annihilated and the union dissolved?"[76] It seems clear that Hamilton believed that, even under the Articles of Confederation, treaties of their own force already preempted inconsistent state law.

John Jay shared Hamilton's views. As secretary for foreign affairs, Jay had concluded that refusal to observe the 1783 Treaty of Paris was impeding efforts to reach commercial agreements with Britain, France, and Spain. On October 13, 1786, he presented a report to Congress responding to the British complaints of treaty violations. Jay declared that he "considers the thirteen independent sovereign States as having, by express delegation of power, formed and vested in Congress a perfect though limited sovereignty for the general and national purposes specified in the Confederation," particularly the war and treaty powers. "When therefore a treaty is made," Jay continued, "it immediately becomes binding on the whole nation and superadded to the laws of the land, without the intervention, consent, or fiat of State legislatures." Since the parties to a treaty are the two national sovereigns, "states have no right to accept some Articles and reject others" or to "subject [treaties] to such alterations as this or that State Legislature may think expedient to make."[77]

Jay urged Congress to recommend three measures to the states. The first declared that the state legislatures could not pass any act "interpreting, explaining, or construing a National treaty" or "restraining, limiting or in any manner impeding, retarding or counteracting the operation or execution of the same." The second resolution demanded that state laws violating the Treaty of Paris "be forthwith repealed." As a further safeguard, the third measure recommended that the states repeal any laws that might come into conflict with the treaty in the future, and it recommended that the states grant their courts the power to adjudicate treaty questions, "any thing in the said Acts or parts of Acts to the contrary thereof in any wise notwithstanding." In his proposals, Jay sketched the three elements of treaty supremacy: (1) national sovereignty was vested in Congress, not the states; (2) state laws inconsistent with national treaties were invalid;

(3) state courts were to block the operation of state laws that conflicted with treaties. Following Jay's advice, Congress on April 13, 1787 issued his report in its own name to the states and adopted the three resolutions.[78]

Tellingly, the very form of the resolutions proved Jay (and Hamilton) wrong about the status of treaties under the Articles of Confederation. If the Continental Congress had already enjoyed a legislative power in treatymaking that preempted conflicting state law, then Congress should not have needed to ask the states to repeal their inconsistent laws. Rather than declaring congressional supremacy, the resolutions displayed for all to see that Congress relied on state goodwill to implement its foreign policy. If there had been general agreement on Jay's interpretation of the treaty power under the Articles, the states should have complied quickly with Congress's demands. Seven states did pass such laws, all but one of them from the North, which had the most to gain from more national control over foreign affairs. All but one of the southern states (which had opposed the change in Jay's negotiating instructions in the Jay-Gardoqui affair) refused.[79] Even at the high tide for the treaty supremacy effort during the Critical Period, the power to legislate still rested firmly in the hands of the state legislatures.

During this same period, Jay's and Hamilton's future collaborator, James Madison, was engaged in his own examination of the relationship between the treaty power and the power of legislation. By 1786, according to Madison scholars, he had become disillusioned with the state legislatures, which he believed were subject to demagoguery and were enacting unjust economic legislation. Madison also had become concerned about the sectional divisions sparked by the Jay-Gardoqui controversy. Supporting the opening of the Mississippi as a matter of policy, he feared that the North's use of its majority power would undermine the cause of strengthening Congress's powers. After the failure of the Annapolis Convention to expand Congress's commercial powers, Madison and others turned their attention to broader constitutional overhaul. Madison's innovation, which would set him apart from Hamilton and Jay, was to seek treaty enforcement not in the states or their judiciaries, but in a representative national Congress that truly exercised the power to legislate.[80]

Preparing for the Philadelphia Convention in the spring of 1787, Madison drafted a memo, "Vices of the Political System of the United States," that laid out much of his thinking. States had obstructed the success of the confederation by encroaching on congressional powers, violating treaty obligations, and refusing to cooperate on matters of national interest. As examples of the first, Madison cited wars and treaties between the states and the Indians and unapproved interstate compacts. As examples of the second, Madison recited the violations of the Treaty of Paris, which he traced to the parochial outlook of state legislators. "From the number of Legislatures, the sphere of life from which most of their members are taken, and the circumstances under which their legislative business is carried on," he observed, "irregularities of this kind must frequently happen."[81] Of the third class of problems, Madison pointed to interstate commerce, which witnessed state discrimination against imports and failure to present a common national front on trade. These were not unusual criticisms of the Articles of Confederation system. What made Madison's thinking original, however, was that it linked these problems to the unrestrained nature of popular government in the states.

Madison's "Vices" memo traced the problems of the confederation to the state legislatures. Why had the confederation failed? "[F]rom a mistaken confidence that the justice, the good faith, the honor, the sound policy, of the several legislative assemblies," Madison wrote, "would render superfluous any appeal to the ordinary motives by which the laws secure the obedience of individuals. . . ." Since the people had never ratified the articles, it was no more than "a treaty of amity of commerce and of alliance, between so many independent and Sovereign States," rather than part of every state constitution. Congress could not enforce its directives on the states or individuals, nor could it be confident that state courts would enforce its commands over state laws. "Whenever a law of a State happens to be repugnant to an act of Congress, particularly when the latter is of posterior date to the former, it will be at least questionable whether the latter must not prevail," Madison observed. "[A]nd as the question must be decided by the Tribunals of the State, they will be most likely to lean on the side of the State."[82]

Madison remained unconvinced that a more perfect union ought to rely on state judges and legislatures. "It is no longer doubted that a unanimous and punctual obedience of 13 independent bodies, to the acts of the federal Government, ought not be calculated on," he wrote. Rather, he believed that the federal government needed the power to "operate without the intervention of the States" directly on individuals. "A sanction is essential to the idea of law, as coercion is to that of Government," Madison wrote. "The federal system being destitute of both, wants the great vital principles of a Political Cons[ti]tution." The national government must be fundamentally reorganized to give it three branches of government— legislative, executive, judicial—to exercise the new power to promulgate, execute, and adjudicate the laws. In addition to a federal power that acted directly on individuals, Madison proposed a radical solution: a federal veto over all state legislation. Recalling the Crown's prerogative to review colonial legislation, Madison essentially proposed to make the federal government part of every state legislature; "[w]ithout this defensive power," he believed, "every positive power that can be given on paper will be evaded & defeated." While scholars have focused on the negative as an effort to control state oppression of minorities, it also sought to control state encroachment on federal law by means of institutional and political design, rather than through reliance on state judiciaries.

Madison reconciled the nature of treaties, the power to legislate, and the democratic nature of a new federal government in a way that Hamilton and Jay had not. Hamilton and Jay clothed in supremacy the decisions of an institution that was more of a treaty organization than a representative government. They chose to rely on state courts to enforce the law of a different sovereign—one that did not even function along democratic lines. Most important, their approach to treatymaking and enforcement failed to account for the creation of a representative national government, created by a popularly ratified document, that possessed its own executive, legislative, and judicial branches.

Madison, however, had thought through these questions. The first steps in his reform of the national government placed it on the firmer footing of popular ratification, based representation on population, and vested it with necessary national powers, especially over interstate and foreign commerce. Second, and equally important, the government was to be given the authority to enact and enforce law on individuals through its own independent institutions. Once the national government was reconstituted it would no longer need the states and their judiciaries for implementation of federal law. Madison's approach to treaties and lawmaking can be seen as a part of his broader remedy for the weaknesses of the confederation—a sweeping reconstitution of the national government into a democratic republic.[83]

CONCLUSION

We might fairly say that the Articles of Confederation system followed the traditional operation of the foreign affairs power that began in Great Britain in the 1620s and continued through the American Critical Period of the 1780s. Under the theory and practice of the British constitution during this time, warmaking and treatymaking were widely understood to be executive powers. Parliament could check the exercise of executive power through its legislative powers over funding, the regulation of domestic conduct, and impeachment. To be sure, the American revolutionaries reacted against the perceived abuses of the executive power by the Crown when they broke with Great Britain. When redesigning their state governments, however, they sought to limit executive power by diluting the unity, independence, and energy of the executive as an institution. What the revolutionaries did not do was to transfer executive authority over warmaking and treatymaking to the legislature. The one counterexample of a state constitution that explicitly vested such power in the assembly only underscores the common presumption that such powers lay with the executive.

Instead of taking the foreign affairs power away from the executive, the revolutionaries assumed that the assemblies could provide balance through their traditional legislative. They relied on more than a century of shared Anglo-American constitutional history, in which Parliament had used its formal constitutional authority over funding, legislation, and impeachment to win a functional veto over the Crown's exercise of the war and treaty powers. In rebelling against Great Britain, the revolutionaries had fought to retain this constitutional framework, which they put into practice with the new state governors. This system also guided the design of the Articles of Confederation, in which Congress exercised the executive power delegated by the states. While the executive Congress may have held the "the sole and exclusive right and power of determining on peace and war," it lacked a national legislative power. With the states controlling funding, supplies, and implementation, the nation not only could not wage effective war, it also could not live up to the terms of its peace treaty with Great Britain, which threatened America with disunion and even partition by the European powers.

This understanding of the foreign affairs power framed the debate that would occur during the drafting and ratification of the Constitution. Under the Articles of Confederation, the Continental Congress held the traditionally executive power to make treaties, but lacked the legislative authority to implement them. One response, embodied by the legal and political efforts of Hamilton and Jay, was to argue that national sovereignty resided in the Congress, which could make treaties that had direct legislative effect on individuals. Madison developed an alternate vision that unified the executive treaty power and the legislative power in a different manner. Rather than give treaties a domestic lawmaking dimension, Madison believed that a new constitution ought to vest the national government with the true power to legislate. With the force of popular sovereignty behind it, Congress would wage its own wars, pass its own laws, implement its own treaties, and rely on its own independent organs of government. Both approaches to treaties and lawmaking were debated at the Constitutional Convention, which, while appearing to adopt the Hamilton-Jay system, would provide the grounds for the Madisonian structure that prevailed during ratification.

4

WRITING AND RATIFYING
A FOREIGN AFFAIRS CONSTITUTION

Meeting in Philadelphia in the summer of 1787, the delegates to the Constitutional Convention devoted more of their energies toward creating a stronger national government than detailing its precise internal organization. Beyond establishing the existence and general functions of the three branches, the Framers did not set down in writing the exact allocation of authority over foreign affairs. This silence might indicate that the Framers intended to leave to future presidents, congressmen, and justices the freedom to work out the separation of powers for themselves. Alternatively, the silence might indicate an intention to continue practices and relationships among the branches that were so widely understood as to need no specific description.

This chapter shows that both interpretations partially explain the Framers' approach. In establishing the war and treaty powers, the Framers intended to adopt the traditional system they knew—foreign affairs remained an executive power, distinct from the legislature's authority over funding and domestic lawmaking. Yet, this arrangement left the precise boundaries of the war and treaty powers unfixed and subject, in each case, to the exercise of each branch's constitutional powers. In effect, the Framers demarcated a gray area in which the president and Congress could either cooperate in adopting a common foreign policy war or struggle to achieve conflicting goals.

Delegates came to Philadelphia to repair the defects of the Articles of Confederation, including what they saw as an inability to provide a sufficient defense against invasion. The weakness arose not because the Congress was unable to initiate war, but because it had to rely on the good faith of the states to raise and supply the military. The Framers quickly corrected this problem by expanding federal powers in foreign affairs at the expense of the states. The Constitution not only vested the federal government with the power to raise, supply, and lead the national military, it also divested the states of the ability to maintain peacetime armies and to wage war. While the Framers made clear that the national government, not the states, should exclusively govern the nation's foreign affairs, when it came to the allocation between the president and Congress, the Framers did not seek to place complete power in one branch. Some Framers initially hoped to place Congress at the fore in decisions on war, but this approach did not prevail. Rather, the provisions that they adopted contemplated overlapping competencies and powers held by equal, although structurally different, branches.

When the battle over the Constitution shifted from Philadelphia to the states, criticism forced the Federalists to express their vision of war in more concrete terms. The Federalists responded by defending a system in which the president and legislature would each use their independent powers as they saw fit, and in which the courts and legal sanctions were absent. It was a system that mirrored the British example. As James Madison described it before the Virginia ratifying convention: "The sword is in the hands of the British king; the purse in the hands of the Parliament. It is so in America, as far as any analogy can exist."[1]

A similar approach governed treaties. The Framers maintained the distinction between treatymaking and legislation that characterized British practice and their own thinking during the Revolution and the Critical Period. The Constitution reflects this understanding by allocating treatymaking to the executive branch and lawmaking to Congress. This division of powers did not just empower the Senate by giving it a joint role in treaties, but also protected the lawmaking process by limiting treaties to an executive function. Concern about the antidemocratic nature of the treaty process led at least some of the leading Framers to accept a role for the popularly elected House. In response to criticism that an unlimited treaty power could override individual rights or bargain away important national objectives, Federalists responded that treaties could not accomplish anything so drastic without the participation of the House in implementing legislation. Rather than receiving automatic enforcement within American law, treaties were an executive function—like decisions for war—that could be effectively implemented only if the legislature exercised its own constitutional powers.

THE CONSTITUTIONAL CONVENTION
AND THE VIRGINIA PLAN

When Edmund Randolph of Virginia made the first proposal for a new form of government at the Constitutional Convention on May 29, 1787, the delegates understood that the failure to handle foreign affairs effectively was one of the chief defects with the Articles of Confederation. Yet they did not have a clear remedy in mind. Randolph identified the chief problem with the Articles as its inability "to prevent a war nor to support it by [its] own authority." He cited examples that showed "that [the United States] could not cause infractions of treaties or of the law of nations, to be punished." This was particularly dangerous to the Union, he said, because "particular states might by their conduct provoke war without controul," a war that the Continental Congress did not have the resources at its command to fight and win.[2] To address these challenges, Randolph proposed a reconstituted national government with new powers, known as the "Virginia Plan."

The Virginia Plan addressed the problems of the Articles of Confederation in two ways. First, it proposed a bicameral legislature that would exercise all legislative power and would operate on the basis of popular representation.[3] A national executive, chosen by the legislature, would enjoy the executive powers of government. A national judiciary would adjudicate controversies under federal law, but the job of reviewing the constitutionality of proposed legislation would fall to a council of revision. This new national government would exercise powers over foreign affairs, interstate commerce, areas in which the states were incompetent, and taxation. Randolph's proposal created a government that could act directly on individuals, freeing it from dependence on the states for the execution of national laws and treaties. It did not enumerate the national government's limited powers, but instead resorted to broad grants of authority: the executive would "enjoy the Executive rights vested in Congress by the Confederation," and the "National Legislature" would exercise the "Legislative Rights" of the old Congress.[4]

While the Virginia Plan maintained the traditional vesting of formal war and treaty powers to the executive, it also gave the federal government new means to suppress state laws that interfered with federal treaties. Randolph proposed that the negative extend only to state laws that violated, "in the opinion of the National Legislature the articles of Union," rather than in all cases whatsoever.[5] By a unanimous vote, the convention subsequently approved a motion, without discussion, by Benjamin Franklin to add the words "or any treaties subsisting under the authority of the Union," to make clear that the negative would protect both the Constitution and treaties. Madison's efforts, however, to expand the negative to "improper" state acts—in other words, giving the federal government the power of review over all state laws, whether unconstitutional or not—failed in June. But the Committee of the Whole adopted the limited form of the negative, along with other elements of the Virginia Plan, soon thereafter.[6]

In a situation that would be familiar to modern separation of powers scholars, the Framers did not share an exact definition of executive and legislative powers. Confusion arose over the division of national powers among the branches, and no firm consensus could be reached on whether the foreign affairs powers should be vested solely in the president or in the Senate. Drawing on their British experience, almost all of the delegates who spoke on this question agreed that the powers of war and peace were executive in nature. On June 1, when the delegates discussed the Virginia Plan's provision to transfer the old Congress's executive powers, several speakers protested vesting the executive branch with complete power over war and peace. Mindful of the Crown's efforts to use its foreign affairs powers to encroach on legislative prerogatives, the delegates were unsure whether it would be wise to transfer to the president the Continental Congress's executive authorities in this area. Charles Pinckney's comments were typical: he "was for a vigorous Executive but was afraid the Executive powers of [the existing] Congress might extend to peace & war &c which would render the Executive a Monarchy, of the worst kind, to wit an elective one."[7] John Rutledge "was for vesting the Executive power in a single person, tho' he was not for giving him the power of war and peace." Although James Wilson supported a single executive for its "energy, dispatch and responsibility to the office," he too warned that the convention should not adopt the British division of executive and legislative powers. Wilson "did not consider the Prerogatives of the British Monarch as a proper guide in defining the Executive powers. Some of these prerogatives were of a Legislative nature. Among others that of war & peace &c."[8] At this point in the debate, the Framers seemed to agree that vesting the president with all the "executive powers" of the Articles of Confederation would include the power over war and peace.

For this reason, several delegates opposed transferring all executive power to the president because it would give him authority in war and peace equal to, if not greater than, that enjoyed by the British king. Arguing that the model of the British constitution was ill suited to America, Wilson succeeded early in June in limiting the president to executing the laws, appointing officers, and exercising powers delegated to him by Congress.[9] Although subsequent proposals deviated from the arrangements of the Virginia Plan, they did not reflect a different understanding. William Paterson's alternative to the Virginia Plan, known as the "New Jersey Plan," sought to retain the existing structure of the Articles of Confederation. Supported by the small states, the New Jersey Plan did not create a representative legislature based on population. It only extended federal power to include the regulation of interstate and international commerce and the right to impose import duties.[10] Congress would still represent the states alone, it would still lack the power to act on individuals, and it would still be dependent on the states for supply, for implementation of policy, and for execution of its laws. Nonetheless, even the New Jersey Plan declared that the executive "direct all military operations; provided that none of the persons composing the federal Executive shall on any occasion take command of any troops, so as personally to conduct any enterprise as General."[11] Paterson's suggestion on this point did not meet with the approval of the convention, but his plan nonetheless was sent to the Committee of Detail, which was in charge of translating the various proposals into a draft constitution. Although the New Jersey Plan contained the weakest executive of all the various schemes, one elected and controlled by Congress, it demonstrates that even those most opposed to executive power believed that the future president should control the military.

Alexander Hamilton put forth yet another plan of government. In a lengthy speech, he proposed giving the executive, which he called the

"Governour," "the direction of war when authorized or begun." The Senate would possess "the sole power of declaring war."[12] In his influential work, Charles Lofgren has read Hamilton, even though the most pro-executive figure of the Constitutional Convention, as "inclined to limit severely the executive's role in initiating war" because he appears to require a declaration of war before the president can direct it.[13] This overstates the case. Hamilton could have said that the executive had the direction of war after the Senate had declared it. Certainly, as we have seen, the state constitutions and the Articles of Confederation provided examples of constitutive documents that placed such restrictions on the executive power. In any event, the convention did not adopt anything like Hamilton's explicit restriction on the president's war powers. Indeed, Hamilton recognized that the executive could wage war without a declaration, when war had been "authorized or begun," rather than "declared." Hamilton's plan, which was widely ignored by his colleagues, recognized that both the governor and the Senate would share the powers of the executive branch. Hamilton joined his colleagues in envisioning war powers as an executive power with the Senate acting as an executive privy council rather than as a legislative body.

These early stages of the Philadelphia Convention did not give rise to a change in the existing understanding of the foreign affairs power as executive in nature. Nor did it alter the traditional view of the legislature's powers as fundamentally rooted in funding and domestic legislation. On July 26, however, the convention sent specific resolutions derived from the Virginia Plan to the Committee of Detail. The delegates retained the Virginia Plan's language that the national legislature would exercise the legislative powers of the old Congress, but they removed the vesting of executive power from the executive branch. In its place, they inserted an enumeration of the executive's power as extending only to executing the laws and appointing officers. The resolutions failed to transfer the old Congress's executive powers, including those of making war and peace, to any institution within the new government.[14]

Large and small states experienced more initial disagreement over treaty enforcement, which was only inevitable due to the New Jersey Plan's refusal to create a popular legislature. Instead of the Virginia Plan's negative on state laws, Paterson's scheme included the progenitor of the Supremacy Clause:

> [A]ll Acts of the U. States in Cong[ress] made by virtue & in pursuance
> of the powers hereby & by the articles of confederation vested in them,
> and all Treaties made & ratified under the authority of the U. States shall
> be the supreme law of the respective States so far forth as those Acts
> or Treaties shall relate to the said States or their Citizens, and that the
> Judiciary of the several States shall be bound thereby in their decisions,
> any thing in the respective laws of the Individual States to the contrary
> notwithstanding; and that if any State, or any body of men in any State
> shall oppose or prevent ye carrying into execution such acts or treaties, the
> federal Executive shall be authorized to call forth ye power of the Con-
> federated States, or so much thereof as may be necessary to enforce and
> compel an obedience to such Acts, or an Observance of such Treaties.[15]

Paterson's proposal closely tracked the approach of Hamilton and Jay: treaties are the supreme law of the land, part of the higher law of each state, and must be enforced by state judges. By contrast, the Virginia Plan had created a new, popularly elected legislature that could override state laws both through the negative and through its own powers, or that could avoid state law entirely by acting on individuals directly. It solved the problem of treaty enforcement by raising the power of implementation to the national level. Under the New Jersey Plan, Congress had no such new powers, and as a result it was still dependent on the state governments to give effect to its treaty commitments.

For Madison, the New Jersey Plan's reliance on state judicial review would provide few guarantees for federal supremacy. In a lengthy critique on June 19, he argued that one of the chief defects of Paterson's proposal was its failure to "prevent those violations of the law of nations & of Treaties which if not prevented must involve us in the calamities of foreign wars."[16] As Madison observed, "[t]he tendency of the States to these violations has been manifested in sundry instances. The files of Cong[res]s contain complaints already, from almost every nation with which treaties have been formed. Hitherto indulgence has been shewn to us." Ominously, Madison predicted that "[t]his cannot be the permanent disposition of foreign nations." The New Jersey Plan would do nothing to remedy this state of affairs. "The existing confederacy does not sufficiently provide against this evil. The proposed [Paterson] amendment to it does not supply the omission. It leaves the will of the States as uncontrouled as ever." State judicial review would not solve this problem, Madison argued, because the New Jersey Plan Congress would continue to represent only the states, not the people. "It could not therefore," Madison reasoned, "render the acts of Cong[res]s in pursuance of their powers even legally paramount to the Acts of the States." State judges would have no choice but to follow state law, and state legislatures and executives easily could override federal acts. Representatives of the larger states found the negative and the federal power to legislate far preferable to the smaller states' alternative of coercion and state judicial enforcement.[17]

While the small states put up resistance, initial drafts of the Constitution continued to hew closely to the Virginia Plan. Representation continued to be based on population, but because of concerns about the president's powers, the Committee of Detail vested the Senate with the sole power over war and peace, treatymaking, and the appointment of ambassadors.[18] To Congress, the committee assigned the power "to make War; to raise Armies; to build and equip Fleets"; to the executive, it assigned the power of "Commander in Chief of the Army and Navy of the United States, and of the Militia of the Several States." The president also received the powers to execute the laws and appoint officials, to call Congress and to recommend legislation, to receive ambassadors, and to grant pardons. Under this plan, the Senate served as an executive council of state, modeled on the state councils that shared executive power with the governor. It was to be elected by the members of the House rather than appointed by the state legislatures. Original proposals vested foreign affairs power in the Senate because, it was believed, the Senate would have the continuity and wisdom to handle the difficulties of foreign affairs. With smaller numbers and six-year terms, senators could handle sensitive diplomatic relations and could pursue policies that advanced the long-term national interest.[19] At the same time, the majoritarian impulses of Madison and other large-state delegates were satisfied by the Senate's mode of election by the popularly elected House.

The Great Compromise changed this sanguine view of the Senate. On July 16, the delegates resolved their impasse over representation by agreeing to a bicameral legislature composed of a popularly elected House of Representatives and a Senate in which each state legislature would select two senators.[20] Equal state representation ruined Madison's and Wilson's effort to organize the new government along the principles of national popular sovereignty. Such a Senate would be large, and therefore it would lack the ability to act with the wisdom, stability, and calculation necessary for executive functions. A Senate representing states in their corporate capacity would be unlikely to exercise the negative on state laws, and it would not hold the devotion to the national interest that justified vesting it with the foreign affairs powers.

On the day following the Great Compromise, the convention eliminated Madison's negative by a vote of 7 to 3. Delegates criticized the negative as unnecessary, because "sufficient Legislative authority should be given to the Genl. Government" to override inconsistent state laws; others argued that state courts would invalidate any state laws contrary to federal law; while yet others claimed that the negative would prove a logistical nightmare.[21] Defending his proposal, Madison again expressed doubts about the ability of state courts to correct violations of federal law: "Confidence can[not] be put in the State Tribunals as guardians of the National authority and interests. In all the States these are more or less depend[en]t on the Legislatures." Madison's arguments, however, proved unsuccessful, and the convention instead unanimously adopted a motion by Luther Martin to adopt the New Jersey Plan's Supremacy Clause instead.[22] Once plans for a legislature with broad powers, elected on the basis of population, had been discarded, the momentum for other nationalist mechanisms, such as the negative, no longer had political support.

Transformation of the Senate from a popularly elected body to a representative of state interests profoundly affected the conception of the Senate's role in foreign affairs. The Senate would no longer be a representative of the nation, but instead threatened to be the forum for sectional interests and disunion, as we saw with the Articles of Confederation in the Jay-Gardoqui affair in chapter 3. When the proponents of popular sovereignty lost over the design of the legislature, as Jack Rakove has observed, they began to reconceptualize the presidency as not merely an executor of legislation, but as a new institution that represented the will of the people. As the convention turned to discuss the draft Constitution clause by clause, this new approach to the executive prompted a reallocation of both the war and treaty powers in its favor.

On August 17, the Constitutional Convention famously changed the grant of power to Congress from the power to "make" war to the power to "declare" war.[23] Charles Pinckney of South Carolina opened the debate by arguing that the power to make war should rest in the Senate, because the full legislature's "proceedings were too slow." Pinckney believed that the Senate was superior for both functional and political reasons. Not only would the Senate be "more acquainted with foreign affairs, and most capable of proper resolutions," but it also should have the power to make war because "it would be singularly unique for one authority to make war, and another peace." Pinckney believed the Senate, rather than Congress as a whole, would prove a more appropriate vessel for the war power because it represented the states directly: "The small have their all at stake in such cases as well as the large States."

Others went further than Pinckney in their skepticism of Congress. But instead of seeking to move all war power to the Senate, the seat of sectional interests, they proposed an expansion of the executive role in warmaking through the presidency. Pierce Butler argued for "vesting the power [to make war] in the President, who will have all the requisite qualities, and will not make war but when the Nation will support it." Like his colleague from South Carolina, Butler wanted to reapportion the war power to the executive for both functional and political reasons. Immediately after Butler's comment, Madison and Elbridge Gerry of Massachusetts moved "to insert 'declare,' striking out 'make' war; leaving to the Executive the power to repel sudden attacks." Madison's amendment expanded the executive's power to respond unilaterally to an attack, and it recognized that making war—the entire war power—was a broader power than the power to declare war. Madison's notes, however, fail to answer two significant questions about his proposed change. He did not elaborate on what type of attack would trigger the executive's warmaking authority. While an invasion on American soil would qualify, it is unclear if assaults on American forces, citizens, or property overseas would as well. Furthermore, Madison did not indicate whether he and Gerry described the purpose of their amendment ("to repel sudden attacks") to the whole convention, or whether they introduced the amendment without explanation.

The subsequent confusion over the amendment suggests that Madison and Gerry did not explain its meaning to the assembled delegates. Perhaps the lateness of the hour—the debate occurred at the equivalent of 5 P.M. on a Friday—may have fatigued the notetaker himself. Whatever the reason, the discussion shows quite clearly that the Framers did not possess a clear consensus on the Declare War Clause. Speaking first, Roger Sherman believed Madison's amendment unnecessary. The draft's original version "stood very well. The Executive shd. be able to repel and not to commence war." Sherman appears to have thought that the president already had the power to respond to attacks, and that reducing Congress's power to that of declaring war would permit the executive to commence wars unilaterally. He favored leaving "make" war as it was, because it was "better than 'declare' the latter narrowing the power too much." Sherman correctly realized that the amendment would remove Congress's monopoly over war and permit the president to initiate hostilities as well. His comments, however, confused other delegates. Some interpreted him as opposing the amendment in order to protect executive power by implying that, absent an explicit prohibition, the president possessed the power to declare war. By substituting "declare" for "make" in the enumeration of Congress's powers, the president would lose this power to Congress.

Elbridge Gerry seems to have interpreted Sherman's comments in this way. He rose next to proclaim that he "never expected to hear in a republic a motion to empower the Executive alone to declare war." Gerry's statement seems odd. But, if we view Sherman's comment as expanding presidential power by preserving the executive's authority to begin war, Gerry's exclamation might make more sense. He could have intended to narrow the president's authority to engage in hostilities, so that the executive could not wage unilaterally a formal, declared war. At this point, an understanding of eighteenth-century international law again proves useful. Being familiar with Grotius and other treatise writers, Gerry would have feared any interpretation that gave the president an authority to declare war, because a declaration would represent a legal widening of a conflict at home and abroad. Gerry may have agreed with presidential authority to initiate hostilities, but he did not want the president to have the power to convert the entire nation's relations from peace to one of total, absolute war.

Further debate involving the allocation of both the war and peace powers also reflects the Framers' shared understanding of the meaning of a declaration of war. Pinckney had argued that the same body, the Senate, should exercise the power of peace and war. Oliver Ellsworth of Connecticut responded that "there is a material difference between the cases of making war, and making peace. It shd. be more easy to get out of war, than into it. War also is a simple and overt declaration." In contrast to war's simplicity, said Ellsworth, "peace is attended with intricate & secret negotiations." He shared the understanding that declaring war differed from commencing war, neither of which a Framer would have described as "simple and overt." Like Gerry, Ellsworth was concentrating on the legal aspects of war and peace, rather than their operational meanings. Declarations of war are "simple" because they alter legal relationships and recognize an existing state of hostilities in one shot. In discussing peace, Ellsworth described the negotiation of a treaty, which legally formalizes the end of hostilities.

Rising to support Ellsworth, George Mason differentiated between war and peace: he "was for clogging rather than facilitating war; but for facilitating peace." He "was agst giving the power of war to the Executive, because not safely to be trusted with it; or to the Senate because not so constructed as to be entitled to it," but then curiously backed the change from "make" to "declare." Mason's actions comport with his words only if we view him as concurring in the idea that the "make" war language did not preclude the executive from waging a defensive war, or from declaring war. Ellsworth and Mason may have supported the change to "declare" war because it limited the executive's ability to plunge the nation into a total war.

Some amount of confusion also surrounded the taking of the vote on the Madison-Gerry amendment. Madison's notes show that seven states initially voted to adopt the change, with two states against. After the convention had approved the new language, Rufus King rose to explain that " 'make' war might be understood to 'conduct' it which was an Executive function." Madison records that King's critique of the Make War Clause convinced Ellsworth to change Connecticut's vote to yes, although the amendment had already received sufficient support to pass. However, the official Journal of the convention shows that the Madison-Gerry amendment initially lost by a vote of 4 to 5, with New Hampshire, Connecticut, Maryland, South Carolina, and Georgia voting against, and then on a second vote succeeding by the 8 to 1 tally, with New Hampshire remaining the lone dissenter.[24]

Although the closing events of August 17 are somewhat unclear, we still can venture some tentative conclusions. Changing the phrase from "make" to "declare" reflected an intention to prohibit Congress from en-croaching on the executive power to conduct war. Although the amend-ment only changed Article I, the substitutions recognized the president's powers in one dimension and restricted it in another. Madison and Gerry's explanation of their amendment confirms that the Framers implicitly un-derstood that a reduction in congressional war authority would produce a corresponding expansion in executive authority, even though they failed to explain whether the president's new "power to repel sudden attacks" derived from the clause concerning executive power or the one about the president's role as commander in chief. The change not only increased the minimum level of executive power—repelling sudden attacks—but it also set a limit on its apex as well—declaring war. Adopting the amendment made clear that the president could not unilaterally take the nation into a total war, but also suggested that he might be able to engage the nation in hostilities short of that.

The August 17 debate also raises two other often overlooked points. First, some of the delegates did not envision the executive as Wilson's magistrate charged only with executing the laws passed by Congress. A majority of the Framers probably believed that the president enjoyed a "protective power," as Henry Monaghan has described it, which permitted him to guard the nation from attack, even in the absence of congressional consent or of a constitutional provision expressly delegating such power.[25] Second, another group thought that the president could lay a claim, equal to that of Congress, to representing the people, for he would "not make war but when the Nation will support it."[26] Supporters of a representa-tive presidency resisted proposals to vest Congress with the sole power over peace, which the convention considered after the Madison-Gerry amendment. Although some delegates supported a strong executive hand in peace on the ground that the president could best conduct peace ne-gotiations in secret, their predominant rationale was that the president would better represent the nation. Congress could not be trusted because it might grow to enjoy the enhanced federal powers concomitant with wartime, or because sectional interests might prolong war. A motion to give Congress the sole power of making peace failed 10 to 0 immediately after the vote to give Congress the power to declare war.[27]

A similar transfer of authority from the Senate to the presidency oc-curred when the Constitutional Convention took up the Treaty Clause on August 23. Madison began by observing that "the Senate represented the States alone, and that for this as well as other obvious reasons it was proper that the President should be an agent in Treaties."[28] Professor Rakove has laid out a strong case that these "other obvious reasons" included a concern about the Senate's unrepresentative nature and a new respect for the president's democratic accountability.[29] As Rakove argues, once the president's election by the people is taken into account, Madison's comment gains in significance. It demonstrates that Madison sought to counterbalance the influence of the states in the treaty process by including the republican, representative president.

Other delegates supported an effort to expand the treaty process to include the House. Speaking directly after Madison, Gouverneur Morris declared that he was uncertain whether "to refer the making of Treaties to the Senate at all."[30] Instead, Morris proposed an amendment that "no Treaty shall be binding on the U.S. which is not ratified by a law." Wilson supported the amendment because it did nothing more than recognize the power that the legislature would already have. Analogizing to the British constitution, Wilson observed that Parliament had a voice "[i]n the most important Treaties," despite the royal prerogative, because "the King of G. Britain being obliged to resort to Parliament for the execution of them, is under the same fetters as the amendment of Mr. Morris." In other words, Parliament had to approve implementing legislation for a treaty to take effect in domestic British law. William Johnson responded that "[t]he Example of the King of G. B. was not parallel. Full & compleat power was vested in him." Legislative participation was not needed to ratify the treaty (and thus "make" the agreement), but only to fulfill its obligations. "If the Parliament should fail to provide the necessary means of execution," Johnson said, "the Treaty would be violated." Both Wilson and Johnson agreed that the British Parliament had the authority to block the implementation of a treaty, but they disagreed whether parliamentary action resulted in no agreement being made, or in an agreement being made and then broken. Wilson thought that the legislature's implicit role showed that different bodies could negotiate and ratify; Johnson believed the exact opposite. At the very least, both Wilson's and Johnson's comments suggest that they thought that Congress's legislative powers gave it sole control over a treaty's domestic implementation.

Morris's proposal was defeated by a vote of 8 to 1, leaving the treaty power solely in the hands of the Senate.[31] Majority rule was not so easily defeated, however, as the delegates succeeded in postponing final consideration of the Treaty Clause. As they adjourned for the day, Madison "hinted for consideration," as he put it in his notes, whether the president and Senate ought to share power over peace and alliance treaties, and whether to require a majority vote of the whole legislature for the rest. From there the Treaty Clause was sent to the Committee on Postponed Parts, which was formed to resolve substantial disagreements. On September 4, that committee reported the version that forms the basis for today's clause: the president was given power to make treaties with the advice and consent of two-thirds of the Senate. It also transferred the Treaty Clause from the article governing the Senate to what would become Article II of the Constitution.[32]

While the Committee on Postponed Parts left no record of its deliberations, two members of the South Carolina delegation later discussed the crafting of the clause during their state's ratification process. Pierce Butler, a committee member, stated that it had believed that none of the branches—Senate, president, and the House—alone could be trusted to exercise the power properly. The Senate's sole control "was objected to as inimical to the genius of a republic, by destroying the necessary balance they were anxious to preserve."[33] Although some wanted to vest the power in the president, others opposed this motion on the ground that it would too easily allow him to involve the country in war. The participation of the House was suggested, but the idea was doomed by "an insurmountable objection," in Butler's words, "that negotiations always required the greatest secrecy, which could not be expected in a large body." Confirming Butler's account, a second delegate, General Charles Cotesworth Pickney, observed that agreement existed that the House should not have a role in making treaties because of "the secrecy and dispatch which are so frequently necessary in negotiations."[34] Pickney then explained why the committee had included the president in the treatymaking provision. Some had emphasized the representative feature of the presidency that Madison had raised on August 23: the president "was to be responsible for his conduct, and therefore would not dare to make a treaty repugnant to the interest of his country; and from his situation he was more interested in making a good treaty than any other man in the United States." Others, however, expressed concern that a president might be bribed by a foreign power or swayed by sectional interests. Therefore, Pickney concluded, the committee had vested the power in the president and Senate both.

As Jack Rakove has observed, these two speeches "fill a major gap in the records of the proceedings at Philadelphia."[35] They indicate that the Committee on Postponed Parts altered the Treaty Clause specifically so as to implement two of the themes raised by the earlier debates in the convention. First, the president was inserted into the process not only to check the Senate, but also to represent the nation as a whole. The presidency's republican nature contrasted sharply with that of the Senate, which represented state and sectional interests. Second, the committee, like the majority of the convention, remained hostile to participation by the House in the making of international agreements because they believed it structurally unsuited to the delicacies of international negotiation. The elevation of the president as the representative of the people in foreign affairs also may have led critics to focus on the House's functional inadequacies rather than on its democratic nature.[36]

One last illuminating debate occurred on the two-thirds vote requirement when the convention finally approved the Treaty Clause on September 7–8. Wilson attacked the supermajority provision because it "puts it in the power of a minority to controul the will of a majority."[37] Rufus King agreed that the two-thirds requirement was unnecessary because "the Executive was here joined in the business," which constituted a "check which did not exist in [the Continental] Congress." The convention unanimously adopted an amendment to exclude peace treaties from the two-thirds requirement, "allowing these to be made with less difficulty than other treaties." Madison then proposed allowing peace treaties to be made by two-thirds of the Senate alone. "The President," Madison worried, "would necessarily derive so much power and importance from a state of war that he might be tempted, if authorized, to impede a treaty of peace." His motion was seconded by Pierce Butler, who thought the amendment a "necessary security against ambitious & corrupt Presidents."

On September 7, the delegates defeated by a vote of 8 to 3 Madison's amendment. The next day, the convention reversed Madison's earlier successful motion on peace treaties, and subjected them to the same two-thirds vote requirement for all treaties. Again the vote was 8 to 3. Significantly, some had argued in favor of Madison's scheme of majority vote for peace treaties because they saw it as an *additional* check on the president's war power. Gouverneur Morris, for example, spoke in favor of excluding peace treaties from the two-thirds requirement because he feared that Congress would be hesitant to support necessary wars if it would be difficult to make a peace treaty later. "If two thirds of the Senate should be required for peace, the Legislature will be unwilling to make war for that reason, on account of the Fisheries or the Mississippi, the two great objects of the Union."[38] Second, Morris thought that senatorial control over peace was preferable to the traditional manner of legislative control, which he called "negativing the supplies for the war." Because Morris found the use of appropriations to control both war and peace as "the more disagreeable mode," he wanted to provide Congress with another check on executive war powers. His views represent the consistent understanding that Congress's chief institutional check on executive powers in foreign affairs was the power of the purse. At the same time, Morris like other delegates voted against excluding the president from the peace process. "[N]o peace ought to be made without the concurrence of the President, who was the general Guardian of the National interests," said Morris.[39] While Morris and Madison lost in their efforts to render peace treaties easier to make, Morris prevailed in keeping the representative president the leading figure in the making of treaties.

Critics of presidential powers in foreign affairs often seek their proof in the Federal Convention. The final August consideration of treaties, however, within the context of the war power, only underscores the themes that the Constitution maintained foreign affairs power in the executive branch, with a check through funding and legislation. The Philadelphia Convention sought to modify, rather than transform, the political relationship between the executive and legislative branches in the realm of war powers. The executive would have full command of the military and would play the leading role in initiating and ending war. The executive, however, could not wage war without the support of Congress, which could employ its appropriations power to express its disagreement and, if necessary, to terminate or curtail unwise, unsuccessful, or unpopular wars. The Framers revised the inherited order by vesting the power to declare war in the legislature. In their plans, the clause acted as a method of dual containment. It prevented the president from unilaterally igniting a total war, yet simultaneously barred Congress from encroaching on his exclusive authority to conduct hostilities short of that. Rather than a trumped-up magistrate, the president received the responsibility of guarding the nation and its interests, even if that meant fighting with the legislature to enforce the desires of the people, in war as well as in peace.

If the Declare War Clause bore the interpretation that some have proposed, then Congress would be able to terminate executive warmaking by declaring war not to exist. Or it could force the president into an unwanted war by declaring war to exist, which some scholars construe as the power to begin hostilities. This interpretation, however, is far from the original understanding of the clause. Although the Declare War and Appropriations Clauses assign Congress an important role in determining the breadth and intensity of hostilities with another nation, the Framers did not intend Congress to exercise a similar power in beginning or ending conflicts. When discussing both the Declare War Clause and the treaty power, delegates expressed skepticism concerning the ability of a popular body to represent accurately the best interests of the nation. Rather, the Framers saw the president as the protector and representative of the nation, and they believed that a decision as significant as peace could not be made without his consent. The Framers were not dupes; they remained fully aware of the dangerous possibility that a president might prolong war in order to expand his own political power. Nonetheless, the Framers maintained that if Congress wished to challenge presidential warmaking, it had to turn to "the more disagreeable mode, of negativing the supplies for the war."

Others place great importance on the Federal Convention as proof both that the Senate was to have a role equal to the president's over treaties, and that treaties were meant to have direct legislative effect in the United States. They argue that the president's late inclusion into the treaty process shows that the Framers still considered the Senate as the primary institution.[40] They further argue that the elimination of the Virginia Plan's veto over state laws, and the adoption of the New Jersey Plan's Supremacy Clause, represent a clear decision to make treaties self-executing in U.S. courts and to exclude Congress from treatymaking.[41] Evidence from the convention, however, when considered carefully, is more complex. With regard to the division of the treaty power, delegates clearly shifted authority to the president due to the Senate's transformation from an executive council of state, chosen by the House, into a direct representative of state interests. As "ostensible head of the Union," the president came to possess substantial freedom and discretion in foreign affairs and treaty-making. The Framers underscored their adherence to the customary idea of executive power by locating the treaty power in Article II, giving the Senate an advisory role in treaties and appointments, and providing the president with the power to "make" the treaty.

With regard to treaty enforcement, the Constitutional Convention did select the Supremacy Clause approach over Madison's more aggressive effort to place the federal government in the position of a state legislature of last resort. Nonetheless, the history reviewed here shows that several delegates, including several of the convention's leading members, believed that to have direct effect in domestic law, treaties should be approved by Congress. Once the convention had altered the Senate's method of selection, delegates sought repeatedly to inject more democratic elements into the treatymaking process. Delegates vested the president with the dominant role in treatymaking, again, to provide majoritarian safeguards on the treaty power.

Efforts to include the House would have furthered this goal, but they were derailed by the widespread belief that the House could not participate effectively in diplomatic relations. A House role in the implementation of treaties, but not in their formal negotiation, satisfied both structural concerns. Although it rejected the negative on state laws, the delegates adopted the other major elements of Madison's plan, including a popularly elected branch of the national legislature that had the power to pass laws that applied directly to individuals, and whose laws could be enforced by independent organs of the national government. Further, the proposed Constitution vested Congress with powers, such as those over interstate and international commerce, which would require its cooperation for the implementation of future treaties. Delegates appeared to agree that treaties would require statutory implementation by Congress before they could take domestic effect, and that this—in conjunction with the president's new role in treaties—provided a majoritarian safeguard on treatymaking.

FOREIGN AFFAIRS AND THE RATIFICATION DEBATES

Leading accounts of the war and treaty powers often do not examine the state ratification debates in any detail. John Ely and Harold Koh, for example, virtually ignore the ratification debates in their discussion of war powers, while Jack Rakove focuses on *The Federalist Papers* and a few ratification statements to investigate the question of the scope of the Senate's advice and consent power. Perhaps this is understandable; the Constitutional Convention was a single assembly at a single point in time, one in which we can discern the relationships between different discussions and important votes. The ratification process, on the other hand, was far more unruly. After the Philadelphia Convention, there was no one place or occasion for debate to occur; events moved to the thirteen ratifying conventions, which were separated by both geography and time. Lacking the almost instantaneous modes of communication that we enjoy today, the founding generation relied on open-air and closed-door meetings, and letters and newspapers carried by horse and sea, for political discussion and exchange of information. Nonetheless, the ratification debates are perhaps the most important source for understanding the Constitution. They carried the greatest political legitimacy: as Madison and Wilson admitted, the Federal Convention had no authority to propose a new constitution, and only through a ratification process that involved directly elected state conventions could it receive democratic approval. The ratification also allowed critics, the Anti-Federalists, to challenge the Constitution and force its supporters, the Federalists, to explain the meaning of specific constitutional provisions and how they would work in practice.

When the Constitution went to the states for ratification, the people were without the benefit of Madison's notes, which only appeared posthumously. For guidance, they had the constitutional text and their understandings of the language drawn against the background of Anglo-American political and constitutional history of the preceding century. They did not find in the Constitution the enfeebled governors of many of the early state constitutions, nor the dominant assemblies that had caused many of the problems of the Critical Period. Instead, they discovered a rejuvenated presidency, one that had regained unity in a single person that was independent of the legislature through its own selection by the Electoral College and thereby the people. In light of the eighteenth-century meaning of "declare war" and "commander in chief," and the placement of the treaty clause in Article II, those who participated in the ratification would have viewed the Constitution as creating a structure in which the president played the primary role in war and a significant, if not primary, role in determining peace. Customary executive power over foreign affairs had returned to a unitary, energetic executive, but one that took the form of a republican president rather than a hereditary monarch.

Congress too had undergone significant change. Gone was the weak executive of the Continental Congress under the Articles of Confederation, so dependent on the states for implementation of its policies and funding of its operations. In its place, the Constitution created a representative national legislature, with its own powers of taxation and funding, and the authority to directly regulate individual conduct. It had significant foreign affairs powers of its own, including the authority to raise and fund the military, to declare war, to define punishments for violations of international law, and to regulate interstate and international commerce. Yet, it no longer had "the sole and exclusive right and power of determining on peace and war," nor the sole authority of "entering into treaties and alliances," as under Article IX of the Articles of Confederation. Given their shared history, the Framers would have assumed that this separation of power between president and Congress would lead to executive initiation in war and peace, checked by legislative control over funding and domestic regulation.

The only odd duck was the Senate. It seemed to violate the clean separation of powers envisioned by Montesquieu and Locke. At times it was part of the executive branch: it gave its advice and consent to the president's making of treaties and appointment of officers. At other times it was part of a bicameral legislature. In still other times it was even judicial—as a court to try impeachments. The people and their delegates to the ratifying conventions would not have known about the evolution of the Senate during the Federal Convention from an executive advisory council to a representative body for the states as part of the Great Compromise. Nor would they have known of the transfer of foreign affairs authority at the end of the convention from the Senate to the president. Instead, they saw only an institution that seemed to play the function of both representing states and disrupting a seamless unity in the executive branch.

Naturally enough, Anti-Federalists seized on this new distribution of powers as a repudiation of the constitutional principles that Americans had fought for in the Revolution. They saw the president as a monarch, a Congress that overrode state sovereignty, and a Senate whose existence violated the separation of powers. Federalists initially justified the Constitution's allocation of war powers based on the need for a strong national government in a hostile world. Anti-Federalists, however, argued that this arrangement would produce a tyrannical national government capable of oppressing the states. In light of these predictions, Federalists discarded their earlier claims of exigency and developed new arguments drawing on the formal division of powers between Congress and the presidency. They invoked the example of Parliament's funding powers as a check on executive warmaking. They also used the rhetorical strategy of exaggerating the powers of the British monarchy in order to make the president's role appear more benign. Although it would have been to their advantage, the Federalists did not argue that Congress's power to declare war, or the possibilities of judicial review, would check the president's foreign affairs power.

Possibly unlimited in scope and shared by the president and Senate, the Treaty Clause also generated significant controversy during the ratification process. Anti-Federalists cited the clause as proof that the Constitution violated the separation of powers and threatened individual liberties. They argued that the Senate's role in the making of treaties violated the separation of powers, that the treaty power threatened an unlimited legislative power that could destroy the states, and that the House of Representatives was needed to check the other branches. Some Federalists, such as John Jay, responded that House participation was impractical because of its large size and the need for secrecy. When this explanation did not prove convincing, it fell to others, such as James Wilson in the Pennsylvania ratifying convention and James Madison in the Virginia ratifying convention, to return to the traditional separation of treatymaking and lawmaking between the executive and legislative branches. As we will see, the conclusion of the ratification process yielded an understanding of the treaty power that fell well within the traditional Anglo-American constitutional categories.

THE ANTI-FEDERALIST ATTACK

Initial Federalist explanations of the war power quickly became an easy target for Anti-Federalist writers and politicians. Alexander Hamilton argued in an early *Federalist Paper* that the federal government must possess the means to respond to unpredictable events and foreign dangers:

The authorities essential to the care of the common defence are these—to raise armies—to build and equip fleets—to prescribe rules for the government of both—to direct their operations—to provide for their support. These powers ought to exist without limitation: Because it is impossible to foresee or define the extent and variety of national exigencies, or the correspondent extent & variety of the means which may be necessary to satisfy them. The circumstances that endanger the safety of nations are infinite; and for this reason no constitutional shackles can wisely be imposed on the power to which the care of it is committed.[42]

In *The Federalist* No. 41, Madison built on Hamilton's thesis by justifying exclusive federal war powers on a realist view of the world:

With what colour of propriety could the force necessary for defence, be limited by those who cannot limit the force of offence? If a Federal Constitution could chain the ambition, or set bounds to the exertions of all other nations: then indeed might it prudently chain the discretion of its own Government, and set bounds to the exertions for its own safety. . . . How could a readiness for war in time of peace be safely prohibited, unless we could prohibit in like manner the preparations and establishments of every hostile nation? The means of security can only be regulated by the means and the danger of attack. They will in fact be ever determined by these rules, and by no others.[43]

Madison hoped that the political unity brought by the Constitution itself would deter European interference in America. But if that were not enough, the Constitution had to permit the federal government to take any steps necessary for the national security: "It is in vain to oppose constitutional barriers to the impulse of self-preservation." According to Madison, exigency justified the expansion of government authority in war and peace.

Anti-Federalists met the Federalist argument head-on. "Brutus," perhaps the most capable Anti-Federalist writer, told the voters of New York that the requirement of an emergency would prove no obstacle to a large federal army: "[T]here will not be wanting a variety of plausible reasons to justify the raising [of an army], drawn from the danger we are in from the Indians on our frontiers, or from the European provinces in our neighborhood."[44] If the government needed to safeguard against surprise attacks, Anti-Federalists argued, let the Constitution provide only for sufficient forces to staff outposts and garrisons during peacetime. This would enable the states to retain their exclusive control over military supply as a popular counterweight to a standing army.[45] If the states did not impose these restrictions, Anti-Federalists warned, the federal government eventually could toss aside the Constitution and impose a dictatorship on the states. Said Brutus:

> [T]he evil to be feared from a large standing army in time of peace, does not arise solely from the apprehension, that the rulers may employ them for the purpose of promoting their own ambitious views, but that equal, and perhaps greater danger, is to be apprehended from their overturning the constitutional powers of the government, and assuming the power to dictate any form they please.[46]

Anti-Federalists recalled the king's actions that provoked the revolution. A tyrannical government in London had used a standing army to violate the constitutional rights of the colonists. Even less extreme Anti-Federalists greatly feared the possibilities of federal military rule. Perhaps the best representative of moderate Anti-Federalist thought, the "Federal Farmer," acknowledged the need for a federal government with exclusive powers over "all foreign concerns, causes arising on the seas, to commerce, imports, armies, navies, Indian affairs, peace and war." But, he warned:

> The general government, organized as it is, may be adequate to many valuable objects, and be able to carry its laws into execution on proper principles in several cases; but I think its warmest friends will not contend, that it can carry all the powers proposed to be lodged in it into effect, without calling to its aid a military force, which must very soon destroy all elective governments in the country, produce anarchy, or establish despotism.[47]

To Anti-Federalists, both president and king held the same powers over war and peace, and thus threatened the same tyranny. In several widely circulated pamphlets, those opposed to the Federalists argued that the textual grants of power to the president mirrored those of the king. "Cato" asked, "[W]herein does this president, invested with his powers and prerogatives, essentially differ from the king of Great-Britain [?]"[48] Similarly, "Old Whig" scolded the Federalists for not "making the kingly office hereditary" since they were asking the people "to receive a king." He warned:

> [The President] appears to me to be clothed with such powers as are dangerous. To be the fountain of all honors in the United States, commander

in chief of the army, navy and militia, with the power of making treaties and of granting pardons, and to be vested with an authority to put a negative upon all laws, unless two thirds of both houses shall persist in enacting it . . . is in reality to be a king as much a King as the King of Great-Britain, and a King too of the worst kind;—an elective King.[49]

Like Cato, Old Whig asked his readers "what important prerogative the King of Great-Britain is entitled to, which does not also belong to the President during his continuance in office."

Anti-Federalists were especially troubled by the president's power as commander in chief. They were familiar with historical examples demonstrating that an army, once given to an executive, was difficult to take away. They remembered kings who had maintained their own standing armies during their battles with Parliament. Most vivid in their memory, however, was the recent example of General George Washington, who had given up the reins of power and returned to private life against the wishes of many of his officers and troops. Anti-Federalists doubted that future commanders in chief would display the same civic virtue and restraint that made Washington's action instantly famous around the world. Old Whig urged his readers:

[L]et us suppose, a future President and commander in chief adored by his army and the militia to as great a degree as our late illustrious commander in chief; and we have only to suppose one thing more, that this man is without the virtue, the moderation and love of liberty which possessed the mind of our late general, and this country will be involved at once in war and tyranny.[50]

With a standing army at hand, the president would encounter little difficulty in using his constitutional powers to impose an unconstitutional dictatorship. As "Philadelphiensis" pleaded to the voters of Pennsylvania:

Who can deny but the president general will be a king to all intents and purposes, and one of the most dangerous kind too; a king elected to command a standing army? Thus our laws are to be administered by this tyrant; for the whole, or at least the most important part of the executive department is put in his hands.[51]

Some Anti-Federalists were aware that the exercise of the British monarch's prerogatives in war and peace, as broadly described by Blackstone, were subject to parliamentary funding. Hence, Cato correctly concluded that in the realm of practical politics, the president's authority under the Constitution did not differ in important measure from that of the king. Anti-Federalists questioned whether Congress could control the president, when the executive in Great Britain had come to such power even in the face of formal parliamentary powers over the purse.

Other Anti-Federalists believed that the Constitution gave the president even more freedom from legislative control than that enjoyed by the Crown. "Tamony," who was widely published in the key states of Pennsylvania, New York, and Virginia, dismissed Federalist attempts to pass off "the office of president" with "levity" and as "a machine calculated for state pageantry."[52] Rather, Congress's power to fund the military for two years, Tamony believed, would place the president in a more advantageous position than the king, who had to seek military appropriations every year. Said Tamony:

> Suffer me to view the commander of the fleets and armies of America, with a reverential awe inspired by the contemplation of his great prerogatives, though not dignified with the magic name of King, he will possess more supreme power, than Great Britain allows her hereditary monarchs, who derive ability to support an army from annual supplies, and owe the command of one to an annual mutiny law. The American President may be granted supplies for two years, and his command of a standing army is unrestrained by law or limitation.

Some Anti-Federalists even feared that Congress would collude with the president to make him the equivalent of a king.[53]

Implicit in the attack on the Federalists was an understanding of the British constitution consistent with the one offered here. Practice and political history were the guiding precedents, not just Blackstone's description of the royal prerogative. Anti-Federalists recognized that Congress would possess the same check on the president that Parliament exercised against the king. They doubted, however, whether Congress would put its funding power to good use. Completely missing, moreover, was the Declare War Clause, which the Anti-Federalists never mentioned as another possible check on presidential authority. Perhaps it was not in their interests to acknowledge the clause because they were intent on exaggerating the president's Article II powers. The Anti-Federalists, however, did not criticize everything in the Constitution, and the more sophisticated writers were not reluctant to praise the provisions they liked. It seems that they simply did not notice the Declare War Clause. To them, the important point was that the Constitution adopted the basic allocation of war powers between the executive and legislature that had existed in recent British history. Given their conclusion that Parliament and Congress controlled the "sinews of war," and that the king and the president directed the military, they had every reason to believe that the new Constitution would produce a warmaking system similar to Great Britain's.

The Anti-Federalist attack on the Treaty Clause raised the same specter of an unlimited power that could be turned to tyranny. But in this instance the culprit was the Senate, rather than the president. Anti-Federalists argued that the Senate, in collusion with the president, would use the Treaty Clause to serve its own ends at the expense of the public good. As George Mason's widely published *Objections to the Constitution* argued:

> [T]heir other great Powers (vizt. their Power in the Appointment of Ambassadors & all public Officers, in making Treaties, & in trying all Impeachments) their Influence upon & Connection with the supreme Executive from these Causes, their Duration of Office, and their being a constant existing Body almost continually sitting, join'd with their being one compleat Branch of the Legislature, will destroy any Balance in the Government, and enable them to accomplish what Usurpations they please upon the Rights & Libertys of the People.[54]

At the root of this fear was the concern that the Constitution vested the Senate with legislative, executive, and judicial authorities. To any student of Montesquieu, this combination of authority in the same body was a clear violation of the separation of powers. Well-regarded Anti-Federalists argued that the treaty power, because of the Supremacy Clause, had become tantamount to the power to legislate. Mason's *Objections* was illustrative: "By declaring all Treaties supreme Laws of the Land, the Executive & the Senate have, in many Cases, an exclusive Power of Legislation. . . ." Not only had Montesquieu warned against the dangers of combining the executive and legislative powers, but the Framers also believed that the British Parliament had won the right to defend the liberties of the British people by keeping the power to legislate distinct from the Crown's power to enter into treaties. An effort to subsume the legislative power into the treaty power would have recalled the corruption of Parliament by the Crown.

Anti-Federalists complemented this criticism with a second attack on the treaty power. Foreshadowing the debate on the limits of the treaty power that continues to this day, some Anti-Federalists charged that the legislative aspect of the treaty power was potentially unbounded, because it was not subject to the limits of Article I. The influential Federal Farmer wrote on October 12, 1787:

> By the [Supremacy Clause], treaties also made under the authority of the United States, shall be the supreme law: It is not said that these treaties shall be made in pursuance of the constitution—nor are there any constitutional bounds set to those who shall make them: The president and two thirds of the senate will be empowered to make treaties indefinitely, and when these treaties shall be made, they will also abolish all laws and state constitutions incompatible with them. This power in the president and senate is absolute, and the judges will be bound to allow full force to whatever rule, Article or thing the president and senate shall establish by treaty, whether it be practicable to set any bounds to those who make treaties, I am not able to say: If not, it proves that this power ought to be more safely lodged.[55]

By giving treaties supremacy effect, the Anti-Federalists argued, the Constitution had vested in only the president and the Senate the power to enact laws. Because the Senate was an aristocratic body, it could corrupt the president—already a monarchical figure—and enlist his cooperation in the oppression of the people. As Anti-Federalist writer Brutus observed:

> The power to make treaties, is vested in the president, by and with the advice and consent of two thirds of the senate. I do not find any limitation, or restriction, to the exercise of this power. The most important Article in any constitution may therefore be repealed, even without a legislative act. Ought not a government, vested with such extensive and indefinite authority, to have been restricted by a declaration of rights? It certainly ought.[56]

Without a Bill of Rights, open-ended grants of power like the Treaty Clause would allow the new national government to violate individual freedoms.

The third element in the Anti-Federalist attack was the Constitution's failure to take the necessary corrective measures to contain the treaty power. In addition to a Bill of Rights, Anti-Federalists wanted to maintain the Anglo-American distinction between the power to make treaties and the power to legislate, so that at least the popularly elected House could block abuses of the treaty power. The Constitution's treatment of the treaty power, Mason observed, "might have been avoided, by proper Distinctions with Respect to Treaties, and requiring the Assent of the House of Representatives, where it [could] be done with Safety."[57] Mason asserted that the Constitution was dangerous because it departed from the usual separation between the power to legislate and the power to make treaties. He responded that treaties must remain distinct from laws, and that treaties must be implemented by a popularly elected legislature. Without such checks, Anti-Federalists feared, the president and Senate could use the treaty power to threaten individual liberties, which were not explicitly enumerated (and therefore not protected) by the Constitution.[58]

FEDERALIST RESPONSES

Pennsylvania. The initial Federalist response to these challenges came in the first major ratifying convention, Pennsylvania's. There are several reasons to pay close attention to that convention. Strong Anti-Federalist opposition made Pennsylvania "the first state in which the Constitution was seriously debated."[59] Unlike Delaware, it was the first large and strategically important state to ratify, which it did on December 12, 1787 by a vote of 46 to 23.[60] Pennsylvania was not just the keystone state in terms of its population, central location, and economic clout; it was also one of the symbolic centers of American politics. Philadelphia had been home to the Continental Congress, it was the scene of the signing of the Declaration of Independence, and it was host to the Constitutional Convention. Pennsylvanian Federalists and Anti-Federalists realized that their actions took on significance not just within the state, but nationally. As one historian has written, "the Pennsylvania debates took on a special significance, delineating, as it were, the terms of discourse, the grammar, syntax, and vocabulary of ratification."[61]

In the first public defense of the Constitution by a Federal Convention delegate, James Wilson gave a speech in the Pennsylvania State House Yard on October 6, 1787 that sought to quell Anti-Federalist concerns. Wilson's speech is remembered today mainly for the point that the federal government's limited powers made a Bill of Rights unnecessary; a Bill of Rights would imply that the federal government had general powers to affect individual rights.[62] Wilson, however, also responded to the charge that the Senate violated the separation of powers. At first, he acknowledged that the Senate had violated Montesquieu's famous dictate that executive and legislative powers must be kept distinct and separate.[63] Yet this did not mean that the Senate exercised unlimited authority: "In its legislative character it can effect no purpose, without the co-operation of the house of representatives, and in its executive character, it can accomplish no object, without the concurrence of the president." Wilson argued that Senate participation in a power did not change the essential nature of that power—hence, a Senate role in consenting to treaties did not make the power legislative, just as Senate participation in funding decisions did not make appropriations suddenly executive.

Anti-Federalists remained unconvinced. Responding directly to Wilson, an Anti-Federalist writing under the pseudonym "An Old Whig" argued that "the president and two thirds of the senate have power to make laws in the form of treaties, independent of the legislature itself."[64] For example, the president and Senate could enter into a treaty "upon terms which would be inconsistent with the liberties of the people and destructive of the very being of a Republic," yet the Treaty and Supremacy Clauses "will give such a treaty the validity of a law." In tyrannies, "[w]here all power legislative and executive is vested in one man or one body of men," Old Whig commented, "treaties are made by the same authority which makes the laws. . . ." A republic, however, is "where the legislature is [distinct] from the executive, [and] the approbation of the legislature ought to be had, before a treaty should have the force of a law. . . ." Things were not this bad even in Great Britain:

> [E]ven in England the parliament is constantly applied to for their sanction to every treaty which tends to introduce an innovation or the slightest alteration in the laws in being, the law there is not altered by the treaty itself; but by an act of parliament which confirms the treaty, and alters the law so as to accommodate it to the treaty.

In attacking the foreign affairs power, the Pennsylvania Anti-Federalists resorted to the odd claim that the new Constitution was not British enough.

Once the Pennsylvania ratifying convention itself began in late November, Anti-Federalists reiterated these objections to the Treaty Clause. On December 3, William Findley argued that "[n]otwithstanding the legislative power in Article I, section 1, the power of treaties is given to the President and Senate. This is [a] branch of [the] legislative power."[65] In Great Britain, by contrast, the king "makes [treaties] ministerally, and the legislature confirms them." Federalist Timothy Pickering responded that treaties, under the Constitution, did not have the force of law. "According to common acceptation of words, treaties are not part of the legislative power," Pickering responded, citing the powers of the British king. Turning Findley's argument to his own purposes, Wilson argued that "[t]he President and [Senate] in this Constitution make[ ] the treaty ministerially." Anti-Federalists agreed. John Smilie said, "[s]upreme laws cannot be made ministerially, but legislatively. . . . In Great Britain, a law is frequently necessary for the execution of a treaty." Observed Robert Whitehill: "When a treaty is made in Great Britain it binds not the people, if unreasonable. Treaties are binding by acts of Parliament and the consent of the people." Both Anti-Federalists and Federalists agreed that under the British system of government, the power over foreign affairs, such as the making of treaties, and the power to legislate were kept distinct, and that treaties could have no domestic effect without confirming legislation. Where they disagreed was whether the Constitution incorporated this principle. Fearful of unlimited federal powers, Anti-Federalists argued that the Constitution did not. Searching for a democratic check on the treaty power, Federalists argued that it did.

From the sketchy records that we have, it appears that the Anti-Federalists were unmoved. On December 7, they again attacked the combined effect of the Treaty and Supremacy Clauses. "A treaty is not constitutionally guarded," Findley complained.[66] "It may be superior to the legislature itself. The House of Representatives have nothing to do with treaties." On December 11, Wilson began an elaborate defense of the treaty power. First, he argued that the president would serve as a popular check on treatymaking: "[H]ere[, the senators] are also under a check, by a constituent part of the government, and nearly the immediate representative of the people," Wilson said. "I mean the President of the United States. They can make no treaty without his concurrence."[67] Wilson's second argument suggested that treaties were not really laws at all because of their status as international agreements. "But though treaties are to have the force of laws," Wilson at first suggested, "they are in some important respects very different from other acts of legislation. In making laws, our own consent alone is necessary. In forming treaties, the concurrence of another power becomes necessary. . . . ." Treaties, therefore, are not really laws on their own; instead, they "are truly contracts, or compacts, between the different states, nations, or princes, who find it convenient or necessary to enter into them." Although Anti-Federalists wanted the House of Representatives to have a formal role in treatymaking as in lawmaking, Wilson responded that the large size of the House made a direct, formal role impracticable. "[S]ometimes secrecy may be necessary, and therefore it becomes an argument against committing the knowledge of these transactions to too many persons."

Wilson's third, and most directly responsive argument, was that even without a formal role the House would still enjoy the same power over treaties as Parliament. Even though the British constitution had recognized that all formal power over treatymaking belonged to the Crown, constitutional custom and political reality had given the Commons the final say over treaties in their domestic effects. "[T]hough the House of Representatives possess no active part in making treaties," Wilson remarked, "yet their legislative authority will be found to have strong restraining influence upon both President and Senate." Analogizing to the British system, Wilson admitted that no treaty could have direct legislative effect without the participation of Congress. "In England," Wilson continued,

> if the king and his ministers find themselves, during their negotiation, to be embarrassed, because an existing law is not repealed, or a new law is not enacted, they give notice to the legislature of their situation and inform them that it will be necessary, before the treaty can operate, that some law be repealed or some be made. And will not the same thing take place here?[68]

Safety from tyranny was not to be found in giving the House a formal role, but in understanding that Congress's control over legislation and the purse would give it a working check on the exercise of the treaty power.

What is important for interpretive purposes is what Wilson left unsaid. He did not respond by admitting that the Supremacy Clause had the effect that Anti-Federalists claimed, but that it was necessary to control state encroachments on federal treaties. Wilson even could have defended the Supremacy Clause as a compromise in favor of states' rights. Instead, he responded by emphasizing that the treaty power was subject to strong controls by the popularly elected branches of the government. To deflect Anti-Federalist criticisms of the effect of the Treaty Clause and the Supremacy Clause, Wilson offered a narrow reading of the latter clause that left the customary separation-of-powers principles unchanged.

While the Pennsylvania ratifying convention focused on the foreign affairs power through the subject of treaties, the issue of war powers arose tangentially. Discussing the virtues of the national government, Wilson argued that its new unity and strength would deter the Europeans from partitioning America. He further hoped that the increasing strength of the United States and the vastness of the Atlantic Ocean would prevent the new nation from "mix[ing] with the commotions of Europe."[69] Wilson remarked, "No, sir, we are happily removed from them, and are not obliged to throw ourselves into the scale with any." Presumably, Wilson here referred to the prospect of a splendid isolation from the balance-of-power politics of the Continent. Wilson then embarked on an unprompted discussion of the war power:

> This system will not hurry us into war; it is calculated to guard against it. It will not be in the power of a single man, or a single body of men, to involve us in such distress; for the important power of declaring war is vested in the legislature at large: this declaration must be made with the concurrence of the House of Representatives: from this circumstance we may draw a certain conclusion that nothing but our national interest can draw us into a war.[70]

Advocates of congressional war powers, such as Ely, Louis Fisher, and Charles Lofgren quite correctly place great emphasis on Wilson's speech.[71] Wilson's statement that "[t]his system will not hurry us into war," however, may have been intended to contrast the treaty power with the war power. He was not expounding on the checks between president and Congress, but instead was reassuring his audience that the president and the Senate alone could not obligate the nation to enter a full-scale war because of treaty obligations—a fairly common practice in a period of European great power politics. Wilson's emphasis that neither "a single man" nor "a single body of men" meant that only the legislature as a whole could decide the question of total war. He quite correctly understood that the treaty power could not trump the Declare War Clause.[72] Nonetheless, Wilson was a leading Federalist who relied on the Declare War Clause as a limitation on the war power; the history will show, however, that he was the only one.

New York. After Pennsylvania had ratified, the next two significant hurdles for the Constitution were New York and Virginia. New York witnessed more vigorous debate in the press, although ratification by that state was virtually ensured once word arrived that Virginia, where the Anti-Federalists made their strongest effort to forestall ratification, had approved the Constitution on June 25, 1788. For this reason, New York's convention lacked the sharpness of argument and discussion that characterized the Pennsylvania and Virginia conventions.[73] It is worthwhile, however, to examine the debates in New York that occurred in the press, as many of these writings (such as *The Federalist*) were reprinted throughout the other states and formed the basis of arguments in those conventions.

Anti-Federalist criticisms received a full airing in the New York newspapers. Soon after Pennsylvania's ratification, for example, that state's defeated Anti-Federalist minority published a dissent that circulated widely in New York.[74] Significantly, there was no criticism of the distribution of war powers, nor a claim that the Constitution had significantly changed the usual balance between executive and legislative powers. This, however, was not the Anti-Federalist approach to treaties. The dissenters repeated their criticisms that the Senate's participation in treaties violated the separation of powers, that the open-ended nature of the treaty power threatened individual liberties, and that Congress ought to enjoy Parliament's right to confirm treaties through legislation. "It is the unvaried usage of all free states," the dissenters declared, referring specifically to Parliament's implementation of a recent commercial treaty with France, "whenever treaties interfere with the positive laws of the land, to make the intervention of the legislature necessary to give them operation."[75] The minority wanted the Constitution to declare formally what Wilson promised would occur informally. George Mason's *Objections to the Constitutions* and the Federal Farmer's *Letters,* with their similar arguments, appeared in the New York press in October and November 1787.

Prominent New York Anti-Federalists also took up the charge. As we have seen, writers such as Cato, Brutus, and the Federal Farmer, who were published primarily in New York, attacked the president's war power as monarchical in nature and threatening tyranny. Although recognizing that Congress's funding power would resemble Parliament's ability to check the Crown, they believed it would not pose much in the way of practical obstacle to the president, just as they believed it had not in Great Britain. They saved most of their energies, however for the treaty power. "Complete acts of legislation, which are to become the supreme law of the land, ought to be the united act of all the branches of government . . . ," wrote Cato in December 1787.[76] "[B]ut there is one of the most important duties may be managed by the senate and executive alone, and to have all the force of the law paramount without the aid or interference of the house of representatives; that is the power of making treaties."[77]

Instead of relying on the Declare War Clause, as had Wilson, Federalists attacked the notion that the American Constitution merely mimicked the British. Federalists stressed the formal differences between the American and British plans of government: the separation of war powers between the branches, the exaggerated powers of the king, and the relative weakness of the president. In so doing, the Federalists engaged in rhetorical excess and intentionally distorted Anti-Federalist arguments to permit their easy dismissal. In *The Federalist* No. 69, Hamilton directly responded to the concerns of Tamony, Cato, and their associates. Arguing that the Federal Convention had stripped the executive of the power of declaring war and raising armies, Hamilton portrayed the president as something of a second-rate king:

> [T]he President is to be Commander in Chief of the army and navy of the United States. In this respect his authority would be nominally the same with that of the King of Great-Britain, but in substance much inferior to it. It would amount to nothing more than the supreme command and direction of the military and naval forces, as first General and Admiral of the confederacy; while that of the British King extends to the declaring of war and to the raising and regulating of fleets and armies; all which by the Constitution under consideration would appertain to the Legislature.[78]

At the end of *Federalist 69,* Hamilton contrasted more explicitly the powers of the American president with the British monarch:

> The President of the United States would be an officer elected by the people for four years. The King of Great-Britain is a perpetual and hereditary

prince. The one would be amenable to personal punishment and disgrace: The person of the other is sacred and inviolable. The one would have a qualified negative upon the acts of the legislative body: The other has an absolute negative. The one would have a right to command the military and naval forces of the nation: The other in addition to this right, possesses that of declaring war, and of raising and regulating fleets and armies by his own authority.[79]

Some have read Hamilton's defense as an acknowledgment that Congress must give its approval to all wars. Even if we were to accept *Federalist 69* as the authoritative explanation of the Constitution, this view overstates Hamilton's meaning. Hamilton carefully avoided explaining whether the formal powers transferred from king to Congress would result in any actual change in the making of foreign policy. Indeed, Hamilton did nothing to undermine the prevailing belief that a declaration of war was unnecessary for waging war. As Hamilton had observed in *Federalist 25*, "the ceremony of a formal denunciation of war has of late fallen into disuse."[80]

The Federalist No. 69 also engaged in the common Federalist rhetorical practice of inflating the king's powers in order to give the president a more modest appearance. For example, Hamilton claimed that the British monarch had the sole authority to raise and regulate the armies and navies. By the middle of the eighteenth century, however, Parliament had assumed at least co-equal authority in these areas; as a practical matter the Crown could not pursue its military policies without the assent of the legislature. Hamilton also implied that the king could conduct war and foreign policy on his own. As we have seen, however, the record of history showed that Parliament had used its funding powers to achieve a powerful voice in these areas sufficient to frustrate an effective foreign policy. Hamilton answered Anti-Federalist concerns by contrasting Blackstone's formal (and incomplete) description of the allocation of war powers with the American Constitution's more balanced approach.[81]

Hamilton also misrepresented the Anti-Federalist argument and the nature of Parliament-Crown relations in defending the Constitution's allocation of the treaty power. Hamilton attributed to the Anti-Federalists the argument that Parliament ratified treaties made by the king, which implied that the president—who made treaties subject to Senate approval—

again exercised powers identical to that of the monarch.[82] Hamilton then stated that Blackstone proved that the king made treaties alone, and hence the American president was much weaker. But the Anti-Federalist whom Hamilton answers, Cato, suggested only that Parliament plays a role in the treaty process because the king chooses to consult with it because of its fiscal powers. "[F]or though it may be asserted that the king of Great-Britain has the express power of making peace or war, yet he never thinks it prudent so to do without the advice of his parliament from whom he is to derive his support."[83] Once again, the Anti-Federalists raised the issue of British constitutional practice, which Hamilton answered with the formal British constitution.

Anti-Federalists correctly argued that the Constitution's system did not deviate all that much from the British constitution, as it existed in practice. Thus, the force of their arguments—that the Parliament already exercised substantial control over war and foreign policy via the spending power—forced Hamilton to distort the British separation of powers in order to defend the presidency. Federalists never fully confronted the Anti-Federalist claim that Congress would satisfy the president's military requests as readily as Parliament had cooperated with the king. Indeed, the Federalists appear to have ceded to the Anti-Federalists the truth of their arguments, and even failed to emphasize the point that the Anti-Federalists had conceded: that the executive needed legislative approval in the form of funding for its foreign policy.

Federalist 69 also served as a major response to Anti-Federalist concerns about treaties. The first paper devoted to the treaty power, *The Federalist No. 64*, appeared on March 5, 1788. One of the few papers written by John Jay, it contained a very different understanding of the treaty power than Wilson had offered in Pennsylvania. Jay began by praising the Constitution for vesting the treaty power in the president and Senate, which he believed would be composed of men of the highest character.[84] While the president could manage foreign negotiations with "perfect secrecy and immediate dispatch," the Senate would bring "talents, information, integrity, and deliberate investigation[]. . . ." A large body like the House of Representatives, Jay argued, was incapable of participating in diplomacy. There was no reason why the treaty power had to be vested in the same body that made laws. "All constitutional acts of power," Jay responded, "whether in the executive or in the judicial departments, have as much legal validity and obligation as if they proceeded from the legislature. . . ." It is up to the people, Jay reasoned, to decide where to vest the different functions of government. "It surely does not follow that because they have given the power of making laws to the legislature," Jay wrote, "that therefore they should likewise give them power to do every other act of sovereignty by which the citizens are to be bound and affected." Because the Constitution represented the people's choices concerning the structure of their government, they could allocate lawmaking authority as they chose.

In Jay's mind, the Constitution's grant of federal supremacy to treaties represented no innovation at all, for this had already been the law of the land under the Articles of Confederation. Treaties were binding on the nation, state laws to the contrary notwithstanding, and the only power that could override treaties lay with the nations themselves. "[T]reaties are made not by only one of the contracting parties but by both," Jay maintained. "[C]onsequently that as the consent of both was essential to their formation at first, so must it ever afterwards be to alter or cancel them." Under both the Constitution and the Articles of Confederation, neither state laws nor unilateral action by other branches of government could modify or break a treaty obligation. "The proposed constitution therefore has not in the least extended the obligation of treaties," Jay concluded. "They are just as binding, and just as far beyond the lawful reach of legislative acts now, as they will be at any future period, or under any form of government." Although consistent with his views as the Continental Congress's secretary for foreign affairs, Jay's arguments on this score contradicted political reality and the views of most other Federalists. For example, although Wilson had maintained that the size of the House prevented it from making treaties, he also had acknowledged that the House would retain the power to legislate, which would control the domestic implementation of treaties. Jay's views, and certainly his aristocratic tone, seem out of place with the more republican notes sounded by Madison and Hamilton.

Perhaps sensing that Jay's views were too extreme, Hamilton in *The Federalist* No. 69 sought to demonstrate that comparisons between the British king and the American president regarding treaties were unfounded. In contrast to the president's joint role with the Senate in making treaties, Hamilton argued, the "King of Great-Britain is the sole and absolute representative of the nation in all foreign transactions."[85] Hamilton acknowledged the Anti-Federalist argument that Parliament played a significant role in implementing treaties, but he emphasized the informal nature of Parliament's participation. "It has been insinuated," Hamilton observed, "that his authority in this respect is not conclusive, and that his conventions with foreign powers are subject to revision, and stand in need of the ratification of Parliament." Citing Blackstone, Hamilton concluded that Parliament simply did not participate in making treaties. Nonetheless, he admitted that Parliament did control domestic implementation. "The Parliament, it is true," Hamilton wrote, "is sometimes seen employing itself in altering the existing laws to conform them to the speculations in a new treaty. . . ." On this point, however, Hamilton did not press home Wilson's argument that the legislature's role would constitute yet another check on the treaty power. Parliament's role here, Hamilton argued, arose not from any role in foreign policy, but "from the necessity of adjusting a most artificial and intricate system of revenue and commercial laws to the changes made in them by the operation of the treaty. . . ." A treaty creates a "new state of things," according to Hamilton, to which Parliament must adapt "new provisions and precautions" in order to "keep the machine from running into disorder."

Hamilton joined Wilson and others who emphasized the legislative checks on treaties. Hamilton did not deny that Parliament's control through the legislative power allowed it to implement treaties, nor did he argue that in the United States a different relationship would take hold. A month earlier, Madison had suggested in *The Federalist* No. 53 that the House would enjoy this right. In defending the two-year term for members of the House, Madison had argued that such terms were necessary so that members could become knowledgeable about foreign affairs. "[A] federal representative," he maintained, needed to understand American treaties and foreign nations' commercial policies in order to regulate "our own commerce."[86] He ought "not be altogether ignorant of the law of nations," because that too might be "a proper object of municipal legislation." When it came to treaties, Madison observed:

> [A]lthough the house of representatives is not immediately to participate in foreign negotiations and arrangements, yet from the necessary connection between the several branches of public affairs, those particular branches will frequently deserve attention in the ordinary course of

legislation, and will sometimes demand particular legislative sanction and co-operation.

Hamilton's comments certainly do not contradict Madison's on this score, and indeed they might be seen as harmonious. Perhaps Hamilton consciously avoided contradicting either Jay or Madison, which may have produced the tensions in his own contributions to *The Federalist.* Or Hamilton, having begun with Jay's views, may have gradually developed a more republican vision similar to Madison's.

Hamilton continued his ambiguity in his next paper on the treaty power, *The Federalist* No. 75. Again, Hamilton seemed to be cleaning up after Jay's arguments in *Federalist 64.* Instead of praising the aristocratic nature of the Senate, Hamilton suggested that the Constitution's allocation of the treaty power made sense because "[t]he power in question seems . . . to form a distinct department, and to belong properly neither to the legislative nor to the executive." Hamilton explained:

> The essence of the legislative authority is to enact laws, or in other words to prescribe rules for the regulation of the society. While the execution of the laws and the employment of the common strength, either for this purpose or for the common defence, seem to comprise all the functions of the executive magistrate. The power of making treaties is plainly neither the one nor the other. It relates neither to the execution of the subsisting laws, nor to the enaction of new ones, and still less to an exertion of the common strength. Its objects are CONTRACTS with foreign nations, which have the force of law, but derive it from the obligations of good faith. They are not rules prescribed by the sovereign to the subject, but agreements between sovereign and sovereign. The power in question seems therefore to form a distinct department, and to belong properly neither to the legislative nor to the executive. The qualities elsewhere detailed, as indispensable in the management of foreign negotiations, point out the executive as the most fit agent in those transactions; while the vast importance of the trust, and the operation of treaties as laws, plead strongly for the participation of the whole or a part of the legislative body in the effect of making them.[87]

Here, Hamilton appears to have been straddling the Jay and Madison/ Wilson positions. All seem to agree that treaties would "have the force of law" between sovereign nations under international law. Agreeing with Jay, Hamilton suggested that treaties may be given "the operation of laws." But, at the same time, Hamilton also suggested that treaties were "contracts" between sovereigns, rather than rules given by the sovereign to the subject, and did not relate to the enactment of new laws. Employing similar language in the Pennsylvania convention, Wilson had declared that treaties would have the "operation of laws," but that Congress's cooperation would be necessary to achieve domestic effect. Hamilton, however, did not openly follow Wilson in assuming that the treaty power, to be made meaningful, would depend on subsequent action by the branches, although he pointed out that treaties by themselves did not fall to the executive in the "exertion of the common strength" or the legislative in prescribing rules for the citizen. While some have read *Federalist 75* as sketching a broad role for treaties in setting domestic rules of conduct, a closer reading shows Hamilton to have been far more ambivalent toward the executive treaty power—somewhere between Jay on the one hand and Madison/Wilson on the other.

Hamilton's contributions to *The Federalist Papers* on the treaty power are noteworthy on two other points. First, he emphasized, as Jay had not, the argument made in the Constitutional Convention that the presence of the president was necessary to provide a voice for the representative of the people. The mixture of powers was seen as a benefit, because it allowed the republican president to safeguard the interests of the people in making treaties with the Senate, the representatives of the states. Second, in the formal distribution of the treatymaking power, Hamilton also continued Jay's criticism of the structural defects of the House in the field of foreign relations. Wrote Hamilton: "[T]he fluctuating, and taking its future increase into the account, the multitudinous composition of [the House], forbid us to expect in it those qualities which are essential to the proper execution of such a trust."[88]

Anti-Federalist reaction was mixed. Some still pressed to give the House a formal role in the ratification of treaties. Anti-Federalists in the Maryland convention criticized the expansive nature of the treaty power, which they feared would "control the national legislature, if not supersede the Constitution of the United States itself."[89] Others came away from the discussions of the treaty power with an understanding, seemingly shared by Federalist writers, that Congress's legislative powers would check treaties. Most notably, the Federal Farmer, who had attacked the Treaty Clause in October 1787, accepted the argument that Congress's plenary power in other areas, especially commerce, would require its cooperation with international agreements. In a second series of letters, published in May 1788, the Federal Farmer declared that "[o]n a fair construction of the constitution, I think the legislature has a proper controul over the president and senate in settling commercial treaties."[90] Because of Article I, Section 8, Congress had a monopoly on the authority to regulate trade and commerce with foreign nations. On the other hand, Article II, Section 2 gave the president the authority to make treaties, of which the Federal Farmer believed there were three kinds: treaties of commerce, treaties of peace, and treaties of alliance. In order to ensure that the Constitution is "consistently construed," he concluded, "it shall be left to the legislature to confirm commercial treaties." Recognizing Congress's authority over commerce maintained the traditional separation between the power to legislate and the power to make treaties. Such agreements "are in their nature and operation very distinct from treaties of peace and alliance," the Federal Farmer observed. Although treaties of peace and alliance may require secrecy, and so may justify the exclusion of the House, "very seldom" do "they interfere with the laws and internal police of the country." "[T]o make them," the Federal Farmer argued, "is properly the exercise of executive powers," and therefore the Constitution did not grant the legislature any authority to interfere with them.

But commercial treaties were an entirely different matter:

> As to treaties of commerce, they do not generally require secrecy, they almost always involve in them legislative powers, interfere with the laws and internal police of the country, and operate immediately on persons and property, especially in the commercial towns: (they have in Great-Britain usually been confirmed by Parliament;) they consist of rules and regulations respecting commerce; and to regulate commerce, or to make regulations respecting commerce, the federal legislature, by the constitution, has the power. I do not see that any commercial regulations can be made in treaties, that will not infringe upon this power in the legislature; therefore, I infer, that the true construction is, that the president and senate shall make treaties; but all commercial treaties shall be subject to be confirmed by the legislature. This construction will render the clauses consistent, and make the powers of the president and senate, respecting treaties, much less exceptionable.

The Federal Farmer made the Federalists' case as clear as could be. Treaties of peace and alliance, generally executive in nature, did not require legislative participation because they did not affect domestic conduct. Treaties of commerce, however, did require congressional participation because they "interfere with the laws and internal police of the country" and "operate immediately on persons and property." Unlike treaties of peace and alliance, concerns about secrecy did not require the exclusion of the House from participation in commercial agreements. The Constitution's grant of commerce power in Article I would ensure that Congress could police this distinction between legislation and treaties.

Our review of the Federalist and Anti-Federalist discussion in the press shows that a complex debate occurred concerning the relationship between treaties and the legislative power. Anti-Federalists made the Treaty Clause part of their general criticism of the Constitution, claiming it violated the separation of powers and contained open-ended power grants that threatened individual liberties. From Jay's haughty praise of the vesting of foreign affairs powers in the best and brightest, Federalist responses evolved into Hamilton's, and then Madison's, defense of the treaty power as not invading the legislative power, except in those areas, such as commerce, where Congress would have a checking role in implementation. Published near the end of the ratification battle in the press, the Letters of the Federal Farmer show that some of the leading Framers—both Federalist and Anti-Federalist—had reached a shared understanding that treaties would not have direct effect in areas within Congress's Article I powers, although they still disagreed, perhaps, on whether this arrangement would provide a sufficient check on the powers of the national government.

With regard to the war power, Anti-Federalists predicted that the president's powers would rival that of the British Crown, and that the legislature's powers would prove no obstacle to a tyrannical executive. Federalists first responded that a dangerous world demanded executive speed and unity of action in foreign affairs and then contrasted the formal weaknesses of the presidency with an inflated version of the British Crown. Yet, as the debate moved to other states, Federalists began to emphasize in war powers the same arguments they were making with regard to treaties. This shift in focus from formal law to applied politics is demonstrated by a letter from Samuel Holden Parsons, a lawyer, major general, and Federalist leader in Connecticut, to William Cushing, future Supreme Court justice and Massachusetts Federalist. Parsons wrote to explain Connecticut's ratification, in the hopes of assisting passage in her neighbor, Massachusetts:

> I think we involve ourselves in unnecessary doubts about our security against an undue use of the powers granted by the Constitution, by not clearly distinguishing between our present condition and that of the people of Great Britain. There, the supreme executive is hereditary. He does not derive his powers from the gift of the people; at least, if the contrary is true in theory, its practical operation is not such. He there holds, as his prerogative, the power of raising and disbanding armies, the right to make war and peace with many other very great and important rights independent of any control. That the armies are his armies, and their direction is solely by him without any control. The only security the people there have, against the ambition of a bad king, is the power to deny money, without which no army can be kept up. Here the army, when raised, is the army of the people. It is they who raise and pay them; it is they who judge of the necessity of the measure; tis they who are to feel the burthens and partake the benefits. . . . It is therefore our army and our purse, and not the sword or purse of a king.[91]

Soldiers drawn from the people, Parsons argued, would feel no personal attachment to the president, especially when Congress had called them up and paid their salaries. Congress would also check the president through its "power to deny money, without which no army can be kept up." These political forces would prevent an executive tyranny. As we will see in Virginia, Federalists turned to these arguments to win ratification for both the war and treaty powers.

The Crux of Ratification: Virginia. Events in Virginia put these understandings of the foreign affairs power to the test. During the crucible of ratification in that critical state, Federalists and some Anti-Federalists agreed that Congress's power over funding and legislation would check the executive's powers over war and peace. There are several reasons why the views expressed in the Virginia convention have a weight greater than that of any other state convention. Virginia was perhaps *the* critical state in the ratification effort. Geographically it linked the South and the North, and its political leadership in the nation was such that even Alexander Hamilton doubted that the Constitution could survive in New York without

Virginia's approval.[92] It is difficult to imagine the Union succeeding, even if the necessary states had ratified, without the state of Washington, Jefferson, Madison, and John Marshall, among others. As Forrest McDonald has written, "Virginia's ratification was almost as important to the Federalists as that of the first nine states. Without those nine states the Constitution could not be put into operation. Without Virginia, George Washington, the man whose unrivalled prestige made him the obvious choice for office, could not be elected president."[93]

Nor was the Constitution railroaded through Virginia. According to the records that survive, Virginia experienced the fullest, and most contentious, debate of all of the ratification conventions. Anti-Federalist political leadership was perhaps stronger in Virginia than anywhere else. Initially, the opposition included George Mason and Edmund Randolph, both of whom had attended the Constitutional Convention and refused to sign the Constitution. Their rhetorical leader was Patrick Henry. Federalists countered by relying on the reputation of George Washington, the analyses of Madison and Marshall, the prestige of Edmund Pendleton, and the knowledge of local affairs of George Nicholas. As Lance Banning has observed, "this state convention brought together nearly every public man of major influence in Virginia for a brilliant and dramatic recapitulation of the larger national debate."[94] In the Virginia convention we can see the arguments for and against the Constitution made clearly and fully by some of the leading Federalists and Anti-Federalists of the day.

The closeness of the political contest in Virginia also gives added significance to the proceedings. Federalists had won by only a narrow margin in elections for the state ratifying convention, and Anti-Federalists had made inroads in converting many of them to their cause.[95] The Anti-Federalists' final motion to send the Constitution back to the states for amendments lost by only 88 to 80.[96] The Virginia convention probably presented the toughest obstacle that the Constitution and the Federalists were to face in the drive to ratification. As a result, we should pay particular attention to the arguments and counterarguments made to secure its passage in Virginia. While neither the Federalist nor the Anti-Federalist vision of the Constitution was more correct or true, the debates surrounding them reveal common areas of agreement, similarities in reasoning, and sometimes a shared understanding of constitutional texts.[97]

Virginia Anti-Federalists chose to focus their attacks on the foreign affairs power regarding treaties, but inevitably war powers became part of the debate. Massachusetts had opened up new political possibilities because Federalists there agreed to recommend amendments to the Constitution as the price of ratification.[98] In response to a May 1788 letter from New York Anti-Federalists to prominent Virginia Anti-Federalists seeking cooperation, George Mason proposed a list of amendments. One of the amendments sought to vest the treaty power in the president and an advisory council, rather than the Senate.[99] Further, Mason recommended, "all Treaties so made or entered into, shall be subject to the Revision of the Senate and House of Representatives for their Ratification." In Mason's view, commercial agreements ought to be subject to a two-thirds vote, and treaties disposing of territory, fishing, or navigation claims were to require an even higher, three-fourths vote for approval. With regard to war powers, Anti-Federalists wanted to restore the basic framework of the Articles of Confederation, which allowed the states to control foreign affairs by holding the power of funding and supply. Anti-Federalists recommended restoring funding power to the states, banning standing armies in peacetime, and returning control over the militias to the states.[100] Although eight out of the necessary nine states had already adopted the Constitution by the time of their convention, Virginia Anti-Federalists planned to stall the Federalist drive by conditioning ratification on the acceptance of such amendments.

These amendments targeted Anti-Federalist concerns about the Jay-Gardoqui controversy discussed in chapter 3. By 1788, navigation of the Mississippi had become one of the major issues in Virginia politics.[101] Virginia's territory included the present-day states of West Virginia and Kentucky, and settlers there depended on the Mississippi River to transport their goods. Failure to gain navigation rights to the Mississippi threatened to close off western expansion, which was seen as primarily benefiting the South. As William Grayson, a former president of the Continental Congress and leading Anti-Federalist lawyer, put it, "If the Mississippi was yielded to Spain, the migration to the Western country would be stopped, and the Northern States would, not only retain their inhabitants, but preserve their superiority and influence over that of the Southern."[102]

From a political perspective, the Mississippi River question became *the* issue of the Virginia convention, more so than even slavery, because it symbolized the threats of sectional division.[103] It contrasted the voting strengths of North and South on a sectional question that might be replicated in the Senate. It brought to the forefront their different economic interests. While the South, and particularly Virginia, viewed western expansion as critical to its economic growth and important for the continued health of an agriculturally centered economy, the North—at least in southern eyes—was based far more on trade, manufacturing, and commerce, and so had been all too willing to barter away future growth in the West for a trade agreement with Spain. The Mississippi issue might even have expressed different, perhaps nascent, differences between North and South about broader issues of political economy. Southerners might have believed that expanding westward, and keeping open routes for the shipping of American raw materials to Europe, would allow America to remain a nation of republican yeoman-farmers. Virginians also might have viewed northern trade policies as efforts to engage in the rapid economic growth and urbanization that had produced political corruption in England. Finally, the Jay-Gardoqui affair demonstrated not only that the North had more votes by state, and that it differed with the South politically and economically, but also that the North, given the opportunity, would press its advantage to enter agreements that benefited only its region.

Patrick Henry began a broad attack on the Constitution's distribution of the foreign affairs on June 5, 1788. First, he attacked the president's executive power over the military. Anti-Federalists claimed that because the states would have no means to control the national government's ability to make war, the president would become a military despot. Henry argued:

> If your American chief, be a man of ambition, and abilities, how easy is it for him to render himself absolute! The army is in his hands, and, if he be a man of address, it will be attached to him; and it will be the subject of long meditation with him to seize the first auspicious moment to accomplish his design . . . . If we make a King, we may prescribe the rules by which he shall rule his people, and interpose such checks as shall prevent him from infringing them: But the President, in the field, at the head of his army, can prescribe the terms on which he shall reign master, so far that it will puzzle any American ever to get his neck from under the galling yoke. . . . If ever he violates the laws . . . [h]e [may] come at the head of his army to carry every thing before him . . . . [W]here is the ex-

isting force to punish him? Can he not at the head of his army beat down every opposition? Away with your President, we shall have a King: The army will salute him Monarch; your militia will leave you and assist in making him King, and fight against you: And what have you to oppose this force? What will then become of you and your rights? Will not absolute despotism ensue?[104]

Anti-Federalists proposed amendments to restore to the states their control over funding and supply, and the command of the militia. It was not enough that the Constitution placed the purse and sword in different hands, Anti-Federalists wanted the purse and sword in different governments.

With regard to treaties, Henry followed his attack on war powers with a strange claim that large states like Virginia lacked protection because only a quorum of senators was needed to approve a treaty. "The Senate, by making treaties may destroy your liberty and laws for want of responsibility," he told the Virginia convention.[105] "Two-thirds of those that shall happen to be present, can, with the President make treaties, that shall be the supreme law of the land: They may make the most ruinous treaties; and yet there is no punishment for them." This odd argument, however, became the jumping off point for the argument that the interests of large states could only be protected by including the House of Representatives in treatymaking. Using the threat of a Mississippi closure to good effect, Anti-Federalist attacks on the treaty power may have begun to turn the tide against ratification as the convention reached the middle of June.[106]

James Madison had spent the previous month preparing for Anti-Federalist demands for amendments to the Constitution's foreign affairs power. In a striking letter written on May 17, 1788, only two weeks before the beginning of the convention, Madison laid out a strategy to Federalist ally George Nicholas that primarily focused on the treaty power, but proposed common arguments to defend the war power as well.[107] Madison recommended that Federalists should stress that a stronger national government would give the United States the international respect and power to achieve its foreign policy goals, such as opening up navigation of the river, and would protect expanded settlement in the West. Federalists tried these arguments, to little effect, in early June. Madison also emphasized the majoritarian aspects of the treaty process. First, Federalists were to focus attention on the republican character of the president.

His participation in treaties "is an advantage which may be pronounced conclusive," said Madison, because the president was "elected in a different mode, and under a different influence from that of the Senate."[108] Because of his accountability to the people, the president would oppose the use of the treaty power for sectional purposes. "As a single magistrate too responsible, for the events of his administration, his pride will the more naturally revolt against a measure which might bring on him the reproach not only of partiality, but of a dishonorable surrender of a national right." A president's need to return to the electorate every four years would safeguard the nation's interests. As Madison observed, "[h]is duration and re-eligibility are other circumstances which diminish the danger to the Mississippi."

Even if the president fell victim to corruption or sectional interest, however, the people still had another safeguard—the House of Representatives. "It is true that this branch is not of necessity to be consulted in the forming of Treaties," admitted Madison. Nonetheless, he argued, the House could use its legislative powers to exercise an almost equal role in treatymaking. Any significant treaty would require an implementing statute that must come from Congress. The House's "approbation and co-operation," Madison maintained, "may often be necessary in carrying treaties into full effect." As he had in *The Federalist* No. 53, Madison was pressing the distinction between making a treaty and making the laws necessary to carry it out.

Madison's third plan of defense sought refuge in the House's plenary control over appropriations. Here Madison argued that Congress's control over funding would enable the House to influence the war and treaty decisions of the executive branch. "[A]s the support of the Government and of the plans of the President & Senate in general must be drawn from the purse which [the House of Representatives] hold[s]," he explained to Nicholas, "the sentiments of this body cannot fail to have very great weight, even when the body itself may have no constitutional authority." The House's power on this score did not apply uniquely to the treaty context, but instead applied to all of foreign affairs. It appears that Madison would not have looked askance at efforts to refuse to fund a navy, to defund diplomatic negotiations, or to link the funding of government operations to presidential agreement with the House. Certainly Madison would have approved if the House were to refuse to fund the conduct of wars or the implementation of treaties with which it disagreed.[109]

Madison concluded by sketching out a tripartite system of foreign affairs that weighed in favor of republicanism rather than sectionalism:

> [U]nder the new System every Treaty must be made by 1. the authority of the Senate in which the States are to vote equally. 2 that of the President who represents the people & the States in a compounded ratio. and 3. under the influence of the H. of Reps. who represent the people alone.

Without the approval of the president, the Senate, and the House, no foreign policy could succeed, and in this system both the president and the House represented the people. Rather than relying on Blackstone, Madison developed an approach that depended on the practical interaction of the branches rather than simply their formal government powers. It not only maintained but depended for its lifeblood on the distinction between the executive war and treaty powers, and the legislature's monopoly over funding and lawmaking.

While Patrick Henry engaged in a rambling, four-day attack on the Constitution, James Madison and George Nicholas set their responses in motion. First, they rose to defend the treaty power. Following Madison's memorandum, Nicholas answered Henry's criticisms by invoking the president's role in the process and his direct accountability to the people. He continued to predict that if the president were to deviate from his duty to defend the national interest, he "will be degraded, and will bring on his head the accusation of the Representatives of the people—an accusation which has *ever been,* and always *will be,* very formidable."[110] The House, moreover, would perform a function that went beyond the mere criticism of executive actions. "Although the Representatives have no immediate agency in treaties," Nicholas said, "yet from their influence in the Government, they will direct every thing. They will be a considerable check on the Senate and President."

On June 13, 1788, Madison defended the Treaty Clause in similar terms. He argued that three bodies—the Senate, the presidency, and the House—would play a role in international agreements. Besides the Senate, Madison emphasized, "the House of Representatives will have a material influence on the Government, and will be an additional security."[111]

Commercial interests, Madison predicted, "will have little or no influence" in the House, rendering the Mississippi secure. Furthermore, the president's responsibility and accountability to the people would prevent any unfavorable treaty, such as one that would cede the Mississippi, from being concluded with another nation. "As the President must be influenced by the sense and interest of his electors, as far as it depends on him (and his agency in making treaties is equal to that of the Senate) he will oppose the cession of that navigation." And if anyone had missed the point that popular sovereignty would protect the Mississippi, Madison added, "[a]s far as the influence of the Representatives goes, it will also operate in favor of this right."

Patrick Henry remained unmoved. He continued to predict that the president and the Senate would conspire to make treaties that favored sectional interests, and he responded that the House had no formal role in the treaty process. The Federalist response was important, because it underscored the roles of the president and the House, and their accountability to the people rather than to the States. "Will [the President] not injure himself, if he injures the States, by concurring in an injudicious treaty?" Nicholas directly asked Henry.[112] "How is he elected? Where will the majority of the people be?" Regarding the House, Nicholas observed that Henry had treated the representatives of the people "with great contempt." Nicholas then compared the treatymaking powers of the House of Representatives to those of the English House of Commons. Even though neither body had any formal constitutional role, they had a significant voice in foreign policy:

> How is this business done in [Henry's] favorite Government? The King of Great-Britain can make what treaties he pleases. But, Sir, do not the House of Commons influence them? Will he make a treaty manifestly repugnant to their interests?—Will they not tell him, he is mistaken in that respect as in many others?

One does not need to guess what Nicholas's answers to those questions were. "This gives them such influence that [the House] can dictate in what manner [treaties] shall be made." The necessity of the consent of the House of Representatives for any treaty, especially commercial treaties, by statute or by funding was subsequently repeated by other Federalists throughout the debates.

The next day, Madison and Nicholas returned to the same themes to re-
but Henry's accusation that the president's unchecked war powers would
allow the creation of a military dictatorship. Importantly, Federalists *never*
described Congress's power to declare war as a check on the president,
even though it was very much in their interest to do so. Rather, they relied
on the traditional legislative check on executive warmaking: funding. This
created a double security against tyranny. First, the federal government's
power to make war itself would be divided, and, second, Congress would
have a powerful means of controlling presidential military adventurism.
Said Nicholas:

> Under the new Government, no appropriation of money, to the use of
> raising or supporting an army, shall be for a longer term than two years.
> The President is to command. But the regulation of the army and navy
> is given to Congress. Our representatives will be a powerful check here.
> The influence of the Commons in England in this case is very predomi-
> nant.[113]

In other words, the warmaking relationship between president and Congress would operate just as did the one between Crown and Parliament. It
is significant that Anti-Federalists did not disagree about the workings of
the British system. Indeed, during his long harangue against the Constitution, Henry had observed that in Great Britain Parliament's control over
funding gave it authority to check the conduct of war.[114] Anti-Federalists
appear only to have believed that the conspiring branches of the federal
government would combine these powers to oppress the states.

Madison followed with a powerful rejection of Henry's critique. He
criticized Henry's view that the purse and sword had to be held by different governments (in other words, the states and the national), and explicitly analogized to the British experience:

> What is the meaning of this maxim? Does it mean that the sword and
> purse ought not to be trusted in the hands of the same Government? This
> cannot be the meaning. For there never was, and I can say there never will
> be, an efficient Government, in which both are not vested. The only ratio-
> nal meaning, is, that the sword and purse are not to be given to the same
> member. Apply it to the British Government, which has been mentioned.
> The sword is in the hands of the British King. The purse is in the hands of
> the Parliament. It is so in America, as far as any analogy can exist.[115]

Like Nicholas, Madison never invoked Congress's power to declare war as a legislative check on the executive. Rather, he relied directly on Congress's control over funding and even predicted that Congress's powers over warmaking would operate in a manner identical to those of Parliament. Madison further emphasized that the funding power, in addition to Congress's other powers over the military, would prove to be more than enough of a check on the president.

> The purse is in the hands of the Representatives of the people. They have the appropriation of all monies. They have the direction and regulation of land and naval forces. They are to *provide* for calling forth the militia— And the President is to have the command; and, in conjunction with the Senate, to appoint the officers.[116]

It is important to take note of what Madison did not argue. He did not assert that the Declare War Clause would check presidential power. Nor did he claim that the Constitution imposed specific and formal rules for the warmaking process, as it did for the legislative process. Instead, Madison argued that the branches would develop their war policies through the conflict or cooperation of their plenary constitutional powers. Although Henry's arguments had an effect, Madison and Nicholas had managed to stop his political momentum. Some historians even identify these days in June as the decisive moment that turned the Virginia convention toward ratification.[117] Shortly after these arguments about war, peace, and lawmaking, Virginia ratified the Constitution.

These arguments during the Virginia ratifying convention represent the Federalists' best effort to explain the republican nature of the foreign affairs power. Federalists' reliance on the presidency's republican character and the House's control over implementing legislation and funding is significant for interpretive purposes, because it came during the most critical stage of the ratification process. Federalist arguments came specifically in response to Anti-Federalist criticisms of the war and treaty powers. Together, Federalists and Anti-Federalists engaged in a reasoned debate, and the understanding that emerged—that the people would have a voice through the president and the informal role of the House—indicates the meaning that Virginians gave to the Constitution's allocation of the foreign affairs power. As Virginia was the key state in the process of ratification, this evidence powerfully suggests what original meaning we should attach to the relative roles of the president, Senate, and Congress in wielding the foreign affairs power.[118]

CONCLUSION

In the state ratifying conventions, we see the reaction to unlimited legislative power at work. When the delegates arrived in Philadelphia for the Federal Convention, they were propelled by a political turmoil caused by weak executives and a burst of legislative activity. They responded in two ways. First, they established a new national executive unified in one person, its independence guaranteed by national election, and its energy restored through its traditional powers. During this period, the executive nature of warmaking and treatymaking had never metamorphosed into legislative powers, but instead had been married to weak state executives. Second, the Framers ended the harmful effects of excessive decentralization. Under the Articles of Confederation, the states had exercised the power of a national legislature that could frustrate national policies by withholding funds or refusing to enact implementing legislation. To be sure, the Framers added the Supremacy Clause to the Constitution in order to give the federal government the power to implement treaties. But more importantly, they created a new national legislature that had its own power to directly regulate individuals and to tax and spend, and which was no longer dependent on the states for implementation of its policies.

With both a restored executive and a truly national legislature, the customary constitutional balance in foreign affairs could function normally. When the ratification is viewed comprehensively, with attention to the three most significant state conventions, the evidence indicates that the Constitution's supporters understood the war and treaty functions to be executive powers that were distinct from, and could not supplant, Congress's power to legislate or fund. The president or the president-and-Senate might have the energy, independence, and unity to respond to the necessity imposed by unforeseen international events, but they could not wage war without Congress's active cooperation in funding and raising a military, nor could they execute treaties domestically without legislation. No new check on the restored executive was needed because the Framers understood that the new Congress would check the president just as Parliament had balanced the Crown. That is why the power to declare war, at its root a legalistic function that defines relationships and status under international law, is absent from the debates over war and peace in the Federal Convention and the state ratifying conventions. It was not necessary as a check on an executive who had to convince Congress to provide funds, troops, and laws to pursue his foreign policies.

5

WAR POWERS FOR A NEW WORLD

The preceding chapters provide us the opportunity to deepen our understanding of the constitutional text and structure as they regulate the war power. Rather than creating a specific legalistic process, mirroring that for statutes, the Framers believed that separating the president's executive and commander-in-chief powers from Congress's powers over declaring war and funding would create a political system in which in each branch could use its own constitutional powers to develop foreign policy. A close reading of the constitutional text and structure shows that the original understanding of the war power is fully reflected in the Constitution. The Constitution's flexible warmaking system is especially pronounced when compared to other constitutional texts, and to the more formalistic processes established for other forms of government action.

This approach finds that the practice of the political branches in making war since the end of World War II has fallen within the constitutional design. While Congress never declared war in Korea or Vietnam, among many other places, it had every opportunity to control those conflicts through its funding powers. That it did not was a reflection of a lack of political will rather than a defect in the constitutional design. A more flexible approach also allows us to understand America's newest military interventions. Recent wars in Iraq, Afghanistan, and Kosovo were constitutional, even though in none of them was there a declaration of war and Kosovo received no statutory authorization, because Congress has had the full opportunity to participate in decisionmaking elsewhere. This chapter explores the interaction between the Constitution's system of war powers and the demands of international cooperation, as reflected in the questions surrounding international justifications for the use of force and multilateral military commands.

WAR AND THE CONSTITUTIONAL TEXT

Scholars like John Hart Ely, Michael Glennon, Louis Henkin, and Harold Koh have regularly criticized the wars of the Cold War by appealing to the intentions of the Framers. Arguing that the Framers "pursued a substantive end (the limitation of war to the absolutely necessary) by procedural means (requiring the concurrence of both houses of Congress as well as the president)" through the Declare War Clause, Professor Ely proclaims that the Framers' intent has "complete contemporary relevance."[1] Historian Louis Fisher argues that the "constitutional framework adopted by the Framers is clear in its basic principles. The authority to initiate war lay with Congress. The President could act unilaterally only in one area: to repel sudden attacks."[2] Recently, younger scholars, such as Michael Ramsey, Jane Stromseth, and William Treanor, have agreed that the framing materials demonstrate that Congress must give its approval before the use of force abroad (except in cases of responding to a direct attack on the United States).[3] A smaller group of defenders of enhanced executive power has responded by invoking the record of practice, the imperatives of a dangerous world, and the structural advantages of the executive branch.[4] These scholars, such as Robert Bork, argue that functional considerations, not original intent, should determine the Constitution's allocation of power among the branches of government.

These scholars, however, have not focused on the starting point for constitutional interpretation: the constitutional text and structure. Important and long-overlooked insights about the nature of the war power come to light through close examination of the text. First, it is apparent that Congress's power to "declare war" is not synonymous with the power to begin military hostilities. Professor Ramsey's article in the *University of Chicago Law Review* best expresses the opposite view. He argues that the Framers understood the power to "declare war" as the giving Congress the sole power to decide on whether to commence military hostilities against other nations. Under international and domestic law at the time of the ratification, therefore, "declare war" must have been shorthand for "begin war" or "commence war" or "authorize war."[5] Only once Congress had issued this authorization could the president trigger his commander-in-chief authority and fight the war to its conclusion. At best, the president has a limited authority to use force without congressional consent only when the United States has suffered an attack. Thus, the Declare War Clause both expands Congress's war powers and restricts those of the president. As Glennon has written, the clause not only "empowers Congress to declare war," but also "serves as a limitation on executive war-making power, placing certain acts off limits for the President."[6]

The constitutional text, however, simply does not support such an expansive reading. First, the Constitution uses the word "declare" war, rather than "make," "begin," "authorize," or "wage" war. At the time of the Constitution's ratification, "declare" carried a distinct and separate meaning from "levy," "engage," "make," or "commence." Samuel Johnson's English dictionary (perhaps the definitive dictionary at the time of the framing) defined "declare" as "to clear, to free from obscurity"; "to make known, to tell evidently and openly"; "to publish; to proclaim"; "to shew in open view"; or "to make a declaration, to proclaim some resolution or opinion, some favour or opposition."[7] This definition suggests that declaring war recognized a state of affairs—clarifying the legal status of the nation's relationship with another country—rather than authorized the creation of that state of affairs.

Second, if this view were correct, we would expect the Framers to have repeated the phrase "declare war" elsewhere in the Constitution when addressing the same subject. They did not. When discussing war in other contexts, the Constitution's phrasing indicates that declaring war referred to something less than the sole power to send the nation into hostilities. As we have seen, Article I, Section 10 declares that states may not "engage" in war. If "declare war" meant the same thing as initiate hostilities, Article I, Section 10 should have forbidden states from declaring war. Granting Congress the sole authority to "engage" the nation in war would have been a much clearer, direct method for vesting in Congress the power to control the actual conduct of war.

To take another example, Article III of the Constitution defines the crime of treason, in part, as consisting of "levying War" against the United States. Again, "levying" appears to be broader in meaning than merely declaring. If the Framers had used "levy War" in Article I, Section 8, they certainly would have made far clearer their alleged intention to grant

Congress the sole power to decide on war. Conversely, if the step of declaring war were as serious as some believe, Article III ought to have defined treason to occur when a citizen "declares war" against the United States. To be sure, as Adrian Vermeule and Ernest Young have argued, while there may be serious doubts about demanding a consistency in meaning between constitutional provisions, which have been added to the Constitution during different periods of time by different groups of legislators and delegates, this is not true of the original 1787 Constitution.[8] The unamended Constitution was drafted at one time and ratified at one time, and so it is not unreasonable to expect words used on the same subject to convey a common meaning throughout.

The structure of Article I, Section 10 deals an even heavier blow to the pro-Congress reading. It states:

> No State shall, without the Consent of Congress, lay any Duty of Tonnage, keep Troops, or Ships of War in time of Peace, enter into any Agreement or Compact with another State, or with a foreign power, or *engage in War, unless actually invaded, or in such imminent Danger as will not admit of delay* (emphasis added).[9]

This provision creates the *exact* war powers process between Congress and the states that scholars critical of the presidency want to create between Congress and the president. It makes resort to force conditional on the "Consent of Congress," and it even includes an exception for defending against sudden attacks. Pro-Congress scholars have argued that the Framers understood the Declare War Clause to contain an unexpressed exception that permits the executive to use force in response to an attack without having to seek a declaration of war from Congress. Otherwise their strict interpretation would prevent the president from engaging in even defensive uses of force without congressional approval and have proven utterly unworkable in the real world. Article I, Section 10, however, shows the faults of this approach, because it requires us to believe that the Framers did not know how to express themselves in one part of the Constitution but did in another part of the Constitution on exactly the same subject.

Pro-Congress scholars have never attempted to account for the difference in language between Article I, Section 8 and Article I, Section 10.[10] If they assume that specific texts have specific meanings, they also must believe that different texts should be interpreted to have different meanings. If the pro-Congress reading were correct, the Framers naturally should have written a provision stating that "the President may not, without the Consent of Congress, engage in War, unless the United States are actually invaded, or in such imminent Danger as will not admit of delay." Or, Article I, Section 10 should have said that "no state shall, without the consent of Congress, declare war." Instead, the Constitution only allocates to Congress the declare war power and to the president the commander-in-chief power, without specifically stating—as it does in Article I, Section 10 with regard to the states—how those powers are to interact. The Constitution's creation of a specific, detailed war powers process at the state level, but its silence at the federal level, shows that the Constitution does not establish any specific procedure for going to war.

Two additional clues suggest that "declare war" served as a recognition of the legal status of hostile acts, rather than as a necessary authorization for hostilities. Congress's power to declare war does not stand alone, but instead is part of a clause that includes the power to "grant Letters of Marque and Reprisal" and to "make Rules concerning Captures on Land and Water."[11] Placement of the power to declare war alongside these other two is significant, because they clearly involve the power of Congress to recognize or declare the legal status and consequences of certain wartime actions, and not the power to authorize those actions. Ironically, the Marque and Reprisal Clause serves as the linchpin for some defenders of an expansive reading of Congress's war powers. Jules Lobel and Jane Stromseth, for example, who rely on the work of Charles Lofgren, argue that letters of marque and reprisal had come "to signify any intermediate or low-intensity hostility short of declared war."[12] In part, they respond to the history of the 1980s, in which presidents conducted "police actions," smaller conflicts, and covert activity that fall well short of World Wars I and II. When combined with Congress's control over declaring war, Stromseth, Lobel, and Lofgren argue, the Marque and Reprisal Clause provides Congress with full control over the initiation of all military hostilities, whether they be total war or covert actions.

Such interpretive moves, however, rip the constitutional text from its historical context. By the time of the framing, letters of marque and reprisal had come to refer to a fairly technical form of international reprisal, in which a government gave its permission to an injured private party to recover, via military operations, compensation from the citizens of a foreign nation. Without a letter of marque and reprisal, such actions—usually conducted on the high seas—would constitute piracy; with a letter, they were legitimate forms of privateering condoned by sovereign consent. While marque and reprisal certainly are one category of what we today might call "low-level conflict," it does not follow that marque and reprisal must refer to *all* forms of conflict short of war. Recent work suggests that, during the American Revolution, letters of marque and reprisal authorized a rather narrow form of commercial warfare that was conducted for profit and regulated by prize courts, in contrast to military actions by regular armed forces.[13] What seems fairly clear is that marque and reprisal did not refer to all forms of undeclared war, especially those with purely military and political goals, but rather with the legal implications of one species of commercial warfare.[14]

Other foundational documents of the period demonstrate that the Framers thought of the power to begin hostilities as different from the power to declare war. Under the Articles of Confederation, the nation's framework of government until the ratification, Congress operated as the executive branch of the United States.[15] As we have seen, Article IX vested Congress with "the sole and exclusive right and power of determining on peace and war."[16] Here the Framers (several of whom had served in the Continental Congress) had at hand a text that clearly and explicitly allocated to Congress the "sole and exclusive" authority to decide whether to fight a war. If the Framers had intended to grant Congress the power to commence military hostilities, they could easily have imported the phrase from the Articles of Confederation into the Constitution, as they did with other, related powers.[17] Instead, they changed Congress's power to "declare war" from "determining on peace and war." For the pro-Congress position to be correct, the Framers would have had to be clumsy draftsmen indeed.

Presidential critics also fail to take into account the next most important founding-era documents: the state constitutions. Most of the state constitutions did not explicitly transfer to their assemblies the power to initiate hostilities, but rather sought to control executive power by disrupting the structural unity of the executive branch.[18] One state, however, chose to create exactly the type of arrangement contemplated by pro-Congress scholars. In its first 1776 constitution, South Carolina vested in its chief executive the power of commander in chief, but then declared that "the president and commander-in-chief shall have no power to make war or peace . . . without the consent of the general assembly and legislative council."[19] In its 1778 constitution, South Carolina reaffirmed its decision that the legislature first must authorize war by stating that "the governor and commander-in-chief shall have no power to commence war, or conclude peace" without legislative approval. South Carolina's 1776 and 1778 constitutions bear two important lessons. First, they show that the Framers did not understand the phrase "declare war" to amount to the power to "make war" or "commence war"—phrases the South Carolina constitution used to refer specifically to initiating war. Second, the South Carolina constitutions provide an example of constitutional language that clearly and explicitly created a legislature-dominated warmaking system—one that the Framers did not adopt.

Usage of these words during the late eighteenth century further supports the distinction between "declare" and "begin" or "commence." Recall that Article I, Section 10 uses the phrase "engage in War," and Article III uses "levying War." Johnson's dictionary, for example, defined "engage" as "to embark in an affair; to enter in an undertaking," or "to conflict; to fight." Johnson defined "levy" as "to raise, applied to war."[20] Other dictionaries of the period drew a similar distinction between "declare" and "engage" or "levy." Nathan Bailey's English dictionary defined "declare" as "to make known, to manifest, publish, or shew," while "engage" meant "to encounter or fight," and "levy" to "raise."[21] Thomas Sheridan's dictionary defined "declare" as "to make known," "engage" as "to conflict, to fight," and levy as "to raise, to bring together men."[22] All three defined "commence," as used by the South Carolina constitution, as "to begin." Even today, we commonly think of the statutes that establish public programs and mandates as "authorization" statutes (to be followed by appropriations), not "declaring" statutes. A declaration does not authorize or make, it recognizes and proclaims.

When the Framers employed "declare" in a constitutional context, they usually used it in a juridical manner, in the sense that courts "declare" the state of the law or the legal status of a certain event or situation. An example from early American political history—the Declaration of Independence—illustrates this narrower meaning. The Declaration did not "authorize" military resistance to Great Britain. At the time that the

Continental Congress met to draft the Declaration, hostilities had existed for more than a year, and Congress had been exercising sovereign powers—negotiating with Britain, sending representatives abroad, seeking aid—for at least two years.[23] Rather than authorize hostilities, the Declaration announced the legal relationship between the mother country and its former colonies. Thus, the Declaration of Independence appears in the form almost of a complaint, in which the revolutionaries recount their grievances (taxation without representation, suspension of the laws, use of bench trials), the remedy sought (independence), and the applicable law ("the Laws of Nature and of Nature's God"). The Declaration's importance was not in authorizing combat, but in transforming the legal status of the hostilities between Great Britain and her colonies from an insurrection to a war between equals. As historian David Armitage has observed, "in order to turn a civil war into a war between states, and thus to create legitimate corporate combatants out of individual rebels and traitors, it was essential to declare war and to obtain recognition of the legitimacy of such a declaration."[24] The Declaration of Independence was the nation's first declaration of war.

Professor Ramsey's response appears to be that, under international law, declaring war was basically useless. He argues that a declaration of war is not necessary to give armed conflict the status of "war" under international law; it merely happens when conflict begins. Because declarations of war are essentially unnecessary, the grant of authority in Article I, Section 8 must mean something else, and that something must be the power to initiate hostilities. There are several problems with this view. First, if it were correct, the United States should never have issued a Declaration of Independence; events themselves demonstrated that hostilities had been authorized with the mother country. Nevertheless, the Declaration mattered because it openly proclaimed that the colonies had broken away, and it allowed other countries, such as France, to define their own legal relationships with the new nation. Second, the United States should never have taken the trouble to declare war the few times that it has. In each of the five declared wars, the United States could claim that it, its citizens, or its forces had been attacked. The United States could have carried on hostilities, and the legal status of warfare would have been automatically recognized by international law—no declaration was needed. Third, no nation should ever declare war, because apparently the launch of an offensive attack is sufficient. Yet, the British declared war several times in conflicts preceding the framing period—even though these declarations often came after hostilities had broken out.[25]

Declarations of war serve a purpose, albeit one that does not amount to the sole authority to initiate hostilities. Declarations do simply what they say they do: they declare. To use the eighteenth-century understanding, they make public, show openly, and make known the state of international legal relations between the United States and another nation. This is a different concept than whether the laws of war apply to the hostilities; two nations could technically not be at war, even though their forces might be engaged in limited combat (which would be governed by the laws of war). During the eighteenth century, declarations often took the form of a legal complaint in which a nation identified the grounds for waging war, explained the new rules that would apply to interaction between the two nations, and outlined the remedy. Declarations are also important for domestic constitutional purposes. Textually, a declaration of war places the nation in a state of total war, which triggers enhanced powers on the part of the federal government. The Fifth Amendment, for example, says that "[n]o person shall be held to answer for a capital, or otherwise infamous crime, unless on a presentment or indictment of a Grand Jury, except in cases arising in the land or naval forces, or in the Militia, when in actual service in time of War or public danger."

Congress has recognized the distinction between declared total wars and nondeclared hostilities by providing the executive branch with expanded domestic powers—such as seizing foreign property, conducting warrantless surveillance, arresting enemy aliens, and taking control of transportation systems, to name a few—only when war is declared.[26] Even the Supreme Court has suggested that in times of declared war, certain actions by the federal government would survive strict scrutiny but would certainly fail if attempted in peacetime. Thus, the terrible internment of Japanese Americans during World War II was justified only because the United States was in the midst of a war declared by Congress.[27] One doubts whether the courts would have allowed the wholesale internment of Panamanian Americans during the 1989 Panama War, or of Yugoslavs during the Kosovo conflict, or of all Iraqis Americans during the recent invasion and occupation of Iraq. Only a declaration of war from Congress could trigger and permit such extreme measures reserved only for total war.

WAR AND THE CONSTITUTIONAL STRUCTURE

Considerations of constitutional structure reveal, in even sharper contrast, problems with interpreting the Declare War Clause to require congressional authorization of hostilities. According to pro-Congress scholars, the Constitution establishes a strict procedure that requires Congress first to declare or authorize war before the president, as commander in chief, can prosecute hostilities. If the nation is attacked first, then the president can respond without seeking a declaration of war. Yet, the Constitution itself nowhere describes such a process, nor does it explain how the Declare War Clause and the commander-in-chief power must interact. The Framers simply gave the former to Congress and the latter to the president, and left it at that.

Pro-Congress arguments really are structural ones. Professor Ramsey, for example, reads the Declare War Clause to mean more than a power to issue a declaration of war because otherwise it would impose no substantive limit on the president. Implicit in this central idea is that the Constitution's structure requires that there be a check on the president's war powers. This argument, which also runs throughout the work of Ely, Glennon, and Koh, misunderstands the nature of the Constitution's basic structure. Congress needs no check on the president through the Declare War Clause because it already possesses all the power it needs. Congress at any time may use its power of the purse to counter presidential warmaking. Indeed, all Congress need do is nothing: by refusing actively to authorize the existence of armed forces or appropriate additional money to fund wars, Congress can prevent the nation from conducting any effective hostilities. Reading the Declare War Clause to check the president solves a constitutional problem that is not really there.

One way to understand the constitutional structure in order to better see this point is to compare the warmaking process to other decisional processes in the Constitution. Pro-Congress scholars simply believe that the Constitution divides the war power between the president and Congress, with Congress playing the chief role in deciding whether to wage war and the president controlling how to wage war. When the Constitution, however, divides and allocates executive powers through a specific process, it does so far more clearly. The treaty and appointments powers provide a useful illustration. Article II, Section 2 states that the president "shall have Power, by and with the Advice and Consent of the Senate, to make Treaties, provided two thirds of the Senators present concur." By establishing a minimum process for making treaties, this provision makes clear that the president cannot make treaties without senatorial consent. Similarly, Section 2 states that the president "shall nominate, and by and with the Advice and Consent of the Senate, shall appoint Ambassadors, other public Ministers and Consuls, Judges of the Supreme Court, and all other Officers of the United States." This requires senatorial participation in the making of appointments, another power that was executive in nature under the British constitution.

If the Framers had sought to establish a system that requires *ex ante* congressional approval, should they not have used the same framework to achieve the same ends? Article II, Section 2 should have included an additional clause that the president "shall have Power, by and with the advice and consent of Congress, to engage in War." This would have made clear that the Constitution requires Congress's permission when beginning military hostilities, just as the president needs senatorial consent before making treaties or appointing Supreme Court justices. A different reading requires us to believe that the Framers chose ambiguous, obtuse language to allocate war powers in such a manner as to reach *the same functional result* as the Treaty and Appointments Clauses. To be sure, these provisions raise their own interpretive questions, but they take the form of crystals of brilliant clarity when placed beside the War Power Clauses.

The absence of a textually mandated and defined system for going to war is especially clear because the Constitution, in other areas, provides for such processes when they are wanted. Compare war powers to the process for enacting statutes. Although one of the signal defects of the Articles of Confederation was its inability to directly regulate the private conduct of individuals, the Framers still sought to render the passage of legislation difficult. As Brad Clark has pointed out in his articles on federalism and the federal common law, Article I, Section 7 sets out a finely wrought method for making public laws, with explicit provisions when the consent of different parties, such as the president, is required.[28]

It does not describe the legislature's role in lawmaking in Article I, and then the president's veto power in Article II, while leaving blank how the twain shall meet. Similarly, Article V describes a process for amending the Constitution—one in which Congress can exercise the initiative—in which the consent of several actors is precisely outlined.

Contrast this with the process advocated by pro-Congress scholars for warmaking. They believe that making war should be just as precise: Congress must provide a declaration of war (presumably by simple majority vote) before the president can exercise his commander-in-chief functions on the battlefield. If warmaking were to have such process features, involving congressional initiative and consent, we would expect the constitutional text to establish as detailed a procedure for warmaking as for lawmaking or amending the Constitution. Surely, the Framers would have thought war to be as important as the latter two subjects.

A final structural point is worth emphasizing. Much of the support for broadly interpreting the power to declare war arises out of concerns about unchecked presidential warmaking.[29] This argument characterizes the writers on war powers during and immediately after the Vietnam War who believed that President Johnson had unilaterally led America to the worst military defeat in its history, as well as more recent authors.[30] They claim that declarations of war must portend some greater power, even if it is not borne by the text's actual meaning. Thus, they seek to convert declaring war, which specifically functioned under international law to determine the legal status of hostilities, into a domestic legal check on the executive branch.

Such concerns, however, misunderstand the Constitution's grants of power to Congress in war matters, which give it an effective role in the commencement of military hostilities. As noted earlier, Congress can block a president bent on war simply by doing nothing. By refusing to cooperate, by not taking the affirmative step of voting funds, Congress can prevent the commander in chief from conducting any significant military hostilities. This pattern has been repeated in our recent modern wars. In the wars in Iraq and against the al Qaeda terrorist organization and the Taliban militia in Afghanistan, for example, President George W. Bush sought additional funding for military operations, giving Congress the opportunity to oppose hostilities. Similarly, in 1999 President Clinton sought emergency funding for military operations in Kosovo and Serbia. In both cases, Congress could have effectively blocked the conduct of hostilities by refusing to appropriate the funds. Critics of the American warmaking process simply look for the answer in the wrong places. There is no doubt that the Constitution provides Congress with a powerful check on warmaking, but it comes through the authority to grant or deny funds to wage war.

Finally, brief consideration of the interaction between the power to declare war and the president's powers suggests that Congress cannot have the sole authority to commence hostilities. Suppose Congress wanted to engage in war with France against the president's wishes. Even if Congress were to declare war against France, the president could still prevent hostilities from breaking out simply by refusing to order the armed forces to attack. All Congress can do is declare the state of the legal relationship between the United States and France under international law. Congress's power to declare war *cannot* amount to the sole power to initiate hostilities, because the Commander-in-Chief and Executive Power Clauses provide only the president with the power to conduct military operations, and thus a functional veto over any congressional effort to start a war. Congress could even construct a navy and army and fund its operations, but without the commander in chief's cooperation, no real war would occur. Once again, it is the interaction of the executive power with funding that determines the real outcome.

PRACTICE AND THE CONSTITUTION

A more flexible approach to the allocation of war powers shows that, rather than violating the Constitution, the American way of war during the last decade has complied with the constitutional design. It is worth taking a closer look at recent conflicts to show that Congress has had an ample opportunity to consider and to check presidential initiatives in warmaking. In 2001 Afghanistan and 2003–4 Iraq, no declaration of war issued, but Congress did enact statutes "authorizing" the president to engage in armed combat. In response to the September 11, 2001 attacks, for example, Congress quickly enacted Senate Joint Resolution 23 "to authorize the use of the United States Armed Forces against those responsible for the recent attacks launched against the United States."[31] It found not only that the September 11 attacks constituted an "unusual and extraordinary threat to the national security and foreign policy of the United States" but also declared that "the President has authority under the Constitution to take action to deter and prevent acts of international terrorism against the United States," an admission, it seems of the president's inherent authority to use force without congressional permission. Congress then authorized the president to use military force against "those nations, organizations, or persons he determines planned, authorized, committed, or aided the terrorist attacks" of September 11, or "harbored such organizations or persons." In the course of enacting this legislation, Congress had a full opportunity to debate the merits of using military force abroad, particularly in Afghanistan.

Even if such legislation had never been considered, Congress had several other moments to block presidential efforts to wage war against al Qaeda. Military operations in Afghanistan have required additional funds, which President Bush initially requested as part of a $20 billion emergency appropriations bill in October of 2001, which was granted by Congress. The expense of modern war has required ongoing demands for appropriations, with another bill enacted on July 23, 2002 that appropriated more than $4 billion for continuing operations in Afghanistan. Even before the war in Iraq, military operations in Afghanistan and around the world generated approximately $2.5 billion in additional costs per month that require periodic supplemental appropriations to refill the Pentagon's coffers. In the fall of 2001, Congress also enacted a Defense Department authorization bill that determines the military's size, force structure, and weapons systems. If Congress had wanted to prevent the war in Afghanistan, or if it had disagreed with the continuing role of American troops there, it could have refused to provide the funds needed to pay for the personnel, material, and operational expenses of waging the war. War went ahead without a declaration, and Congress had every chance to consider the merits of the conflict and to prevent it.

Congress similarly had ample opportunity to prevent President Bush from ordering the invasion of Iraq. To be sure, Congress enacted legislation authorizing the use of force in Iraq. In an October 2002 joint resolution, Congress authorized the president to use force against Iraq to enforce United Nations Security Council resolutions or to protect the national security of the United States.[32] While this authorizing statute demonstrated Congress's political support for the war, it was not truly necessary. If Congress had wanted to stop the invasion, it could have with-held appropriations. The additional costs for the war in Iraq were so large that Congress approved almost $80 billion in supplemental appropria-tions to fund the war. Defense Secretary Donald Rumsfeld estimated that, even after the end of major combat operations, the costs of military opera-tions and rebuilding expenses in Iraq amounted to $3.9 billion per month. In July of 2003, with reconstruction efforts continuing, Congress adopted an overall appropriation for the Defense Department of $369 billion. At any of these points, Congress could have effectively prevented the inva-sion of Iraq by refusing to fund the billions in expenses needed to keep an American offensive military force in the field and operating. Congress never did.

With both Iraq and Afghanistan, a supporter of the Declare War Clause theory of war powers may well have felt the Constitution satisfied be-cause of the two statutes authorizing hostilities—even though these schol-ars have never explained why authorizing statutes satisfy the requirement for a declaration of war. They have no way of explaining the Kosovo con-flict, however, aside from concluding that the war was unconstitutional. In Kosovo, Congress never enacted an "authorizing" statute, and the presi-dent for the first time exceeded the sixty-day limit on combat imposed by the War Powers Resolution (WPR). For that reason, Kosovo is perhaps the most notable example of the manner in which the spending demands of modern war provide Congress with the functional ability to prevent presidents from waging war, and it requires perhaps a more detailed ex-amination of Congress's actions with regard to that conflict.

In 1998, Serbia launched a crackdown in Kosovo that killed dozens of Albanians and led thousands of others to flee. In March 1999, Serbian military forces began a broad offensive aimed at driving the Albanian population out of the province. Most Albanians went into hiding, fled to neighboring countries, or were killed or detained. On March 23, af-ter the Clinton administration's special envoy left Belgrade with no hope for a negotiated settlement, the Senate passed a concurrent resolution authorizing the president to "conduct military air operations and missile strikes in cooperation with our NATO allies against the Federal Republic of Yugoslavia (Serbia and Montenegro)."[33] The House, however, refused to enact any authorization for hostilities. Nonetheless, the next day Amer-ican warplanes, in conjunction with other NATO forces, began attacking

Serbian forces in Kosovo. In a nationally televised address, President Clinton argued that air strikes were necessary to protect innocent Albanians, to prevent the conflict from spreading to the rest of Europe, and to act with our European allies in maintaining peace.[34] President Clinton also declared that the military's mission would be "to demonstrate NATO's seriousness of purpose," to "deter an even bloodier offensive against innocent civilians in Kosovo," and "to seriously damage the Serbian military's capacity to harm the people of Kosovo." American air and missile operations expanded beyond Serbian units in Kosovo to include military, strategic, and civilian targets within Serbia itself, such as air defense, electrical, communications, and government facilities.

Presidential initiative in warmaking produced congressional funding support, but nothing more. On the same day that air strikes began, the House of Representatives passed a resolution by 424 to 1 that declared its support for American troops, but refused to authorize the use of force.[35] On March 26, President Clinton sent a message to Congress justifying the use of force on his "constitutional authority to conduct U.S. foreign relations and as commander-in-chief and Chief Executive."[36] While he welcomed Congress's demonstrations of support, President Clinton made clear that he did not need its authorization. Following the examples of Presidents Reagan and Bush, Clinton described the report as "consistent" with, rather than "pursuant to," the WPR, demonstrating a refusal either to recognize the WPR's constitutionality or to comply with its terms.[37] On April 28, the House of Representatives first rejected, by a vote of 427 to 2, a joint resolution declaring war on the Federal Republic of Yugoslavia.[38] It then rejected, by a tie 213 to 213 vote, a Senate resolution authorizing the use of force.[39] The House also defeated, by a 290 to 139 vote, a concurrent resolution that would have required the president to remove all American troops from Yugoslavia operations. The House then passed a bill that barred the use of any funds for the deployment of American forces in Yugoslavia without specific congressional authorization, which the Senate did not consider. On May 20, Congress doubled the administration's request for emergency funding for Yugoslavia war operations, to the tune of $11.8 billion, but did not authorize the war.[40] On May 25, President Clinton reported to Congress that he had deployed even more aircraft and combat ground troops to the region to support deep strike operations in Yugoslavia.

Conclusion of the Kosovo conflict highlighted the WPR's impotence in constraining presidential decisionmaking. Bombing attacks against Serbian targets both in Kosovo and in Serbia proper did not end until June 10, 1999, seventy-nine days after the war first began and nineteen days after the resolution's sixty-day clock had ended.[41] As part of the peace terms accepted by Serbia, NATO sent fifty thousand troops, seven thousand of them American, into Kosovo to maintain peace and security during the transition to Kosovar self-government. Congress has never authorized the insertion of American troops, who remain in Kosovo to this day. Congress, however, agreed to provide supplementary appropriations for a long-term military presence in Kosovo, and in the years since has continued to appropriate funds to support the American peacekeeping deployment there. Congress could have stopped the war, if it had possessed the political will, merely by *refusing* to appropriate the funds to keep the military operations going.

One might respond that it is unreasonable to expect Congress to use its appropriations powers to cut off troops in the field. Professors Ely and Koh claim that requiring congressmen to cut off funds is unrealistic given the pressure to show support for troops in the field. Surely members of Congress would not take actions that might be interpreted as undermining the safety and effectiveness of the military, once committed and in the midst of hostilities. We should not, however, mistake a failure of political will for a violation of the Constitution. Congress undoubtedly possessed the power to prevent or end the wars in Iraq, Afghanistan, and Kosovo; it simply chose not to use it. Affirmatively providing funding for a war, or at the very least refusing to cut off previous appropriations, represents a political determination by Congress that it will provide minimal support for a war, but that ultimately it will leave it to the president to receive the credit either for success or failure. Recent wars show only that Congress has refused to exercise the ample powers at its disposal, not that there has been an alarming breakdown in the constitutional structure.

Congress's power over funding, rather than broad framework statutes like the War Powers Resolution, provides the legislature with the right to participate in the decision to initiate hostilities. Indeed, the original understanding indicates that the War Powers Resolution is unconstitutional because it attempts to enact general rules limiting the president's commander-in-chief and executive powers to engage in hostilities that do not rise to the level of total war. When critics complained that the president might exercise such a power recklessly, Federalists such as Madison did not respond by asserting that Congress could pass a statute or use its declare war authority to check the executive. Rather, they responded that Congress would use its appropriations power to frustrate presidential warmaking that was not in the nation's interest. The War Powers Resolution's inconsistency with the Constitution's text, history, and original understanding explains, perhaps, why none of the branches, including Congress itself, has respected its terms. Attempting to place a statutory straightjacket on war powers undermines the very flexibility—swift and decisive presidential action combined with congressional participation by way of the funding power—that the Framers understood the Constitution to establish. Even today, after the end of the Cold War, Congress continues to authorize standing armed forces capable of conducting large-scale military operations around the world. It funds weapons systems that allow the United States to engage in a wide variety of interventions, from quick, surgical cruise missile strikes to power projection by carrier groups to invasions by heavy armored forces. By providing long-term funding for a permanent military capable of such operations, Congress has given the executive the means to send troops immediately into combat overseas. By not taking the step of placing conditions on their use, as is often done with domestic spending programs, Congress has implicitly allowed their deployment. Indeed, by keeping the funds flowing once hostilities in Iraq, Afghanistan, and Kosovo had begun, Congress ratified the executive's exercise of initiative in war. The decision to go to war in those places operated well within the boundaries set by the constitutional text and the original understanding of war powers.

War and the Post–Cold War World

The debate over the constitutionality of military operations like those in Kosovo is as old as the Constitution itself. The American political system has struggled with the question of executive war powers ever since Alexander Hamilton and James Madison squared off in the Pacificus-Helvidius debates. This and earlier chapters have demonstrated that the original understanding of the Constitution permits war powers to be exercised as they have over the last two centuries. Recent conflicts, however, provoke questions that go beyond the usual struggle between the executive and the legislature in managing war. They involve perhaps the most important issue facing the American public law system as it enters this century: how the Constitution will adapt to the globalization of political, economic, and security affairs. These wars provide an early example of the constitutional issues that will arise with increasing frequency as governmental power comes to be exercised by international institutions. During the Kosovo operation, for example, the Clinton administration apparently delegated federal authority to non-U.S. officers, suggested that treaty obligations provided justification for the intervention, and acted inconsistently with international law. In Afghanistan, the United States acted without explicit U.N. Security Council authorization, but claimed that the September 11, 2001 attacks triggered the right to self-defense, and was able to draw on the support, both military and financial, of many nations. In Iraq, however, many have argued that the use of force violates international law, and military and financial support from other nations has been less widespread. Future military and nonmilitary cooperation with other nations may raise similar issues about the domestic legal authority of international organizations, the relationships between treaties and constitutional authority, and conflicts between international and domestic law. This section of the chapter asks whether the legality of use of force under international law acts as a legal constraint on the domestic constitutional system, and discusses the ability of American troops to serve in multilateral operations.

Although perhaps not obvious on the surface, the wars in Iraq, Afghanistan, and Kosovo represent the demands placed on the U.S. Constitution by new forms of international cooperation. In the past, American wars were fought primarily against other nation-states, with the objective of complete victory obtained by defeat of the enemy's military in the field and the capture, occupation, and sometimes annexation of its territory or colonies. Sometimes the United States fought with allies at its side, as in World Wars I and II, but often fought alone, as in the Mexican-American and Spanish-American Wars. American war aims were usually self-interested, with early wars including the expansion of American territory at the expense of other nations, and later ones the defeat or containment of hostile nations driven by the dangerous ideologies of fascism or communism.[42]

Today's wars are different. The United States has not used force with an aim of defeating an enemy nation for the purpose of seizing territory or containing the advances of a hostile enemy and its allies. Rather, recent American conflicts have sought to remove threats to a stable international order, such as the mass emigrations and humanitarian disasters in Haiti or Somalia, or the common dangers to international security posed by rogue nations that harbor terrorists or may possess weapons of mass destruction, as with Afghanistan and Iraq. Rather than full-blown total wars characterized by mobilization of the economy and full deployment of the U.S. armed forces, the nation has become involved more often in "low-intensity conflicts," in which civilian leaders employ military force for more diffuse objectives, such as rebuilding nations, enforcing international peace or the status quo, and imposing costs on hostile regimes. These objectives fall short of total military and political victory.

Events in Kosovo serve as a prime example of the sharpening tension between the demands of international cooperation and the American public lawmaking system. The Balkans historically have been a tinderbox for broader European wars that have called on American intervention to restore peace and stability. American and European policymakers feared that conduct that once was considered domestic now threatened to cause wider disruptions to European security. Serbia's course of repression, for example, produced a stream of refugees that threatened to destabilize neighboring countries, and ultimately our European allies. Widespread human rights violations not only offended European and international norms, but might even have provoked intervention by regional powers, raising the possibility of conflict between greater powers and perhaps NATO allies.[43]

Responses to this transnational problem seemed to require a multilateral solution. No individual European nation had the military or political wherewithal to force Serbia to end its aggression. It was equally unlikely that the United States would unilaterally intervene so far from home, in a nation with close cultural and historical ties to its former Cold War enemy, where its direct national interests were hard to define. Operating through the multilateral structure of NATO allowed member nations to gather their collective resources to address the risks posed by events in Kosovo. Multilateralism allowed NATO nations to submerge the identification of any single nation's interest as dominant in the operation. NATO may have presented a less threatening front to nations, such as Russia, that sympathized with Serbia and might have feared an intervention so close to its own borders. Kosovo signaled the transformation of NATO from a defensive alliance, whose primary goals were to contain Soviet expansionism and to promote European reconstruction, to a multilateral organization that engaged in proactive operations to preempt threats to regional security.

Similar considerations played a role in the decision to attack Afghanistan and Iraq. Afghanistan as a nation did not launch the September 11, 2001 attacks. Rather, the al Qaeda international terrorist organization, which operated freely within Afghanistan thanks to the protection of the Taliban militia, did. Attacking Afghanistan and removing the Taliban leadership was akin to "draining a swamp," in the words of American policymakers, that had provided the breeding grounds for terrorism. In other words, removing Afghanistan as a base for al Qaeda operatives did not constitute revenge for the September 11 attacks, rather it addressed a significant threat to international security. Such an effort, however, did not lay within the powers of the United States alone. Not only did other nations provide special forces and policing units, they also helped to prevent al Qaeda fighters from fleeing to new nations, from drawing on finances and resources stored in other countries, and ultimately from reconstituting its base of operations in a new haven. A successful campaign against al Qaeda requires not only direct military action in Afghanistan, but a coordinated multilateral effort to disrupt and destroy its dispersed, decentralized network.

Iraq represented another threat, at least in the eyes of American policymakers, to the stability of the international system. In the wake of its defeat in the Persian Gulf War of 1991, Iraq had continued to defy U.N. Security Council resolutions that ordered it to destroy and to cease development of its stocks of nuclear, chemical, and biological weapons, to end support for terrorism, and to stop its repression of its own citizens. The record made clear that Saddam Hussein had possessed weapons of mass destruction (WMD) and had used them both against external enemies (Iran) and his own citizens.[44] The United States went to war not to gain territory or a colony, nor to defeat an enemy ideology, but to remove a threat to the international order posed by a tyrannical dictator who had previously invaded his neighbors and who remained potentially armed with weapons of mass destruction. Despite the intense dispute among the United States and Great Britain and the other permanent members of the U.N. Security Council, the United States claimed its invasion was authorized under international law and that it was supported by a coalition of international allies.[45] While the United States may not have required allies to rout Saddam Hussein's military, the difficulties of the occupation indicate the need for multilateral cooperation both financially (to fund the reconstruction), militarily (to restore security in Iraq), and politically (to give the war and its aftermath an international, rather than purely American, appearance).

These wars, in which American military power has sought multilateral ends designed to stabilize the international system, raise issues of a constitutional dimension concerning the relationship between international organizations and law, on the one hand, and American domestic law and institutions, on the other. Although the Clinton administration failed to provide a legal justification for its use of military force in the Balkans, the president referred to American obligations to NATO as one of the primary reasons for the war in Kosovo. In Afghanistan, President Bush claimed that the inherent right to self-defense, without need of U.N. authorization, provided a legal basis for the conflict. In Iraq, the Bush administration claimed authorization from a network of U.N. Security Council resolutions and the inherent right to self-defense. Some scholars have suggested that fulfilling our treaty obligations could provide the president with the constitutional authority to use force without further congressional authorization. Such a claim raises two significant foreign relations law questions: whether the president can use treaty obligations to conduct wars without congressional approval, and whether the president can take the United States into war in violation of international law. Practice suggests that the executive gains little additional constitutional authority when acting pursuant to a treaty, but that he remains free to violate international law in the national interest.

The Constitution's model of war powers suggests that the president need not rely on treaty obligations in order to conduct war. One would not have gotten this impression, however, from the previous academic debates. In the aftermath of the Persian Gulf War, for example, several prominent scholars argued about the relevance to domestic war powers of U.N. Security Council Resolution 678, which authorized the use of force against Iraq. Thomas Franck, for example, has maintained that if the Security Council issues a resolution authorizing military intervention, then the president has the independent constitutional authority to send American troops into hostilities. "Such compliance by the President with international law is not prohibited," Professor Franck and Faiza Patel wrote, "indeed, it is required—by the Constitution."[46] Once the Security Council issued Resolution 678, the president had the authority, indeed had the constitutional obligation, to attack Iraq. Professor Glennon took the opposite tack by responding that even if Resolution 678 imposed a mandatory obligation on member nations, a U.N. obligation cannot alter the domestic allocation of war powers.[47] Because Professor Glennon is one of the many academics who believe that Congress must authorize all uses of force, he argued that a treaty obligation cannot eliminate the need for congressional approval of the use of force. Under this view, a treaty obligation would count for little more than, as Eugene Rostow once famously said, a letter from one's mother. Without a statute authorizing the use of force, Professor Glennon must conclude, presidents cannot unilaterally order the use of force even if it complies with the resolutions of the U.N. Security Council or international law.

The text and history of the constitutional allocation of war powers indicate that this argument is beside the point. Because the president already has the domestic constitutional authority to initiate military hostilities without any authorizing legislation, he need not rely on treaty obligations for legal justification. President Clinton did not need permission by the United Nations to deploy troops into Haiti or Somalia or to send the air force into combat in Bosnia or Kosovo, because his commander-in-chief and executive powers already gave him sufficient constitutional power to do so. This is not to say, of course, that the treaty demands of the United Nations or of our allies should not affect the president's decisionmaking concerning the use of force. It should be made clear, however, that treaties exert an impact in the realm of international politics and foreign policy, rather than in constitutional law. Even if treaties had some constitutional emanations on war decisionmaking, the president's flexibility in implementing and terminating treaties (subjects of subsequent chapters) unilaterally allows him to override or obey any treaty obligations.

A more interesting and difficult question is what impact treaties should have, if any, on the other domestic actors in the struggle over the use of force. Even though treaties may provide no constitutional boost to the president's discretion as commander in chief, some still may believe that treaties should exert a pull on Congress in support of presidential warmaking. Under Professor Franck's theory, for example, a president armed with a Security Council resolution could claim that Congress had the constitutional responsibility to fund any use of force authorized by the United Nations or NATO.[48] After all, if the president is constitutionally obligated to use force to uphold our U.N. treaty obligations, then Congress should have a parallel constitutional duty to fund those military operations. Similarly, according to Professor Henkin, "Congress is internationally obligated, and has the power under the Constitution, to enact laws necessary and proper to carry out the obligations and responsibilities of the United States under the [U.N.] Charter."[49] If treaties are laws of the land, then until they are repealed, these scholars argue, Congress has a constitutional duty to fulfill a treaty's terms even if it disagrees with executive foreign policy or the objectives underlying the treaty.

Such claims can trace their roots back to Alexander Hamilton. In 1796, Jeffersonians claimed that Congress could doom the controversial Jay Treaty by refusing to enact implementing legislation. Hamilton responded that because the Supremacy Clause made treaties the law of the land, the House had no right to consider the treaty on the merits or to refuse to enact the necessary legislation. Wrote Hamilton, "Each house of Congress collectively as well as the members of it separately are under a constitutional obligation to observe the injunctions of a [treaty] and to give it effect. If they act otherwise they infringe the constitution; the theory of which knows in such case no discretion on their part."[50] To make treaties dependent on legislative execution, Hamilton concluded, would render the treaty power hollow. "[T]here is scarcely any species of treaty which would not clash, in some particular, with the principle of those objections," Hamilton declared. "[T]he power to make treaties granted in such comprehensive and indefinite terms and guarded with so much precaution would become essentially nugatory." Hamilton's theory would require Congress to fund automatically presidential warmaking, if those wars were undertaken pursuant to valid treaty obligations—which Hamilton argued in 1791 was for the executive branch to determine.

This approach—essentially the theory underpinning the doctrine of self-executing treaties—is inconsistent with the balance struck by the

Constitution between the executive and legislative powers. As we have seen, both the British constitutional struggles of the seventeenth and eighteenth centuries, and the events of the framing and ratification of the U.S. Constitution, indicate that the Framers understood the legislative power to serve as a crucial check on the executive's control over foreign affairs generally, and the treaty power specifically. The Framers resolved the tension between the executive's role in foreign affairs and the legislature's control over funding and legislation problem by explicit analogy to the British model, which allocated legislative authority to Parliament and treatymaking power to the executive. While the executive would enjoy the freedom to manage international relations through the treatymaking power, the Framers believed that the legislative power—with its monopoly over the regulation of domestic affairs—would provide a crucial constitutional and political check on executive power and policies.

Article I's vesting of legislative power in Congress gives it a blocking role in treatymaking. By withholding implementing legislation or funding, Congress can prevent a treaty from taking domestic effect. In light of this understanding of the Constitution, Congress remains free to exercise its constitutional authorities as it sees fit, regardless of the president's claims that he is upholding treaty requirements. Even if the United Nations or NATO directed its member nations to intervene militarily, and even if these directives were considered valid treaty obligations that amounted to the law of the land, Congress has the constitutional discretion to use its funding and legislative powers to prevent the executive from fulfilling those duties. In invoking our obligations under NATO, therefore, President Clinton may have provided a political justification for the war in Kosovo, but not one that could have constitutionally compelled Congress to approve or support the intervention. Similarly, Congress had no constitutional obligation to fund the invasion of Iraq, even if it agreed with President Bush's argument that doing so was necessary to enforce U.N. Security Council resolutions.

These recent American wars renew a second, long-running debate over the president's constitutional authority to enforce international law. Kosovo brings this question into sharper focus than Afghanistan and Iraq. Under the U.N. Charter, which guarantees the sovereignty and independence of its member states, it appears that the attack on Kosovo clearly violated international law. Article 2(4) of the charter decrees that members shall "refrain . . . from the threat or use of force against the territorial integrity or political independence of any state." Article 2(3) calls on nations to settle their international disputes "by peaceful means in such a manner that international peace and security, and justice, are not endangered," and Article 2(7) declares that nothing in the charter "shall authorize the United Nations to intervene in matters which are essentially within the domestic jurisdiction of any state."

A state may still use force, in keeping with the charter, under two conditions. First, if a nation is attacked in violation of Article 2(4), it may act in self-defense. Article 51 of the U.N. Charter recognizes and affirms, but does not limit, that "inherent" right under international law: "Nothing in the present Charter shall impair the inherent right of individual or collective self-defense if an armed attack occurs against a Member of the United Nations, until the Security Council has taken the measures necessary to maintain international peace and security." Despite the longstanding recognition of a nation's right to self-defense, some argue that Article 51 has limited the right to permit only a response to an actual "armed attack." Some even argue that an armed attack must occur across national borders to trigger Article 51.[51] Under this interpretation, however, the U.N. Charter superceded the existing right under customary international law to take reasonable anticipatory action in self-defense. There is no indication that the drafters of the charter intended to limit the customary law in this way, nor that the United States so understood the charter when it ratified. Instead, Article 51 partially expressed a right that exists independent of the U.N. Charter.[52] The customary international law of the right to use force in anticipation of an attack is a well-established aspect of the "inherent right" of self-defense.[53] As Secretary of State Elihu Root argued long ago, every state has "the right . . . to protect itself by preventing a condition of affairs in which it will be too late to protect itself."[54]

Second, a nation may use force against another nation if acting pursuant to Security Council authorization. Under Article 42, the Security Council may call on member nations to engage in "demonstrations, blockade, and other operations by air, sea, or land forces" that it thinks "necessary to maintain international peace and security."[55] Under Article 39, the Security Council may issue recommendations that ask member nations to voluntarily take military action to restore international peace. Unless a nation is acting in self-defense, the U.N. Charter appears to require that the Security Council must authorize all other uses of force. While one can make the argument that a nation must be able to use force to defend its national interests, even if a cross-border invasion has not occurred, the U.N. Charter and many international legal scholars exclude this possibility. If this is right, then the United States cannot engage in military hostilities unless attacked or unless authorized by the Security Council. As Professor Henkin has concluded: "By adhering to the Charter, the United States has given up the right to go to war at will."[56]

Under this approach, the attack in Kosovo clearly violated international law, Afghanistan did not, and Iraq is an open question. The United States and its allies violated the territorial integrity of the former Yugoslavia and attacked the civilian and military assets of another sovereign nation. They did not receive either a Security Council decision under Article 42 to engage in a police action, or an authorization under Article 39 to use force to restore international peace and security. It is difficult to claim, with a straight face, that American intervention in Kosovo was necessary for purposes of national self-defense; indeed, the United States never claimed as much. Unless one can substantiate the difficult claim that Serbian activities rose to the level of genocide, and that any nation would be authorized to use military force to stop it, it seems that the tragedies in Kosovo represented domestic matters internal to Yugoslavia.

American attacks on Afghanistan and Iraq, however, can lay claim to justification under international law. In regard to Afghanistan, the United States suffered an attack on September 11, 2001 by the al Qaeda terrorist organization, which was based and operated in Afghanistan with the support of its Taliban militia. The attacks caused about three thousand deaths and thousands more injuries, disrupted air traffic and communications within the United States, closed the national stock exchanges for several days, and caused damage that has been estimated to run into the billions of dollars. There is little disagreement with the conclusion that if the September 11 attacks had been launched by another nation, an armed conflict under international law would exist. The September 11 attacks were a "decapitation" strike: an effort to eliminate the civilian and military leadership of the United States with one stroke. In addition to killing the nation's leaders, al Qaeda sought to disrupt the economy by destroying the main buildings in New York City's financial district. The attacks were coordinated from abroad, by a foreign entity, with the primary aim of inflicting massive civilian casualties and loss. Al Qaeda executed the attacks not in order to profit, but to achieve an ideological and political objective—in this case, apparently, changing U.S. foreign policy in the Middle East. Indeed, the head of al Qaeda, Osama bin Laden, declared war on the United States as early as 1996. Finally, the scope and the intensity of the destruction is one that in the past had only rested within the power of a nation-state, and should qualify the attacks as an act of war, which several international organizations recognized immediately after the September 11 attacks.[57] The United States thus had the right under Article 2(4) of the U.N. Charter to use force against al Qaeda in its self-defense, and against the Taliban militia that harbored it, to prevent future attacks on the United States.

The argument with respect to Iraq is more complex. As I have argued elsewhere, the spring 2003 invasion of Iraq was justified under international law.[58] First, in 1991 the Security Council authorized military action against Iraq to force it out of Kuwait and to enforce any relevant resolution, the most important being a cease-fire that suspended the hostilities of the 1991 Gulf War. That cease-fire required Iraq to destroy its existing weapons of mass destruction and to cease all research and production of the same. Both the United States and the U.N. Security Council in Resolution 1441, adopted in November 2002, determined that Iraq was in material breach of this obligation. Due to Iraq's failure to live up to its WMD obligations, established principles of international law—both treaty and armistice law—permitted the United States to suspend the cease-fire and to resume hostilities to compel Iraqi compliance. Second, U.N. Security Council resolutions notwithstanding, the United States could make a self-defense claim that the magnitude of the threat posed by a hostile Hussein regime, one armed with weapons of mass destruction, justified the use of force. To be sure, such a claim of self-defense was more attenuated than the one with regard to Afghanistan, which had supported a direct armed attack on the United States, and it raises difficult questions about the nature of an imminent attack in a world of weapons of mass destruction and terrorism. Nonetheless, both the U.N. Charter and the customary international law right of self-defense provided the United States and its allies with the authority to invade Iraq and remove the Hussein regime.

Under a view promoted by leading scholars, the president's violation of international law should have made Kosovo presumptively unconstitutional. For example, Professors Glennon, Henkin, and Lobel argue that the president has a constitutional duty to enforce customary international law.[59] International law—either through treaty or as federal common law—is part of the "Laws of the Land" under Article VI's Supremacy Clause. According to these scholars, Article II's requirement that the president enforce the laws therefore must include international law. A president may not violate international law, just as he cannot violate a statute, unless he believes it to be unconstitutional. According to Professor Henkin, "[t]here can be little doubt that the President has the duty, as well as the authority, to take care that international law, as part of the law of the United States, is faithfully executed."[60] While some admit that certain forms of constitutional or statutory authority might allow the president to violate international law, others go farther in claiming that the president cannot violate certain forms of international law regardless of his domestic authority.[61]

Although the inclusion of customary international law as federal common law is open to serious doubt, such arguments might be on firmer ground when it comes to treaties, which are explicitly mentioned in the Supremacy Clause.[62] If customary international law is binding on the executive branch, then certainly courts can enjoin the president from violating a more concrete form of international law—namely, the U.N. Charter. Kosovo, however, shows the weakness of these arguments. What was striking in the American public debate over Kosovo was the almost complete absence of any arguments that the war's apparent violation of international law should pose any domestic legal difficulties for President Clinton. While arguments did appear about the legitimacy of the war in Iraq under international law, no one appeared to argue that this alleged infirmity restricted the president's discretion to act as a domestic constitutional matter. In neither Kosovo nor Iraq did international law impose a restraint on presidential action, nor were federal courts about to enforce treaty obligations so as to restrict the commander-in-chief power.

Kosovo, Afghanistan, and Iraq demonstrate the flaws in these theories about the binding nature of international law. The constitutional text nowhere brackets presidential or federal power within the confines of international law. When the Supremacy Clause discusses the sources of federal law, it only enumerates the Constitution, "the Laws of the United

States which shall be made in Pursuance thereof," and treaties. International law, or the "law of nations" as it was known at the time of the framing, does not appear. As we will see, even the inclusion of treaties in the Supremacy Clause does not render treaties automatically self-executing in federal court, not to mention self-executing against the executive branch. Constitutional text aside, allowing international law and treaty obligations to block presidential warmaking could undermine the president's control over foreign relations, his commander-in-chief authority, and even his freedom to participate in the making of international law. At the level of democratic theory, conceiving of international law as a restraint on presidential warmaking would allow norms of questionable democratic origin to constrain actions validly taken under the U.S. Constitution by popularly accountable national representatives. Allowing international law and treaties to interfere with the president's war power would expand the federal judiciary's authority into areas where it has little competence, where the Constitution does not textually call for its intervention, and where it risks defiance by the political branches.

Some scholars concede that if the president is acting pursuant to an inherent constitutional authority, he may violate international law. Kosovo might not directly raise the question of the relationship between the president and international law, then, because President Clinton was acting pursuant to his commander-in-chief powers. While this had been suggested by Professor Henkin, it is not the view shared by others, such as Professors Glennon, Franck, and Lobel.[63] Efforts to save the primacy of international law demonstrate the internal contradictions of this approach. The president always must act pursuant to some authority either directly granted by the Constitution or delegated to him by Congress. Otherwise, he is acting *ultra vires* and without legal authority of any kind. To say that the Commander-in-Chief Clause provides the president with the power to violate international law is to admit that any valid presidential action can violate international law, whether it be taken pursuant to the Executive Power Clause, the president's sole organ power, or the war power. One might make the argument that presidents cannot violate international law pursuant to a legislatively delegated power, but that would mean that Congress cannot violate international law. Nonetheless, Kosovo provides a clear demonstration that presidents are not constitutionally or legally bound by international law. While the legitimacy of the wars in

Afghanistan and Iraq stand on much firmer footing than Kosovo, to the extent that those wars violated international law, they too show that international law is not binding within the American legal system.

MULTILATERAL WARFARE: THE QUESTION OF COMMAND

Notwithstanding the benefits of multilateral action, recent American wars raise a second set of difficult questions concerning the interaction of international organizations with domestic constitutional structures: whether the president can send American troops to serve under foreign command. During the Kosovo operation, for example, overall command of the intervention remained in the hands of General Wesley Clark, an American officer who served both as NATO's Supreme Allied Commander Europe (SACEUR) and as commander in chief of the U.S.-European forces. Although he answered to President Clinton, the secretary general of NATO, and the heads of NATO's member nations, Clark's dual role meant that strategic command of U.S. forces rested in the hands of an American general. American troops, however, could serve under Clark's various subordinates, some of whom were non-U.S. officers, such as British General Sir Michael Jackson, who commanded the sixteen thousand NATO troops stationed in Macedonia during the air war, and then led the NATO ground forces stationed in Kosovo.[64] While the conflicts in Afghanistan and Iraq remained under direct U.S. control, the situations there may not remain so clear cut. An international security force now patrols Kabul, and there may be a need at some point to place American troops under non-U.S. control. While American troops in Iraq serve solely under American command, proposals have arisen to place the Iraqi occupation under the overall command of a U.N. force.

President Clinton's willingness to send American troops into combat in Kosovo under the command of non-U.S. officers appears to be unprecedented. Before analyzing the constitutional nature of the administration's approach to multilateral operations, it is useful first to distinguish among four different levels of military command. First is policy command, which refers to policies that guide the conduct of national strategy. Second, these policies establish the objectives for strategic command, which translates national policy into more concrete military plans. These are developed by the Joint Chiefs of Staff and the secretary of defense. Third, strategic plans guide officers who exercise operational command over corps and divisions and are charged with supervising subordinate officers, organizing forces, and directing their missions, but who do not actually issue orders directly to troops. Fourth, those officers directly in control of troops, who employ units in combat and determine their specific use, exercise tactical command.[65]

American experience in modern alliance warfare suggests that while the political branches have allowed the transfer of certain levels of command to non-U.S. officers, they have reserved most forms of command solely for American military officers. President Woodrow Wilson and General John Pershing, for example, resisted efforts during World War I to incorporate American troops immediately into British and French units. Throughout the conflict, President Wilson maintained policy command, General Pershing retained operational command, and subordinate American officers exercised tactical command of the American Expeditionary Force. In response to Germany's last-ditch offensive in March 1918, however, the allied political leadership delegated strategic command to French General Foch, although American officers from General Pershing on down retained operational and tactical command. During World War II, President Roosevelt and General George Marshall decided to develop both policy and strategic plans jointly with the British prime minister and the British chiefs of staff. Although officers of different nationalities could exercise operational command—British Field Marshal Bernard Montgomery led the Normandy invasion under the command of the Supreme Allied Commander in Europe, General Dwight Eisenhower—tactical command generally remained in the hands of their national commanders. Only American officers exercised the authority to both coerce and discipline American units and troops.[66]

Postwar conflicts do not appear to have changed this practice. Although the U.N. Charter called for the creation of a U.N. military force composed of national units placed at the Security Council's disposal, the ideal of an international military force died with the advent of the Cold War. Like other major military powers, the United States never concluded the necessary agreements to place designated units under U.N. command and control. In the two large-scale military conflicts sanctioned by the United Nations, the Korean War and the Persian Gulf War, American generals exercised strategic command over the allied military, while American officers maintained operational and tactical command over American troops.[67] As American interventions, the use of force in places such as Vietnam, Grenada, and Panama did not raise questions of multilateral command.

Kosovo appears to be the first time that a U.S. commander in chief placed American troops directly under the operational and tactical command of a foreign officer. Responding to congressional efforts to stop this new policy, the Clinton administration claimed a broad constitutional power in the president to delegate military command authority to any person. In an opinion by the Office of Legal Counsel of the U.S. Department of Justice (OLC), the administration asserted that congressional proposals to prohibit foreign command of U.S. troops violated the president's commander-in-chief and foreign affairs powers.[68] According to OLC, the Commander-in-Chief Clause "commits to the President alone the power to select the particular personnel who are to exercise tactical and operational control over U.S. forces." To prevent the president from "acting on [his] military judgment concerning the choice of the commanders," even if that commander is an agent of the United Nations, would impermissibly violate both his commander-in-chief power and his constitutional ability to conduct diplomacy. Because "U.N. peacekeeping missions involve multilateral arrangements that require delicate and complex accommodations of a variety of interests and concerns, including those of the nations that provide troops or resources," OLC argued, a mission's success may depend on the commander's nationality, or on the "degree to which the operation is perceived as a U.N. activity" and not that solely of the United States.

While it identifies and addresses the heart of the issue, the Clinton administration's justification fails to convince, primarily because it constructs a boundless principle that does not account for historical practice. According to OLC, the president's commander-in-chief power allows him to select anyone to lead American troops into potentially life-or-death situations, even non-U.S. officials. OLC appears to maintain that the president has complete discretion over the decision; he need not even believe that delegating all aspects of command authority is necessary for reasons of national security. OLC's opinion also seems to contemplate that the president could delegate command to individuals regardless of their relationship, if any, to the federal government. Under OLC's reasoning, the president could place in command a senator or Supreme Court justice, any state official, or even private individuals, in addition to international officials, foreign officials, or even foreign private citizens, without having to appoint them officers of the United States. This is not to say that the president cannot "deputize" American private citizens to assist him in executing the laws, only that when he does so they must become officers of the United States, as required by the Appointments Clause, and become subject to the oath requirement of Article VI. The Appointments Clause, in combination with other provisions of Article I, however, seems to bar the appointment of foreign officials as officers of the United States without specific congressional consent.

Further, the Clinton administration's argument runs up against the unbroken historical practice of previous commanders in chief. Presidents apparently have never agreed to delegate either policy or tactical command to non-U.S. officers. Indeed, in only one instance, under the specter of an Allied collapse in World War I, has a president transferred strategic command outside the U.S. command structure. Even though presidents have granted operational control to foreign commanders, they have circumscribed that delegation by reserving coercive and disciplinary authority over American troops for American commanders only. Even in the recent war against Serbia, American military leaders sought to avoid continuous service by American troops under foreign command by giving each national military contingent a separate sector of Kosovo to administer. OLC's approach, however, would allow the president to vest even for the first time tactical control over American forces to foreign commanders, would permit foreign commanders to exercise coercive and disciplinary authority over American soldiers, and would even provide for the amalgamation of American soldiers into foreign or international military units.

Most importantly, the Clinton administration's legal justification for multilateral command fails to respect the Constitution's limitations on the transfer of federal power to entities that are not directly responsible to the American people. First, placing American troops under foreign command seems inconsistent with the Supreme Court's recent jurisprudence interpreting the Appointments Clause.[69] While much recent academic writing on the clause has focused on the relative roles of the president and Senate in appointing judges,[70] the Court has articulated the clause's broader function in ensuring that federal power is exercised only by federal officers accountable to the people's elected representatives.[71] As first stated by the Court in *Buckley v. Valeo,* the Appointments Clause requires that those exercising substantial authority under federal law must undergo appointment according to the clause's terms.[72] According to the Court's subsequent opinions, this rule prevents Congress from transferring executive law-enforcement authority to individuals not responsible to the president or his subordinates. The transfer of military command, pursuant to NATO or U.N. obligations, threatens this principle by allowing the president or the treatymakers to transfer executive power to individuals independent of presidential control.[73]

Furthermore, the Appointments Clause plays more than a separation-of-powers role in maintaining the balance between the Congress, the treatymakers, and the president. As Chief Justice Rehnquist has written for the Court, "The Clause is a bulwark against one branch aggrandizing its power at the expense of another branch, but it is more: it 'preserves another aspect of the Constitution's structural integrity by preventing the diffusion of the appointment power.' "[74] According to the Court, the clause prevents the diffusion of federal power by limiting its exercise only to those who undergo the appointment process. The Framers, the justices believed, centralized the appointments power because they feared the vesting of power in officeholders who were not accountable to the electorate.

A centralized appointments process prevents the national government, as a whole, from concealing or confusing the lines of governmental authority and responsibility so that the people may hold the government accountable. Allowing the transfer of command authority to non-U.S. officers threatens this basic principle of government accountability. International or foreign officials have no obligation to pursue American policy, they do not take an oath to uphold the Constitution, nor can any American official hold them responsible for their deeds. Granting military command to such individuals undermines the clause's purpose in promoting a certain level of government accountability because it transfers federal power to those who lie outside the control of the people.

Second, the Constitution's creation of a unitary executive militates against the delegation of command authority to a foreign commander. Whether one agrees with the formalist or functionalist side in the debate over the separation of powers,[75] transferring power outside of the federal government fundamentally conflicts with the concept of unified executive power. For formalists, any exercise of federal authority by an individual who is not a member of the executive branch, and thus is not removable by the president, violates the separation of powers because it prevents the president from fully controlling the implementation of federal law.[76] Once the president delegates authority to a foreign commander, he cannot issue orders to that commander, backed up by the threat of removal and discipline, as he could to an American officer, even though that foreign official may issue directives to subordinate American soldiers. In fact, as the Clinton administration has noted, the independence of such foreign commanders from American control is crucial to the success of their missions. One of the very purposes of multilateralism is to create the impression that a military operation falls under the aegis of a neutral international organization that does not represent the interests of a single nation. While functionalists may be willing to accept some conditions on the removal power, they have not endorsed the delegation of federal power to those who are completely insulated from presidential control.[77] Further, functionalists should object to foreign command of American troops because it undermines accountability in government. Voters cannot hold either the executive or Congress accountable if decisions are made by those who are not members of either branch.[78]

Third, the nondelegation doctrine reinforces the limitations imposed by the Appointments Clause and the unitary executive on the transfer of command authority outside of the American military. As formulated by the courts, the doctrine prohibits Congress from delegating its enumerated power to another branch unless it has stated an objective, prescribed methods to achieve it, and articulated intelligible standards to guide administrative discretion.[79] These standards provide the courts, Congress, and the public with some objective factors to review whether the power is being exercised within the limits of the delegation. Transfer of military command to foreign or international officials threatens the purposes of this rule. If the president delegates command authority over American troops entirely outside of the federal government, neither Congress nor the public can determine whether foreign or international commanders are exercising their authority according to American standards, nor can they enforce their policy wishes through usual legal or political methods.[80]

A brief examination of the original understanding supports this reading of the Constitution's promotion of government accountability. Rejecting the idea that sovereignty resided in a king, or even in the government, the revolutionaries located sovereignty in the people, for whom government officials serve as agents. One of the colonists' chief complaints against the British was the rule of imperial officials appointed by a king, and the lack of representation in government. "There is," John Adams wrote in 1776, "something very unnatural and odious in a Government 1000 Leagues off. [A] whole government of our own Choice, managed by Persons whom We love, revere, and can confide in, has charms in it for which Men will fight."[81] The ideal of popular sovereignty, which infused the revolutionary and ratification periods, conceived of all government servants as ultimately answerable to the people. In drafting a new system of government, the Framers sought to advance this principle by dividing the appointments power between the president and Senate to prevent either a single individual or a legislative faction from abusing appointments to their personal or group advantage.[82]

Delegation of military command to foreign or international officers undermines these principles. Individuals who have not undergone the executive, congressional, and public scrutiny that attends appointments, and who are not responsible to the American political system, might exercise authority to issue orders to American soldiers in life-threatening situations. Independent of the executive branch, foreign commanders need not obey presidential directives, need not follow American laws and regulations, and cannot be removed or disciplined by the president. If Congress or the people disagree with military policy or disapprove of the execution of a military operation, they have no political avenue to oversee the officials who are in command. They cannot demand that the president remove an official for incompetence, failure to obey orders, or disagreement over policy. This runs counter to the basic goal of the Appointments Clause, which is to guarantee that the people have a voice in the selection of officials who exercise federal powers, and to allow the people, through the political system, to hold their elected representatives accountable for "an ill appointment."

Although previous presidents have allowed command to flow through foreign commanders, particularly those allied with the United States in World Wars I and II, they did so in very different, and important, ways. The precise structure assumed by those forms of cooperation, however, preserved rather than undermined principles of government accountability. It appears that no commander in chief before President Clinton had delegated policy or tactical command to non-U.S. officers, nor had any president allowed a non-U.S. officer to coerce or discipline American troops. Only one clear case exists in which a non-U.S. officer exercised strategic command over American troops. When presidents have delegated command, it has usually been at the operational level. Operational command, however, does not raise the same problems posed by tactical or policy command. It does not vest foreign officers with the power to actually issue directives to American soldiers that have the force of law behind them. Rather, American military officers, in consultation with American political and military leaders—who still retain policy and strategic command—can determine whether to comply with those orders at the tactical level.[83]

On this point, the delegation of operational command resembles the relationship of American domestic law to certain international norms. International organizations and conventions can place legal obligations on the United States, such as a WTO panel finding that American environmental regulations violate GATT national treatment rules, or they can even call on the United States to meet some nonbinding, aspirational goal.[84] The United States still remains free, however, to choose how best to implement its international obligations, or even whether to violate them and suffer retaliation. In either case, officers of the United States make the decisions and exercise the power of federal law to enforce them. Similarly, if non-U.S. commanders possess operational command, but do not have the authority to coerce or discipline American troops who disobey their orders, they exercise no greater power than any other international organization whose rulings the United States is free, as a matter of domestic law, to adopt or reject. American commanders at the policy and strategic levels still may countermand any order, and American officers at the tactical level are responsible for deciding whether to implement orders of non-U.S. commanders. The decision, therefore, whether and how to harmonize the actions of the American government with international requirements still rests with officers of the United States, who are appointed pursuant to the Appointments Clause and remain accountable in the American political system.

In raising the prospect that non-U.S. officers may receive tactical command, the Clinton administration threatened to introduce an unprecedented approach to American military intervention. In seeking to submerge appearances of American unilateralism within broader multilateral organizations, President Clinton placed American forces at the disposal and command of foreign or international officials. While this may be necessary in order to achieve the goals of working through an independent, neutral international organization, it creates significant tension with American constitutional principles of government accountability and popular sovereignty, as promoted by the Appointments Clause, the unitary executive, and the nondelegation doctrine. One approach that might resolve this potential conflict between international cooperation and American constitutionalism is for presidents and military leaders to transfer only strategic or operational command to non-U.S. officers. Retaining policy and tactical command, combined with the right to coerce and discipline soldiers, would ensure that control over the exercise and enforcement of federal law would remain with individuals responsible to the American government, as required by the Constitution.

6

INTERNATIONAL POLITICS AS LAW?

Interpreting and Ending Treaties

Unlike the war power, the Constitution creates a specific process that governs the making of treaties. Under Article II, Section 2, the president cannot make a treaty without the consent of the Senate. Nonetheless, the constitutional text does not explicitly address a host of other questions, such as those surrounding treaty interpretation and termination, the legal effect of treaties as domestic law, and the interchangeability of treaties with other instruments of national policy. While this constitutional ambiguity has given rise to a dynamic of presidential initiative combined with senatorial and congressional participation through legislation and funding, it has also led some scholars to sharply criticize governmental practice as "counter to the language, and spirit, and history of . . . the Constitution," in the words of Louis Henkin.[1]

Yet, as with the war power, a closer examination of the constitutional text and structure yields important insights. These questions are not as unsettled (and hence so subject to appeals that we look outside the Constitution itself to democratic theory, or normative judgments, for their solution) as some might think. In light of the original understanding of the foreign affairs power, these sources suggest that governmental practice is not unconstitutional, but rather represents the practical outcome of the struggle between the executive and legislative branches provided for by the Constitution. As we will see, the line separating Articles I and II of the Constitution provides Congress with a significant check on the executive's treatymaking power, just as it does on the war power and on the conduct of foreign affairs more generally.

TREATY TERMINATION

As we saw earlier, the Framers understood the conduct of foreign affairs to be executive in nature, while the legislature controlled funding and domestic regulation. This distinction found its expression in the fundamental separation of executive and legislative powers in Articles I and II of the Constitution. The Framers contemplated that the president would exercise plenary control over the conduct of foreign policy, a point that met with rare agreement by Thomas Jefferson, Alexander Hamilton, and Chief Justice John Marshall. On the relatively few occasions where it has addressed foreign affairs, the Supreme Court has lent its approval to this interpretation of the president's powers. Responsibility for the conduct of foreign affairs and for protecting the national security are, as the Supreme Court has observed, " 'central' Presidential domains."[2] The president's constitutional primacy flows from both his unique position in the constitutional structure and from the specific grants of authority in Article II that make the president both the chief executive of the nation and the commander in chief.[3] Due to the president's constitutionally superior position, the Supreme Court has consistently "recognized 'the generally accepted view that foreign policy [is] the province and responsibility of the Executive.' "[4] This foreign affairs power is exclusive: it is, in the words of *Curtiss-Wright*, "the very delicate, plenary and exclusive power of the President as sole organ of the federal government in the field of international relations—a power which does not require as a basis for its exercise an act of Congress."[5]

These principles support what the constitutional text suggests: that the treaty power remains fundamentally executive in nature. First, by locating the Treaty Clause in Article II, the Constitution defines the treaty power as executive, except for any specific exceptions, such as the Senate's participation as an advisory council. It is the president who *makes* treaties, not the Senate and not the Senate and president. Second, Article II's structure confirms that executive power in this area is broader than the authorities listed in Article II, Section 2. Simply because the Treaty Clause does not specifically detail the location of relevant corollary powers does not mean that such powers lie in the hands of the Senate. Rather, these powers must remain within the president's general executive power. Third, Article II's Vesting Clause requires that we construe any ambiguities in the allocation of executive power in favor of the president. If Article II, Section 2 fails to allocate a specific power, then Article II, Section 1's general grant of the executive power serves as a catch-all provision that reserves to the president any remaining federal foreign affairs powers.[6]

This understanding of the constitutional text and structure has led to the recognition that the president enjoys powers, such as the removal of executive branch officials, unenumerated in the text. There is substantial debate over whether this principle is true for domestic affairs, but it certainly holds in foreign affairs. Treaties represent a central tool for the exercise of the president's plenary control over the conduct of foreign policy. In the course of protecting national security, recognizing foreign governments, or pursuing diplomatic objectives, the president may need to decide whether to perform, withhold, or terminate U.S. treaty obligations. As the U.S. Court of Appeals for the D.C. Circuit has observed, "the determination of the conduct of the United States in regard to treaties is an instance of what has broadly been called 'the foreign affairs power' of the President. . . . That status is not confined to the service of the President as a channel of communication . . . but embraces an active policy determination as to the conduct of the United States in regard to a treaty in response to numerous problems and circumstances as they arise."[7] Construing the Constitution to grant unenumerated treaty authority to another branch could prevent the president from exercising his core constitutional responsibilities in foreign affairs.[8]

Thus, treaty-related powers not specifically detailed in Article II, Section 2, such as the powers to terminate or suspend treaties unilaterally, remain with the executive branch. It is the president alone who decides whether to *negotiate* an international agreement, and it is the president alone who controls the subject, course, and scope of negotiations. The president has the sole discretion whether to *sign* a treaty and even whether to choose to submit it for Senate consideration. The president may even choose not to ratify a treaty after the Senate has approved it.[9] Because the Constitution does not specifically excerpt the termination and interpretation of treaties from the president's executive power in Article II, they remain presidential powers.

This conclusion receives additional support from the constitutional structure. An initial point of comparison is between the Treaty and Appointments Clauses. As Laurence Tribe has cogently argued in his criticism of the conclusions reached by Bruce Ackerman and David Golove, interpretations of the Treaty Clause should look to the Appointments Clause because they are adjacent to each other in Article II, Section 2 and share a parallel structure.[10] When fully excerpted, the parallel is clear:

> [The president] shall have Power, by and with the Advice and Consent of the Senate, to make Treaties, provided two thirds of the Senators present concur; and he shall nominate, and by and with the Advice and Consent of the Senate, shall appoint Ambassadors, other public Ministers and Consuls, Judges of the supreme Court, and all other Officers of the United States, whose Appointments are not herein otherwise provided for, and which shall be established: but the Congress may by Law vest the Appointment of such inferior Officers, as they think proper, in the President alone, in the Courts of Law, or in the Heads of Departments.

Both provisions divide what had once been solely executive powers between the president and the Senate, which acts in an executive capacity for these functions. Both provisions also make clear that the president enjoys the initiative: it is he who makes the treaty, and it is he who first nominates and then appoints officers. Neither provision, however, prescribes any rule about the relative roles of the president and Congress once the treaty is made or the officer is appointed. They both fail to address the interpretation of the treaty or the management of the officer—they do not specify who may terminate a treaty or who may remove an officer.

Comparison of the development of the law regarding appointments suggests that presidents should retain control over the interpretation and termination of treaties. When the first Congress created the initial agencies, debate arose over the removal of their officers—known as the "Decision of 1789." Significantly, the question came up during the creation of the secretary of state and his department. Some believed that because the Senate had given its consent to the appointment, its approval was needed to remove the secretary. Others argued that the secretary worked for Congress and so the president had no removal authority at all. Madison believed that the Constitution gave the president the authority to remove executive officers, and he criticized the contrary view as a threat to the president's ability to guide the executive branch. It would reduce the "power of the President to a mere vapor; in which case his responsibility for execution will be annihilated."[11] Madison articulated the principle that all executive power was vested in the president, and that the Senate's Article II roles were exceptions to be narrowly construed:

> The constitution affirms, that the executive power shall be vested in the President. Are there exceptions to this proposition? Yes, there are. The constitution says, that in appointing to office, the Senate shall be associated with the President . . . . Have we a right to extend this exception? I believe not. If the constitution has invested all executive power in the President, I venture to assert that the Legislature has no right to diminish or modify his executive authority. The question now resolves itself into this, Is the power of displacing, an executive power? I conceive that if any power whatsoever is in its nature executive, it is the power of appointing, overseeing, and controlling those who execute the laws.[12]

Congress ratified this understanding by refusing to place any conditions on the president's authority to remove cabinet members. In creating the Departments of Foreign Affairs and War, Congress explicitly acknowledged their status as "executive Departments" subject to presidential control.[13] In several cases, the Supreme Court has ratified the link between presidential control over the execution of the laws, the executive branch, and the removal of executive officers, and has found that the president's Article II executive authority must include the power to remove executive officers.[14]

Given the parallels between the Appointments and Treaty Clauses, it makes sense as a matter of textual interpretation to give them similar readings. Although the Constitution requires Senate advice and consent for appointments, the vesting of the executive power in Article II gives the president authority over the control and removal of federal officers. Likewise, the Constitution's comparable treatment of the treaty power suggests that the president has the authority to control the interpretation and termination of treaties. Indeed, the reasons given for control over officers prove only more pressing in the foreign affairs context. With appointments, Madison and a majority of the first Congress believed that removal power was critical to the president's ability to control how officers executed the laws. With treaties, the president's need for control extends beyond mere administration of Congress's dictates to the implementation of his own independent constitutional obligation to develop and direct foreign policy. Part of the management of the day-to-day conduct of our international relations involves the interpretation and reevaluation of the nation's international commitments, as established in part by treaties. Presidents cannot carry out the nation's foreign policy without interpreting treaties or, when they are inconsistent with policy goals, terminating them.

Another significant difference between treaties and statutes occurs in their process of enactment. The process for statutes is familiar. After members of Congress introduce bills on the floor, they are referred to the relevant committees. Committees hold hearings on legislation, analyze and amend their provisions, and report them to the floor for full consideration. If a bill receives majority votes in both chambers, and undergoes further adjustment in conference committee between the Houses, it is sent to the president for approval. If the president vetoes the bill, the House and Senate may override his veto by a two-thirds vote. Only passage of a second, repealing statute can terminate a statute. The center of gravity of this process naturally settles in Congress, which initiates legislation, terminates legislation, and even enacts legislation without the approval of the president. This process, and its balancing of authorities between the House, Senate, and president has not developed through practice or theory, but was instead finely calibrated by Article I, Section 7.

Compare this careful process to the Constitution's treatment of treaties. The president decides to initiate an international agreement. Because of his monopoly over the conduct of diplomatic relations, he controls the drafting of treaty provisions. The president supervises treaty negotiations and decides whether to submit a completed agreement to the Senate for its consent. The president's control over the process is so complete that he may refuse to make a treaty even after the Senate has given its advice and consent. In an almost reverse mirror image of the process for statutes, the treaty process shifts the center of gravity to the president, who initiates treaties, and who exercises an unconditional veto over their making. Given the president's control over every aspect of the treaty process, aside from the Senate's advice and consent role, there is no textual reason to infer a joint mechanism for a treaty's termination or interpretation.

This difference in the process for making treaties and statutes is only a manifestation of the different roles of the executive and legislature in foreign affairs. In the domestic sphere, Congress is the nation's primary lawmaker, though its power is subject to the limited check of the president's veto. In the international sphere, the president is the nation's primary lawmaker vis-à-vis other nations, subject only to the check, in treaty-making, of Senate advice and consent. The president's power to terminate treaties must reside in the executive as a necessary corollary to the exercise of the president's other plenary foreign affairs powers. For example, a president may need to terminate a treaty in order to implement his decision to recognize a foreign government. Or the president may wish to terminate a treaty that has become obsolete, to sanction a treaty partner for violations, to protect the United States from commitments that would threaten its national security, to condemn human rights violations, or to negotiate a better agreement.

Practice has borne out the implications of the constitutional structure. As Green Hackworth has observed, "[i]n some cases treaties have been terminated by the President, in accordance with their terms, pursuant to action by Congress. In other cases action was taken by the President pursuant to resolutions of the Senate alone. In still others the initiative was taken by the President, in some cases independently, and in others his action was later notified to one or both Houses of Congress and approved by both Houses. No settled rule of procedure has been followed."[15] About half of all treaties terminated by the United States have been at the hands of the president acting alone. The first example appears to have occurred when President Lincoln notified Great Britain of the U.S. withdrawal from the Rush-Baggot Convention, a naval disarmament agreement relating to the Great Lakes.[16] A second example did not follow until 1911, when President Taft terminated an 1832 commercial treaty with Russia. While Taft unilaterally terminated the treaty, he then asked the Senate for its approval, but always claimed that he had acted on his sole authority.[17] Many examples of presidential termination have followed, including treaties under Presidents Coolidge, Franklin Roosevelt, Eisenhower, Kennedy, Carter, Reagan, and now George W. Bush. These agreements have ranged from the somewhat insignificant, such as the Protocol to the General Inter-American Convention for Trademark and Commercial Protection (terminated by FDR in 1944), to the important, such as the Mutual Defense Treaty with Taiwan (Carter), the acceptance of the compulsory jurisdiction of the International Court of Justice (Reagan), and the ABM Treaty (Bush). While some elements of the historical record may be debatable, no other method of treaty termination has shown equal durability or commanded equal recognition.

Judicial rejection of challenges to the presidential termination of treaties has acknowledged the executive's textual and structural authority
in foreign affairs. In *Goldwater v. Carter*, Senator Goldwater challenged
President Carter's unilateral termination of the mutual defense treaty
with Taiwan. The District Court agreed that the Constitution required
both the president and Congress to take formal action before a treaty
could be terminated.[18] Sitting en banc, the U.S. Court of Appeals for the
D.C. Circuit reversed and upheld the president's unilateral power to terminate treaties.[19] The *per curiam* court offered eight general reasons why
the president enjoyed this authority:

1. The president had a unilateral power over removal of federal officials.

2. The constitutional text is silent as to treaty termination.

3. The Senate's advice and consent role is extraordinary and should
not lightly be extended.

4. The president is the constitutional representative of the United
States in its foreign relations.

5. Congress's power over domestic implementation of a treaty is irrelevant to the question of termination.

6. Requiring Senate consent for the termination of treaties "would be
locking the United States into all of its international obligations, even if
the President and two-thirds of the Senate minus one firmly believed that
the proper course for the United States was to terminate a treaty."

7. Even though historical evidence has provided many different examples of treaty termination, "in no situation has a treaty been continued in
force over the opposition of the President"; meanwhile, the conduct of the
United States in regard to treaties is part of the executive's plenary power
over the conduct of foreign affairs.

8. No judicially manageable standards exist for drawing distinctions
among treaties based on their substance, in order to determine any implied role for the Senate in treaty termination in regard to particular
treaties.

On appeal, the Supreme Court vacated the D.C. Circuit opinion and remanded the case to the District Court with directions to dismiss the complaint on the ground that the question raised was nonjusticiable.[20] Justice
Brennan, the only justice who reached the merits, would have affirmed
the D.C. Circuit, while a majority of justices found the case not capable

of judicial resolution. The Supreme Court's dismissal of the case indicates that any presidential termination of a treaty would be unreviewable in the courts. This has the practical result of leaving any unilateral presidential decision to terminate undisturbed.

These issues came to a head with President Bush's decision in December 2001 to withdraw from the Anti-Ballistic Missile (ABM) Treaty. He reached this decision unilaterally, after failure to come to agreement with Russia about modifications to allow development of a limited defensive system. Under the analysis presented here, this decision was fully within the president's constitutional powers. This did not have the effect, however, of leaving Congress powerless. Congress easily could have prevented President Bush's decision from having any practical meaning by refusing to fund further research and development of a National Missile Defense (NMD) system. Through its funding powers, Congress could have forced U.S. compliance with the substance of the ABM treaty, even if the United States had withdrawn from it as a matter of form. Instead, Congress had pursued the opposite result for several years. Under President Clinton, the executive branch had chosen to adhere to the ABM Treaty, even as rogue nations such as North Korea began to develop both nuclear weapons and ballistic missile capabilities. In 1999, Congress enacted the National Missile Defense Act, which declared that it was "the policy of the United States to deploy as soon as technologically possible an effective National Missile Defense against limited ballistic missile attack."[21] Congress continued to fund the NMD program both before and after President Bush's decision to terminate the ABM Treaty. Congress had every opportunity to prevent President Bush from achieving his foreign policy goal, but chose not to. On this score, the constitutional system relies on the same dynamics in the treaty termination area as it does in war powers—allowing for substantial presidential initiative, subject to the potential congressional check provided by funding and legislation.

TREATY INTERPRETATION AND THE CONSTITUTIONAL TEXT AND STRUCTURE

A similar logic applies to presidential authority over treaty interpretation. While scholars and the political branches have struggled over individual treaties, it seems clear that treaty interpretation is so tied up in the setting of foreign policy that the power has come to rest with the executive branch. Formally, the Constitution does not address the power to interpret treaties on behalf of the nation. The same approach—Hamilton's as Pacificus—that gives the power to terminate treaties to the president would do the same with interpretation. Functionally, interpreting American treaty obligations is such a critical part of setting and implementing day-to-day foreign policy that it is difficult to imagine how it could be separated from the president's responsibility to represent the nation in foreign affairs.

Debate over the question arose most notably when President Reagan sought to interpret the ABM Treaty to permit the research and development of a space-based anti-missile system (the SDI program). Senators and many legal scholars argued that the president had to abide by the understanding of the treaty jointly held by the president and Senate at the time of ratification. The controversy boiled down to whether the treaty's prohibition on all anti-missile missile systems (defined as including ABM missiles, launchers, and radar) extended to space-based ABM systems using "exotic" technologies such as lasers and radiation devices. Senators claimed that during the 1972 consideration of the treaty, the Nixon administration had assured the Senate that the agreement prohibited all current and future ABM systems, including space-based types, although the evidence for this view relied on a few sentences in the voluminous Senate record.[22] Reagan administration critics argued that just as legislative history should guide the courts in the interpretation of federal statutes, the understandings of the treatymakers—both the president and Senate—should determine the meaning of a treaty. Any effort by a president to interpret a treaty at variance with the Senate's understanding would be an unconstitutional attempt to infringe on the Senate's treaty role. Professor Tribe, for example, testified before the Senate Foreign Relations and Judiciary Committees that "the Constitution itself could become the first casualty of Star Wars, and that [SDI] is quite needlessly starting out with an offensive against the separation of powers and an assault on the Senate's constitutionally specified role in the treatymaking process."[23]

Contrary to these views, the analysis presented here indicates that the president should have the leading role in treaty interpretation and reinterpretation. As a textual matter, the Constitution does not speak directly to the issue of treaty interpretation. As a foreign affairs power, therefore, the structure of the Constitution's allocation of the executive power and Article II's Vesting Clause would reserve it to the president. Indeed, if the president has the power to terminate treaties, and to perform all other corollary functions with regard to treaties except for the Senate's advice and consent power in making them, then the president should have the power to interpret them as well. This makes functional sense too, as the president must constantly interpret treaties as part of the day-to-day conduct of foreign affairs. Presidential swiftness and secrecy in foreign affairs, one of the primary benefits of a unitary executive in the eyes of the writers of *The Federalist Papers,* would encounter difficulties if presidents had to constantly confer with the Senate or Congress every time they sought to interpret a treaty while dealing with a foreign nation.

Granting the president the power to interpret treaties goes little beyond the existing executive power to interpret, and even violate, international law in the course of executing foreign policy. Just as the president must interpret international law in the course of managing international relations, so too must the president interpret our treaties as part of the day-to-day execution of foreign affairs. Both functions flow from the president's constitutional and functional position in foreign affairs. Even in the administration of domestic statutes, where the rights of Congress are more clearly established than is the case with treaties, the courts grant the executive branch substantial discretion in interpreting ambiguous laws due to its superior expertise and its democratic accountability.[24] Critics of President Reagan's ABM treaty interpretation sought to impose limits on presidential power at its zenith, the execution of foreign policy, rather than at other moments, such as treaty formation, where the Senate has a better claim to joint participation.

In light of the executive's leading role in foreign affairs, there seems to be little constitutional reason to privilege senatorial understanding of a treaty over those promoted by the president. To be sure, the Senate's advice and consent is necessary before the president can make a treaty. But the Senate votes on the treaty text, expressing its own understandings during the advice and consent process. To give the Senate's understandings of the treaty independent force, especially when the Senate does not directly express those understandings in the treaty text through reservations, allows one party to the treatymaking process to avoid the supermajoritarian hurdles imposed by the Treaty Clause. It also allows the Senate to intrude into the management of international relations by projecting its unenacted wishes into the nation's future conduct under the treaty.

Another way to view this question is to analogize it to the federal common law. Federal courts often face gaps in statutes, either because Congress neglected to complete a statutory scheme or because it did not anticipate the statute's application to future circumstances.[25] Courts fill those gaps by inferring how Congress would have completed the statute or how it would have applied the statute to an unforeseen case. Because Congress often cannot act in such situations, it falls to the courts to exercise some lawmaking authority, one constrained by the legislature's intentions as expressed in other statutory provisions and the law's structure. When courts act to fill gaps, however, questions about the extent of their policymaking authority often arise, especially when Congress provides little guidance concerning the policies to be promoted by a federal common law rule.

Treaty reinterpretation involves the same basic issues as those surrounding the federal common law. Treaties often have gaps, as statutes do. With SDI, for example, the president and Senate failed to reach a conclusive agreement about the meaning of the text in regard to exotic anti-missile systems. In 1972, neither the United States nor the Soviet Union seriously anticipated or considered the possibilities of futuristic weapons systems based on lasers. The reinterpretation fight essentially boiled down to a struggle over which branch would have the authority to fill that gap in the ABM Treaty. In the federal common law context, courts ordinarily would look to indications of the legislature's intentions, in part because Congress's institutional barriers to enacting laws prevent it from addressing every possible issue.

In the treaty context, however, the situation is quite different. Often international relations will call on the president rather than the courts to adapt the text to new circumstances. Further, the president does not suffer from institutional handicaps that might prevent him from creating a treaty "common law" rule. Because of his participation in the treaty process and his constitutional role as representative of the nation in foreign affairs, the president both can read the text of a treaty in line with its intentions and harmonize that interpretation with current foreign policy demands. He does not suffer from the problems of legitimacy that beset the federal courts in their role of making common law, as the president is both nationally elected and constitutionally charged with conducting the nation's foreign relations.

Finally, the president's control over the interpretation of treaties makes sense when viewed in light of the combination of the executive's foreign affairs and treaty powers. At a functional level, for example, reinterpretation of the ABM Treaty only served as a shortcut to a goal that President Reagan could have achieved under his other executive powers. In the absence of any treaty at all, President Reagan possessed the commander-in-chief and sole organ powers. Instead of interpreting the ABM Treaty, he could have abrogated it, or terminated only those portions that seemed to restrict SDI. He could have used his other constitutional powers to declare that the United States would adhere unilaterally to the treaty's non-SDI-related terms as long as the Soviets did. The Reagan administration pursued exactly this course with the second Strategic Arms Limitation Treaty with the Soviet Union (SALT II), which restricted the size of each nation's nuclear arsenal. While both Presidents Carter and Reagan declined to seek Senate ratification of SALT II in the wake of the Soviet invasion of Afghanistan, the Reagan administration promised to adhere to its limits so long as the Soviets did.[26] An approach combining termination with unilateral declaration would have reached the same outcome as treaty interpretation. President Reagan would even have been free to negotiate a sole executive agreement with the Soviets that would have kept much of the ABM Treaty's restrictions on current technologies intact. Allowing the president to reinterpret treaties simply provides the executive with a more effective method that bears more benefits for American foreign policy, without incurring the international political costs of formally breaking a treaty.

Reagan's critics argued deference to the executive in foreign affairs ought to give way before clear evidence of the Senate's understanding of a treaty. Using a legislative history approach, however, fails to appreciate the significant differences between treatymaking and lawmaking. These differences make the adoption of doctrines of statutory interpretation inappropriate in the treaty context. To be sure, the Senate's understanding of an enacted statute is clearly important, because its consent jointly controls the meaning of that text. Yet even in that context, as described below, the use of legislative history remains controversial. Proponents of a greater Senate role in treaty interpretation must carry the additional burden of showing why such legislative history ought to matter in an area over which the president has enhanced competence and authority. Examining the more sophisticated theories of statutory interpretation, in fact, demonstrates that privileging legislative history is even less useful in the treaty context than it might be in the statutory context.

TREATY INTERPRETATION AND STATUTORY INTERPRETATION

To understand the problems with using legislative history in treaty interpretation, we should recall the vast differences between treaties and statutes as instruments of national policy. The president decides to initiate an international agreement. Due to his monopoly over the conduct of diplomatic relations, he controls the drafting of treaty provisions. He also supervises treaty negotiations and even decides whether to submit a completed agreement to the Senate for its consent. The president's control over the process is so complete that he may refuse to make a treaty even after the Senate has given its advice and consent. Unlike the repealing of statutes, Senate participation is not needed to terminate a treaty: the president can do it unilaterally. In an almost reverse mirror image of the process for statutes, the treaty process shifts the center of gravity to the president, who initiates and terminates treaties, and who exercises a complete veto over their making. This difference in process and in institutional arrangements indicates that, rather than privileging Senate understandings of a treaty, the president's positions ought to control the interpretation of an international agreement.

There is an ongoing debate in legal academia over the value and legitimacy of legislative history, such as committee reports and floor statements, in the interpretive enterprise. Textualists, such as John Manning and Adrian Vermeule, urge courts to abjure reliance on legislative history for several reasons, including its lack of approval by majority vote, its unreliability, and judicial incompetence in its use.[27] Critics of the "new textualism," such as William Eskridge and Philip Frickey, respond that legislative history provides the necessary context without which an effort to give meaning to a text would be futile.[28] This debaté has significant, yet largely overlooked, implications for the dispute over treaty interpretation.

The most compelling constitutional argument on behalf of textualism is that legislative history is at odds with the constitutional structure. Statutory text is the clearest indicator of congressional understanding because the text alone received the approval of both Congress and the president. Relying on legislative history conflicts with the constitutional structure because it gives legal effect to materials that do not undergo the bicameral approval and presentment required for all statutes by Article I of the Constitution. Permitting unenacted legislative history to determine the meaning of statutes allows groups within Congress to usurp the power of Congress as a whole, or, as Manning has argued, allows Congress to delegate to itself law-interpreting functions constitutionally vested in the judiciary and the executive branch.

Related to this argument is the textualist claim that the use of legislative history expands the judicial function beyond its proper boundaries. While they admit that gaps exist in statutes, textualists claim that silence alone does not authorize courts to resort to legislative history. Rather, the separation of powers requires that judges defer to Congress to fill in statutory gaps. As public choice theorists have argued, it is notoriously difficult to claim that collective bodies such as Congress have any unified intention at all, which provides yet another reason to focus exclusively on the statutory text. Even if such intent did exist, legislative history may be an unreliable indicator of that intent because it is the product of compromise and political maneuvering, and judges may be incompetent at construing it properly. As Justice Scalia has written, legislative history "is more likely to produce a false or contrived legislative intent than a genuine one."[29]

The arguments against using legislative history to interpret statutes apply with equal, if not greater, force in the treaty context. Floor colloquies or hearing statements about treaties never undergo approval by two-thirds of the Senate or ratification by the president. Part of the reason that the Framers established the two-thirds supermajority requirement for treaties was to render treaties difficult to make and to protect the interests of the states. Allowing treaty-related legislative history to escape that requirement defeats the Framers' substantive purposes in erecting a difficult procedural hurdle. In this sense, the use of treaty-related legislative history may represent an even greater affront to the Constitution than the use of statutory legislative history, because it evades an even higher vote requirement.

Legislative history avoids yet another barrier that does not apply to statutes. Treaties involve not just the president and Senate, but a third party—namely, the foreign treaty partner. Legislative history does not become part of the treaty text, and it is never formally communicated to the other nation as part of the documents that are ratified by both nations. The few pieces of legislative history expressed in the Senate concerning futuristic ABM systems never made it into the ABM Treaty text and therefore cannot be said to have received Senate consent, presidential ratification, and Soviet agreement. President Reagan's approach to treaty interpretation can be seen as an effort to give effect to meanings drawn solely from the treaty text. His interpretation can also be understood as an outright rejection of any use of legislative history as failing to meet the supermajority requirements of the Treaty Clause.

Other standard textualist arguments against the use of legislative history carry equal, if not greater, force in the treaty setting. It is difficult to know whether the Senate had any unified understanding of the ABM Treaty. Even proponents of the Senate's prerogatives in treaty interpretation could identify only a few isolated incidents when the subject of futuristic anti-missile technologies arose. It calls for a leap of faith to attribute the thoughts expressed in those sparse interchanges, between two or three senators, say, and hearing witnesses, to a collective legislative body with a hundred members. Even if the Senate could be of one mind on the fine points of the ABM Treaty, it is difficult to be sure that we today are properly reading the legislative history of 1972. It may be a danger (as with all legislative history) that such materials merely provide a useful arena for interested parties to read their own policy preferences into the treaty. Rather than search for an uncertain, possibly nonexistent, collective Senate intent, textualism suggests that interpretation ought to focus on the treaty text, as read by the democratically responsible branch vested with the day-to-day management of foreign affairs.

Textualism, of course, does not appeal to everyone. Other approaches to interpretation, often at odds with textualism, yield similar results in this specific case; indeed, they may lead even more clearly toward a presidential power of treaty interpretation. The main intellectual response to the new textualism has arisen in the dynamic interpretative theories developed by William Eskridge and Philip Frickey, who argue that statutory interpretation is a continuous process in which the courts exercise substantial discretion in reaching policy solutions. Judges do not leave gaps unfilled for Congress, nor do they seek to find the right answer as evidenced by congressional intent. Rather, judges use a wide variety of contextual sources, influenced by their own policy values and those of the political and legal climate around them, to inform their practical reasoning about the meaning of statutes. However, statutes do not retain forever the fixed understandings held by the lawmakers at the time of enactment. Rather, their meanings evolve as federal courts adapt the law to new situations in line with changing public and legal values.

In the world of dynamic statutory interpretation, the role of continual interpreter of the law rests with the federal courts. If we were to accept the Eskridge and Frickey model, it seems clear that the function of interpreting treaties would fall on the president rather than the judges. Just as courts must interpret statutes in the course of fulfilling their constitutional function of resolving disputes, the president's constitutional role as manager of American foreign policy requires him to continually interpret treaties to apply to new international situations. As the functionally superior actor in foreign relations, the executive branch can more effectively harmonize new readings of treaty texts in light of evolving U.S. national security goals and the geopolitical context. As head of the most democratically accountable branch in the national government, the president can also ensure that current treaty interpretations comport with publicly supported foreign policies. Ultimately, the people can hold the president directly accountable for his interpretation of a treaty, something that the polity can do only indirectly with the courts in the statutory interpretation context.

TREATIES AND THE NEUTRALITY PROCLAMATION

The issue of the president's authority over treaties arose early in the Republic's history. The reading given here of the constitutional text and structure—that the president has an independent power to terminate and interpret treaties—was put on display by President Washington in issuing the Neutrality Proclamation of 1793. Many of the leading figures in the administration and in Congress at that time were members of the Federal

Convention or the state ratifying conventions, most notably George Washington, Alexander Hamilton, and James Madison. Their actions can help confirm this reading of the original understanding of the Constitution. The Washington administration set many of the precedents that guide the interaction of the branches of government to this day. Early postratification history suggests that those who first put the Constitution into practice believed that the president had plenary authority to terminate and interpret treaties.

The Neutrality Proclamation had its roots in the French Revolution. After beheading King Louis XVI, France declared war on Great Britain and Holland on February 1, 1793.[30] The new regime's ambassador to the United States, Edmund Genet, landed in early April, about the same time that news reached the United States of events on the Continent. The news threw the American government into a quandary concerning its obligations under the 1778 treaties with France, which had been crucial to the success of the American Revolution. Article 11 of the 1778 Treaty of Alliance called on the United States to guarantee French possessions in America, which meant that France could now call for American defense of the French West Indies from British attack.[31] Article 17 of the separate 1778 Treaty of Amity and Commerce gave French warships and privateers the right to bring prizes into American ports, while denying the same right to her enemies.[32] Article 22 prohibited the United States from allowing the enemies of France to equip or launch privateers or sell prizes in American ports.

Washington's cabinet was deeply split over whether to observe these treaty obligations. Upon learning of the French declaration of war, Treasury Secretary Hamilton, "with characteristic boldness" in the words of Jefferson, began to press for a suspension of the French treaties.[33] Hamilton feared that providing military assistance to the French, or even allowing French warships to use the United States as a base, would provoke British retaliation against the United States. While a change in government did not automatically void treaties with another state, he argued that the uncertain status of the French government and the dangerous wartime situation allowed the United States to suspend the 1778 agreements.[34] While Secretary of State Jefferson agreed that American military participation in the European war was out of the question, he favored observance of the 1778 agreements because of his sympathy toward the French Revolution and his suspicion of political ties with Britain.

On April 18, Washington sent a list of thirteen questions concerning the position to take on the war to Hamilton, Jefferson, Secretary of War Henry Knox, and Attorney General Edmund Randolph, and ordered a cabinet meeting for their discussion the next day.[35] Almost all of Washington's questions involved the interpretation of the 1778 French treaties. Question four, for example, asked: "Are the United States obliged by good faith to consider the Treaties heretofore made with France as applying to the present situation of the parties." Washington also requested the cabinet to consider whether Article 11 of the Treaty of Alliance applied to an offensive war by France, whether the United States could observe the treaties and remain neutral, and under what conditions the United States could suspend or terminate the 1778 agreements. While most scholars today discuss the Neutrality Proclamation as an example of executive declaration of international law, or of the integration of international and domestic law, they have ignored the neutrality debate's core as a question of treaty termination and interpretation.

Washington's questions produced a deceptive unanimity in the cabinet. Everyone answered that a proclamation of neutrality should be issued, but in order to assuage Jefferson's concerns, the word "neutrality" was not used. Washington issued the proclamation, drafted by Randolph, on April 22.[36] Acknowledging a state of war between France and the other European powers, he declared that the United States "should with sincerity and good faith adopt and pursue a conduct friendly and impartial toward the belligerant [sic] Powers." President Washington further saw fit to "declare the disposition of the United States to observe the conduct aforesaid towards those Powers respectfully" and "to exhort and warn the citizens of the United States carefully to avoid all acts and proceedings whatsoever, which may in any manner tend to contravene such disposition." The proclamation also stated that the federal government would prosecute those who "violate the law of nations, with respect to the Powers at war." The cabinet realized that the United States was in no position to be anything but neutral, and there was immediate agreement to issue the proclamation.[37]

Two other questions met with unanimous answers. The cabinet agreed that the president should receive Genet. Finally, the cabinet unanimously answered Washington's last question in the negative: "Is it necessary or advisable to ask together the two Houses of Congress with a view to the present posture of European affairs? If it is, what should be the particular objects of such a call?" Adjourning the meeting without reaching the other ten questions, Washington asked his advisers to submit written responses on the suspension or termination of the 1778 treaties.

In his response of April 28, Jefferson argued that nothing in international law allowed for the suspension or annulling of a treaty simply because of a change in government.[38] He also argued that France was unlikely to ask the United States to fulfill its obligation to defend the West Indies, and that it would be better to wait for a request before deciding whether to terminate the treaty. Hamilton, joined by Knox, argued on May 2 that the uncertain outcome of the civil war in France justified the United States in temporarily suspending the operation of the treaty.[39] They also argued that the treaty applied only to defensive wars, not one in which France had declared war first, and that international law would justify termination of the treaties due to the dangerous circumstances. Randolph's opinion, entered on May 6, agreed with Jefferson. Telling Jefferson the next day that he "never had a doubt about the validity of the treaty," Washington decided against suspension.[40] On the question of the Article 11 obligation to defend the French West Indies, Washington decided to remain silent, a wise choice, as Jefferson's prediction that the French would not affirmatively invoke the provision proved correct.

These events show that President Washington and his cabinet unanimously assumed that interpretation of the 1778 French treaties rested solely within presidential authority. Washington's April 22 proclamation was not just a declaration that the United States would remain neutral in the European conflict. It was a presidential determination that American treaty obligations did not require entry into the war on the side of the French. Only after Washington reached that interpretation could he declare the United States to be neutral in the conflict. Washington did not act pursuant to any congressional authorization to interpret the treaties. Indeed, the cabinet unanimously agreed that the president should not call Congress into session. More than a year later, Congress finally stepped in, providing legislation for federal prosecution of those who violated American neutrality.[41] This legislative act accepted Washington's interpretation of the 1778 treaties and implemented it at the domestic level.

The Washington administration's approach to the European war demonstrated sensitivity to the distinction between treaty interpretation, which belonged to the executive, and domestic implementation, which was the province of Congress.

A second lesson to emerge from these events comes from the manner in which Washington and his cabinet construed the Franco-American treaties. The Continental Congress had conducted the negotiation and ratification of the 1778 treaties.[42] Washington, however, never asked what understanding the Continental Congress held concerning American obligations under the agreement, nor did any of his cabinet members (including Jefferson, who wanted to interpret the treaty in the light most favorable to France). Rather, both Hamilton and Jefferson grounded their appeals in the national interest, international law, considerations of power politics, and reason and common sense. Neither Washington nor his cabinet ever mentioned consulting the journals of the Continental Congress or the papers of the negotiating team in Paris. None of them expressed a belief that consultation with the existing Congress or Senate was necessary or advisable. Washington and the leading figures of his administration proceeded on the assumption that it was the exclusive province of the executive branch to interpret treaties on behalf of the United States.

A third lesson is that Washington and his cabinet seemed to agree that the president had the authority to terminate the 1778 treaties on his own authority. Washington's April 18 questions to his cabinet asked whether the "general plan of conduct for the Executive" should include "renounce[ing]" the treaties with France "or hold[ing] them suspended." Washington evidently did not think that the executive branch needed to consult with Congress or the Senate before taking this step. In replying, Hamilton demonstrated his belief that the president could terminate the treaties, but recommended only that they be suspended. Jefferson, who was fighting a rearguard action to prevent a break with France, did not raise the constitutional argument that termination required congressional or senatorial consent, but only that international law would not justify termination. As Professors Prakash and Ramsey have similarly concluded, the Neutrality Proclamation controversy demonstrates that several of the leading American officials of the Washington administration, including apparently Washington himself, Hamilton, and Jefferson, agreed that the president's constitutional powers include the right to terminate treaties unilaterally.[43]

Critics of this reading of the historical record might turn to the Pacificus-Helvidius debates for support of a greater congressional role in treaty interpretation. In those essays, which appeared during the summer of 1793, Hamilton, under the pseudonym of Pacificus, defended the president's constitutional authority to issue the Neutrality Proclamation.[44] He argued that Washington's authority to declare the nation's neutrality derived from the Constitution's Article II, Section 2 executive Vesting Clause; for him, the Senate's role in making treaties was only a narrow exception from the general grant of executive power to the president. When the Constitution sought to transfer traditionally executive powers away from the president, Hamilton argued, it did so specifically, as with the power to declare war. Writing as Helvidius, James Madison responded that Hamilton's reading exaggerated the president's authority.[45] He argued that Article II, Section 2 did not incorporate all of the British Crown's executive powers, and claimed rather unpersuasively, according to historians, that the Constitution placed strict limits on the president's foreign affairs powers.[46]

It is important to recognize, however, that Madison did not take issue with Hamilton's claim that the power to interpret or terminate treaties was fundamentally an executive power. Indeed, it was difficult for Madison to deny that the power emanated from Article II, Section 2. During the First Congress, after all, Madison had argued that the president enjoyed the power to unilaterally remove federal officers, despite the fact that the removal power was not explicitly allocated by the Constitution. Rather, Madison rested his constitutional claim on the far narrower point that the president could not interpret treaties in a manner that prevented Congress from exercising its own plenary constitutional powers. Washington's proclamation was defective, in Madison's eyes, not because the president interpreted a treaty without congressional participation, but because it declared the nation's neutrality in the European war. According to Madison, Washington had interpreted the treaty in a way that might preclude Congress from exercising its own power to declare war. "The declaring of war," Madison argued, "is expressly made a legislative function."[47] Thus, the "judging of the obligations to make war, is admitted to be included as a legislative function." Therefore, "[w]henever then a question occurs whether war shall be declared, or whether public stipulations require it, the question necessarily belongs to the department to which these functions belong." If the treaty had not involved a military alliance, Madison could not have maintained his argument against presidential treaty interpretation. Madison's point, it should be noted, is unconvincing. The Neutrality Proclamation did not prevent Congress from declaring war, if that were its wish. In fact, Washington's actions had the effect of preserving the *status quo ante* so that Congress could still choose war or peace at its discretion.

If Madison's (and Jefferson's) constitutional opposition to the Neutrality Proclamation extended no further, it seems that actors in the first government under the Constitution assumed that the president enjoyed the power to interpret treaties. Madison and Jefferson were making the structural point that the executive could not exercise its freedom to interpret treaties, or any of its other executive powers, so as to supplant congressional powers. The president could not interpret a treaty to require the United States to remain at peace, just as he could not interpret a treaty to forbid Congress from lowering or raising tariffs as it wished. In either case, the Constitution's explicit grant of a specific power to Congress prevents the president from usurping that power. Indeed, this is a logical corollary of the Constitution's separation of the treaty and legislative powers. Thus, the Neutrality Proclamation episode not only demonstrates the president's freedom in treaty interpretation, it also underscores the check on that power provided by Congress's Article I powers.

Conclusion:
Treaties and the Bush Administration

Events such as the Neutrality Proclamation, the termination of the Mutual Defense Treaty with Taiwan, or even the Reagan-era struggle over the SDI program may seem of limited relevance to today's challenges of rogue nations, the proliferation of weapons of mass destruction, and terrorism. Recent efforts, however, designed to respond to such problems only highlight again the centrality of treaties to the conduct of foreign affairs. Treaty termination and interpretation has proven central in the debate over how to respond to the proliferation of nuclear weapons and ballistic missiles, and the legal status of al Qaeda and Taliban fighters captured in Afghanistan and throughout the world. On these questions, the Constitution's flexibility toward the distribution of the foreign affairs power has given the president the tools to promote U.S. foreign policy, but at the same time has ensured that Congress has the ability to block policies with which it disagrees.

It is more than mere coincidence that the primary treaty controversy of the 1990s should involve the very same treaty as that of the 1980s. While the substantive legal questions were certainly different, both involved a contest between conflicting interpretations of the ABM Treaty. Those interpretations served as proxies for deeper disagreements concerning strategic nuclear weapons policy in the post–Cold War world. With the reduction in superpower tensions during the 1990s, the strategic theories that had motivated the ABM Treaty no longer worked. First, the Soviet Union was no longer the clear nuclear threat that it had once been. As the Soviet Union began to dismantle its empire, the United States and the Soviet Union (and later Russia) began the process of normalizing relations. In January 1993, President Bush and President Boris Yeltsin signed the START II agreements, which eliminated all multiple-warhead ICBMs and reduced the superpowers' strategic nuclear stockpiles by two-thirds.[48] Mutually assured destruction (MAD) became less central to American national security as the threat of a Russian first strike receded.

Second, the nuclear threat from other nations dramatically increased. In the Persian Gulf War, Iraq not only used ballistic missiles to attack American and allied forces, but also turned out to have engaged in a secret nuclear weapons development program. A 1998 bipartisan commission headed by Donald Rumsfeld (later the secretary of defense) concluded that the intelligence community had underestimated the ability of rogue nations to develop nuclear-armed missiles. In 1999, the U.S. intelligence community concluded that North Korea had advanced to the point where it could begin testing a ballistic missile capable of hitting the United States.[49] That same year, India and Pakistan both successfully tested nuclear warheads. North Korea had already been pursuing a covert nuclear weapons program during this period. Nuclear proliferation and the rise of rogue nations eroded yet another piece of MAD, which had relied on a single rational opponent who could understand the nuclear balance of terror.

In conjunction with these changes in the strategic environment, American missile defense goals shifted from countering a Soviet first strike to preventing limited ballistic missile attacks on the United States. In his January 29, 1991 State of the Union address, President Bush asked that the SDI program be refocused to provide protection from a strike of a few dozen warheads.[50] With the 1991 Missile Defense Act, Congress declared that the nation should deploy a NMD system "capable of providing a highly effective defense of the United States against limited attacks of ballistic missiles."[51] The goal was not to alter the strategic balance with a collapsed Soviet Union, but to defend against "accidental or unauthorized launches or Third World attacks." As it had with the Reagan administration's SDI program, Congress conditioned funding for the reoriented ABM program on continued compliance with a strict reading of the ABM Treaty. To the extent an NMD system might become inconsistent with this understanding of the treaty, Senate leaders urged the president to negotiate amendments that would allow deployment of a limited system.

The dissolution of the Soviet Union on December 25, 1991 dashed any hope of a swift negotiated solution. Fifteen independent states emerged in place of the Soviet Union, and four of them (Russia, Belarus, Kazakhstan, and Ukraine) came into possession of portions of the Soviet nuclear arsenal. Replacing one nuclear adversary with four potential ones not only undermined the theory of mutually assured destruction between the two superpowers, it also destabilized the bargain struck in the ABM Treaty that the superpowers would limit themselves to a single ABM system each. Even if each republic of the former Soviet Union agreed to adhere to the treaty, each could still build one ABM system around its capital. In other words, the Soviet Union's breakup now meant that fifteen ABM systems could exist within its former territory.

The Soviet Union's collapse also raised the possibility that the ABM Treaty was no longer in force because of the disappearance of one of the two state parties to the agreement. Under international law, a change in government alone generally does not alter a state's obligations to honor its treaty commitments. A different and more difficult question arises, however, when an imperial state itself dissolves—an issue known as *uti possidetis* in international law.[52] Initially, the Bush administration decided to conduct a treaty-by-treaty review of U.S. agreements with the Soviet Union to determine which of them remained in force.[53] In 1997, the Clinton administration negotiated agreements, known as Memoranda of Understanding (MOUs), with the Russian Federation, Belarus, Kazakhstan, and Ukraine to expand the ABM Treaty to the four nuclear powers that emerged from the Soviet Union's collapse.[54] President Clinton, however, never submitted these agreements to the Senate, where they likely would have encountered stiff resistance from supporters of an NMD system. Nevertheless, President Clinton claimed that the "ABM Treaty itself would clearly remain in force" even if he never submitted the multilateralization agreements to the Senate, or even if the Senate were to reject them.[55] Some Republican senators, on the other hand, claimed that the fall of the Soviet Union automatically terminated the ABM Treaty, and that a new treaty would have to be submitted to the Senate for any of its provisions to continue in force. In an effort to prevent the administration from continuing the ABM Treaty in force without senatorial consent, both chambers approved provisions, one statutory and one a treaty condition, that declared that the United States would not be bound by any substantial modification of the ABM Treaty that did not undergo the treaty process.[56] Despite this pressure, the Clinton administration continued to act as if the ABM Treaty remained in force between the United States and the Soviet Union's successor states.

Regardless of the answer, under international law, to the question whether the dissolution of the Soviet Union ended the ABM Treaty, the central question for American foreign relations law remains which branch of the federal government had the primary authority to determine whether the United States would continue to comply with the agreement. President Clinton's decision to continue adherence to the ABM Treaty, despite the legal effects caused by the collapse of the Soviet Union, drew its constitutional justification from the approach developed here concerning the executive power in foreign affairs. If the president has the authority to interpret treaties, he certainly must have the power to interpret less concrete forms of international law. At the very least, executive interpretation of international law should receive substantial deference from the other branches, just as the Supreme Court currently gives deference to the president's reading of treaties and statutes. Presidential power thus allows the executive to determine not only whether the ABM Treaty survives the collapse of the Soviet Union, but also the rules of international law concerning the obligations of successor states.

In addition to his power to interpret the international rules of state succession, the president has the constitutional authority to interpret the ABM Treaty on behalf of the United States. The president's formal role as the maker of treaties and his function in conducting our international relations vest the executive with the power to interpret treaties. This authority allowed President Clinton to permit multilateralization without the need for a treaty amendment, a move that resembled the Reagan administration's broad interpretation of the ABM Treaty more than fifteen years before. In that instance, the executive branch argued that ambiguity or silence in the treaty text allowed it to move forward with a new form of anti-ballistic defense, one unanticipated by the negotiators in 1972. Similarly, the ABM Treaty did not address multilateralization in the event of the collapse of the Soviet Union; the prospect of its disintegration was probably as remote in the negotiators' minds as the idea that the United States might someday devolve into fifty states. President Clinton could have claimed that in the absence of clear prohibitory language in the treaty, he had the power to fill the lacuna left by the treatymakers of 1972. As the primary interpreter of federal law and policy in foreign affairs, this function would properly rest with the president when, in the domestic statutory context, it normally would fall to the federal courts.

Third, the president's other foreign affairs powers provided independent justification for the continuation of the ABM Treaty's obligations. In managing our foreign affairs, the president often makes executive agreements with other nations without the consent of the Senate or of Congress. These agreements can be made pursuant to preexisting authorization by treaty or statute, or they can be made under the president's commander-in-chief or other executive authority. Indeed, a great deal of the nation's foreign relations must be conducted by agreements, of varying levels of formality, between the executive and the representatives of other nations. The executive branch can enter into an informal agreement whereby it promises to refrain from a particular action in exchange for similar restraint on the part of the other party. Although SALT II never underwent senatorial advice and consent, the United States acted consistently with its terms as a matter of executive branch policy, so long as the Soviet Union did the same. Even less formally, the executive branch has entered into voluntary restraint agreements whereby foreign exporters limit their imports into the United States in exchange for executive refusal to pursue trade sanctions.[57] At even lower levels, the executive branch enters into memoranda of understandings that express a commitment to other nations, but do not even rise to the level of a legal obligation. Indeed, as arms control agreements and other international regulatory regimes grow more specific and complex, it is almost inevitable that the executive branch will need to rely on less formal methods of agreement to fill in gaps in international agreements and to reach more flexible methods of cooperation.

While accepting the president's unilateral authority to interpret treaties, our flexible approach to the foreign affairs power also recognizes that the Senate and the Congress could use their own plenary powers to shape underlying policy. Even when an international agreement is formally embodied in a treaty, the legislature has the constitutional discretion to frustrate or even countermand its obligations. For example, the Framers understood the legislative power, in particular Congress's monopoly over funding and the domestic implementation of international obligations, to impose a check on the executive's control over treatymaking. Thus, Congress could use its power over the purse to require the president to deploy an NMD system by a certain date, even if inconsistent with the ABM treaty. Indeed, Congress came close to this very outcome by declaring in the 1999 Missile Defense Act that the United States ought to develop such a system as soon as technologically feasible. Congress could go even further by ordering the deployment of a primitive ABM system, even if it represented a poor risk at huge cost, solely to provide some defense against an accidental launch or an attack by a rogue state. Congress could further declare, as it in fact has, that any agreement made by the executive concerning the ABM Treaty would not bind the United States unless it underwent the treaty process. Because Congress, under the last-in-time rule, also has the power to terminate treaties, it could certainly deny any nontreaty international agreements the status of a binding national obligation. While such a law could not constrain the executive's discretion to conduct foreign policy as it saw fit, it could release the nation or any of its branches from either international or domestic obligations to uphold the ABM Treaty's successor agreements.

The lack of a formal treaty also invites Senate intervention into ABM policy. At present, it does not appear that the Senate, acting alone, has the authority to terminate treaties. In a situation where the executive pursues international agreements without the treaty form, however, the Senate can use its role in the treaty process to promote its own wishes. During its 1997 consideration of the Conventional Forces in Europe (CFE) Flank Document, which adjusted the CFE agreement in the wake of the Soviet Union's collapse, the Senate conditioned its approval of the treaty on the submission of any ABM multilateralization agreement for Senate advice and consent. While not legally enforceable, the Senate's condition implicitly threatened that the Senate would refuse to approve subsequent arms control agreements until it received the ABM successor agreements. As with Congress's power vis-à-vis the executive's treatymaking authority, the Senate can use its constitutional powers to achieve the political end of ensuring that it can participate in any decision involving ABM policy.

When President George W. Bush took office in 2001, presidential authority to both interpret and terminate treaty became central to the resolution of the NMD/ABM Treaty quandary. Committed to developing a limited NMD system, the administration had substantial flexibility to maintain much of the ABM Treaty structure by arguing that the agreement contained a significant lacuna. The treaty's main focus was on antiballistic missile systems that provided a continental defense against the nuclear arsenal of the Soviet Union; its text did not specifically address systems that create a more limited security against only a few missiles launched by others or by accident. Consistent with the Constitution, the president could have interpreted the ABM Treaty to maintain its ban on an NMD system that could defeat the large Russian nuclear deterrent, but still allow the deployment of a limited system in response to accidental launches or rogue states. This does not stretch presidential powers any further than did President Washington in interpreting the 1778 French treaties as allowing American neutrality in 1793, than did President Reagan in the 1980s in interpreting the ABM Treaty to allow SDI research, or than did President Clinton in the 1990s in claiming that the ABM Treaty continued to exist despite the disappearance of the Soviet Union. While no doubt some would argue that this is inconsistent with the ABM Treaty's blanket prohibition on ABM systems, the president enjoys the final constitutional authority on the interpretation of treaties such as this; opposition to his interpretation would have to work its way through the spending and legislative powers of Congress.

Ultimately, the Bush administration was unable to come to agreement with the Russians about reinterpreting the ABM Treaty to permit deployment of limited NMD systems. This amounted to a failure of diplomacy rather than a lack of constitutional power. The Bush administration then made use of a combination of its formal powers in foreign affairs to arrive at the same result as a reinterpretation of the ABM Treaty. President Bush unilaterally terminated the ABM Treaty in December 2001, as permitted by the terms of the treaty itself, to allow research and development of a limited "hit-to-kill" system to go forward, with possible deployment in Alaska by 2005 to counter a possible North Korean ICBM threat. He then set the policy of the United States as adherence to the rest of the treaty's terms in regard to comprehensive ABM defenses, so long as the Russians do so as well, even though there was no longer any treaty requiring such compliance. The Bush administration no doubt has expressed this policy through an informal understanding with the Russians, rather than through a new treaty. Of course, the more informal the arrangement, the more significant become the powers of Congress and the Senate, which could influence NMD policy through spending and legislation, or by leveraging its power over the approval of other international agreements. Instead, the Congress, which had been more aggressively promoting NMD programs than the Clinton administration, supported President Bush's funding requests for NMD research and possible deployment. If Congress had disagreed with President Bush, however, it could have forced the United States to effectively adhere to the substantive terms of the ABM Treaty simply by refusing to fund any NMD work by the Pentagon.

The importance of the power to interpret treaties, and its allocation between president, Senate, and Congress, was again put on display during one of the most heated international legal issues in the war on terrorism— the legal status of detainees captured in the war against the al Qaeda terrorist network and the Taliban forces that harbored it. Under common article 2 of the Third Geneva Convention of 1949 (GPW Convention), if state parties engage in an international armed conflict, members of their armed forces taken in combat are accorded prisoner of war (POW) status.[58] Certain volunteer and militia forces associated with a state party are similarly entitled to POW status, so long as they fulfill four basic conditions: they are under responsible command, they wear a recognizable insignia, they bear their arms openly, and they obey the laws of war. If entitled to POW status, al Qaeda and Taliban prisoners would enjoy the same conditions and rights as members of regular armed forces in a conventional state-to-state war, including detention in group barracks and the right to be released at the end of the conflict. Some legal scholars and human rights groups argue that prisoners in the war on terrorism are entitled to such POW status, if not the status of regular criminal defendants in the civilian justice system.

On February 7, 2002, the White House announced that President Bush had interpreted the GPW Convention to find that al Qaeda and Taliban members are not entitled to POW status.[59] At the same time, he ordered that the detainees receive treatment in a manner consistent with the GPW Convention, so long as consistent with military necessity. The administration's public reasoning ran thus.[60] First, the al Qaeda terrorist organization is not a nation state, and therefore it could not and did not sign the GPW Convention. Since, under article 2 of the convention, it applies only to international armed conflicts between state parties, the GPW Convention simply does not govern the treatment of al Qaeda prisoners. Second, even if the Taliban militia were the regular armed forces or militia of Afghanistan, they still do not fulfill the four basic conditions for POW status required under article 4 of the GPW Convention. The latter reading is based in part on the facts available to the president concerning the manner in which the Taliban organized itself and conducted itself on the battlefield. As this chapter has made clear, President Bush had the constitutional authority to interpret and apply the convention without requiring the consent of the Senate or Congress.

The political system has accepted that President Bush enjoyed the power to interpret the Geneva Convention in this manner, despite the fact that he did not consult with or seek the consent of the Senate or Congress. This acceptance is suggested by the fact that, as far as I could tell, no members of Congress took to the House or Senate floor, or held committee hearings, to question the president's authority to make this decision on behalf of the United States. Recent Supreme Court cases addressing the reach of federal habeas corpus jurisdiction to the detention of al Qaeda and Taliban detainees have studiously avoided any judgment on President Bush's determination that the Geneva Conventions did not provide enemy combatants in the war on terrorism with POW status.[61] Rather than an usurpation of authority, President Bush's power to interpret and apply the Geneva Conventions was rooted in the text, structure, and history of the Constitution.

Opposing views on treaty interpretation risk yielding a far more confusing and undesirable result. It is clear that the convention, by its text, purports to establish rights for individual POWs. Some scholars, such as Michael Van Alstine and Carlos Vázquez, argue that federal courts should adjudicate treaty rights that favor individuals.[62] This would require the courts to review the legal status of enemy prisoners and potentially issue decisions that conflicted with President Bush's interpretation, which is part of his conduct of the ongoing war against terrorism. These scholars might even countenance deference to international organizations, such as the International Committee of the Red Cross, which may interpret the Geneva Convention differently. Under this approach, a federal court could determine al Qaeda and Taliban prisoners to be POWs, even though doing so would interfere with decisions made by the president, as commander in chief, regarding the manner in which to detain prisoners captured on the battlefield, the resources to devote to their detention, the amount of security to assign, and even whether to release still-dangerous prisoners. The Supreme Court long ago recognized that such matters should rest solely in the discretion of the president, and until 2004 it had found that U.S. courts had no jurisdiction over the detention of enemy aliens held outside the United States.[63] Even with the decision in *Rasul v. Bush* to permit federal habeas corpus jurisdiction to extend to the detention of enemy combatants held at the Guantanamo Bay naval station, the Supreme Court has so far not taken up pleas that it review the president's interpretation of the Geneva Convention.

The current controversy over the Geneva Convention illustrates the reasons why the Constitution vests treaty interpretation authority in the president. It is the president who must interpret treaties as part of the day-to-day conduct of foreign affairs and as part of his constitutional responsibility to fulfill the nation's international obligations while also protecting its security. Determining the legal status of the detainees forms a central part of the executive branch's strategy in successfully fighting the war against the al Qaeda terrorist network. Similarly, interpreting and ultimately terminating the ABM Treaty was an important element in promoting the administration's NMD policies to cope with the threat of rogue nations armed with ballistic missiles and nuclear weapons. Congress still retains the ability to check these policies by refusing to fund NMD programs or by conditioning funds for the war on terrorism to require treatment of detainees consistent with the Geneva Convention. Congress's positive response to these presidential initiatives demonstrates that it agreed politically with the executive branch, not that it lacked effective tools to influence foreign policy.

7

Treaties and the Legislative Power

Struggle for control over the termination and interpretation of our international obligations is not the only significant issue raised by treaties in the constitutional system. A second issue is whether the president and Senate can engage in the regulation of domestic conduct through the use of treaties, rather than through statutes enacted by Congress, even in areas that fall within Congress's exclusive Article I, Section 8 control. The tension between international agreements and the domestic authority of Congress has been relieved through the doctrine of non-self-execution, which holds that a treaty will not apply of its own legal force without implementing legislation. Courts usually presume that when the text of a treaty is silent, it is generally non-self-executing. Non-self-execution has the virtue of leaving foreign affairs in the hands of the political branches, keeping the judiciary out of a policymaking role, and providing the national government with the constitutional flexibility to determine how best to live up to our international obligations.

Much like a judicial presumption in favor of non-self-execution, the reservations, understandings, and declarations (RUDs), which are attached to treaties during the Senate's advice and consent review, help preserve Congress's control over legislation. Rather than requiring self-execution, the Constitution allows the House and Senate to use their constitutional and political powers over legislation and funding to prevent direct treaty implementation. Congress may use its powers in specific cases to establish the broad principle that any treaty that infringes on the scope of the domestic legislative power must be implemented by legislation, or it can use its powers on a case-by-case basis. After this process of cooperation or struggle, the branches may even arrive at a rule of complete non-self-execution, depending on historical and international circumstances, the relative power of the branches, and the people's wishes.

This approach to treaties has received harsh criticism from some scholars. As we saw in chapter 1, they argue that—both as a violation of the plain text of the Supremacy Clause of Article VI and as a betrayal of the Framers' original intention—judicial refusal to directly implement treaty provisions as domestic law is unconstitutional. This book's analysis of the history of the foreign affairs power, however, reveals a different understanding. Emerging from the political thought and the British constitutional struggles of the seventeenth and eighteenth centuries, non-self-execution embodied a deeper structural principle that separated the executive power, which controlled treatymaking, from the legislative power, which regulated domestic conduct.

Americans during the colonial and early national periods sought to maintain this distinction, which checked the power of the central government and ensured that local representatives promulgated the laws. Dissatisfaction with the inability to enforce treaties, however, contributed to the calling of the Constitutional Convention. While some leaders believed that treaties were supreme law and should be enforced by state judges, others, particularly James Madison, sought to establish a truly representative national government that would make, and enforce, treaties by its own means. Tradition and history established a constitutional rule that treaties were not to take domestic effect without legislative implementation; Madison sought to work within this rule by establishing sufficient legislative power at the national level to enforce treaties directly.

In this chapter, we turn to non-self-execution as a lens to understand the relationship between treaties and domestic legislation. Non-self-execution alleviates the conflicts between the growing demands of the international system and the expanding scope of treaties by maintaining the House's control over domestic legislation. We then examine an important, early debate over the implementation of the first significant international agreement made under the Constitution, the Jay Treaty, to see the practical workings of the separation between the executive and legislative powers. Insights from the constitutional text and structure, and the lessons of the history from the early Republic, will then give us the perspective to approach the questions raised by globalization concerning the effect of today's treaties as domestic law.

NON-SELF-EXECUTION AND THE CONSTITUTIONAL
TEXT AND STRUCTURE

Examination of constitutional text and structure yields unnoticed insights concerning the relationship between treaties and domestic law. I argue that the constitutional text and structure establish a core distinction between treaties on the one hand, and other forms of federal lawmaking on the other. The notion of self-executing treaties seeks to blur this line by using an executive power contained in Article II to engage in the domestic regulation of private individuals and their conduct, which is usually Congress's province.

If all treaties were self-executing, in the sense that they would automatically become federal law on a par with statutes, they would undermine important aspects of the separation of powers, federalism, and popular sovereignty. Self-execution would vest in the executive branch a legislative power broader in scope than Congress's. Self-executing treaties arguably would be free of the constraints of federalism and the separation of powers. Non-self-execution, in contrast, harmonizes treaties with constitutional structure and maintains the important distinction between foreign relations and domestic lawmaking.

As we have seen, the most significant textual difference between a treaty and a statute is found in the treaty power's placement in Article II, which vests the executive power in the president, rather than in Article I, which vests all "legislative Powers herein granted" to the Congress. The Treaty Clause's location shows that treaties are executive, rather than legislative, in nature. The Senate's participation alone does not convert treaties into legislation, just as the Senate's participation in appointments does not transform them into legislative acts, or the president's wielding of the veto transforms legislation into executive acts. Instead, the Constitution appears to include the Senate both to dilute the unity of executive action in the area of treaties, and perhaps to impart more continuity to the conduct of foreign affairs. With their six-year terms (two years longer than the president's), senators provide "a sense of national character" and stability, much like that supplied by the privy council in England and the governors' councils in the states, and can restrain abuses of power by the executive.[1] The Constitution centralizes public lawmaking into a tortuous process to make the exercise of legislative authority more difficult, thereby protecting the states and the people from unwarranted exercises of federal power. In the few cases articulating the distinction between legislative and executive power, the Supreme Court has defined the executive power by its very lack of the power to make laws. "In the framework of our Constitution," Justice Black wrote for the Court in *Youngstown Sheet & Tube Co.,* "the President's power to see that the laws are faithfully executed refutes the idea that he is to be a lawmaker."[2]

Moreover, self-execution invites a conflict between the textual grants of the executive and legislative powers and resolves the clash by allowing the treatymaking authority to trump Congress's Article I powers. According to the conventional academic view, the president and Senate may resort to the treaty process to address any matter, so long as it is "an agreement between two or more states or international organizations that is intended to be legally binding and is governed by international law."[3] Louis Henkin's views are representative of the consensus: "[I]f there are reasons in foreign policy why the United States seeks an agreement with a foreign country, it does not matter that the subject is otherwise 'international,' that the treaty 'makes laws for the people of the United States in their internal concerns,' or that—apart from treaty—the matter is 'normally and appropriately . . . within the local jurisdictions of the States.'"[4] Despite the Court's recent federalism decisions, which Curtis Bradley has argued should also apply to the treaty power, separate articles by David Golove and Edward Swaine have sought to reinforce the argument that treaties are not subject to the federalism limitations that apply to Congress. According to Professor Golove, for example, "the President and Senate can make treaties on any subject appropriate for negotiation and agreement among states," regardless of the federalism restrictions on Congress's Article I powers.[5]

If treaties enjoy this broad scope, and if they are always self-executing, then the treatymakers can regulate any area that lies within Article I's enumerated powers. For example, a self-executing treaty could make certain actions federal crimes, despite the Constitution's allocation to Congress of authority to "define and punish Piracies and Felonies committed on the high Seas, and Offences against the Law of Nations." Likewise, the treatymakers would be free to establish new commercial or environmental regulations, though the power to regulate interstate commerce is vested in Congress. If the United States forges multilateral agreements addressing problems that were once domestic in scope, treaties could replace legislation as a vehicle for domestic regulation. Gerald Neuman has even argued that treaties can be used to overrule Supreme Court decisions limiting Congress's Commerce Clause or Fourteenth Amendment enforcement powers. In *City of Boerne v. Flores,* for example, the Supreme Court rejected Congress's effort, in the Religious Freedom Restoration Act (RFRA), to expand religious exemptions from state laws; the Court found that the law went beyond Congress's enforcement powers under the Fourteenth Amendment and intruded into areas of regulation reserved to the states.[6] Nevertheless, according to Professor Neuman, Congress could simply reenact RFRA—and effectively overturn *Boerne*—by implementing an international treaty that guarantees religious liberty. Once the United States ratified the International Covenant on Civil and Political Rights, it acquired a treaty obligation to ensure that the freedom to "manifest religious beliefs in action would not be infringed without proportionate justification," Professor Neuman writes.[7] "Whether that treaty obligation was validly acquired depends on whether it conflicts in some way with the Constitution. The mere fact that the treaty may require the extension of religious exemptions within areas of traditional state regulation creates no obstacle to its validity."

Recognizing these problems, some foreign relations scholars and that general statement of the conventional scholarly wisdom, the *Restatement (Third) of the Foreign Relations Law of the United States,* admit certain exceptions to self-execution. For example, the *Restatement* declares that treaties cannot take direct effect as American law if legislation is "constitutionally required."[8] Yet several foreign relations scholars argue that the treatymakers can exercise the Commerce Clause power, among others, without resorting to statute.[9] Professor Vázquez, for example, argues that the treatymakers can exercise Article I, Section 8 powers granted to Congress.[10] But if he is correct, then the treatymakers must be able to exercise all of Congress's legislative powers. The constitutional text, which treats all of these powers in Article I, Section 8, does not make any distinctions among them. The one exception is the Appropriations Clause, which declares that "[n]o money shall be drawn from the Treasury, but in Consequence of Appropriations made by Law."[11] Professor Henkin and the *Restatement* admit that use of the term "by Law" indicates that appropriations can only be made by a statute, rather than by a treaty.[12] Yet this reading undermines their approach to the Supremacy Clause, which is built on the idea that a treaty is not constitutionally different from a "Law."

Nonetheless, those who support self-execution admit that the doctrine cannot apply to all treaties, regardless of subject matter. They concede that legislation is necessary to implement a treaty if it calls for a declaration of war, an appropriation of money, the raising of taxes, or the punishment of criminal conduct.[13] Yet, they do not provide any principled distinctions between those areas that can be the subject of treaties and those that cannot. Without such a distinction, their view must result in a conclusion that treaties may regulate any matter within Congress's legislative authority. As we will see, Madison argued during the Jay Treaty debates that "if the Treaty-power alone could perform any one act for which the authority of Congress is required by the Constitution, it may perform every act for which the authority of that part of the Government is required."[14]

In making treaties self-executing, the *Restatement* view would create a potentially limitless legislative power. While Article I, Section 8 vests Congress with enumerated plenary powers, the Constitution subjects these grants to the limitations of Article I, Section 9, such as the prohibition on *ex post facto* laws and bills of attainder. Even some important elements of the Bill of Rights apply textually only to Congress. If the *Restatement* is right that the treatymakers can exercise legislative power without resort to Article I's lawmaking process, then self-execution allows the federal government to legislate without opposition from the textual checks on congressional powers. As Madison worried, "if the legislative powers specifically vested in Congress, are to be no limitation or check to the Treaty power, it was evident that the exceptions to those powers, could be no limitation or check to the Treaty power."[15] While the Supreme Court has rejected the argument that treaties can infringe on individual rights,[16] textually the Constitution would seem to permit this result, once we agree that treaties are self-executing.

Self-execution also may permit the treatymakers to act outside the constraints of the separation of powers, constraints that several scholars believe not to apply with full strength to treaties. Professor Henkin, for example, argues that the treaty power "is not limited by the powers of Congress," and he concedes only that "it is assumed to be subject to other radiations from the separation of powers."[17] He does not, however, identify any separation of powers principles that would check the treaty power, aside from a prohibition on the admittedly "hypothetical" possibility of a treaty that redistributed wholesale certain powers among the three branches. If this view is right, then the treatymakers can create new governmental arrangements that would violate the Constitution if undertaken domestically. The president and Senate could delegate to international organizations powers that ordinarily inhere in the executive branch, such as authority over law enforcement or administrative rulemaking. Or a treaty could transfer authority from Congress to the executive branch or to an international organization, as Thomas Franck argues has occurred with the U.N. Charter and Congress's power to declare war.

If treaties are interchangeable with statutes, but are free from the usual structural constraints of the separation of powers, then the treatymakers could restructure government to regulate domestic affairs in ways not permitted to Congress. Perhaps a treaty could be used to justify the creation of an administrative agency, charged with enforcing and administering the treaty, whose officers could be made completely immune from presidential removal and supervision, or who could be made responsible to Congress. If undertaken by statute, however, such maneuvers would be unconstitutional under Supreme Court cases upholding the limited removal provisions of the independent counsel law or invalidating the administrative role of the comptroller general (a creature of Congress) in the Gramm-Rudman-Hollings deficit reduction act.[18]

Self-execution also would free the treatymakers and their legislative power from federalism limitations. Several leading scholars believe that federalism does not restrict treaties in the same manner as it does statutes. This would allow the president and Senate to make policy for the nation on any subject, regardless of the limited enumeration of federal powers or the Tenth Amendment. The Tenth Amendment presents no bar, these authorities argue, because its reservation of powers is inapplicable to the treaty power, which was expressly delegated to the federal government. As usual, Professor Henkin's view represents the conventional wisdom. "Since the Treaty Power was delegated to the federal government, whatever is within its scope is not reserved to the states: the Tenth Amendment is not material," Henkin argues. "Many matters, then, may appear to be 'reserved to the States' as regards domestic legislation if Congress does not have power to regulate them; but they are not reserved to the states so as to exclude their regulation by international agreement."[19] Anything that the treaty power can touch upon is, by definition, excluded from the Tenth Amendment. This argument, Henkin concludes, "is clear and indisputable."

In *Missouri v. Holland,* the Supreme Court suggested its agreement with this proposition.[20] *Holland* raised the question whether Congress had authority to enact the Migratory Bird Treaty Act of 1918, which implemented a 1916 treaty between the United States and Great Britain that protected migratory birds. The treaty barred the hunting or capture of any of the birds protected by the treaty, an action that the federal courts at the time had held lay outside Congress's Commerce Clause powers. According to an opinion by Justice Holmes, the treaty power was not to be limited by some "invisible radiation from the general terms of the Tenth Amendment" that required invalidation of the Migratory Bird Treaty Act. Rather, Holmes concluded, "there may be matters of the sharpest exigency for the national well being that an act of Congress could not deal with but that a treaty followed by such an act could, and it is not lightly to be assumed that, in matters requiring national action, a power which must belong to and somewhere reside in every civilized government is not to be found." Because treaties concerned "a national interest of very nearly the first magnitude," Holmes observed, they could not be limited by the Tenth Amendment or Congress's enumerated powers in Article I, Section 8.

Whether *Missouri v. Holland* makes sense today is much debated among legal scholars. At one level, *Holland* has a certain logic because the treaty power is an executive power located in Article II, which is not subject to the textual limitations that apply to Article I. But exemption from the restrictions on Congress's Article I power does not logically compel the conclusion that treaties are freed from federalism altogether. As the Supreme Court had stated before *Holland,* the treaty power must be exercised "consistent with the distribution of powers between the general and state governments."[21] Before the Rehnquist Court's reinvigoration of federalism, the generous interpretation given to the Commerce Clause relieved the government of relying on the broad extent of the treaty power for its actions. Even today, there can be little doubt that the Migratory Bird Treaty Act would be constitutional without the need of a treaty. In recent years, however, the Supreme Court has placed new limits on the extent of the federal government's powers. In *United States v. Lopez,* which struck down a federal law banning handguns in school zones, and *United States v. Morrison,* which struck down a federal law prohibiting violence against women, the Court has restricted Congress's authority under the Commerce Clause for the first time since the New Deal.[22] In other cases, the Court has restricted Congress's authority to enact legislation to enforce the Fourteenth Amendment's Equal Protection Clause, has held states immune from damages lawsuits, and barred federal "commandeering" of the agencies of state government.[23]

Professor Bradley has cogently argued that these limits should apply to treaties as well. Otherwise the Constitution would allow an almost limitless power to the treatymakers—a result at odds with the structure of the federal government as one of limited, enumerated powers.[24] Professor Golove has replied, however, that this view is at odds with the original understanding of the Constitution and early treaty practice, both of which support the notion that treaties are not limited by standard federalism principles.[25] Regardless of the result of this debate, *Holland*'s expansive reading of the treaty power underscores the severe textual and structural difficulties created by the theory of self-execution. The *Restatement (Third) of Foreign Relations Law* says that "the Tenth Amendment does not limit the power to make treaties and other agreements," and that "the United States may make an agreement on any subject suggested by its national interests in relations with other nations."[26] When combined with the claims that all treaties have the same legal force as statutes, that they automatically preempt inconsistent state law, and that they are to be immediately enforced by the federal and state courts, the treaty power becomes an almost unlimited authority to legislate. Requiring Congress to implement treaties would prevent such a limitless power.

Maintaining a clear separation between the executive treatymaking power and Congress's authority over domestic legislation serves functional goals as well. In almost all domestic spheres of activity over which the federal government has jurisdiction, the Constitution grants the power to legislate to Congress. As a matter of accountability, when the government imposes rules of conduct on individuals, those rules ought to be made by members of the legislature who directly represent the people. Non-self-execution better promotes democratic government in the law-making process by requiring the consent of the most directly democratic part of the government, the House of Representatives, before the nation can implement treaty obligations at home. To be sure, the president provides a safeguard against an antimajoritarian treaty, but presidential participation is not a complete protection for majority rule, especially during a second term. Establishing a process in which the House takes part through implementing legislation provides yet another safeguard for popular sovereignty.

Non-self-execution also produces benefits for the system of public law-making described by different theories of the legislative process. Some students of legislation believe that Congress primarily acts as a forum for making deals between interest groups.[27] Although some public choice scholars are dubious that the legislative process advances the "public interest," pluralists view interest groups as desirable because they facilitate stability, moderation, and broad satisfaction with the political system.[28] Other theories of the legislative process suggest that if international agreements are implemented by the full Congress, more committees and groups will become involved, bringing to bear greater legislative and policy expertise, producing more information on legislative choices, and fostering communication between the different political players.[29] The more steps that exist in implementing treaties, the more open the process and the greater the chances for reasoned discussion about the policies involved.[30] A requirement that treaties receive implementing legislation exposes international agreements to the benefits of a more open political process, which promotes stable policymaking and broader political acceptance.

To be sure, the Framers at times suggested that the House was ill suited to diplomacy because of its size and lack of stability. These secrecy concerns no longer seem compelling in light of the large size of the Senate, the role of the House in foreign affairs, and the nature of modern regulatory treaties, which can resemble domestic legislation in purpose and effect. Today's Senate, with one hundred members, is 50 percent larger than the original House of Representatives, and incumbency rates in the House today average about 90 percent.[31] The House today plays an equal role in foreign policy, with committees on international relations, national security, and intelligence that routinely handle sensitive information and oversee legislation related to foreign affairs. Even if the Senate is better disposed to diplomacy than the House, multilateral treaties that impose domestic rules of conduct do not demand secrecy or speed of action. Only those treaties that have the least domestic effect, and hence need no implementing legislation, such as military or political alliances, demand secrecy. A presumption of non-self-execution would not affect the nation's ability to negotiate these types of treaties. Furthermore, the Senate never assumed the active role in diplomatic negotiations that some Framers may have hoped for. For example, after President Washington sought to consult with the Senate on a treaty, the noise and confusion in the Senate chamber led to the matter's being deferred to another day. President Washington left in a huff and, according to one account, declared that "he would be damned if he ever went there again."[32] The Senate's formal role in treatymaking has become one of after-the-fact consent, while the president assumes primary responsibility for setting foreign policy and conducting diplomatic negotiations.

Self-execution distorts the public lawmaking process by removing the procedural checks on the exercise of legislative authority. In place of the parallel House and Senate procedures for studying and adopting legislation, the treatymaking process shifts the center of policymaking from Congress to a president unencumbered by bicameralism. The development of treaty provisions and the understanding of treaty negotiation and drafting is dominated by the president, rather than by the legislature, as would be the case with domestic statutes. The termination of treaties also demonstrates how treaties would distort the public lawmaking process. Statutes require the consent of both houses of Congress and the president, or two-thirds of Congress without the president, before they can be repealed. As we saw in chapter 6, the Constitution gives the president the authority to unilaterally terminate treaties. As with treaty formation, the president retains this authority on the strength of his preeminent position in foreign affairs and his structural superiority in managing international relations. If the nation regulates certain domestic conduct by statute, the president cannot terminate the rules without congressional approval. If the nation should regulate the same conduct by self-executing treaty, however, the president may terminate the regulation at will.

Furthermore, under the consensus view, the "last-in-time" rule allows treaties to supersede earlier statutes, and subsequent statutes to override earlier treaties. In other words, if the terms of a statute and of a treaty come into conflict, the provision that was enacted most recently will pre-empt the earlier version.[33] Allowing treaties and statutes to supersede each other in this way seems inconsistent with the formalist approach to lawmaking articulated by the Supreme Court in *INS v. Chadha*.[34] In *Chadha*, the Court invalidated Congress's creation of the legislative veto, which was used in that case to overturn the attorney general's determination, pursuant to his statutorily delegated power, not to deport an alien. It reasoned that Congress could enact legislation—which it defined as legislative action affecting the rights of individuals outside of Congress—only by passing laws that survived bicameralism and presentment to the president. A decision to repeal earlier legislation—as was the case with the use of the legislative veto in *Chadha*—requires a new law. Viewed in *Chadha*'s light, the last-in-time rule violates the Constitution's structural principles of lawmaking, because it allows the treatymakers to counteract an earlier action by the president, Senate, and House. During the Jay Treaty debates, Madison rejected this possibility out of hand because "it involved the absurdity of an Imperium in imperio; or of two powers both of them supreme, yet each of them liable to be superseded by the other."[35]

Automatic self-execution of all treaties also errs in assuming that all forms of federal law are self-executing. According to Professors Henkin and Vázquez, treaties are listed as one of the three forms of federal law in the Supremacy Clause, along with the Constitution and federal statutes; if the latter two are self-executing law, then treaties should be as well. This simple logic falters because courts have refused to adopt the same blanket rule of self-execution for constitutional and statutory provisions that some urge for treaties. In the statutory context, federal courts generally have refused to recognize a claim, even when brought by an injured plaintiff, unless the statute clearly grants a private cause of action.[36] Although the Court once adopted a more generous approach toward the implication of private rights of action, it since has employed a narrower approach that requires an expression of congressional intent in either the statutory text or the legislative history.[37] The Court's strict test on private rights of action means that numerous federal statutory provisions cannot be enforced in court. Administrative law schemes recognize that certain federal mandates are to be enforced by the executive branch rather than by Congress or the courts.[38]

Judicial refusal to enforce statutory provisions may be even more pronounced when the case involves foreign affairs. In *Tel-Oren v. Libyan Arab Republic,* for example, the D.C. Circuit refused to hear a claim by the survivors of a terrorist attack on a civilian bus in Israel.[39] In his concurrence, Judge Bork concluded that courts should not infer a cause of action under the alien tort statute because, under the cause of action analysis, a court must examine the particular character of the issues presented for decision. Drawing on both the act of state and the political question doctrines, Judge Bork found that the separation of powers required courts to defer to the political branches in foreign affairs, so as to avoid interference with the functions of the other branches and to prevent the judiciary from deciding issues that were not fit for judicial resolution. Taking "into account the concerns that are inherent in and peculiar to the field of international relations," Judge Bork concluded that the centralization of the conduct of foreign relations in the political branches constituted " 'special factors counseling hesitation in the absence of affirmative action by Congress.' "[40] While Judge Bork's opinion is not offered here as representative of a broad practice by the courts, it exemplifies judicial reluctance to give self-executing effect to federal statutory provisions in the foreign affairs area. Judge Bork's *Tel-Oren* concurrence also explains judicial unwillingness to intervene in other foreign affairs questions, as expressed in the political question doctrine, the act of state doctrine, the reluctance to engage in dormant foreign affairs preemption, and the presumption against extraterritoriality.[41]

Mistaking the Supremacy Clause to require automatic judicial enforcement of treaties is more dramatic when considered in light of the non-self-executing nature of constitutional provisions. Certain constitutional clauses cannot receive judicial implementation because the Constitution vests execution in the political branches. To take one example, much of Article III is non-self-executing, which leaves to Congress the decision whether to create the lower federal courts and to define their jurisdiction.[42] In the Judiciary Act of 1789, the first Congress did not provide for federal jurisdiction over all of the cases and categories provided for in Article III. Indeed, for much of our nation's history, Congress did not provide for general federal question jurisdiction, and even today the diversity jurisdiction statute does not fully vest the lower courts with the full extent of jurisdiction possible under Article III, Section 2. Nor, for that matter, was Article III self-executing as to the creation of the federal court system.[43] If something as vital to the constitutional system as the organization and jurisdiction of the judiciary is non-self-executing, despite the Supremacy Clause, it is difficult to understand why all treaties benefit from a contrary rule. Well-known justiciability doctrines, such as standing, mootness, and ripeness, further preclude courts from adjudicating all cases that raise questions of federal law.[44]

Of particular importance for our discussion is the political question doctrine, which is relevant not only as another example of the judicial underenforcement of constitutional norms, but because it suggests that foreign affairs cases may receive less judicial attention than others. Despite withering criticism, as we have seen with regard to war powers, the courts seem intent to enforce the doctrine where foreign affairs are concerned. Federal courts famously have refused to hear cases challenging the president's use of military force without a declaration of war, both during the 1980s and 1990s and during the Vietnam War, and most recently with the wars in Iraq and Kosovo.[45] Treaty cases also have triggered the political question doctrine. In *Goldwater v. Carter,* as we saw in chapter 6, a four-justice plurality agreed that the question whether the president could terminate treaties without the consent of the Senate presented a nonjusticiable political question. And as Justice Brennan wrote for the Court in *Baker v. Carr,* "[n]ot only does resolution of [foreign affairs] issues frequently turn on standards that defy judicial application, or involve the exercise of a discretion demonstrably committed to the executive or legislature; but many such questions uniquely demand single-voiced statement of the Government's views."[46] In earlier cases, according to the Court, these reasons had led it to apply the political question doctrine to avoid reviewing foreign affairs decisions of the political branches.[47] A similar concern about a lack of judicial ability has led lower courts since *Baker* to dismiss challenges by individuals against government actions involving foreign affairs.[48]

The *Baker* Court's discussion of the political question doctrine indicates that the courts are reluctant to intervene in foreign affairs cases because of their lack of competence. Another factor, however, also animates the doctrine's operation in this field: the structural superiority of the other branches. In this respect, Justice Brennan's views echoed Justice Sutherland's opinion for the Court in *United States v. Curtiss-Wright,* in which the Court observed that the force of the nondelegation doctrine ought to be significantly relaxed in foreign affairs. In raising political question concerns in *Goldwater v. Carter,* Justice Rehnquist also relied on Sutherland's language in *Curtiss-Wright* to urge deference to the political branches. To be sure, academics have rightly criticized *Curtiss-Wright* on a number of grounds.[49] Nonetheless, these criticisms do not address *Curtiss-Wright*'s judgment that the political branches, acting together, are structurally superior to the judiciary in managing the nation's foreign affairs, and that their decisions ought to receive some amount of judicial deference.

Non-self-execution better accords with the constitutional allocation of the foreign affairs power than a broad rule requiring that courts automatically enforce all treaties. By refusing to enforce treaties without implementing legislation, the courts can avoid the difficult policy questions inherent in determining how best to execute the nation's international obligations. These are problems for which the federal courts are ill suited from a functional point of view, and for which they ought to defer to the other branches. Both the president and Congress possess institutional capabilities and resources that render them superior to the courts in shaping how the nation should live up to its treaty commitments. Because the Constitution does not compel a rule of self-execution even for all constitutional or statutory provisions, the courts have the flexibility to adopt a rule that better makes sense of the Constitution's textual division of the treaty and legislative powers and honors the political branches' leading role in foreign affairs.

In response to these arguments, academic defenders of self-executing treaties rest their hopes almost entirely on the Supremacy Clause. Professor Vázquez, the most thorough critic of non-self-execution, argues that the Supremacy Clause makes treaties law, on a par with the Constitution and federal statutes, that must be enforced by courts in properly brought suits by individuals.[50] The Supremacy Clause, he concludes, demonstrates the intent to "adopt[ ] the very same mechanism for enforcing treaties, federal statutes, and the Constitution itself."[51] Professor Henkin writes that "[i]n some constitutional systems, treaties are only international obligations, without effect as domestic law; it is for the parliament to translate them into law, and to enact any domestic legislation necessary to carry out their obligations."[52] That, he argues, is not the law in the United States because the Supremacy Clause makes treaties "the supreme Law of the Land." "That clause, designed principally to assure the supremacy of treaties to state law, was interpreted early to mean also that treaties are law of the land of their own accord and do not require an act of Congress to translate them into law." Refusal to enforce treaties, therefore, represents a serious judicial violation of the Constitution. "The distinction found in certain cases between 'self-executing' and 'non-self-executing' treaties," Jordan Paust declares, "is a judicially invented notion that is patently inconsistent with" the Supremacy Clause.[53] In fact, Professor Paust continues, "such a distinction may involve the most glaring of attempts to deviate from the specific text of the Constitution."

The most glaring fault with these arguments is that they mistake the Supremacy Clause—a provision aimed at ensuring that federal law preempts inconsistent state law—for a separation of powers provision. Yet, the text of the clause does not clearly call for immediate judicial execution of all treaty provisions, and it instead allows the political branches to take the lead in determining how the nation shall observe its international obligations. To be sure, making a species of federal enactment a "law of the land" expresses its superiority over inconsistent state law. But the "law of the land" phrase does not address how that supremacy is to be achieved. A constitutional, statutory, or treaty provision can achieve "law of the land" status through presidential or congressional, rather than judicial, action. One might even read the "law of the land" phrase as an affirmative duty of the federal government, as a whole, to give effect to constitutional, statutory, or treaty obligations. This would give treaties domestic effect outside of the courts, although the executive and legislative branches would remain free to break a treaty.

Contrary to the arguments of Henkin and Vázquez, the Supremacy Clause does not specify what branch or branches within the federal government bear the primary responsibility for treaty implementation. Mere use of the phrase "law of the land," by itself, does not establish a priority of obligation that requires the judiciary to act first, in the absence of guidance from the political branches. In fact, if their reading were correct, then the third part of the clause would have proven unnecessary. If they were right that making a type of federal enactment the "law of the land" obviously vests it with automatic judicial enforcement, then requiring state judges to give effect to the Constitution and laws, "any Thing in the Constitution or Laws of any State to the contrary notwithstanding" would have been surplusage. If "law of the land" obviously meant "immediate judicial enforcement," then the Supremacy Clause need not have mentioned state judges at all.

The meaning of "law of the land" is not the only textual problem with the pro-self-execution reading of the Supremacy Clause. What should be clear, on a cursory reading of the clause, is that it fails to address the relationship of the treaty power and the legislative power. While the clause does declare the supremacy of federal law over state law, it does not alter the existing relationships between different types of federal law and their methods of enforcement. The Supremacy Clause did not address the division of the legislative and executive treaty powers because that allocation had already been made by the Constitution. As Madison put it during the debates over the Jay Treaty, "[T]he term *supreme,* as applied to Treaties, evidently meant a supremacy over the State constitutions and laws, and not over the Constitution & laws of the U. States. . . ."[54]

The Supremacy Clause's federalism purpose becomes even clearer when one examines the governmental actors it regulates. The clause requires only state judges to give effect to federal laws, even when they come into conflict with state constitutional or legislative provisions. It does not discuss the relative roles of the president, Senate, and House. It does not even address the duties of federal judges in giving supremacy effect to treaties, not to mention the obligations of state executives and legislatures. If the Supremacy Clause does not even address whether and how state executives and legislatures must give effect to treaties, it is hard to read it as establishing a rule concerning the relative roles of the political branches and the federal judiciary on treaty implementation. If the Supremacy Clause were to shoulder the burden that Vázquez and Henkin place on it—overturning the traditional separation of the treaty and legislative powers—one would expect it to say so.

The clause's placement in Article VI further underscores its federalism purpose. The provisions that allocate the powers of the three branches are found in the first three articles of the Constitution. By the time one reaches Article IV, the Constitution no longer addresses the powers of the branches vis-à-vis one another, but instead turns to powers that had to be vested in the nation as a whole. Article VI addresses whether pre-constitutional debts are valid against the new government, the nature of the oath to the Constitution that is to be taken by federal and state officials, and the supremacy of federal law. None of these provisions seeks to play any role in the separation of powers. If the Constitution had sought to reallocate part of Congress's legislative power to the president and Senate acting by treaty, then Article VI would have been an odd place indeed to have done so. It would have been as if the Constitution, in Article VII, had included a clause allowing Congress to shield all federal officers from presidential removal or direction.

Professor Vázquez has responded that interpreting the Supremacy Clause to not compel self-execution reads the word "treaties" out of the clause.[55] If all treaties required legislative implementation, there would have been no need for "treaties" in Article VI because every treaty would already have been implemented by a statute. This is perhaps the best textual claim in support of self-execution. It would only apply, however, if non-self-execution applied to all treaties, regardless of whether or not they fell within Congress's Article I powers. However, treaties that touch on areas that are regulated by the states do not, by their very definition, infringe on Congress's legislative powers. While non-self-execution allows us to read the treaty power in harmony with Article I's vesting of the legislative power in Congress, it is unnecessary when the treaty power involves matters within the jurisdiction of the states.

Acknowledging that certain treaties may extend beyond Congress's powers gives meaning to the word "treaties" in the Supremacy Clause while preserving Article I's vesting of the legislative power. If a treaty regulates a matter within the jurisdiction of the states, then the word "treaty" in the Supremacy Clause provides Congress with the authority to enact a statute preempting state law to give effect to the treaty. Without the word "treaty" in the clause, a federal statute that sought to implement such treaty obligations would run afoul of the Tenth Amendment or other federalism protections. Giving the word "treaty" this role is more consonant with the clause's overall objective of preventing states from resisting the enforcement of federal law, rather than giving it the completely different separation of power purpose of vesting treaties with aspects of the legislative power. This reading also accounts for the result in *Missouri v. Holland*. *Missouri*'s reasoning has troubled commentators because it fails to explain exactly where, in the Constitution, the federal government receives the power to enforce treaties that go beyond Congress's Article I powers. As Professor Bradley has observed, there is significant "concern after [*Missouri*] that the treaty power might not be subject to *any* constitutional restraints, including the individual rights provisions of the Bill of Rights."[56] Reading the word "treaty" in the Supremacy Clause in the manner suggested here provides *Missouri* with the textual hook that it has lacked. At the same time, it does not prevent the president and Senate from modifying a treaty commitment through reservations, understandings, and declarations to prevent treaties from having such an effect. As Professors Bradley and Goldsmith have argued, the ability to sign multilateral human rights treaties, while taking reservations from those provisions that would have such a *Missouri v. Holland* federalism effect, makes it more likely that the United States will enter into those agreements.[57]

Professors Vázquez and Henkin have also suggested that non-self-execution robs treaties of any significance. If a treaty cannot take effect without an implementing statute, what is the point of having a treaty in the first place? This argument has a pedigree that goes back to Alexander Hamilton, who argued that Congress had a constitutional obligation to appropriate money and pass legislation to implement treaties. As Hamilton wrote, "there is scarcely any species of treaty which would not clash, in some particular, with the principle" that treaties cannot exercise Article I power.[58] If such were the case, he continued, then "the power to make treaties granted in such comprehensive and indefinite terms and guarded with so much precaution would become essentially nugatory." This argument, however, considers treaties only in terms of their domestic effects, rather than as instruments of international relations. Even if a treaty were not implemented domestically, it is, once made, an instrument governed by international law that imposes obligations on the United States. Treaties still remain the primary vehicle by which the United States makes long-term commitments of a political or military nature with other nations. If anything has made treaties less meaningful, it is not non-self-execution, but the growing use of congressional-executive agreements, which are examined in the chapter 8.

The theory of self-execution suffers just as much at the hands of practice as at the hands of text and structure. There are many instances in which courts refuse to enforce treaties in properly brought cases, and the doctrine of non-self-execution has been a part of American law since as early as Chief Justice Marshall's decision in *Foster v. Neilson* in 1829.[59] The political branches have long engaged in a practice of attaching reservations, understandings, and declarations (RUDs) to treaties that have rendered parts or all of them non-self-executing. These reservations often are not even part of the text of the treaty itself, but are instead sometimes expressed in the Senate's resolution approving the treaty, and sometimes only in the legislative history. While the practice of attaching such RUDs has been much criticized, there is also little doubt that they are regularly used to protect the prerogatives of Congress and of the states under our constitutional system.[60]

TREATIES IN THE NEW REPUBLIC: THE DEBATE OVER THE JAY TREATY

Events during the early years of the Republic further support the relationship developed here between treaties and legislation. While not as relevant as the records of the ratification debates—arguments and events after 1788 cannot have influenced the minds of those who adopted the Constitution in 1787—postratification evidence can show how the Constitution's structures worked in practice. The pre–Revolutionary War debts continued to raise the issue of treaties and legislation, which was finally resolved only with the ratification of the Jay Treaty between the United States and Great Britain in 1795. Some scholars place great store on the postratification treatment of the debt issue, because they read the Supreme Court's decision in *Ware v. Hylton* as adopting a doctrine of self-execution toward the 1783 treaty. A broader examination of the prewar debt issue, however, shows that a principle of non-self-execution eventually emerged. Controversy over the Jay Treaty's handling of the war debts, in fact, would lead to the articulation of a rule of non-self-execution by the Jeffersonian Republicans and later by Chief Justice Marshall in *Foster v. Neilson*.

Foreign relations became the focus of the nation's affairs and the chief source of political conflict under the new Constitution. As we have seen with the Neutrality Proclamation, at issue was the basic policy that the United States should pursue toward Great Britain and revolutionary France. Hamilton and his supporters wanted to restore the favorable trade and commercial ties that had existed with Great Britain before the Revolution. Jefferson and Madison opposed closer relations because of both sympathy for France and dislike of the new financial, industrial, and social developments in Great Britain. These divisions over political economy and foreign policy spurred the formation of political parties in the early Republic and led to sharp differences over the allocation of the constitutional powers of foreign affairs when the Federalists retained control over the presidency and the judiciary, while the Jeffersonians gained power in Congress.[61]

These developments came to a head during the controversy over the Jay Treaty of 1795. The Jay Treaty resolved several contentious issues between Great Britain and its former colonies, such as the evacuation of the British from the northwestern forts, British compensation for American merchant ships seized during the war with France, and reduced trade barriers. One of the treaty's signal accomplishments was the resolution of the issue of prewar debts owed by American borrowers to British merchants. During the Critical Period most of the states had refused to enforce Article IV of the 1783 Treaty of Paris, which had declared that creditors should meet with "no lawful Impediments" in recovering prewar debts. Widespread opposition throughout the states led to defiance of Congress's claims to treaty supremacy. Once the war ended, British merchants found that state legislatures and courts refused to hear their claims, especially in Virginia, whose citizens owed approximately 2 million of the nation's 5 million pounds in debts. Whether the federal courts would enforce Article IV of the 1783 treaty remained an open question during the early years of the new Republic.[62]

Opposition to collection of the debts led to several efforts to prevent the new federal courts from hearing British claims against American debtors. Seeking to limit judicial involvement in the debt question, Congress placed a five-hundred-dollar minimum amount in controversy on the jurisdiction of the circuit courts, which had the effect of excluding the majority of debt claims from federal court. Opposition to debt repayment even contributed to the ratification of the Eleventh Amendment, enacted in reaction to the Supreme Court's decision in *Chisolm v. Georgia* in 1793.[63] In *Chisolm,* the Supreme Court ignored claims of state sovereign immunity and allowed a citizen of South Carolina to bring an action for damages against the state of Georgia. Although *Chisholm* did not involve the peace treaty, its implications for the debt issue were clear. Without state sovereign immunity, British merchants and property owners could sue states in federal court for confiscation and sequestration of their American property. Passage of the Eleventh Amendment ensured that British creditors would be unable to bring suit in federal court against the states, some of which had allowed American debtors to pay their debts into the state treasury in exchange for a release from their debt under state law.

The Eleventh Amendment, however, did not protect the original debtors from suit, and it was this avenue that British creditors pursued in *Ware v. Hylton*. [64] In 1774, Hylton, a Virginian, had issued a bond to pay three thousand pounds to William Jones, a British merchant. Under Virginia's wartime sequestration law, Hylton had paid part of the sum, in depreciated paper dollars, into the state treasury and received a discharge of the debt. Because the Virginia courts had refused to hear British creditor claims, Jones did not file for recovery until a federal trial court became available in 1790. The case was tried between 1793 and 1794 before a Circuit Court in Richmond composed of Chief Justice Jay, Justice Iredell, and Judge Griffin. John Marshall, then a Federalist lawyer practicing in Richmond, argued on behalf of Hylton that the Virginia sequestration law barred recovery, that the British had been a wartime enemy and could not recover in court, and that the British had violated the peace treaty and so could not benefit from its terms. The plaintiff replied that Article IV of the 1783 treaty suppressed any state laws that stood in the way of the enforcement of a debt claim.

Justice Iredell, writing for a 2 to 1 majority, found for the Virginia debtor. Although he was reversed by the Court on appeal, his views are worth pursuing because they receive substantial attention from supporters of the self-execution thesis. First, Iredell concluded that Article IV "could only be effected by the legislative authority," and that whenever "a treaty stipulates for anything of a legislative nature, the manner of giving effect to this stipulation is by that power which possesses the legislative authority." Drawing on the British example for this point, Iredell extensively discussed a 1786 Anglo-French commercial treaty that had required parliamentary cooperation to give it effect. Second, Iredell observed that the Supremacy Clause had acted to give treaties more than just moral effect. "Under this constitution," Iredell wrote, "so far as a treaty constitutionally is binding, upon principles of *moral obligation,* it is also by the vigor of its own authority to be executed in fact. It would not otherwise be the *Supreme law* in the new sense provided for. . . ." Each branch of government, Iredell concluded, therefore had an obligation to use its powers to execute treaties. Third, Iredell seemed to suggest that because state law had frustrated the implementation of Article IV, ratification of the Supremacy Clause essentially repealed those laws. Fourth, however, Iredell found that the treaty did not specifically require the states to repeal any "impediments" to debt recovery, and so the federal courts could not infer a repeal. It is unclear whether Justice Iredell was adopting a presumption that treaties were to be non-self-executing unless they clearly said otherwise, or whether he believed that it was the primary obligation of the states to repeal their impeding laws before federal courts could enforce the treaty. Chief Justice Jay dissented in an unreported opinion that has not survived.

Justice Chase wrote the main opinion for a unanimous Court in reversing Iredell. Like Jay, Chase believed that even before the Constitution, Congress had the authority to adopt a treaty that overrode state laws regarding the British debts. "It seems to me," Chase wrote, "that treaties made by Congress, according to the Confederation, were superior to the laws of the states; because the Confederation made them obligatory on all the states." Any doubts on this subject were "entirely removed by" the Supremacy Clause. "It is the declared will of the people of the United States that every treaty made by the authority of the United States, shall be superior to the Constitution and laws of any individual State." Therefore, Justice Chase concluded, the Supremacy Clause required the Court to suppress the Virginia sequestration statute in favor of Article IV of the peace treaty. Unlike a "stipulation that certain acts shall be done, and that it was necessary for the legislatures of individual states, to do those acts," Justice Chase interpreted Article IV as "an express agreement, that certain things shall not be permitted [in] the American courts of justice." Because only a court could hear a creditor's claim for recovery, only the courts could give effect to Article IV.

Defenders of self-execution judge *Ware* to be an early victory. "*Ware v. Hylton* establishes that, when a treaty creates an obligation of a state vis-à-vis individuals," observes Professor Vázquez, "individuals may enforce the obligation in court even though the treaty does not, as an international instrument, confer rights directly on individuals of its own force."[65] They are correct to place such confidence in *Ware;* it stands as the most authoritative declaration in favor of self-executing treaties from the framing period. Nevertheless, *Ware* does not provide the grounds for such broad lessons. First, Justice Iredell's opinion stood for quite the opposite proposition—that the 1783 treaty was not self-executing. Second, his opinion appears unclear on whether the Supremacy Clause actually reversed the British rule on treaties. Justice Iredell seems to have believed that treaties that require legislative action must continue to be implemented by the legislature. Third, Justice Chase's opinion also contains language that suggests that treaties calling for legislative action still must be implemented by Congress—hence his discussion that only the courts could give effect to Article IV of the peace treaty. Fourth, Article IV did not actually give British plaintiffs a cause of action to sue in federal court. Rather, the treaty only preempted a defense created by state law; the cause of action itself arose under state common law. Finally, as Justice Iredell suggested, the 1783 treaty may not have required congressional implementation because, unlike treaties that would be made after the ratification, it had been reached under the Articles of Confederation and thus may have been implemented directly by the Supremacy Clause.

At best, then, *Ware* can stand for only a very limited form of self-execution. Justices Iredell and Chase could make their statements about judicial enforcement of Article IV because the peace treaty did not call for action by the national legislature. Indeed, Article IV could not do so because, at the time of the treaty's ratification, Congress did not have the authority under the Articles of Confederation to interfere with state laws concerning contracts. While today such matters might fall within the scope of the Commerce Clause, as interpreted by the Supreme Court, it seems doubtful that in 1796 the framing generation would have considered private loans to be the subject of congressional power. *Ware,* therefore, did not involve a conflict between the treaty power and the power to legislate because Congress could not legislate in the area regulated by Article IV of the Treaty of Paris. Rather, the peace treaty required action by the states to conform their local laws to its terms, and by the courts, which supplied the only forum for its actual implementation. Indeed, both Justice Iredell's and Justice Chase's opinions made statements that were consistent with the idea that if a treaty fell within the legislative powers enumerated in Article I, it would have to be implemented by Congress.

Very little attention surrounded the *Ware* decision when it was handed down; the political system was focused on the controversy over the Jay Treaty, which finally resolved the problem of the prewar debts by transferring British debt claims to an international commission. Only after a contentious debate in which Congress declared that treaties that conflicted with its power to legislate were non-self-executing was the treaty implemented. Rather than supporting self-execution theories, the war debt story indicates that self-execution produces severe strains on the separation of powers. With the Jay Treaty, the political system relieved that stress by articulating and following the opposite rule.

As recounted by Professors Elkins and McKitrick in *The Age of Federalism,* relations with Great Britain in 1794 had deteriorated to the point where a war scare was brewing in the United States. In addition to retaining the vital northwestern forts since the end of the Revolution, Britain had continued to pursue commercial policies that discriminated against American shipping and goods. In late 1793, Britain initiated an offensive against the French West Indies, which called for the seizure of neutral ships trading in the area. British ships captured more than 250 American merchant vessels; the cargoes and vessels were condemned as prizes and some of their sailors were impressed into the British navy. President Washington appointed Jay, who was still serving as chief justice, as ambassador to seek compensation and to resolve other outstanding issues, such as the prewar debts and the forts, which threatened to spark war between the two nations. Jay left in the spring of 1794, a year after dissenting in *Ware* in the Circuit Court, and returned a year later with the new treaty.

In seeking to negotiate a new agreement with the British, the Washington administration was not confident enough to count on the courts to implement the Peace Treaty of 1783. Even Chief Justice Jay, whose Court would rule on the issue in *Ware,* was unwilling to represent to the British that the American court system ought to be relied on. Instead, Jay proposed an entirely different mechanism to adjudicate the claims of British creditors and American shippers. Article VI of the treaty established an arbitral commission, composed of two British and two Americans and a fifth to be chosen, to adjudicate the claims. British claimants could appeal to the commission from American courts and were not bound by the rules of evidence that obtained there. The U.S. government would assume the debts and pay the claims as determined by the commission. Rather than rely on state and judicial implementation, the Jay Treaty finally resolved the prewar debt problem by relying on federal action undertaken by federal institutions. Although *Ware* would decide that the 1783 treaty was self-executing, the political branches in the Jay Treaty turned to other methods to live up to the nation's obligations.

This was a striking conclusion to the British debt problem, given that it was the institutional head of the federal judiciary who negotiated the arrangement. It was all the more surprising in light of Chief Justice Jay's own dissent in *Ware* and the positions that he had taken as secretary for foreign affairs in 1787 and as author of *The Federalist* No. 64. Jay's treaty had rendered *Ware v. Hylton,* as it would be decided by the Supreme Court in 1796, practically irrelevant. Although the chief justice personally believed that treaties, as the supreme law of the land, ought to be immediately executed in the courts, he must have concluded that the ongoing constitutional and political controversy concerning the enforcement of Article IV of the Treaty of Paris had demonstrated that self-execution was not in the judiciary's best interests. Concludes historian Richard Morris: "When one reflects on the hostility with which the nation reacted to *Chisolm v. Georgia,* it might well appear that Jay demonstrated prudence and common sense in keeping this emotionally charged political issue from further undermining the authority of the Court."[66] A doctrine of self-execution placed the judiciary at risk because it could bring the courts into conflict with the political branches concerning the conduct of foreign policy.

Efforts to implement the treaty provoked a sharp political and constitutional struggle over the treatymaking power and the power to legislate. In the end, the treatymakers included the most democratic body of government into the process in order to make treaties meaningful under domestic law. By promising to assume the debts and to improve the treatment of British shipping and goods, the Washington administration was forced to turn to the House for the necessary implementing legislation. As David Currie has observed, this sparked one of the great constitutional battles of the early National Period.[67] Among other things, Jeffersonians in the House challenged the treaty's failure to win broader neutrality rights for American ships and sailors. They also sought to block the treaty for bringing the nation unacceptably close to Great Britain. They began to wage a campaign to convince the Senate to reject the treaty because it guaranteed British citizens the right to own land, which the Jeffersonians argued rested outside federal powers, and because it adopted most-favored-nation status toward British goods, which they claimed ought to be the subject of congressional legislation. These efforts ultimately proved unsuccessful, as the Senate approved the treaty by a party line 20-to-10 vote on June 24, 1795.[68]

The battle moved to the House. In the press and in Congress, Hamilton and other Federalists strongly pressed a self-execution argument. Because the Supremacy Clause made treaties the law of the land, the House had a constitutional obligation to implement the Jay Treaty. It had no right to consider the treaty on the merits, nor could it refuse to pass the necessary implementing legislation. In "The Defence," published as the House began consideration of whether to implement the treaty, Hamilton wrote: "[E]ach house of Congress collectively as well as the members of it separately are under a constitutional obligation to observe the injunctions of a [treaty] and to give it effect. If they act otherwise they infringe the constitution; the theory of which knows in such case no discretion on their part."[69]

To make treaties dependent on legislative execution, Hamilton argued, would make the treaty power a hollow one. "[T]here is scarcely any species of treaty which would not clash, in some particular, with the principle of those objections . . . ," Hamilton argued. "[T]he power to make treaties granted in such comprehensive and indefinite terms and guarded with so much precaution would become essentially nugatory."

In response, members of the House made a bold claim—bold because it directly challenged President Washington's authority—that the Jay Treaty was non-self-executing. Madison and Albert Gallatin argued that no treaty that regulated a subject within Congress's enumerated powers could take effect without legislative authorization. They based their arguments on the fact that the Constitution vested legislative power in Congress and that Congress exercised the same powers that Parliament did in regard to treaties made by the king. After describing Parliament's authority, Gallatin declared that "in the same manner is [the treatymaking power] limited here, not however merely by custom and tradition, but by the words of the Constitution, which gives specifically the Legislative power to Congress."[70] Therefore, the House had the right to diplomatic information about the treaty in order to decide whether to implement it. The House had "a *right* to ask for the papers . . . because their co-operation and sanction was necessary to carry the Treaty into full effect, to render it a binding instrument, and to make it, properly speaking, a law of the land."[71] Criticizing Hamilton's view, Madison supported a resolution that the Constitution "left with the President and Senate the power of making Treaties, but required at the same time the Legislative sanction and cooperation, in those cases where the Constitution had given express and specific powers to the Legislature."[72] Congress had no duty to im-plement treaties, according to Madison. "It was to be presumed, that in all such cases the Legislature would exercise its authority with discretion. . . . [T]his House, in its Legislative capacity, must exercise its reason; it must deliberate; for deliberation is implied in legislation." After several weeks of debate, the House passed the resolution 62 to 37 on March 24, 1796, demanding Jay's negotiating instructions.[73]

President Washington refused. Following Hamilton, he argued that the House had a constitutional obligation to implement the treaty, because it was already the law of the land, and that the House had no discretion to examine the agreement on the merits.[74] Washington specifically cited the Constitutional Convention's rejection of the proposal that all treaties re-ceive congressional ratification. In response, the House debated whether to fight congressional exclusion from treaties. On April 6, a Republican representative introduced a resolution declaring that treaties involving matters within Congress's enumerated powers could not take effect with-out implementing legislation, and that the House had full discretion to decide whether to pass such laws. That same day, Madison rose to de-fend Congress's role in implementing treaties, one that specifically drew upon the ratification debates of the Constitution. President Washington was correct, Madison admitted, that the Constitutional Convention had rejected an amendment to give the House a formal role in treatymaking. That, however, was not the power claimed by the resolution, which sought control only over the implementation, not the making, of treaties. In any event, evidence from the Constitutional Convention was not controlling because it was the state ratifying conventions that had "accepted and rat-ified the Constitution."[75] An examination, Madison claimed, of the Penn-sylvania, Virginia, and North Carolina ratification debates would show that the Framers believed that treaties could not exercise domestic legislative effects without congressional implementation. Not wishing to recite full passages from these debates, Madison said he "would only appeal to the Committee [of the Whole] to decide whether it did not appear, from a candid and collected view of the debates in those Conventions, and particularly in that of Virginia, that the Treaty-making power was a limited power; and that the powers in our Constitution, on this subject bore an analogy to the powers on the same subject in the Government of Great Britain. He wished, as little as any member could, to extend the analogies between the two Governments; but it was clear that the constituent parts of two Governments might be perfectly heterogeneous, and yet the powers be similar."[76]

Convinced by these arguments, the House adopted the resolution the next day by another lopsided vote of 57 to 35. Having established its constitutional authority in treatymaking, the House then began a lengthy debate on the treaty's merits. Pressure from Jeffersonian supporters in the West, who stood to benefit from American control of the northwestern forts and a subsequent reduction in Indian resistance to expansion into the Northwest territories, convinced House leaders to approve implementing legislation. The House approved appropriations by a close vote of 51 to 48.[77] Yet, approval of the treaty's substance did not undermine the House's constitutional position. The House had laid claim to the procedural right to evaluate the treaty because it was non-self-executing in those areas under Congress's authority. The House then approved the treaty because it was, as Professor Currie has concluded, a good one for the nation under the circumstances.

What makes the Jay Treaty episode important is not just that the treaty itself removed the issue of the prewar debts from the federal courts, but that it made clear the reasons why the Jeffersonians believed that non-self-execution was constitutionally required. As articulated by Madison and Gallatin, Article I vested the legislative power in Congress, while Article II established treatymaking as an executive function. Therefore, any treaty that pledged to undertake an action within Congress's Article I power had to receive legislative implementation. In defending this conclusion, Madison argued not just that the Constitution had incorporated British practice, but that this had been the original understanding of the Framers. On this score, Madison had remained fairly consistent from the writing of his "Vices" memo, through the Constitutional Convention, to the Virginia ratifying convention. His purpose had shifted from creating a truly representative national government to ensuring that the legislature maintained sufficient checks on executive power. The Jay Treaty episode confirms the Framers' belief that treaties that regulated areas within Congress's Article I powers required legislative implementation, and it showed how those principles could work in practice.

CONCLUSIONS: NON-SELF-EXECUTION AND MULTILATERALISM

Non-self-execution provides a ready means to solve some of the tensions between the treaty and legislative powers. International events now influence numerous areas of life that were formerly the preserve of regular legislation, while domestic conduct has produced effects on problems of an international scope. Correspondingly, the scope of international agreements has broadened, which has expanded the potential reach of the treaty power. Meanwhile, nationalization of the American economy and society has produced an expansion in the powers of Congress, particularly through its commerce and spending powers. International efforts to regulate areas such as the environment, arms control, the economy, or human rights, therefore, will come into conflict with Congress's constitutional powers, just as treaties threatened to do—albeit in more limited subject-matter areas—during the framing and early National Period. In short, the globalization of affairs produces substantial tension with a constitutional system that maintains a strong distinction between the power to make treaties and the power to legislate.

Non-self-execution provides a means to solve this tension. It prevents international political commitments, entered through treaties, from automatically imposing domestic legal obligations on the government until the political branches have determined the manner in which to implement them. It reserves to the most popular branch of government, Congress, its authority over the domestic regulation of individual citizens and their private activity, while also creating a presumption that protects the normal regulatory prerogatives of the states under our federal system of government. It also preserves the discretion of the president and/or Congress to choose to disregard international rules without violating the domestic Constitution.

The values served by non-self-execution become clearer when we examine two different sets of issues raised by globalization: the multilateralization of the use of force and the death penalty. Turning first to the use of force, it will be recalled that the U.N. Charter prohibits the use of force unless in self-defense or on authorization by the Security Council. The United States ratified the U.N. Charter as a treaty at the end of World War II. Thus, some argue, in ratifying the charter the United States gave up its right to initiate hostilities unless in conformity with its terms. Because a treaty is part of the "law of the land" under the Supremacy Clause, and hence on a par with the Constitution and other federal law, the president has a constitutional obligation, in seeing that the laws are faithfully executed, not to order the use of force that would violate the U.N. Charter. If a Congress funds a presidential war at odds with the U.N. Charter, one imagines that Congress is acting unconstitutionally as well. "By adhering to the Charter," according to Professor Henkin, "the United States has given up the right to go to war at will."[78]

Two disruptions of the constitutional structure flow from this position. First, it renders any presidential use of force that is not taken in self-defense or authorized by the Security Council not only illegal, but unconstitutional. Presidential discretion to use force in foreign affairs, as envisioned by the Framers and established in the constitutional text and structure, is unarguably reduced as a result. Under this approach to treaties, the violation of international law by the United States and its allies in Kosovo also amounted to a violation of the Constitution by President Clinton. After all, the United States could not claim seriously—nor did it try—that Serbia was armed with weapons of mass destruction and their delivery systems and that it posed a threat sufficient to trigger the U.S. national right of self-defense. Due to Russia's veto, the Security Council never issued a resolution authorizing the use of force. In using force against Kosovo, the United States violated the U.N. Charter and President Clinton, under a self-execution theory, failed to perform his constitutional duty to enforce the laws of the land.

Second, equating treaties with statutes has the effect of transferring the authority to decide whether to use force in international relations to an international organization. Under the Constitution's original design, the president and Congress decide on war through the interaction of their constitutional powers. Putting to one side the use of force in self-defense, many scholars believe both that the United States cannot wage war without Security Council permission, and that if the Security Council authorizes war—as it did in the 1991 Persian Gulf War—the United States must use force to meet the goals set out by the Council. In other words, the Security Council has the authority under the charter to impose both a negative duty (not to attack) and an affirmative duty—to use force to enforce council resolutions. The Constitution's usual procedure of relying on the president and Congress to make these decisions, under this approach, is effectively within the control of the Security Council. In those cases, however, where the United States can make an actual claim of self-defense, as in Afghanistan and probably Iraq in 2003, the United States—and thus the president and Congress—would still have their usual room for decisionmaking.

Of course, the United States has used force many times since the end of World War II, and not all of those cases met the requirements of the U.N. Charter. In fact, in only two instances has the use of force been authorized by the Security Council, in Korea in 1950 and in the Persian Gulf four decades later. During this period, some conflicts undoubtedly qualified as national exercises of the right to self-defense under international law—Afghanistan being the easiest example. Others, however, may not have—such as the uses of force in Kosovo, Bosnia, and Lebanon—although there is usually a healthy debate over each one.[79] Non-self-execution explains why these interventions did not violate the Constitution. If we consider treaties to be diplomatic commitments in the realm of international politics, rather than automatic laws enforceable in the United States, then the president has no constitutional obligation to enforce the U.N. Charter, nor does Congress have any obligation to fund actions to comply with it. Rather, the political branches can decide whether and how the nation should obey a Security Council resolution, or they can even decide to violate the charter, as in Kosovo. Non-self-execution also precludes any real delegation of authority to the United Nations, as the decisions of that international organization remain—from the perspective of the American constitutional system—only the demands of international politics. Security Council decisions may bind the United States as a matter of international law, but the president and Congress decide how they are to be implemented, if at all.

It should come as no surprise that the federal courts have adopted this approach in cases involving the decisions of the organs of the United Nations. In *Diggs v. Richardson* (1976), for example, the U.S. Court of Appeals for the District of Columbia Circuit confronted a Security Council resolution sanctioning South Africa because of its occupation of Namibia.[80] Plaintiffs sought an injunction, based on the Security Council resolution, ordering the U.S. government to cease economic relations with South Africa involving goods from Namibia. Dismissing the case, the D.C. Circuit held that the resolution was not self-executing and was not enforceable federal law. In *Committee of United States Citizens Living in Nicaragua v. Reagan* (1988), the D.C. Circuit faced a suit demanding that the Reagan administration cease all aid to the contra resistance in Nicaragua, as the United States had been ordered to do by the International Court of Justice (ICJ).[81] The D.C. Circuit again dismissed the case, holding that ICJ decisions are not self-executing, and that any requirement in the UN Charter to obey ICJ decisions was similarly non-self-executing.

Recent litigation over the death penalty raises the same tensions and ultimately may require the same solution. Aliens arrested and tried in the United States for capital murder sometimes have not received notification, at the time of their arrest, that they have the right of access to consular representatives from their countries, as guaranteed by the Vienna Convention on Consular Relations. In two cases, one involving a citizen of Paraguay, the other two brothers from Germany, all convicted of murder and sentenced to death, the International Court of Justice ordered the United States to "take all measures at its disposal" to stop their execution. In refusing to order a stay of execution in the first case, *Breard,* the Supreme Court suggested that the ICJ order was not self-executing federal law, and found that 1996 changes to the federal death penalty statute had overridden any treaty obligations.[82] In the second case, *LaGrande,* the Court also refused to issue a stay, with the executive branch informing the Court that the ICJ decision was not binding federal law, but was instead a matter of international politics.[83] In yet a third case, decided in 2004, the ICJ ordered the United States to stay the execution of fifty-one Mexicans on death row and to provide them a judicial forum for review and reconsideration of their convictions.[84]

According to some scholars, failure to obey the ICJ's decision constituted a violation of federal law. In regard to the *Breard* case, Professor Henkin argues that the ICJ order was self-executing federal law.[85] Professor Vázquez similarly argued that if the ICJ order was binding it must also be self-executing, a view shared by Anne-Marie Slaughter. If this were correct, then the Supreme Court violated federal law by refusing to issue a stay of execution, and the president failed to uphold his duty to enforce federal law by not ordering Virginia or Oklahoma to stop the execution. Indeed, this view conceivably would have the president send in federal marshals to stop state prison officials from carrying out the sentences, as his authority to execute federal law would preempt the state law imposing the death penalty. It would also expand the powers of the federal government at the expense of the states, because without the ICJ order there was no basis, under the Bill of Rights or the federal habeas statute, to halt the executions.

Presidents are not about to issue unilateral orders to state prisons halting the executions of foreign nationals duly convicted of capital murder. And the Supreme Court has not (at least not yet) issued stays of executions when the only violation of federal law asserted is a failure to notify a defendant of his rights under the Vienna Convention. Contrary to leading academic views, however, this does not constitute a violation of the Constitution. Rather, it is a recognition of the manner in which non-self-execution works as a practical matter to allow the political branches of government to decide how to implement our international obligations, with due regard for constitutional principles of the separation of powers and federalism. By treating the Vienna Convention and the U.N. Charter provisions concerning the ICJ as nonbinding, the Supreme Court leaves it to the president and Congress to decide whether and how to obey ICJ orders. The president and Congress simply chose not to exercise their powers to enforce these orders. Non-self-execution also preserves the Court's own authority to interpret, as a final matter, all species of federal law, rather than allowing that power to be transferred to the ICJ. Finally, non-self-execution in this context protects the prerogatives of the states, which have the primary responsibility for enforcing criminal laws such as murder.

A presumption that treaties are non-self-executing thus plays two important roles. First, as William Eskridge and Philip Frickey have argued, such presumptions allow the judiciary to avoid difficult constitutional questions and to protect the constitutional structure, without having to block actions by the political branches.[86] While protecting the constitutional line between the executive treaty power and legislation, it also leaves to the political branches the flexibility to decide whether and how to implement the nation's international obligations. Second, a clear statement rule helps contain the potential for unlimited lawmaking at a time when the line between domestic and international affairs is disappearing. Globalization, plus the interaction of several broad doctrines about the unbounded subject matter of treaties, their freedom from the restraints of the separation of powers and federalism, and their alleged interchangeability with statutes, threatens to give the treatymakers a legislative power with few limits. Non-self-execution ensures that treaties, like the Constitution itself and all other species of federal law, are true to the notion that the national government is one of limited and separated powers.

8

Laws as Treaties?

Statutes as International Agreements

Only twice in the last century, in 1919 with the Treaty of Versailles and in 1998 with the comprehensive Nuclear Test-Ban Treaty, has the Senate rejected a significant treaty sought by the president.[1] In both cases, the international agreement received support from a majority of the senators, but failed to reach the two-thirds supermajority required by Article II, Section 2 of the Constitution. The failure of the Versailles Treaty resulted in a shattering defeat for President Wilson's vision of a new world order based on collective security and led by the United States. Rejection of the Test-Ban Treaty amounted to a major setback for the Clinton administration's arms control policies and its efforts to promote American participation in international efforts at regulatory cooperation. In both cases, presidents raised the concern that a minority of the Senate could frustrate an internationalist American foreign policy and thereby turn the nation toward isolationism.

According to many scholars and legal authorities, however, both presidents could have avoided this result by submitting their international agreements as statutes. Instead of navigating Article II's advice-and-consent process, presidents have sent international agreements to both houses of Congress for simple majority approval through a process known as a "congressional-executive agreement." While in the first fifty years of American history, the nation concluded twice as many treaties as nontreaty agreements, since World War II the United States has concluded more than 90 percent of its international agreements through a nontreaty mechanism.[2] Between 1939 and 1989, the nation has entered into 11,698 executive agreements, made either by statute or by the president alone, but into only 702 treaties that have undergone the supermajority process required by Article II, Section 2.[3]

Despite the fact that the constitutional text includes a specific Treaty Clause but no other means to enter into international agreements, a broad intellectual consensus exists that congressional-executive agreements may serve as full substitutes for treaties. Louis Henkin, for example, has written that "it is now widely accepted that the Congressional-Executive agreement is available for wide use, even general use, and is a complete alternative to a treaty."[4] This is known as the idea of "interchangeability": statutes are interchangeable with treaties. Bruce Ackerman and David Golove share this view, but only if one agrees with their theory that the Constitution can be amended without actually adopting an amendment; without their theory, congressional-executive agreements are unconstitutional. Some, however, such as Laurence Tribe, argue that the Treaty Clause is exclusive and that congressional-executive agreements violate the Constitution's supermajority requirements for treaties.

It is fair to say that interchangeability of statutes and treaties represents a consensus among academics. According to the *Restatement (Third) of Foreign Relations Law,* there is no line between treaties and congressional-executive agreements, so "[w]hich procedure should be used is a political judgment, made in the first instance by the President."[5] Professor Henkin even openly acknowledges that the statutory form should be used precisely to evade the Treaty Clause. Such agreements, he advises, "remain[ ] available to Presidents for wide, even general use should the treaty process again provide difficult."[6] Not surprisingly, presidents have followed suit. In submitting an international agreement for approval, President Truman told Congress: "I am satisfied that either method is constitutionally permissible and that the agreement resulting will be of the same effect internationally and under the supremacy clause of the Constitution whether advised and consented to by the Senate or whether approval is authorized by a joint resolution."[7] If this is true, presumably congressional-executive agreements benefit from the same broad doctrines that many scholars believe apply to treaties, such as freedom from subject matter, federalism, or separation-of-powers limitations.

This striking divergence between the constitutional text on the one hand, and practice supported by academic opinion on the other, is not just a matter of intellectual curiosity. International agreements today are assuming center stage in efforts to regulate areas such as national security, the environment, trade and finance, and human rights. As international agreements increasingly assume the function of statutes, the treaty power threatens to supplant the domestic lawmaking process, even in areas within Congress's Article I, Section 8 competencies. At the same time, interchangeability raises the prospect that statutes could fully replace treaties, which raises the problem that Congress could exercise executive powers in areas where treaties have force beyond domestic statutes. While this may not have presented much of a practical problem in an era when the reach of the Commerce Clause was thought to be virtually limitless, the Supreme Court's recent federalism decisions make clear that significant areas still exist where treaties may provide the sole constitutional source for national regulatory power. Interchangeability would permit statutes to evade the restrictions on Congress's Article I, Section 8 powers, just as globalization threatens to allow the treaty power to supplant the domestic lawmaking process.

Explaining the constitutionality of the congressional-executive agreement is a matter not just of intellectual coherence, but of practical economic and political importance. Today, about one-quarter of the gross national product arises from international trade, whose rules are set by the North American Free Trade Agreement (NAFTA) and the World Trade Organization (WTO) agreement. If all international agreements must undergo the supermajority treaty process, America's ability to participate in a new world of international cooperation will be hampered. On the other hand, use of a constitutionally illegitimate method would throw America's participation in the world trading system into doubt. Not only would constitutional questions undermine the validity of current congressional-executive agreements, they also would raise problems for America's ability to engage in ever more intensive international cooperation. Uncertainty about the constitutionality of the congressional-executive agreement may undermine novel efforts to craft international solutions in response to the effects of globalization on areas such as finance and economics, security, the environment, and human rights.

Our analysis of the Constitution's approach to international agreements and domestic law develops a legitimate foundation for congressional-executive agreements. It provides a clear dividing line between situations in which treaties must be the sole instrument of national policy and those that can be dealt with by statute. We will confirm theory by evaluating the record of practice by the political branches, rather than making normative claims derived from different theories of constitutional interpretation. Practice suggests that complete interchangeability has been rejected because it creates severe distortions in the American public lawmaking system. Allowing statutes completely to replace treaties eliminates the restrictions on Congress's enumerated powers and undermines the separation of powers in foreign affairs. Nor is treaty exclusivity an acceptable alternative. Congressional-executive agreements still have a legitimate place in the constitutional conduct of foreign policy because they preserve Congress's constitutional powers over such matters as international commerce. A proper place still exists for treaties, even in a world of expanded congressional powers, for regulating subjects that rest outside of Congress's Article I powers. While the lawmakers run into their constitutional boundaries in areas outside the Commerce Clause, the treaty-makers may still use their powers to reach beyond the limits of Article I, Section 8 and the Tenth Amendment. Treaties also are required for the national government to act in areas that are the subject of the concurrent powers of the executive and legislative branches.

THE UNEASY CASE FOR INTERCHANGEABILITY

Given the important role played by the congressional-executive agreement, an absence of convincing textual or structural support ought to be a matter of great concern. The Constitution explicitly grants the federal government the power to make international agreements only in Article II, Section 2's Treaty Clause, and it refers to treaties only three other times. In order to justify the use of congressional-executive agreements at the end of World War II, scholars such as Myres McDougal read an implicit authorization for nontreaty, international agreements in Article I, Section 10's prohibiting of states from entering into any "agreement or compact" with a foreign power. From this, they suggested that the Constitution recognizes a broader class of international agreements than just "treaties." Why would the Framers preclude the states from exercising the power to make an "agreement or compact," but then not give it to the federal government?[8]

Constitutional silence, however, can cut both ways. The canon of *expressio unius est exclusio alterius,* by which the presence of one term implies the exclusion of others, suggests that the Framers understood all of the federal government's power to make international agreements to rest in the Treaty Clause. If the presence of the words "agreement or compact" in the text demonstrates that the Framers understood international agreements to take forms other than the treaty, then we can expect them to have used those words in Article II if they meant to grant a broader power to the national government. An examination of the original understanding shows no support for the idea that the Framers believed that the federal government possessed some free-floating, nontextual power to make international agreements. Rather, as we have seen, the attentions of both Federalists and Anti-Federalists during the ratification debates focused exclusively on the Treaty Clause. Instead of worrying about whether statutes could do the job of treaties, the Framers argued over whether treaties might invade the province of statutes.

Further, reading prohibitions on the states as empowering the federal government to do the opposite is an unpersuasive and ultimately dangerous interpretive technique. Section 2 of the Fourteenth Amendment, for example, prohibits states from denying citizens the equal protection of the laws. Adopting a McDougal-like approach would require us to infer the lack of a similar prohibition on the federal government as an implicit constitutional authorization to do otherwise. A similar interpretive approach would read the Fifteenth Amendment's prohibition on state efforts to block access to the ballot based on race as confirming the federal government's power to so discriminate. It does not appear that the Court would agree with these propositions, nor would most constitutional theorists today.

One might suggest, as Professors Ackerman and Golove have, that the Necessary and Proper Clause provides Congress with the authority to make international agreements in aid of its other powers.[9] In one of their rhetorical moments, they characterize this as a "Marshallian" reading of the Constitution because it builds on the approach of Chief Justice Marshall in *McCulloch v. Maryland.*[10] As all law students learn, *McCulloch* upheld the constitutionality of a national bank, even though it was nowhere mentioned in the constitutional text, as an appropriate means to achieve congressional powers to regulate commerce, establish the treasury and currency, and fund government operations. Claiming to follow the same logic, Ackerman and Golove assert that so long as Congress has decided that a congressional-executive agreement is "appropriate" to achieve the full use of a constitutional power, and so long as the "end [is] legitimate," then the congressional-executive agreement is constitutional. While this argument better engages the textual problem, it suffers from several flaws. It confuses constitutional meaning with Supreme Court decisions that limit the Court's own discretion in reviewing the constitutionality of legislation. *McCulloch*'s language about the link between ends and means serves the purpose of removing *the Court* from the job of reviewing legislative judgments. It does not relieve the president or Congress from determining whether certain means actually are constitutional, and it was precisely on this ground that President Jackson vetoed the bill chartering the Second Bank of the United States.[11]

A greater problem is that this approach misapplies *McCulloch*'s federalism implications to the separation of powers. *McCulloch*'s reading of the Necessary and Proper Clause only countenances expansions in federal powers, vis-à-vis the states, when necessary to achieve legitimate federal aims. Recent cases, such as *United States v. Printz,* which prohibited the federal government from "commandeering" state officials to implement federal law, even indicate that state sovereignty may impose some limit on the reach of the clause.[12] What is important to recognize, however, is that *McCulloch* does not allow Congress to deploy the Necessary and Proper Clause so as to rearrange the separation of powers. Reading the clause to justify congressional-executive agreements transfers the power to make international agreements from the executive branch (made up of president and Senate) to the legislature. If this reading were correct, a variety of other congressional efforts to restructure government should have been equally constitutional. Congress, for example, could have used the Necessary and Proper Clause not just to condition the removal of an independent counsel in order to protect against interference in the investigation of high executive officials, but to shield the office from presidential control altogether. Congress could have relied on the clause to justify the creation of the legislative veto or the vesting of budget reduction authority in the comptroller general. While it may be very well to read the clause as allowing a power to establish a national bank where none had been granted to the federal government, it is quite a different matter to read the clause as allowing Congress to seize from the president and Senate the power to make international agreements.

In order to give interchangeability its full due, we should examine the work of an older generation of scholars—including Edwin Corwin, Quincy Wright, and Myres McDougal and Asher Lans—who successfully argued in favor of congressional-executive agreements as World War II neared its conclusion.[13] Initially, they built their case on precedent. They pointed to a long line of examples—the first congressional authorization of international postal agreements, the annexations of Hawaii and Texas, and various reciprocal trade laws—that allegedly demonstrated almost 150 years of interchangeability. Suffice it to say, however, that none of these precedents evidenced a decision to replace the treaty with a statutory process in which Congress gives its *ex post* consent to a presidentially negotiated agreement. Rather, many of these examples fall within the other types of interbranch cooperation—sometimes erroneously conflated with the distinct type of congressional-executive agreement addressed here— in which Congress delegates factfinding or rulemaking authority to the president.

Defenders of the constitutionality of congressional-executive agreements claimed that two Supreme Court cases, *Field v. Clark* (1892) and *B. Altman & Co. v. United States* (1912), provide legitimacy for the practice of interchangeability.[14] As Professors Ackerman and Golove have argued, however, these cases lend little support for the idea that statutes could substitute for treaties. In *Field v. Clark,* the plaintiff argued that Congress could not delegate to the president factfinding authority for a reciprocal tariff law. This arrangement is a very different creature from the *ex post* congressional-executive agreement of today, and, in fact, it does not even require an agreement with another nation. *Field v. Clark* only rejected the claim that the reciprocal tariff statute violated the nondelegation doctrine, and nothing more. It could not find that the *ex post* congressional-executive agreement was constitutional because there was no such congressional-executive agreement involved.

B. Altman similarly did not call on the Court to review the constitutionality of a statutory method for making international agreements. The case involved a different kind of mechanism, in which Congress provided the president with *ex ante* authorization to reach trade agreements, within specified criteria, with different nations. *B. Altman* did not raise the question of the constitutionality of the use of this procedure in place of the treaty. Instead, it asked only whether a statute that provided the Court with appellate review over claims based on "treaties," could be read to include this novel form of executive and legislative cooperation, a question the Court answered in the affirmative. *B. Altman* did not come close to approving the interchangeability of congressional-executive agreements and treaties.

Once we dispel the notion that the congressional-executive agreement has received the approval of historical practice or judicial decision, the genuine reason for its modern use comes into focus. Congressional-executive agreements represented an effort to replace what was seen as an outmoded method for dealing with international affairs with a more efficient, democratic process. New Deal legal scholars and their progeny believed that providing the Senate with a checking role in making international agreements, included by the Framers to protect sectional interests, had been a dismal failure. With only a small minority needed to block an international agreement, the treaty process allowed isolationism to reign over American foreign policy. While the constitutional difficulty in making treaties expressed a bias against international entanglements, New Deal intellectuals believed that isolationism was a disease that threatened to cripple America in a new, interdependent world. Isolationist senators had blocked American participation in the League of Nations, which had led to the failure of the peace, the rise of Hitler, and the return of world war.

New Deal intellectuals and their successors believed that the congressional-executive agreement substituted a more democratic mechanism for a state-dominated process.[15] International agreements reached through a statutory process reflect the will of the majoritarian president and of both houses of Congress. Approval by the most democratic branches was particularly important for new types of international agreements. These agreements were just as significant to the nation's welfare as any domestic legislation, and with national economies and societies becoming more interdependent, they directly impacted American lives. The congressional-executive agreement would better promote democratic government by requiring the consent of the most popular part of the government, the House of Representatives, before the nation undertook international obligations.

No doubt, these criticisms of the treaty process have substantial truth to them. The Framers understood that the treaty process would have antidemocratic features. A desire for greater democracy, however, standing alone does not provide sufficient reason for rejecting a clear textual provision. The same arguments that New Deal scholars levied against the Senate's role in treatymaking easily could be repeated against many other features of the Constitution. Take the Senate as a whole. States representing a minority of the population can block treaties; states representing a minority of the population can block normal legislation as well. Senators representing a minority of the population can block the appointment of cabinet officers and federal judges. Senators representing a minority of the states can block constitutional amendments, as can an even smaller minority of state legislatures. Or take the Supreme Court's power of judicial review. Every time the Court invalidates a federal law, a small number of unelected officials have prevented the majority from acting. As Henry Monaghan has asked in criticizing similar efforts to devise more "democratic" methods of constitutional amendment, do all of these antidemocratic elements of the Constitution demand that the political branches devise non-text-based methods for their evasion?[16]

Indeed, the weakness of the New Deal-era defense of congressional-executive agreements is further revealed by an unwillingness to take the promajoritarian case to its logical conclusion. If the objective is to increase the democratic nature of making international agreements, there is no reason to stop with a statutory process. As Jesse Choper has pointed out, even the constitutionally prescribed method for making laws suffers from antimajoritarian features. Senators from the least populous states can block a statute supported by the majority; an even smaller number can use the filibuster to prevent even a majority of senators from voting; committee chairs and majority leaders can impose their wishes at variance with that of the majority; interest groups may succeed in manipulating the legislative process to engage in rent-seeking. If supporters of the congressional-executive agreement were to pursue their quest for democracy full bore, they ought to centralize the making of international agreements in the president alone, who (aside from the vice president) is the one federal officer chosen by the entire electorate.

Such an outcome, obviously, would conflict with the text and structure of the Constitution. This approach not only would read the text of the

Treaty Clause out of the Constitution, it also would allow the president to encroach on Congress's Article I, Section 8 powers in foreign affairs, such as the regulation of international commerce. If it were acceptable, however, to allow statutes to replace the Treaty Clause as a method for making international agreements, despite the Constitution's sole mention of the federal government's power to do so in Article II, Section 2, then it would be equally legitimate to allow unilateral presidential decree to replace the congressional-executive agreement. Perhaps, in defense of the New Deal approach, one might say that the statutory process still ensures that some form of checks and balances exists in the making of international agreements. Maintaining checks and balances, though, does not explain why the congressional-executive agreement is to be preferred to the treaty process; the treaty process itself contains both checks and balances *and* a majoritarian element through the participation of the president. Making the Constitution more majoritarian includes no principle to limit its application.

In order to rehabilitate the case for interchangeability, Professors Ackerman and Golove propose a theory that requires acceptance of the idea that the Constitution is capable of "transformation" by popular will, without expression in a constitutional amendment. In their minds, political struggle over the treaty power during the birth of the postwar order amounted to a nontextual constitutional change that eliminated the exclusivity of the Treaty Clause. Professors Ackerman and Golove argue that a group of professors and government officials, scarred by the Senate's refusal to approve the Versailles Treaty, waged an intellectual campaign before and during World War II to make congressional-executive agreements interchangeable with treaties.[17] They believe, however, that neither scholarly opinion nor political practice before World War II supported the interchangeability of statutes and treaties. Rather, they conclude that the New Deal scholars misread precedent and made blatant appeals to policy in order to set the stage for the mothballing of the treaty process. Building on elite opinion, the centrally important event in legitimating the congressional-executive agreement occurred in the 1944 elections, in which the American people allegedly lent their overwhelming approval to the reelection of President Franklin D. Roosevelt and his postwar plans for intensive participation in international institutions. Opinion polls and newspaper editorials at the time, according to Ackerman and Golove, indicate that the electorate supported the elimination of the Senate's chokehold over treaties as part of a ground swell against isolationism. In response, the Senate dropped its objections to congressional-executive agreements under consideration at the end of World War II, and practice since has codified the new constitutional arrangement.

The most nagging flaw with this transformationist position, as with the internationalist approach, is that it essentially reads the Treaty Clause out of the Constitution. If congressional-executive agreements are fully interchangeable with treaties, and if congressional-executive agreements are not mentioned in the Constitution while treaties are, then the New Dealers are guilty of amending the Constitution without resort to the Article V process. Responding to this challenge, made most forcefully by Professor Tribe against the constitutionality of the congressional-executive agreements approving NAFTA and the Uruguay Round, Ackerman and Golove invoke Ackerman's controversial theory of amending the Constitution outside of Article V.[18] Ackerman believes that the Constitution provides for two types of lawmaking: higher/constitutional lawmaking and ordinary/political lawmaking. The latter occurs most of the time, when people make ordinary policy through regular elections. The former occurs at revolutionary "moments," when the citizenry becomes consumed with more profound constitutional and political issues, debates them, and resolves them in ways that fundamentally alter the nature of constitutional government.

Ackerman and Golove view the adoption of the congressional-executive agreement as another episode in one such moment—namely, the New Deal. As the end of World War II neared, intellectual and political leaders sought to avoid a repeat of Versailles by engaging in an end run around the treaty's supermajoritarian requirement. Overwhelming popular majorities agreed with elite internationalist opinion to replace the treaty with a more democratic process. Ackerman and Golove view the 1944 triumph of Roosevelt and the Democratic Party as legitimating the substitution of the pro-internationalist, congressional-executive agreement for the treaty. With public opinion polls in favor of a two-house process for international agreements, and in the face of proposed constitutional amendments in the House to strip the Senate of its monopoly over the treaty power, the Senate backed down. Its endorsement of the statutes approving the Bretton Woods agreements, according to Ackerman and

Golove, signified the Senate's acquiescence to a new constitutional settlement. By 1947, "[i]nterchangeability had become part of the living Constitution," and it was firmly "codified" in the 1950s, 1960s, and 1970s.[19] This became part of the larger constitutional change wrought by the New Deal, which transferred power from the states to the national government and from Congress to the administrative state. Similarly, the internationalist victory produced more populist lawmaking in foreign affairs by removing the anachronistic ability of a minority of the states, through their votes in the Senate, to keep the nation on an isolationist path. Rather than evolution, the move to the congressional-executive agreement was a sharp, and quite conscious, break from the past.

While certainly colorful and provocative, the transformationist argument suffers from a number of defects. First, it bears the same problems that afflict Ackerman's general theory of constitutional interpretation. Other scholars, such as Tribe, Richard Posner, Daniel Farber and Suzanna Sherry, and Michael Klarman, have engaged in full-scale critiques of the "constitutional moments" theory, so only some of the main points need be summarized here.[20] There is little doubt that the Framers conceived of constitutional lawmaking as distinct from ordinary lawmaking, but Ackerman provides little evidence that the Framers believed higher lawmaking could occur outside of Article V, but within the normal constitutional framework. If the people were to act outside of Article V, they would be altering and abolishing their previous form of government completely, rather than making minor adjustments. To act within the framework of the Constitution, amenders must include a text that can identify exactly what supermajorities of the people have agreed to change, and whether permanent supermajorities on the question indeed exist. Both the framing and reconstruction are distinct from 1944 in that the first two constitutional moments resulted in formal amendments that embodied the revolutions that occurred, while the New Deal and the 1944 moment did not. If popular support for the congressional-executive agreements were indeed so overwhelming, its supporters should have guaranteed its future legitimacy by ratifying a constitutional amendment. Legal instruments, such as statutes or constitutional amendments, allow the polity itself to judge whether large, inchoate majorities will translate into concrete changes in social and political norms. Indeed, without the text of an amendment, it is difficult if not impossible for later interpreters to determine what changes the majority actually understood it was making in the governing structure and how long-lasting they would be.

Second, even accepting that constitutional change may legitimately occur outside the context of a formal amendment, Ackerman provides no sure way to identify when an amendment-less constitutional moment has occurred. If periodic elections are the product of lesser, sordid, ordinary political lawmaking, it seems contradictory to assert that they also can reflect higher lawmaking, unless accompanied by a constitutional amendment. To take the 1944 elections as an example, Ackerman and Golove are forced to assume that voters actually had the congressional-executive agreement issue in mind when they voted for the Democratic Party or for President Franklin D. Roosevelt for the fourth time. But voters had any number of issues on their minds during the 1944 elections: Roosevelt's enormous personal popularity; maintaining political stability during the endgame of the war; dislike of the Republican presidential candidate, Governor Thomas Dewey (who was so uninspiring a candidate that contemporaries compared him to "the bridegroom on the wedding cake, the only man who could strut sitting down, a man you really had to know to dislike, the Boy Orator of the Platitude"); and approval of the Democratic administration's wartime policies. [21]

Ackerman and Golove's defense of interchangeability, in other words, suffers from a level-of-generality problem. It seems safe to conclude that the Democrats' more internationalist approach to the postwar order had something to do with their 1944 victory. Ackerman and Golove, however, provide no compelling reason why we must interpret general political approval for the Democrats and distaste for the Republicans as a mandate for a constitutional amendment on the far narrower issue of congressional-executive agreements. They fail to point to any significant campaign speeches or statements where FDR or Dewey mentioned interchangeability, congressional-executive agreements, or the Senate's constitutional role in treatymaking; they do not identify any facts that show that the electorate was conscious of the constitutional difficulties created by the Senate's supermajoritarian check; nor do they demonstrate that party leaders believed this to be a significant issue in the campaign. Instead, Ackerman and Golove are left to infer that, because the electorate wanted a more secure, internationalist postwar order, they would have agreed to lesser-included measures to achieve that goal, such as interchangeability.

Historians of the period have reviewed the same evidence and have not reached similar conclusions. Indeed, while a recent work by historians Townsend Hoopes and Douglas Brinkley recognizes the 1944 electoral results as "a clear-cut mandate for American participation in the United Nations and for a large American role in the postwar world," they also point out that Roosevelt had won by only 3 million votes, the tightest margin of victory since 1916 and a reflection of concerns about FDR's health and long term in office.[22] The 1944 elections provided a vague mandate for internationalism, but nothing more concrete or defined.[23]

It is dubious, for example, whether the 1944 elections and the passage of the Bretton Woods agreements serve as convincing evidence of a constitutional moment. While the 1944 elections may have provided support for a more internationalist foreign policy, it does not appear that any of the major political leaders viewed the election results as a mandate to do away with the treaty. Neither Roosevelt nor Dewey engaged in any serious debate or discussion during the campaign about the shape of the postwar world or the United Nations—in fact, the presidential candidates had negotiated a truce to keep the question of international organization out of the wartime elections.[24] Franklin Roosevelt's campaign activity during the summer and fall of 1944 shows no mention of the Senate's treaty role or of congressional-executive agreements. In his most significant speech concerning foreign affairs during the election, President Roosevelt only saw fit to discuss broad policy differences with the Republican Party—namely, his claims that Republicans had always championed isolationism—rather than process issues like the Senate's power over treaties.[25]

Evidence is similarly absent concerning the approval of the Bretton Woods and U.N. Charter agreements. President Truman's memoir does not discuss any constitutional deal, nor even the issue of the interchangeability of congressional-executive agreements. Dean Acheson, who at the time was assistant secretary of state for congressional relations, never mentions the issue in his detailed account of the period.[26] It does not appear that either senators or members of the House understood the passage of Bretton Woods to impart any meanings of constitutional significance. While Ackerman and Golove rely on statements in the congressional record, committee reports, and the occasional campaign speech or party platform, they do not place these records in the context provided by numerous available primary sources, such as the *Foreign Relations of the United States* series, presidential library materials, memoirs, and oral histories—all standard sources for diplomatic and presidential historians of the origins of the Cold War.

Secondary historical and political science works reveal that Ackerman and Golove's reading of the construction of the postwar world has little support. Standard biographies of FDR, both old and new, do not mention interchangeability, congressional-executive agreements, or the Senate's role in treatymaking in the context of the 1944 elections.[27] More specialized works on Franklin Roosevelt and foreign policy, such as Robert Dallek's *Franklin D. Roosevelt and American Foreign Policy, 1932–1945*,[28] and more recent studies,[29] make no mention of interchangeability—indicating again that neither Roosevelt nor the voters in the 1944 elections thought much about the issue. If anything, the secondary works indicate that FDR respected the Senate's treaty role and sought ways to work with leading senators on important international agreements, such as the U.N. Charter, rather than avoiding the Senate through new constitutional loopholes.[30] Leading histories of President Truman's establishment of the Cold War national security state and of the policy of containment by John Lewis Gaddis, Melvyn Leffler, and Michael Hogan are similarly silent—further confirmation that no one of any political significance believed that passage of the Bretton Woods or the U.N. agreements signified the acceptance of interchangeability.[31]

THE UNEASY CASE FOR TREATY EXCLUSIVITY

Other leading scholars have responded to congressional-executive agreements with a theory of treaty exclusivity, which holds that the Treaty Clause provides the only constitutional method for reaching significant international agreements. Although this view has received the support of various academics over the years, including Edwin Borchard and Raoul Berger, Professor Tribe's recent criticisms of Ackerman and Golove has been the most recent and thoughtful expression. Tribe argues that the statutory process for making international agreements violates the Constitution. While much of his argument hits home, he fails to provide an explanation for the constitutionality of the congressional-executive agreement, or to identify a distinction between treaties and statutes for purposes of making international agreements. Rather, Professor Tribe is left arguing that the Treaty Clause is the exclusive method for making significant international agreements, that the WTO and NAFTA agreements are unconstitutional, and that American presidents and Congresses have built much of the postwar world order on unconstitutional foundations.

Tribe effectively criticizes Ackerman's approach to constitutional interpretation on several grounds. He accuses Ackerman and Golove of ignoring the basic architecture of the Constitution, as expressed in the manner in which its text and structures fit together. Rather than attempting to harmonize the Constitution's different provisions, Ackerman and Golove read them only as "suggestions" or "illustrations" of many possible governmental structures.[32] Any gap, therefore, in the constitutional text—such as the absence of a provision making clear the Treaty Clause's exclusivity—constitutes an opportunity to provide for an extratextual means of lawmaking. The Necessary and Proper Clause notwithstanding, the Supreme Court's approach to the separation of powers demonstrates the faults of the Ackerman and Golove approach. In *INS v. Chadha,* for example, the Court did not infer any extracongressional power to provide for the legislative veto, while in *New York v. United States* the Court did not allow the Necessary and Proper Clause to permit for the commandeering of state legislatures.[33] In both cases, the Constitution's structural guarantees for the protection of the other branches of the federal government and of the states barred the transformation of a constitutional gap into a new form of federal lawmaking. As with the legislative veto and commandeering state governments, Tribe concludes, so it is with the congressional-executive agreement.

Tribe makes several less abstract textual and structural arguments that more directly undermine Ackerman and Golove's approach. In perhaps his most insightful textual response, Tribe claims their reading conflicts with the Court's understanding of the Appointments Clause. According to Ackerman and Golove, the Treaty Clause is nonexclusive because it does not expressly prohibit any alternative methods for making international agreements. The Appointments Clause, however, which sits adjacent to the Treaty Clause in Article II, expressly provides for alternative methods: while it requires Senate approval of principal officers of the United States, it allows Congress to vest the appointment of inferior officers in the president, heads of departments, or the federal courts. Thus, in Article II,

Section 2 itself, the Framers made exclusive senatorial advice and consent to the appointment of principal officers, and then explicitly created an alternate procedure for inferior officers. Application of the canon of *expressio unius*, Tribe argues, indicates that there is no alternate procedure for the making of international agreements.[34] If the Framers had wanted to provide for other methods for making international agreements, they knew how.

Tribe's second point draws on the presidential veto over statutes. As we have seen, the president has the plenary authority to refuse to ratify a treaty, even after the Senate has consented to it. Under Article II, it is the president who "makes" the treaty, subject only to Senate advice and consent, giving him an absolute veto over treaties. But the president has only a conditional veto over statutes, which Congress may override by a two-thirds vote. A statutory method for making international agreements allows Congress to make international agreements over presidential objection. If Congress can use the Necessary and Proper Clause, Tribe asserts, in combination with its enumerated powers to override presidential opposition, then it also could use the same powers to appoint its own ambassadors and to conduct its own negotiations with foreign powers. Use of the congressional-executive agreement reduces the president's constitutional prerogatives in foreign relations.

Tribe effectively identifies interpretive, textual, and structural problems with interchangeability. He fails, however, to develop a convincing theory to take its place. Tribe's uncompromising reading of the text forces him to conclude that the treaty power is the *only* method for making significant international agreements, although he concedes that the president can make other nontreaty agreements alone as sole executive agreements. For Tribe, deciding whether an agreement must receive the consent of a Senate supermajority depends on whether the "agreement constrains federal or state sovereignty and submits United States citizens or political entities to the authority of bodies wholly or partially separate from the ordinary arms of federal or state government."[35] Absent from Tribe's analysis is any examination of the treaty power in light of the Constitution's allocation of powers to other branches of the government, or of the historical controversies concerning the treaty power's scope.

Tribe's distinction is both too broad and too narrow. He believes that the nation must use treaties whenever it constrains its sovereignty or subjects its citizens to another sovereign power, but he fails to define "sovereignty" and to explain whether the political branches can delegate it. Tribe fails to understand the difference between international obligations on the one hand, and their implementation according to domestic constitutional processes on the other. This leads him to confuse sovereignty in its international sense and sovereignty in its domestic constitutional sense. Any international obligation, whether assumed by the president alone, by the president and the Senate, or by the Congress as a whole, constrains the sovereignty of the people of the United States. That is the very nature of an international obligation. If Tribe believes that any international agreement that constrains federal or state sovereignty must undergo the treaty process, then *all* such pacts must be executed as treaties. Tribe himself, however, refuses to go that far, as he accepts the constitutionality of sole executive agreements.

Tribe's effort to develop an exclusivist theory also fails to understand sovereignty in its domestic sense. The difficult question is not whether an international agreement constrains or delegates national sovereignty, but whether the branches of government will live up to it. While a treaty creates an international obligation, it is the Constitution's allocation of powers to the three branches that provides the powers to fulfill it—no treaty can constrain the lawmaking authority of the federal government. According to the last-in-time rule, for example, Congress is free at any time to override a treaty simply by passing a statute. As we saw in chapter 7, even the president, acting alone, can effectively terminate a treaty. A treaty cannot permanently alter the sovereignty of the United States or of the American people; it cannot change the allocation of authority between federal and state governments as established by the Constitution. Only a constitutional amendment could achieve that result.

A constitutional amendment, not a treaty, would also be required to achieve the second class of actions envisioned by Tribe: subjecting American citizens directly to international rules and organizations. The Constitution makes no explicit provision that would allow for the transfer of federal power to entities—outside of the American governmental system—that are not directly responsible to the American people. Placing American citizens under the direct regulation of international law and organizations seems inconsistent with the very Appointments Clause that provides Tribe with such ammunition. As the Supreme Court has observed, the broader function of that clause ensures that only federal officers accountable to the people's elected representatives may exercise federal power. This rule prevents Congress from transferring executive law enforcement authority to individuals not responsible to the president or his subordinates. It also prevents the national government, as a whole, from concealing or confusing the lines of governmental authority and responsibility so that the people may hold the actions of the government accountable. This approach to the transfer of government authority is further bolstered by Article II's creation of a unitary executive and the nondelegation doctrine.

An examination of the congressional-executive agreement marking American entry into the WTO demonstrates the dual faults of Tribe's approach. He believes that the Uruguay Round agreements, which established the WTO, constrains American national or state sovereignty sufficiently to require a treaty. In one sense, Tribe is correct in observing that the WTO limits American sovereignty by constraining the nation's ability to engage in trade-related measures, such as raising tariffs, enacting discriminatory import restrictions, and barring foreign corporations from certain markets. Every international agreement, however, imposes some type of obligation on the United States for which it receives some benefit. Unless Tribe believes that every international agreement requires a treaty, his definition of sovereignty at this level is far too broad. This is an extreme position that even Tribe does not espouse, and one that is at odds with two centuries of national practice.

Along the domestic dimension of sovereignty, Tribe's account of the WTO similarly misses the mark. Even though the WTO may place international obligations on U.S. trade practices, it places no binding restrictions on American sovereignty or power in the constitutional sense. Upon agreeing to the new WTO system, the United States agreed to live up to certain trade provisions, but the agreement itself does not directly act on American citizens. It remains within the purview of the federal government whether to, and how to, live up to the WTO's requirements, consistent with domestic constitutional procedures. For example, the WTO creates a dispute-settlement procedure in which other nations may bring actions to challenge American trade practices. A decision by a WTO dispute-settlement panel, however, has no binding legal effect within the United States, nor does it have any constitutional impact on the branches of the national government. A WTO body could not order the State of California, for example, to cease discriminatory import restrictions on computer equipment imports from abroad, nor could it compel the United States to treat South American agricultural imports on an equal footing with American produce. The United States can choose to ignore the WTO decision and keep its laws and policies intact; there is no supranational body that can force the United States to obey. While aggrieved nations might receive permission from the WTO to impose retaliatory sanctions on American imports, there is no direct regulation of American citizens or parties by any international organization. Tribe's definition of the scope of treaties, therefore, provides little help on this score because neither the WTO, NAFTA, nor any international agreement can restrict American sovereignty—the Constitution itself gives to the political branches the discretion whether to comply or to ignore any international obligation.

Arguments that all congressional-executive agreements violate the Constitution sweep too far. If Tribe were correct, about 90 percent of the international agreements made by the United States since World War II would be invalid. These agreements include not just postal exchange agreements, but many of the foundations of the postwar economic order, such as Bretton Woods and GATT, and America's recent efforts to expand free trade after the end of the Cold War, such as NAFTA and the WTO. Further, the exclusivist view ignores competing constitutional structures and texts that cut against it. Tribe argues, for example, that the Necessary and Proper Clause cannot justify the congressional-executive agreement, but he provides no explanation for the reach of Congress's plenary power over international commerce. Even if Congress cannot send its own ambassadors or ratify its own international agreements, Congress can still pass statutes involving international commerce that unilaterally accept international obligations.

Tribe's view also has its own structural distortions. In order to expand the reach of treaties, the exclusivist view must engage in a corresponding reduction in Congress's constitutional powers. If treaties are the exclusive method for entering into international agreements, and treaties are self-executing, then the treatymakers can legislate on almost any subject, so long as it is addressed by an international agreement. This would allow the treatymakers to exercise Congress's Article I, Section 8 powers to regulate domestic and international commerce. To take but one example, if the nation wanted to change the length of time for patents, it generally would use a statute to do so because of Congress's Article I, Section 8 authority to regulate intellectual property. If an international agreement is involved, however, authority over this subject suddenly would transfer to the treatymakers. This dilemma could be avoided if most treaties are non-self-executing. As we saw in chapter 7, non-self-execution permits a harmonization of the treaty power and the legislative power by precluding treaties from exercising any power granted to the legislature in Article I, Section 8. If all domestic implementation remains in the hands of Congress, we can avoid structural contradictions created by the potential overlap of the treaty and legislative powers.

Constitutional Text and Structure and Congressional-Executive Agreements

Critics of interchangeability make an important point: allowing statutes to replace treaties distorts the constitutional structure of foreign affairs and eliminates important constitutional limitations on federal power. A closer examination of the textual and structural problems of interchangeability here may lead the way to a theory of congressional-executive agreements that is more fully in keeping with the Constitution. We then discuss how practice maintains the line between executive power and the legislative power, and undermines the case for both interchangeability and treaty exclusivity.

Interchangeability's most obvious distortion of the constitutional structure lies in its weakening of the president's formal foreign affairs powers. As we saw in chapter 7, the constitutional text and structure place the president in the central position in treaty affairs. The president, not the Senate, chooses to initiate the treaty process, and the president can still refuse to make a treaty even after the Senate has approved it. A statutory process for making international agreements threatens to oust the president from this dominant position and negates his absolute veto over foreign policy. If an agreement takes the form of a public law, then Congress can initiate the process without presidential approval, just as it can propose any statute. Even if the president unequivocally opposes an agreement and vetoes it, Congress can still override with a two-thirds majority vote. These structural implications conflict with the Constitution's centralization of foreign affairs power in the executive branch. As we have seen, the constitutional text and structure, as well as long executive and legislative practice reaching to the very beginnings of the Republic, recognizes that the president is constitutionally responsible for the conduct of foreign policy. Creating an alternate process for making international agreements, one that excludes the president, would allow Congress to pursue its own foreign policy and interfere with the executive's leadership role.

Interchangeability further warps the president's foreign affairs powers after the public lawmaking process ends. Statutes require the consent of both houses of Congress and the president, or two-thirds of Congress without the president, before they can be repealed. As we saw in chapter 7, today most commentators, courts, and government entities agree that the president may terminate a treaty unilaterally. The president retains this authority because of his leading role in foreign affairs and his structural superiority in conducting international relations. If the nation were to regulate certain domestic conduct by statute, the president could not terminate the rules without congressional approval. If the nation were to regulate the same conduct in concert with a treaty, however, the president enjoys the power to terminate the regulation at will.

Interchangeability, however, upsets this structure in either one of two ways. On the one hand, it could mean that Congress can bind the nation to an international agreement that the president could not terminate unilaterally, which would represent a serious curtailment of the executive's foreign affairs powers. On the other hand, defenders of interchangeability might allow the president the same ability to terminate congressional-executive agreements as he has to terminate treaties. This, however, would provide the president with the heretofore unknown power to repeal statutes. It would be tantamount to granting the president a direct share of the legislative power—a result, as Henry Monaghan has argued, at odds with our understanding of the executive power.[36]

Interchangeability also undermines the Constitution's structure by allowing Congress to escape the restrictions on its enumerated powers. If the statutory process is a perfect substitute for the Treaty Clause, then congressional-executive agreements must enjoy the same constitutional benefits that accrue to treaties. Interchangeability could allow statutes to enjoy the less stringent application of the separation of powers to treaties.

This could happen in one of two ways. First, treaties could transfer powers among the branches, or create hybrid forms of government power, that would prove unconstitutional if undertaken solely by domestic law. Second, the treatymakers could delegate authority that normally resides with the executive or judicial branches to international organizations.[37] Under the conventional wisdom, a treaty could transfer authority from Congress to the executive branch or to an international organization, as some argue that the U.N. Charter actually does, when a statute could not. Theoretically, interchangeability allows statutes to enjoy the loosened restrictions that would apply to treaties in these situations.

Used in these ways, congressional-executive agreements can undermine the separation of powers in both of its interbranch aspects. First, suppose that a statute required the transfer of law enforcement or judicial power to an international agency or tribunal. Officials of the international body would not generally be removable by the president, because the very point of creating international regulatory institutions often is to free them from the direct influence of different nation-states. Even under the loose standards of *Morrison v. Olson* or *Mistretta v. United States,* a domestic effort by Congress to completely shield individuals who exercise executive authority from presidential removal would fall afoul of the Appointments Clause, the Article II vesting clause, or the Take Care Clause, while efforts to transfer the federal judicial power might violate Article III's Vesting Clause. Yet, some international and constitutional law scholars, such as Harold Bruff and William Davey, argue that such standards should not apply to international agreements.[38] Second, if statutes are to enjoy the same status as treaties, and if treaties are not subject to the usual structural constraints of the separation of powers, then presumably Congress could restructure the separation of powers when acting through the congressional-executive agreement, even though it could not with an identical statute that concerned domestic affairs.

Interchangeability also threatens to allow Congress to exercise powers that, if exercised domestically, would violate federalism limitations. Before the Rehnquist Court's reinvigoration of federalism, the generous interpretation given to the Commerce Clause relieved the government of relying on the broad extent of the treaty power for its actions. As we saw in previous chapters, however, the Supreme Court recently has placed new limits on the extent of the federal government's powers. Interchangeability provides the lawmakers with a way to avoid these recent restrictions. Leading commentators assert that the treatymakers can make policy on any subject, even where the lawmakers would be prevented from doing so by Article I, Section 8's enumeration of limited congressional powers or by the Tenth Amendment's reservation of powers to the states.[39] If true, then interchangeability threatens to unleash statutes from Article I, Section 8 and the Tenth Amendment. Interchangeability, in other words, creates a subclass of statutory law that is free from the restrictions that apply to ordinary statutes.

Interchangeability provides yet a third way for statutes to escape the normal limitations on their scope. According to the *Restatement (Third) of Foreign Relations Law,* the United States can enter into a treaty on any subject so long as it is "an agreement between two or more states or international organizations that is intended to be legally binding and is governed by international law."[40] Drawn from international law, this definition contains no subject-matter limitations. As everyday life becomes more closely intertwined with international events, systems, trends, and markets, and treaties involve not just military alliances, but individual rights, environment, finance and commerce, and crime, it will become even more difficult to cordon off a domestic sphere that shall remain immune from international agreement. If treaties can be made on virtually any subject, and if congressional-executive agreements and treaties are fully interchangeable, then statutes that embody international agreements can regulate virtually any subject. Congress would be able to enact statutes that are not limited in subject matter, are not limited by Article I, Section 8's enumeration of powers, and are not limited by the Tenth Amendment or federalism.

Constitutional text and history point the way toward solving these structural problems, without falling into the trap of rejecting congressional-executive agreements as instruments of national policy or of adopting a free-floating approach to constitutional amendment. As previous chapters argued, the constitutional text makes a clear distinction between executive power in foreign affairs and Congress's authority over funding and domestic legislation. This distinction suggests that the use of congressional-executive agreements should be restricted to those areas where Congress has plenary authority under Article I, Section 8, and that treaties must be used for matters outside of Congress's powers, such as those involving concurrent executive and legislative powers or those outside its normal authority. Thus, Congress can resort to congressional-executive agreements in areas such as international trade and finance, where any international agreement would require its cooperation for implementation anyway. Treaties, however, still remain the required instrument of national policy when the federal government reaches international agreements on matters outside of Article I, Section 8, such as human rights, or over which the president and Congress possess concurrent and potentially conflicting powers, as in war powers. As argued in chapter 7, treaties may still be concluded in areas of congressional authority, but such treaties must be non-self-executing in order to preserve the Constitution's separation of the executive and legislative powers.

Under the basic framework developed in previous chapters, the treaty power is an executive power that rests in Article II, as distinguished from the legislative authority vested in Congress in Article I, Section 8. Congressional-executive agreements may be used in the arena of international economic affairs because Congress has plenary authority over the area under the Foreign Commerce Clause. Congress could adopt unilaterally the changes in tariffs, customs laws, or national treatment required by NAFTA or the WTO, even in the absence of an international agreement. Not only are congressional-executive agreements acceptable, but in areas of Congress's Article I, Section 8 powers, they are—in a sense—constitutionally required. In order to respect the Constitution's grant of plenary power to Congress, the political branches must use a statute to implement, at the domestic level, any international agreement that involves economic affairs. Congressional-executive agreements preserve Congress's Article I, Section 8 authority over matters such as international and interstate commerce, intellectual property, criminal law, and appropriations, by requiring that regardless of the form of the international agreement, Congress's participation is needed.

Intellectual property protections under recent international trade agreements illustrate this point. Before the Uruguay Round of the GATT, regulation of the length of patents was a matter of domestic law. Congress established the period of patents under its plenary Article I, Section 8 power to "promote the Progress of Science and useful Arts, by securing for limited Times to Authors and Inventors the exclusive Right to their respective Writings and Discoveries." Under an 1861 law, patent terms in the United States ran seventeen years from the time a patent application received approval. Part of the WTO agreement, Article 33 of the Agreement on Trade-Related Aspects of Intellectual Property Rights, altered that term of patent protection to twenty years from the time of the filing of a patent application. Just as Congress would have used a statute to change the term of patent protection unilaterally, it used the same instrument to alter domestic laws in accordance with our international obligations.[41] Under a theory of treaty exclusivity, however, the only way for the United States to have implemented this change was through a supermajority vote of the Senate. Indeed, exclusivity would require the use of the treaty process even though Congress could adopt the twenty-year term unilaterally to bring the United States into harmony with an international agreement that it has not joined. But, according to exclusivists, if the nation were to enter into a formal agreement that achieved the exact same result in substantive law, the federal government must use the treaty form.

Using congressional-executive agreements in areas of plenary congressional authority avoids this constitutional conflict. Whether Congress adopts the new twenty-year period as part of an international agreement or as merely a change in domestic policy, the instrument is the same: a statute that receives the support of simple majorities in both houses of Congress and the signature of the president. This approach implies that the treatymakers could choose to make a treaty on a subject within Congress's Article I powers, but requires that such a treaty be without domestic effect until implemented by Congress. In the end, both the treaty and congressional-executive route would still require a statute to make changes in domestic law within areas under Congress's Article I competence.

Viewing congressional-executive agreements in this way helps clarify the line that separates statutes from treaties. Allowing treaties to expand into areas regulated by Article I, Section 8 would undermine the constitutional structure by excluding the most direct popular representatives in the national government from exercising their control over areas given specifically to Congress. On the other hand, allowing congressional-executive agreements to reach areas outside of Article I, Section 8's enumeration of powers would undermine the Constitution's vesting of a limited legislative power in the federal government. With the growing internationalization of domestic affairs, merely asserting a foreign relations link or the need to comply with a multilateral international agreement could prove too large a loophole. Allowing treaties to regulate subjects outside of congressional powers, while limiting congressional-executive agreements to matters given to the legislature alone by Article I, Section 8, would prevent international agreements from distorting the Constitution's public lawmaking system.

Following this approach would avoid the severe federalism concerns raised by interchangeability. In light of the special role of the Senate, which has a unique interest in defending state prerogatives, the treaty process provides greater political safeguards for the states than the regular statutory process.[42] Even though the Court's reinvigoration of federalism in the last decade has substantially undermined (if not overruled) *Garcia v. San Antonio Metropolitan Transit Authority*,[43] the idea that the structure of the national government provides significant protection for state sovereignty has special force with the Treaty Clause. Unlike the statutory process, which scholars such as Jesse Choper and Larry Kramer believe already provides sufficient political safeguards for federalism, the treaty process requires a supermajority vote in the Senate. Only a constitutional amendment or the override of a presidential veto demand as high a degree of consensus. This requirement presumably provides federalism interests with even greater protection with regard to a treaty than a statute, not only because one-third plus one of the Senate can stop a treaty, but also because these senators can represent an even smaller percentage of the population. Protection of state institutional interests was one of the very reasons why the Framers preserved the Articles of Confederation's supermajority requirement for treaties.

Treaties usually involve matters of foreign affairs that are of great national importance, over which the Constitution already centralizes power in the national government. Putting to one side the serious doubts of some scholars, the Court has observed in cases such as *United States v. Curtiss-Wright Export Corp.* (1936), *United States v. Belmont* (1937), and *United States v. Pink* (1942) that the Constitution's transfer of all of the foreign affairs power to the federal government may have relieved the states of any cognizable interests when international relations are involved.[44] National sovereignty in international relations may allow the federal government to exercise broader powers, vis-à-vis the states, than it could domestically. Even in foreign affairs areas not specifically delegated to the federal government by the Constitution, as Justice Sutherland asserted in *Curtiss-Wright,* the states may have been completely ousted because of the need to unify national sovereignty in the federal government. As Justice Sutherland later wrote in *Belmont,* "[g]overnmental power over internal affairs is distributed between the national government and the several states. Governmental power over external affairs is not distributed, but is vested exclusively in the national government."[45] Although this nationalist view of the foreign affairs power has not gone unchallenged, language in recent cases suggests that it still holds sway among the justices of the Supreme Court.[46] The approach developed here would allow such exercises of national sovereignty to occur through the treaty power, whose supermajority requirement in the Senate and the limitations of non-self-execution would harmonize it with the constitutional structure.

This analysis finds that the domestic area open to control only by treaty is the class of subjects that rests outside of Congress's Article I, Section 8 powers. Because of recent Rehnquist Court decisions defining the limits of federal powers, there are several subjects that could fall within this category. Matters outside the scope of the Commerce Clause, such as garden-variety or gender-motivated crimes, represent one such subject. Expansions of the definition of individual rights beyond the interpretation of the Supreme Court is another. A third is commandeering state officials and overriding state sovereign immunity. While treaties should not be self-executing in areas of plenary congressional authority, they should reach areas that lie outside of congressional powers due to Article I or Tenth Amendment limits.

Human rights agreements, as we will see, are a good example of the difference between the scope of treaties and of statutes. *City of Boerne* made clear that Congress could not use its Section 5 powers to pursue a definition of constitutional rights at variance with the decisions of the Court. While we may live in an age when many important rights are guaranteed by statute, *City of Boerne* still forbids Congress from interfering in areas where the Court has refused to recognize broader constitutional protections. As Gerald Neuman has suggested, however, this limitation on congressional authority may not apply to the treaty power due to *Missouri v. Holland.*[47] The treaty power, Justice Holmes indicated, was not just a different procedure for the exercise of Article I authority, but an independent source of substantive power. This would allow several treaties

that the United States has ratified to alter the definition of certain individual rights contrary to Supreme Court decisions. For example, the International Covenant on Civil and Political Rights prohibits the death
penalty for crimes committed when the criminal offender was under the
age of eighteen.[48] Supreme Court precedent, however, once permitted
states to execute juvenile offenders as young as sixteen years old.[49] That
same treaty sets international standards against cruel, inhumane, or degrading treatment while in prison that go beyond the Court's reading of
the Eighth Amendment. If *Missouri v. Holland* remains good law, then the
political branches theoretically can use the treaty power to reach these results without being limited by Section 5 of the Fourteenth Amendment or
the Commerce Clause. Rather than altering the meaning of the Constitution, as interpreted by the Supreme Court, Congress would merely be
implementing a treaty.

Treaties, rather than congressional-executive agreements, also would
be necessary in areas over which the executive and legislative branches
have concurrent or overlapping powers. Because unilateral action by one
branch cannot bind the other branch as a constitutional matter, the nation may need to assume an international obligation by treaty in order to
commit both branches. Not surprisingly, the exercise of the foreign affairs
power may be the area where treaties are most necessary. As we saw in
earlier chapters, the Constitution often delegates different powers over
the same foreign affairs issue to the two political branches, without speci-
fying the relationship between those powers. War powers provide a ready
example. The Constitution gives the president the commander-in-chief
power and the undefined executive power, while vesting in Congress the
sole power to declare war and to raise and fund the military. The constitutional text does not, however, clearly state which branch has the authority
to initiate military hostilities. Since neither branch can engage in unilateral
action that will result in the sustained commitment of the United States
to make war as part of a political or military alliance, a treaty may be
necessary to allow both branches to commit themselves convincingly. A
congressional-executive agreement could not be used, because it would
essentially allow Congress acting by statute to order the executive to make
an international commitment to use his war powers in a certain way.

We may therefore expect treaties to be used in areas where the
branches possess concurrent powers that require cooperation—rather

than unilateral congressional or presidential action—for their consistent exercise. Political/military alliances and arms control are areas where the participation of both the president and a supermajority of the Senate may be necessary because of the competing allocation of foreign affairs power. The United States, for example, could not live up to its obligations under the North Atlantic Treaty alliance through the unilateral actions of the executive or legislature alone. To be sure, the president could station troops in Europe under the commander-in-chief power, and even order them into conflict on his own authority. Nonetheless, only congressional participation could guarantee that the nation could raise, properly equip, and fund the large, permanent military forces that have guarded Europe for more than fifty years. While Congress could pass a statute creating those armies, it could not constitutionally force the president to deploy them. The treaty form provides the appropriate means to fulfill the nation's obligations under the NATO treaty, because it represents the promise of both the president and a supermajority of the upper house of the legislature to meet demanding, long-term obligations.

Or consider arms control agreements. In the Intermediate-Range Nuclear Forces Treaty with the Soviet Union, the United States agreed to remove an entire class of nuclear weapons from deployment and to cease production and refrain from any future flight-testing of certain missiles and launchers.[50] Implementation of this treaty required both branches to cooperate in the use of their constitutional authorities. The commander-in-chief power controlled the placement and use of existing missiles such as the Pershing II, which President Reagan had deployed to Western Europe in the early 1980s, as well as the potential conversion of other weapons systems into intermediate-range weapons. Legislative participation was necessary to guarantee that Congress would not authorize or fund the development of future intermediate-range nuclear weapons. A similar analysis may be applied to the START treaties, which require the elimination of some existing nuclear weapons and the commitment to ceilings on American nuclear force structures. Contrast these treaties with a trade agreement such as NAFTA or the WTO. Congress could bring domestic law into compliance with NAFTA or the WTO in the absence of any agreement, or even in the face of presidential opposition. For trade, a congressional-executive agreement, or statute, is all that is needed.

Curtailing the subject matter of congressional-executive agreements solves many of the structural problems with full interchangeability. On the one hand, as we have seen, interchangeability allows the legislative power not only to subsume executive functions, but also to escape the limitations imposed by Article I, Section 8. Treaty exclusivity, on the other hand, ultimately fails because it creates irreconcilable conflicts between the treaty power and the legislative power. Although the treaty power fundamentally remains an executive one, several developments—such as the rise of globalization, the doctrine of self-execution, and relaxed structural limits on treaties—threaten to give the treaty power a sweeping legislative dimension. Executive assumption of legislative power assaults the Constitution's vesting of all legislative power in Congress, and it undermines constitutional structures that promote popular sovereignty. Congressional-executive agreements defuse this conflict by continuing to reserve to the legislature the power to regulate those areas given to it under Article I, Section 8, but allowing ample room for treaties to operate outside that field. Such an approach is also faithful to the Framers' original understanding of the Constitution that the executive power in foreign affairs and the legislative power over domestic regulation would remain distinct and separate.

A logic that would make treaties the exclusive means of making international agreements, on the other hand, combined with expansive theories of the treaty power, leads to the conclusion that the treatymakers can exercise virtually any and all of the federal government's legislative powers. This conclusion is fundamentally at odds with the Constitution's reservation of legislative authority to a popularly elected Congress. As we saw in chapter 7, Madison believed that "if the Treaty-power alone could perform any one act for which the authority of Congress is required by the Constitution, it may perform every act for which the authority of that part of the Government is required."[51] Madison further argued that if by treaty "the President and Senate can regulate Trade; they can also declare war; they can raise armies to carry on war; and they can procure money to support armies." Madison believed that this result demonstrated that the treaty power could not be read so far as to enjoy legislative authority, because the Constitution vested Article I, Section 8's powers in Congress specifically to ensure that the House played a determinative role in their exercise. "[A]lthough the Constitution had carefully & jealously lodged the power of war, of armies, of the purse &c. in Congress, of which the immediate representatives of the people, formed an integral part," Madison observed, an exclusivist theory of treaties meant that the "President & Senate by means of Treaty of Alliance with a nation at war, might make the United States parties in the war: they might stipulate subsidies, and even borrow money to pay them: they might furnish Troops, to be carried to Europe, Asia or Africa: they might even undertake to keep up a standing army in time of peace, for the purpose of co-operating, on given contingences [*sic*], with an Ally."[52]

Some scholars wisely concede that only Congress can exercise certain powers, such as appropriations and taxation. The exclusion of these areas from the general rule of self-execution makes sense when viewed as a matter of democratic policymaking. Clearly, matters such as declaring war, raising taxes, and imposing criminal penalties are some of the most vital exercises of the legislative power, and they have never been thought to lie with the judiciary or executive. This principle, however, also argues against allowing the treatymakers to transfer to themselves any of the powers vested exclusively in Congress under Article I, Section 8, because the Constitution itself does not textually distinguish among those powers. As Madison said during the Jay Treaty debates, "[t]hese powers, however different in their nature or importance, are on the same footing in the Constitution, and must share the same fate." Only by requiring congressional-executive agreements in areas that involve Congress's powers, or by adopting a presumption that treaties are non-self-executing, can this conflict between Articles I and II be resolved.

Maintaining the line between executive and legislative power, and between treatymaking and lawmaking, better accords not just with the constitutional text and structure, but also with the Constitution's system of democratic governance and popular sovereignty. In domestic spheres of activity, the Constitution grants the power to legislate to the federal government through the institution of Congress. The Constitution promotes the idea that when the government imposes rules of conduct on private individuals, those rules ought to be made by their most directly accountable representatives. This principle of popular sovereignty seems to demand that Congress usually participate in the promulgation of international agreements that require individuals to act or not act in certain ways, just as Congress is the dominant institutional force in the enactment of domestic laws that have the same effect. As modern international agreements begin to encompass matters such as economics, industrial and environmental activity, individual liberties, and other areas that have usually been the preserve of domestic legislation, congressional-executive agreements impose the same process on the same subjects, regardless of whether the impulse for regulation comes from domestic or international sources. Use of a statutory process for certain international agreements involves the most directly democratic part of the government, the House of Representatives, before the nation can regulate domestic matters through international agreements.

The treaty process allows a minority of senators, representing perhaps an even smaller minority of the national population, to block international agreements. This point also has a flip side. While perhaps unlikely, it is also possible under the treaty process for two-thirds of the Senate to force the nation to enter into a treaty without the support of the majority of the people. According to recent population estimates, two-thirds of the Senate can represent as little as 32 percent of the population. If the sixteen most populous states opposed a treaty, producing thirty-two Senate votes out of one hundred, they would represent 185.6 million of the nation's estimated 272.7 million people, or 68 percent of the population.[53] To be sure, the presence of a popularly elected president provides a safeguard against the chances of an antimajoritarian treaty, but presidential participation is not a complete protection for majority rule, particularly once a president enters his or her second term. Establishing a process in which the House's prerogatives over domestic legislation are preserved by the congressional-executive agreement provides yet another security for popular sovereignty.

Mandating that treaties serve as the exclusive method for making international agreements, on the other hand, would generate tension in the public lawmaking process. Just as complete interchangeability creates textual and structural difficulties by importing doctrines that apply only to statutes into the foreign policymaking process, so too treaty exclusivity disrupts the finely tuned statutory methods for regulating domestic affairs. Allowing treaties to exercise legislative power would shift the locus of lawmaking from the legislature to the executive branch. Although the president surely has a significant political role in the initiation and enactment of legislation, the institutional weight behind domestic policymaking gives Congress at least an equal, if not dominant, role in the passage of statutes. Without congressional-executive agreements, and with a limitless scope on the subject matter of treaties, the treaty could shift the center of gravity in domestic regulation to the executive branch from the legislature.

This would be a significant change to the public lawmaking process because of the differences between making treaties and making statutes. Although the Constitution provides for a senatorial "advice and consent" function, this role has become one of after-the-fact consent. The president, not the Senate, decides whether to negotiate with other countries and on what subjects. It is the executive branch, rather than the House or Senate, that conducts the negotiations and actually concludes the treaty. Indeed, the Constitution forbids Congress from sending its own representatives in foreign negotiations because of the president's plenary power to appoint and receive ambassadors. Further, as we have seen, the Constitution vests the president with the plenary power to serve as the "sole organ" of the nation in its foreign relations. The president takes the primary role in enforcing treaties, and it is often his understanding, as expressed to the Senate during the advice and consent process, that counts in future interpretation of the treaty. Demands for flexibility, speed, and unity of action in foreign affairs have almost inevitably led to the flow of power to the executive. Requiring that treaties enjoy legislative power threatens to import these pro-executive structures into the normal lawmaking process.

Termination of treaties draws these problems into sharp relief. Statutes require a repealing statute to terminate their provisions. As discussed earlier, however, practice shows that treaties may be terminated by unilateral presidential action. This difference creates a serious anomaly in the constitutional structure. If the political branches choose to regulate domestic conduct by statute, the president cannot terminate the rules without Congress's permission. If, however, the political branches should regulate the same conduct by treaty, the president can terminate the regulation at will. Treaty exclusivity, therefore, has the effect of expanding the president's powers as more and more aspects of domestic life can be regulated by international agreement rather than by statute. A doctrine whereby congressional-executive agreements are needed to enter into agreements that have domestic legislative effects preserves the balance of powers among the branches. In conjunction with the theory of self-execution and the growing internationalization of domestic affairs, treaty exclusivity provokes an irreconcilable conflict between the executive and legislative powers. Congressional-executive agreements provide a way to resolve this tension by allowing Congress to retain authority over those matters delegated to it by the Constitution, even when an international agreement threatens to intrude on its plenary powers.

PRACTICE AND CONGRESSIONAL-EXECUTIVE AGREEMENTS

A durable theory of international agreements should take practice into account. Theory should not only explain this record, but also provide a satisfactory account of how the making of international agreements interacts with our general public lawmaking system. Theories that create anomalies and contradictions in the way the branches make laws ought to be rejected in favor of a theory that accounts for practice in a manner consistent with the text, structure, and original understanding of the Constitution. Judged by these standards, the New Deal, Ackerman and Golove, and exclusivist approaches fail. If Corwin, Henkin, or Ackerman and Golove were right, congressional-executive agreements should be used to make all international agreements, while if Tribe were right, treaties would be used exclusively. The political branches continue to use both instruments of foreign policy, and in a way that maintains subject-matter distinctions between the two, something that none of the academic theories canvassed above can explain. This record shows how deeper structural imperatives in the Constitution have led the branches to interact in a way that harmonizes their potentially conflicting powers. A theory of congressional-executive agreements that limits their scope to matters within Congress's Article I, Section 8 powers, while reserving treaties for matters outside Congress's plenary authorities, is the only one that makes sense of practice and reduces distortion to the constitutional text and structure.

Neither complete interchangeability nor treaty exclusivity has been borne out in practice. A review of American postwar international agreements indicates that the political branches have reserved certain areas, specifically national security and arms control, for the treaty process. The political branches' respect for subject-matter distinctions between treaties and congressional-executive agreements not only directly contradicts the interchangeability thesis, but also shows the deeper separation of powers principles at work.[54] What follows is a summary of the manner in which the political branches have reserved agreements in certain subjects for treaties, while others are open to congressional-executive agreements.

Political Agreements. In the early postwar period, a number of significant agreements were reached by treaty: the peace treaties with Japan and Italy; the entry of the United States into the United Nations and the North Atlantic Treaty Organization (NATO); and the current web of U.S. mutual defense agreements, such as bilateral agreements with South Korea, the Philippines, Japan, and Taiwan (terminated in 1978), and multilateral security arrangements, such as the Southeast Asian Treaty Organization, the Australian–New Zealand–U.S. agreement, and the Rio Treaty.[55] Subsequent, less-intensive security agreements, such as promises to defend against threats, training of local forces, or pre-positioning of equipment, have resulted from unilateral executive declarations or sole executive agreements, and none of these have risen to the level of seriousness of America's entry into the United Nations or NATO.[56] Perhaps the most significant international security arrangements to arise from the end of the Cold War were formalized by treaty—the final settlement with regard to Germany and the expansion of NATO to include some of the nations of the formerly communist Eastern Europe.[57] While some exceptions exist, they do not seem to undermine the general subject-matter trend.[58]

Arms Control. Recent experience with arms control cuts even more sharply against interchangeability. Since the end of World War II, presidents have submitted to the Senate as treaties almost every significant arms control agreement, such as the Limited Nuclear Test-Ban Treaty, the Threshold Test-Ban Treaty, the Anti-Ballistic Missile Treaty, the Nuclear Non-Proliferation Treaty, the Intermediate-Range Nuclear Forces Treaty, and the Treaty on Conventional Armed Forces in Europe.[59] These agreements established the policy of nuclear deterrence through mutually assured destruction, restricted the spread of nuclear weapons, and began the demilitarization of Europe. There appears to have been only one exception to this consistent pattern: approval by statute of the first round of the Strategic Arms Limitations Talks (SALT I) between the United States and the Soviet Union, which imposed limits on the nuclear warheads and delivery vehicles possessed by the superpowers.[60] Approval of SALT I by statute, however, cannot serve as a firm precedent for interchangeability. The agreement had a limited duration of only five years; both sides understood that it would be replaced by a permanent pact, SALT II. Indeed, the agreement was formally known as the SALT I Interim Agreement. And when negotiation of SALT II was finally completed, President Carter initially sent the agreement to the Senate for approval as a treaty, but then did not press for its approval in the wake of the Soviet invasion of Afghanistan. Presidents Reagan and Bush never asked the Senate to approve the agreement.[61]

Experience since the Cold War has only reaffirmed the consistent use of the treaty to make arms control agreements. Presidents have submitted to the Senate bilateral agreements between the United States and Russia, such as the Strategic Arms Reduction Talks (START) I and II agreements, which have reduced the level of nuclear warheads and restricted the use of certain delivery systems. Presidents have sent to the Senate agreements that have reduced the positioning of conventional weapons in the European theater of operations, and that have allowed unimpeded overflights to verify compliance with arms control pacts. The political branches have also chosen to use the treaty process to approve controversial multilateral arms control agreements, such as the Chemical Weapons Convention, even when they faced significant opposition in the Senate.[62] Agreements that the United States has not yet signed, such as the Land Mines Convention, and agreements still in development, such as the strengthening of the Biological Weapons Convention, would take the form of treaties, rather than of congressional-executive agreements.[63]

In part, this consistent treaty practice has resulted from Senate efforts to defend its prerogatives. During ratification of the last round of arms control agreements, as Phillip Trimble has observed, the Senate included in the resolution of advice and consent a condition that all future agreements involving military, security, or arms control issues be submitted to the Senate as treaties rather than as congressional-executive agreements.[64] Senate attachment of this condition expresses the intention not to accept the theory of interchangeability, and indicates that the Senate will enforce this understanding of the Constitution by refusing to approve any international agreements that do not take the treaty form. Indeed, the Clinton administration so understood the condition and agreed to abide by it.

Human Rights. In addition to political/military and arms control agreements, one of the most significant areas of recent American foreign policy—human rights—is conducted primarily through treaties rather than congressional-executive agreements. Historically, significant human rights agreements, such as the Hague Regulations on the rules of war and the Geneva Conventions, underwent the supermajority Senate consent process.[65] More recently, the first Bush administration used treaties to formalize American entry into the International Covenant on Civil and Political Rights (ICCPR), which guarantees certain minimum individual rights in the political sphere, and the Genocide Convention, which makes genocide a crime against humanity. President Clinton followed suit. The two important human rights agreements approved during his presidency, the Convention against Torture in 1994 and, that same year, the International Convention on the Elimination of All Forms of Racial Discrimination, took the treaty form. Four other multilateral human rights agreements that supporters once thought that the Clinton administration would seek to join—the Convention on the Elimination of all Forms of Discrimination against Women, the Covenant on Economic, Social and Cultural Rights, the Inter-American Convention on Human Rights, and the Convention on the Rights of the Child—also would take treaty form, even in the face of likely Senate opposition. Indeed, it is difficult to think of a human rights agreement that has gone through two-house approval rather than through the president and Senate alone.[66]

These human rights treaties show that the political branches recognize a distinction between treaties and congressional-executive agreements. Some human rights agreements have languished in the Senate for up to thirty years. The ICCPR, for example, was first proposed in 1966, but was not ratified until 1992. The Genocide Convention was first presented in 1948, but was not ratified by the United States until 1989. Senate leaders opposed several of these treaties out of concern that they require more expansive individual rights than those in the Constitution. To mention one disreputable example, southern senators feared that certain human rights treaty provisions would hasten the dismantling of segregation.[67] If treaties and congressional-executive agreements truly were interchangeable, presidents could have short-circuited this opposition by sending human rights agreements to both houses of Congress for majority approval. This course of action would have been all the more successful once much of the political opposition to the goals of the treaties had disappeared in the wake of the civil rights revolution. Yet it does not appear that presidents have ever attempted to use the alternate statutory procedure to avoid such political opposition in the Senate.[68]

Extradition. Yet another area where the political branches generally have resorted to treaties to reach international agreements has been extradition. Under standard extradition agreements, one nation agrees to surrender a person charged with or convicted of a crime under the law of another state, so that the latter state may try or punish the individual.[69] Although at one time it was thought that nations had a duty to grant extradition freely, customary international law never recognized a general duty to surrender fugitives. As a result, the United States and other nations have entered into a web of bilateral agreements that generally require showing cause to hold a person, that the offense has been created by treaty or statute, that the offense was within the jurisdiction of the requesting country, and that double jeopardy would not be violated.[70] Article 27 of the 1794 Jay Treaty with Great Britain contained the first American extradition provision, and, as Ruth Wedgwood has argued, its implementation by President John Adams produced one of the early Republic's great foreign policy crises.[71]

Extradition poses an interesting question in regard to federal power, as Congress does not appear to possess any textual authority to provide for the seizure of an individual on American soil and for his delivery to a foreign nation for trial. Since the Jay Treaty, however, the political branches have used Article II treaties to reach extradition agreements with more than a hundred nations.[72] Only a single recent example is to the contrary: in 1994 and 1995, the president entered into executive agreements with the International Criminal Tribunals for the Former Yugoslavia and Rwanda to surrender persons within the United States charged or convicted by those tribunals. Rather than approval by treaty, Congress implemented the agreements by expanding federal extradition laws—which until 1996 had implemented treaties—to include the two international tribunals. In a 1999 challenge brought by a Rwandan citizen in the United States indicted by the Rwanda tribunal, a divided panel of the U.S. Court of Appeals for the Fifth Circuit upheld the use of the congressional-executive agreement.[73] In dissent, Judge DeMoss demonstrated that the majority's new exception proves the rule. "Every extradition agreement ever entered into by the United States (before the advent of the new Tribunals) has been accomplished by treaty. . . ."[74] Aside from this sole, rushed example, extradition has stood as another example in which the treaty power has provided the sole mechanism for reaching international agreements.

Environment. In addition to extradition, the president and Senate have used the treaty process for most of the nation's significant environmental agreements. While perhaps not as crucial to national security as alliances or arms control, international environmental treaties may represent the most legislation-like agreements in their setting of norms for domestic private conduct. The United States has entered into agreements limiting pollution, such as the Montreal Protocol, which accelerated the retirement of certain chemicals that harmed the ozone layer, and the Convention on Transboundary Pollution, which seeks to reduce cross-border air pollution, by the treaty process. Agreements that protect certain environments, such as the Antarctic region or outer space, or endangered species, such as whales, polar bears, migratory birds, and seals, also have undergone approval by a supermajority of the Senate. More ambitious regulatory agreements, such as the U.N. Convention on Climate Change, also have undergone the treaty process.[75] As with human rights treaties, presidents have agreed to submit these pacts to the Senate even when they could have avoided significant opposition by resorting to the two-house procedure. Presidents have delayed the submission of controversial environmental agreements, such as agreements that would require the nation to protect biodiversity and to restrict its energy use and industrial pollution, because of likely Senate opposition.[76] Although President Reagan decided against submitting to the Senate one of the most significant international environmental agreements, the Law of the Sea Convention, it is currently under consideration by the Senate again as a treaty, rather than a congressional-executive agreement. Indeed, if the interchangeability theory were correct, a sufficient majority of Congress could have enacted a statute entering into the Law of the Sea Convention over President Reagan's opposition.[77]

Examination of postwar practice by the political branches thus reveals a manageable line between treaties and congressional-executive agreements. The president and Senate have used the statutory process to approve agreements that generally involve international trade and economics. These subjects fall within Congress's Article I, Section 8 power over international commerce and often require modification of existing statutory law to bring the United States into compliance. The president and Senate, it appears, still reserve certain classes of subjects for the treaty process, primarily national security, arms control, human rights, and the environment. These areas bear important constitutional differences from international economics and commerce.[78] Subjects such as national security and arms control, for example, fall primarily within the president's plenary powers as commander in chief and sole organ of the nation in its foreign relations. They also involve concurrent powers on the part of Congress, such as those of appropriations and of declaring war. It is unclear what congressional power could justify extradition—the seizure of persons because of their alleged acts in foreign countries, regardless of their involvement in interstate or international commerce—due to the lack of an explicit enumerated power. Environmental law straddles the line between treaties and congressional-executive agreements—while some environmental matters rest within Congress's powers over interstate commerce, others (especially more recent environmental agreements addressing energy use or biodiversity) might not, in light of the recent restrictions on the Commerce Clause imposed by the Supreme Court.

CONCLUSION

Conceiving of congressional-executive agreements as occupying the sphere of international agreements that involve Congress's Article I powers has important implications for foreign affairs law and the making of international agreements. It predicts what types of future international agreements will undergo the statutory or treaty processes. It indicates how the political branches may address several of the difficulties that will arise with future international agreements. It also provides an understanding of the changing choice of instruments over time. Two developments make the choice of statute versus treaty significant. As domestic affairs become more global, international agreements will come to play a more important role in domestic regulation. At the same time, the Supreme Court's effort to protect state sovereignty and to impose new checks on congressional power removes more areas from the reach of the legislature. This phenomenon may place pressure on the political branches to turn to treaties to engage in the regulation of noncommercial activities or individual rights. Because of these trends, whether the political branches adopt an international agreement by treaty or by statute will bear important consequences for the scope of federal jurisdiction and the substance of national regulation.

While they may appear identical under international law, the difference between statutes and treaties makes a significant difference for domestic purposes. The constitutional differences between the two dictate what form the political branches must use to enter into certain types of international agreements. Future trade agreements or expansion of American free trade areas will continue to undergo the statutory process because they involve Congress's powers over foreign commerce. Agreements that rest outside Congress's plenary powers, such as human rights, political/military, and arms control, will still require use of the Treaty Clause. Some areas, such as the environment, may rest somewhere in between. Although much domestic environmental legislation presumably passes constitutional muster under the Commerce Clause, the noncommercial nature of proposed international environmental agreements and the Supreme Court's new restrictions on the Commerce Clause may require use of the treaty form. As the scope of the Commerce Clause recedes and efforts to harmonize domestic regulation with international standards increase, the Treaty Clause may present a more reliable source for legislative power.

Maintaining this line between congressional-executive agreements and treaties achieves two larger goals. First, it maintains a distinction between the executive and legislative powers, which allows Congress to check executive branch foreign policy that has direct domestic effects. Second, this line comports closely with the practice of the political branches since the end of World War II. If the nation is to enjoy the benefits of a choice of instruments to pursue its foreign policy goals, it needs a constitutional theory to explain the coexistence of both treaties and congressional-executive agreements. An approach that keeps treaties within the executive power and congressional-executive agreements within Congress's Article I powers supplies a durable approach that harmonizes the constitutional text, structure, and history with practice.

9

THE CONSTITUTION AND
THE MULTILATERAL FUTURE

Conventional wisdom on the legal framework governing American foreign relations has suffered from three significant flaws. First, scholars have sought to impose a strict, legalistic process on the interaction of the executive and legislative branches in reaching decisions on war and peace. Second, they have claimed that the original understanding of the framing generation both dictates the limitation of presidential power in foreign affairs and establishes a broad power in the federal government to make and implement international agreements and international law. Third, they rely on judicial intervention to enforce this precise vision of the balance of powers in foreign affairs, backed up as it is by the original understanding.

This book offers a different approach to foreign affairs and American constitutional law. I have argued that rather than a legalistic process, the Constitution establishes a more flexible, dynamic approach to the resolution of questions of war and peace. It is not a strict framework, determined by the original understanding and enforced by the federal judiciary, which enforces checks and balances on the exercise of the foreign affairs power. Rather, foreign policy emerges from the interaction of the plenary powers of the different branches of government. Congress may set its powers over funding and legislation against the president's Article II authorities in war and treatymaking and his structural advantages in wielding power, or the branches may choose to cooperate to reach foreign policy outcomes. Aside from preserving to each branch its core constitutional competencies, the Constitution allows the political branches to shape a variety of processes for deciding on matters ranging from war to peace to international cooperation.

War powers demonstrate the differences in these approaches. Leading scholars believe that the Declare War Clause requires that Congress approve all uses of force before the president may send the military into combat. They claim support from the original understanding, in which the Framers allegedly wanted to clog the channels of war by requiring the most numerous body of government to decide the question. As James Wilson said, "This system will not hurry us into war; it is calculated to guard against it. It will not be in the power of a single man, or a single body of men, to involve us in such distress."[1] If the president wages war without Congress's consent, these scholars argue, the federal courts must declare the conflict unconstitutional.

As we have seen, this proposal runs counter to the pattern of recent history, in which presidents have sent American troops to do battle in such places as Korea and Kosovo without congressional authorization. The Bush administration seems to be the exception that proves the rule by seeking, and receiving, statutory approval by Congress before launching wars in Afghanistan in October 2001 and Iraq in March 2003. Rather than violating the Constitution, however, the practice of unilateral presidential warmaking falls within the permissible bounds of discretion granted to the political branches. With large militaries designed to project overwhelming force throughout the world at his disposal, the president as commander in chief holds the initiative to use force abroad. Congress can always cut off the funding for military adventures, which in the era of modern war may mean simply refusing to appropriate new funds or constructing offensive weapons systems. This effective check on the president's power renders unnecessary any formal process requirement for congressional authorization or a declaration of war before hostilities may begin.

This basic structure, in which the political branches check each other without the need for judicial intervention, defies the conventional academic wisdom. Thus, in the setting of foreign policy, the interpretation of treaties and international law, and the termination of international agreements, the president may enjoy the initiative due to the formal and functional presumptions that the unenumerated foreign affairs power rests with the executive. Nonetheless, Congress can control the practical exercise of these powers by refusing to fund presidential programs, by enacting laws at odds with executive foreign policy, and by structuring a military in keeping with its preferred strategy for international relations. If Congress wishes to force termination of the ABM Treaty, for example, it can fund a national missile defense; if it wants to keep the agreement, Congress can simply defund research and development work into anti-missile systems. Similarly, Congress can control the scope of the treaty power by preventing the domestic implementation of international obligations, which also has the effect of preserving Congress's constitutional authority over the matters reserved to it under Article I, Section 8.

Throughout these debates, evidence concerning the original understanding of the Constitution has held an important place. Leading scholars have relied heavily on the statements of the Framers to support their views on the Constitution and foreign affairs. With regard to war powers, for example, John Ely states bluntly that "the 'original understanding' of the document's framers and ratifiers can be obscure to the point of inscrutability"; but "in this case it isn't." Therefore, the inescapable conclusion is that "all wars, big or small, 'declared' in so many words or not . . . had to be legislatively authorized."[2] Similarly, Michael Glennon has claimed that "original constitutional materials indicate that the Framers intended a narrowly circumscribed presidential war-making power, with the Commander in Chief Clause conferring minimal policy-making authority" except in the case of sudden attacks.[3] In this book, the Framers have also made a central appearance, but not to prove the existence of a specific process imposed by the Constitution in the area of war powers specifically, or foreign affairs generally. Rather, this book's goal is to present a more systematic and complete examination of foreign affairs during the framing period, extending from the context set by the political thought of Locke, Montesquieu, and Blackstone, to the history of the colonies and the Articles of Confederation, to the Federal Convention and the state ratification debates. A more comprehensive approach to these sources reveals that the original understanding does not dictate a specific process for foreign affairs decisions, but instead that the Framers anticipated a more fluid, flexible process in which decisions would be reached through the political interactions of the two branches. History shows that history itself does not demand a single answer to questions of war and peace.

While important in their own right, these timeless questions of war and peace are becoming even more important due to the most significant development in the international system since the end of the Cold War: globalization. Globalization represents more than just the simplistic notion of the spread of market capitalism throughout the world. It also represents an acceleration of the speed of communications, computer networks, and transportation systems that makes possible not just world markets, but also the global dissemination of ideas, news, and values. Globalization is neither wholly good nor wholly bad. It may lower prices and raise living standards, but it also can spread problems quickly to a global level. The growth of disease and crime, the emergence of transboundary pollution and the environmental degradation of global commons, and illicit movements in illegal goods (such as drugs) and human trafficking also arise from the channels of globalization. Indeed, the September 11 hijackings would not have been possible without the easy movement of people and money made possible by rapid transportation and the instantaneous movement of information and capital.

Globalization introduces new twists into the usual debates concerning the Constitution's regulation of international relations. The question whether the president can use force abroad unilaterally, or whether Congress must give its *ex ante* approval, may change when U.N. Security Council approval is required. Similarly, multilateral cooperation in warmaking may raise difficulties concerning the ability of U.S. troops to serve under the command of foreign officers with the compulsion of federal law. With regard to treaties, globalization places stress on existing legal doctrines by prompting international agreements that—in order to effectively coordinate international cooperation—regulate conduct within Congress's control or conduct usually thought of as within the jurisdiction of the states. A treaty on global warming, for example, would limit energy use in the United States, whether residential or industrial. Treaties on human rights require the expansion of individual liberties beyond that currently set by the federal Constitution. Other international agreements raise novel issues concerning government structure, such as whether the International Court of Justice can enjoin state use of the death penalty, whether inspectors for the Chemical Weapons Convention can conduct warrantless searches of U.S. industrial facilities, whether American service personnel can be tried by an International Criminal Court that uses different procedures and enforces different crimes than American criminal law, and whether NAFTA and WTO bodies can adjudicate trade disputes involving American companies.

This book's approach to war powers, treaties, and the relationship between international agreements and domestic law may provide solutions to the tensions between the constitutional structure and the new forms of international cooperation prompted by globalization. International legal scholarship is only beginning to comprehensively address the impact of globalization, which, when combined with the theories of the government's broad powers in foreign relations, places pressure on the basic governmental structure established by the Constitution. Many academics believe, for example, that treaties are not subject to the limits on federal power that apply to federal legislation, but instead may validly regulate any matter that is the subject of an international agreement. At a time when treaties generally involved political/military alliances or most-favored-nation status for imports, the scope of international agreements did not threaten to burst the limits on federal power over private conduct. Modern multilateral agreements, however, seek to create comprehensive international solutions to problems such as environmental protection, human rights, and even arms control, by directly regulating private individuals and their conduct—a function under the Constitution reserved either to Congress or the states. To recall the words of Abram and Antonia Chayes, while "[s]uch treaties are formally among states, and the obligations are cast as state obligations . . . [t]he real object of the treaty . . . is not to affect state behavior but to regulate the activities of individuals and private entities."[4]

These are not insurmountable tensions. By allowing the formal and functional advantages of the executive branch in foreign affairs to remain counterbalanced by Congress's control over funding and domestic regulation, it is possible to retain the main elements of the constitutional structure and permit the United States to take advantage of these new forms of international cooperation. This approach finds support not just in the constitutional text and structure but in the original understanding of the foreign affairs power and, perhaps most importantly, in the practice of the three branches of government. Maintaining Congress's role in managing domestic legislation explains the rise of the judicial doctrine of non-self-execution, of the efforts by the political branches to relieve treaties of domestic effect, and of the use of congressional-executive agreements for international economic regulation.

Resolution of these problems is not purely academic. Clarifying the relationship of the United States to these new forms of international cooperation is proving to be one of the nation's most important foreign policy challenges. Examine, for example, the current controversy over the International Criminal Court (ICC). The United States initially refused to agree to the Statute of Rome, called by some "the most important international juridical institution that has been proposed since the San Francisco Conference in 1945" that established the United Nations.[5] The ICC is a reaction, in part, to the growing problem of war crimes and crimes against humanity committed as part of internecine civil warfare. National solutions have been seen as ineffective, and ad hoc courts such as the U.N. war crimes tribunal for the former Yugoslavia have not been viewed with success. It is understandably hard for countries to try their former leaders for war crimes, and U.N. tribunals have had great difficulty in capturing suspects, defining crimes and procedures, and efficiently conducting their proceedings without sparking resentment from the affected nations. Several critics have also argued that the process of creating ad hoc U.N. tribunals, which requires the approval of the Security Council, slanted things in favor of the big powers. The ICC represents an international solution that would create an independent international organization that would "neutrally" enforce international criminal law, but in a way that directly regulates the conduct of individuals as well as states.

In his last weeks in office, President Clinton signed the ICC treaty. President Bush then withdrew the nation's signature, effectively terminating U.S. participation in the ICC. One of the principal objections to the ICC is that it would allow an international organization to second-guess American decisions about measures to protect its national security, its use of force, and even tactics. Madeline Morris has raised concerns that, in addition to individual criminal culpability, the ICC will be called on to judge the lawfulness of official state actions.[6] Ruth Wedgwood has observed that "the United States has understandably feared that good faith operational questions could be precipitously removed from their usual place of debate in alliance headquarters and military manuals, and be recast in a courtroom's criminal rhetoric."[7] Others, such as Jack Goldsmith, worried that the potential for ICC prosecution of American servicemen for unjustified or ambiguous war crimes might deter the United States from engaging in needed peacekeeping missions.[8] Members of Congress and Secretary of State Colin Powell were concerned that procedures in the ICC would not rise to the level of protections required by the Bill of Rights—the ICC, for example, does not have jury trials.[9] Currently, the United States is engaged in a broad diplomatic effort to sign treaties with ICC nations, which include all of its European allies, to exempt U.S. personnel from the court's jurisdiction. The United States has also threatened to terminate U.N. peacekeeping missions unless U.S. servicemen receive immunity from ICC prosecution, while ICC countries argue that the court should not be subject to the dictates of the Security Council or of the United States. Many of these concerns arise from the interaction between the Constitution and globalization: the relationship between the president's use of force and international rules, the extension of international organizations into areas once governed by domestic law, and the direct international regulation of individual conduct.

In addition to these policy objections, the ICC demands attention because it is a harbinger of things to come. The problems of globalization have prompted the formation of international institutions designed to coordinate a multilateral policy solution. As these international institutions increase in number and authority, they will place increasing pressure on the Constitution's structures for democratic decisionmaking and accountability. Both globalization protesters and those who worry about American sovereignty, such as Jeremy Rabkin and John Bolton, share the concern that the growing institutions of global governance suffer from a serious democracy deficit, an absence of transparency, and weak accountability. Bolton has argued that the costs of global governance, which include "reduced constitutional autonomy, impaired popular sovereignty, reduction of our international power, and limitations on our domestic and foreign policy options and solutions . . . are far too great."[10] Even Dean Joseph Nye, who generally favors American participation in multilateral institutions, recognizes that they easily suffer a lack of democratic legitimacy. "To develop the legitimacy of international governance will require three things," he argues, "1) greater clarity about democracy, 2) a richer understanding of accountability, and 3) a willingness to experiment."[11] For Anne-Marie Slaughter, the "critical question is how to build global democracy to the extent necessary to establish and enhance the legitimacy of existing and emerging international institutions."[12]

As seen through the different lens of a constitutional lawyer, these concerns are not solely a matter of good institutional design. They result from the conflict between the policy need for international institutions and the standards of democracy and accountability established by our constitutional system. Both sides of the debate recognize that in order to be successful, international institutions must have a stronger democratic basis. This book has begun the first steps toward a framework for understanding and addressing how global governance can work within the contours of the American Constitution.

Resolving this tension is important not just for the design of international institutions, but for the stability of American constitutional law and the political system. Events today appear to parallel those of almost a century ago, when the United States underwent nationalization of its markets and society. As the conventional story goes, ways of thinking about the Constitution remained stuck in a prenationalized, agrarian economy. Under this view, the national government did not have the constitutional authority to regulate wages and working conditions, to deal with unemployment or poverty, or to oversee manufacturing or commerce. This view was shared by the Supreme Court, which was still following *Lochner* to prevent regulation of wages and hours, and the *Child Labor Cases* to limit federal control to trade that crossed interstate borders, and even the Democratic Party, which generally emphasized states rights and limited government. [13]

Every student of constitutional law knows the rest of the story. In response to the Great Depression, itself the manifestation of a nationalized economy, President Franklin D. Roosevelt and the Democratic Party swept into office and began the enactment of a recovery program. The New Deal put into place the foundations of the national regulatory state: broad federal power to manage the national economy and independent agencies removed from politics to more precisely and accurately regulate that economy. In 1934 and 1935, the Supreme Court resisted this new institutional design and invalidated the National Industrial Recovery Act and the Agricultural Adjustment Act, two core planks of FDR's recovery program, as well as state and smaller New Deal statutes that suggested that more important programs regulating unions and labor conditions would soon meet their end. [14] Emboldened by a landslide victory in the 1936 elections, President Roosevelt responded with his famous court-packing plan, which attempted to change the Supreme Court's direction by expanding its size.[15] In the "switch in time that saved Nine," the Court headed off the plan by reversing course and upholding, in 1937, a state minimum wage statute, federal labor laws, and social security, when in effect approved the basic elements of the New Deal.

President Roosevelt's court-packing plan went down to defeat, but the Supreme Court and constitutional law suffered no victory either. While Barry Cushman has argued that constitutional doctrine, as it had internally developed by 1935, provided sufficient flexibility to allow the Court to reach its 1937 decisions consistently with its previous cases, even he acknowledges that the lesson learned is that the justices acted in a legally unprincipled, yet politically astute, manner to avoid further political damage to the Court.[16] This resulted in a bloodless constitutional revolution without amendments. As Cass Sunstein has written, the New Deal "altered the constitutional system in ways so fundamental as to suggest that something akin to a constitutional amendment had taken place."[17] Because of what many have seen as the Court's blatantly political switch, the legitimacy of elements of the New Deal revolution remain open to question, either by those who wish to restrict the Commerce Clause or others who believe that elements of the administrative state are unconstitutional.[18]

Globalization has launched a similar transformation, with the same chance of constitutional confrontation and breakdown, as the one that occurred almost a century ago. Just as nationalization created a demand for regulation of the economy at the national level, whether that took the form of suppression of state barriers to trade or uniform rules for manufacturing, so too globalization has increased the need for regulation at the international level. The needs for global regulation parallel those that have arisen in the United States under the administrative state. As John McGinnis and Mark Movsesian have argued, the WTO reduces national trade barriers in much the same way that the dormant Commerce Clause allowed interstate commerce to flow free of state restrictions.[19] International environmental regulation seeks to end the negative externalities of pollution or species extinction in the same way that national environmental regulations have sought the same goals. Like domestic national regulation, international regulation both seeks to keep open the channels of the international marketplace, and to develop collective regulations to address the problems created by that market.

In order to achieve these ends, international regulation has mirrored the legal foundations of the domestic regulatory state: expanded governmental regulation and independent, supposedly neutral, institutions. The New Deal state ushered in a broad power over interstate commerce thought to be virtually limitless until *United States v. Lopez* and *United States v. Morrison* placed some outer limits on the reach of federal regulatory power.[20] Similarly, international agreements seek to regulate all activity in the areas, for example, of human rights or the environment regardless of domestic constitutional structures. The Kyoto accords would limit all energy use, whether subject to congressional or state regulation. Human rights conventions hold both federal and state officials liable to standards that meet or exceed constitutional requirements. Both the New Deal state and the new tools for global governance raise the same questions and difficulties about the scope of federal power, with only the substitution of the Treaty Clause for the Commerce Clause as its source. Whether it is the Treaty or Commerce Clause, however, the questions are the same: what is the appropriate scope of federal power; what relationship must private conduct have to the subjects of federal (or international) regulation; does the Constitution reserve any power to the states?

Parallels also arise with regard to institutions. The New Deal gave birth to an administrative state that ideally is insulated from political pressure and applies technical expertise to its area. Congress has delegated substantial legislative authority to administrative agencies, which are shielded in various ways from direct presidential control. Scholars such as Steve Calabresi, Gary Lawson, and Sai Prakash have criticized the constitutionality of the administrative state precisely for its best attributes.[21] They argue that the administrative state exercises vague, general power unlawfully delegated from Congress, and that independent agencies unconstitutionally disrupt the unity of the executive branch. Only by maintaining a delegation doctrine and making all executive officers accountable to the president, these scholars (and some justices) believe, can the administrative state be rendered democratically accountable and consistent with the separation of powers. International organizations take a similar form, designed as they are to address similar problems, and hence raise the same issues. International institutions, such as the WTO and the Chemical Weapons Convention secretariat, or even the International Court of Justice and the International Criminal Court, suffer from accountability problems and democracy deficits precisely because they are designed to be neutral and independent from the control of any nation or group of nations. This is not to argue that all international institutions raise accountability and separation of power problems, nor that all international regulatory agreements run up against the Constitution's basic framework of a national government with limited, enumerated powers. Rather, at this stage in the development of international law and institutions, I wish only to identify this growing trend toward global governance and how it raises questions for constitutional law similar to those brought forth by nationalization in the United States over the last century. It is the task of foreign relations law scholars to develop an approach that will harmonize these new methods of international cooperation—"the new sovereignty," in the words of Abram and Antonia Chayes—with the forms and structures demanded by the Constitution. This book has sought to identify the general outlines of an answer in the hopes that the American constitutional system need not undergo the same disruption in adapting to globalization that it experienced during the New Deal eighty years ago.

NOTES

PREFACE

1. *The Continuation of Politics by Other Means: The Original Understanding of War Powers,* 84 Cal. L. Rev. 167 (1996); *Politics as Law? The Anti-Ballistic-Missile Treaty, the Separation of Powers, and Treaty Interpretation,* 89 Cal. L. Rev. 851 (2001).

2. *War and Constitutional Text,* 69 U. Chi. L. Rev. 1639 (2002).

3. *Globalism and the Constitution: Treaties, Non-Self-Execution, and the Original Understanding,* 99 Colum. L. Rev. 1955 (1999).

4. *Laws as Treaties? The Constitutionality of Congressional-Executive Agreements,* 99 Mich. L. Rev. 757 (2001).

5. *Point/Counterpoint: Kosovo, War Powers, and the Multilateral Future,* 148 U. Pa. L. Rev. 1673 (2000).

CHAPTER ONE

1. John Hart Ely, War and Responsibility: Constitutional Lessons of Vietnam and Its Aftermath ix (1993).

2. Thomas Franck, Political Questions/Judicial Answers: Does the Rule of Law Apply to Foreign Affairs? 30 (1992).

3. *Campbell v. Clinton,* 203 F.3d 19 (D.C. Cir. 2000) (dismissing challenge to constitutionality of Kosovo conflict); *Doe v. Bush,* 323 F.3d 133 (1st Cir. 2003) (dismissing challenge to legality of war in Iraq).

4. Bruce Ackerman & David Golove, *Is NAFTA Constitutional,* 108 Harv. L. Rev. 799 (1995); Laurence H. Tribe, *Taking Text and Structure Seriously: Reflections on Free-Form Method in Constitutional Interpretation,* 108 Harv. L. Rev. 1221 (1995).

5. Compare Derek Jinks & David Sloss, *Is the President Bound by the Geneva Conventions?* 90 Cornell L. Rev. 97 (2004), with John C. Yoo & James C. Ho, *The Status of Terrorists,* 44 Va. J. Int'l L. 207 (2003), and John C. Yoo, *Treaty Interpretation and the False Sirens of Delegation,* 90 Cal. L. Rev. 1305 (2002).

6. See John C. Yoo, *Globalism and the Constitution,* 99 Colum. L. Rev. 1955, 2080–86 (1999).

7. See, e.g., *Foster v. Neilson,* 27 U.S. (2 Pet.) 253, 314 (1829).

8. See, e.g., Carlos M. Vázquez, *The Four Doctrines of Self-Executing Treaties,* 89 Am. J. Int'l L. 695 (1995).

9. Yoo, *supra* note 6, at 1967–76. This practice is criticized in Louis Henkin, Foreign Affairs and the United States Constitution 201 (1996); Jordan J. Paust, *Self-*

Executing Treaties, 82 Am. J. Int'l L. 760, 760 (1988); Carlos Manuel Vázquez, *Treaty-Based Rights and Remedies of Individuals,* 92 Colum. L. Rev. 1082, 1087 (1992).

10. For a description of this practice, see Stefan A. Riesenfeld & Frederick M. Abbott, *The Scope of U.S. Senate Control over the Conclusion and Operation of Treaties,* in Parliamentary Participation in the Making and Operation of Treaties 261 (Stefan A. Riesenfeld & Frederick M. Abbott eds., 1994).

11. These issues are discussed in greater detail in John C. Yoo, *Politics as Law?: The Anti-Ballistic-Missile Treaty, the Separation of Powers, and Treaty Interpretation,* 89 Cal. L. Rev. 851 (2001).

12. The historical details here are drawn from Stanley M. Elkins & Eric L. McKitrick, The Age of Federalism 303–73 (1993); Forrest McDonald, The Presidency of George Washington 113–37 (1974).

13. The Neutrality Proclamation provoked the famous Pacificus-Helvidius debate between Hamilton and Madison, see Pacificus No. 1 (June 29, 1793), reprinted in 15 Papers of Hamilton at 39 (Harold C. Syrett ed., 1962); Helvidius Nos. 1–5 (1793), reprinted in 15 Papers of James Madison 66–120 (Thomas A. Mann et al. eds., 1985).

14. Louis Henkin, Foreign Affairs and the U.S. Constitution (1996); Harold Hongju Koh, The National Security Constitution: Sharing Power after the Iran-Contra Affair (1990); Michael J. Glennon, Constitutional Diplomacy (1990).

15. *Youngstown Sheet & Tube Co. v. Sawyer,* 343 U.S. 579 (1952).

16. Id. at 634–39.

17. Ely, *supra* note 1, at 3; Franck, *supra* note 2.

18. See, e.g., Curtis A. Bradley & Jack L. Goldsmith, *Customary International Law as Federal Common Law: A Critique of the Modern Position,* 110 Harv. L. Rev. 815 (1997); Jack L. Goldsmith, *Federal Courts, Federalism, and Foreign Affairs,* 83 Va. L. Rev. 1617 (1997); Curtis A. Bradley, *The Treaty Power and American Federalism,* 97 Mich. L. Rev. 390 (1998); Michael D. Ramsey, *Executive Agreements and the (Non)Treaty Power,* 77 N.C. L. Rev. 134 (1998); Saikrishna B. Prakash & Michael D. Ramsey, *The Executive Power over Foreign Affairs,* 111 Yale L.J. 231 (2001).

19. See, e.g., Peter J. Spiro, *Globalization and the (Foreign Affairs) Constitution,* 63 Ohio St. L.J. 649 (2002); Martin S. Flaherty, *History Right?: Historical Scholarship, Original Understanding, and Treaties as "Supreme Law of the Land,"* 99 Colum. L. Rev. 2095 (1999); Carlos Manuel Vázquez, *Laughing at Treaties,* 99 Colum. L. Rev. 2154 (1999); David Golove, *Treaty-Making and the Nation,* 98 Mich. L. Rev. 1075 (2000); William M. Treanor, *Fame, the Founding, and the Power to Declare War,* 82 Cornell L. Rev. 695, 700 (1997); Sarah H. Cleveland, *The Plenary Power Background of* Curtiss-Wright, 70 Colo. L. Rev. 1127 (1999).

20. See Robert J. Delahunty & John C. Yoo, *The President's Constitutional Authority to Conduct Military Operations against Terrorist Organizations and the Nations that Harbor or Support Them,* 25 Harv. J.L. & Pub. Pol'y 487, 503 (2002).

21. *Dames & Moore v. Regan,* 453 U.S. 654, 661 (1981).

22. *Youngstown Sheet & Tube Co. v. Sawyer,* 343 U.S. 579, 610 (1952) (Frankfurter, J., concurring).

23. See, e.g., *Mistretta v. United States,* 488 U.S. 361, 393 (1989) (recognizing the significance of understanding practical consequences when determining the placement of commissions within the federal government); *Youngstown Sheet & Tube Co.,* 343 U.S. at 637 (1952) (Jackson, J., concurring) ("[C]ongressional inertia, indifference or quiescence may sometimes, at least as a practical matter, enable, if not invite, measures on independent presidential responsibility."); *United States v. Midwest Oil Co.,* 236 U.S. 459, 474 (1915) (noting that a "long-continued practice, known to and acquiesced in by Congress" creates a presumption that the practice is legitimate).

24. See, e.g., Eugene V. Rostow, *"Once More Unto the Breach": "The War Powers Resolution Revisited,* 21 Val. U. L. Rev. 1 (1986). See also Robert H. Bork, *Erosion of the President's Power in Foreign Affairs,* 68 Wash. U. L.Q. 693 (1990).

25. See Office of the Legal Adviser, U.S. Dep't of State, The Legality of United States Participation in the Defense of Viet-nam (1966), reprinted in 1 The Vietnam War and International Law 583, 597 (Richard A. Falk ed., 1968) (125 incidents); Congressional Research Serv., Instances of Use of United States Armed Forces Abroad, 1789–1989 (Ellen C. Collier ed., 1989), reprinted in Thomas M. Franck & Michael J. Glennon, Foreign Relations and National Security Law 650 (1993).

26. See *Assignment of Ground Forces of the United States to Duty in the European Area: Hearings before the Senate Comms. on Foreign Relations and Armed Services,* 82d Cong., 1st Sess. 88–93 (1951) (testimony of Secretary of State Acheson); see also Dean Acheson, Present at the Creation: My Years in the State Department 402–15 (1969). In the Korean War, the vast majority of congressmen approved of President Truman's military response to the North Korean invasion, but Congress recessed soon after the initiation of the war and President Truman chose not to ask for formal congressional approval when Congress returned. Id. at 414–15.

27. While presidential critics such as Ely and Henkin generally attack unilateral executive warmaking in the postwar period, they find the Gulf of Tonkin Resolution to amount to acceptable congressional authorization for war, even though it was not a declaration of war. See Ely, *supra* note 1, at 16; Henkin, *supra* note 14, at 101–2. Other critics, however, believe the Vietnam War was unconstitutional as well. See, e.g., Arthur M. Schlesinger Jr., The Imperial Presidency 177–207 (1973); J. Gregory Sidak, *To Declare War,* 41 Duke L.J. 27 (1991); Francis D. Wormuth, *The Nixon Theory of the War Power: A Critique,* 60 Cal. L. Rev. 623, 690–94 (1972).

28. See War Powers Resolution, Pub. L. No. 93-148, 87 Stat. 555 (codified at 50 U.S.C. §§ 1541–48).

29. Presidents Ford and Carter never expressly recognized the resolution's binding force, and President Reagan refused to comply with the resolution when he ordered the use of force in Lebanon, Grenada, Libya, and the Persian Gulf. President George H. W. Bush sent messages notifying Congress of military interventions in Panama and the Persian Gulf that were "consistent with" the WPR, but that did not obey it. During the Gulf War, President Bush dispatched troops to the Middle East for well longer than permitted by the WPR's sixty-day clock. President Bush sent troops to Saudi Arabia within days of the August 2, 1990 Iraqi invasion of Kuwait, and engaged in a build-up that reached more than 430,000 troops by November 8, but did not receive a congressional resolution of support until January 12, 1991, more than five months after the first American deployment. American troops invaded Kuwait and Iraq shortly thereafter. See John C. Yoo, *The Continuation of Politics by Other Means: The Original Understanding of War Powers,* 84 Cal. L. Rev. 167, 186–88 (1996). Even as he asked for a congressional sign of support, President Bush argued that he already had the constitutional authority as president and commander in chief to implement U.N. Security Council Resolution 678, which asked member states to use "all necessary means" to force Iraqi troops out of Kuwait. When he signed Congress's joint resolution supporting the use of force to implement U.N. Resolution 678, H.R.J. Res. 77, 102d Cong., 1st Sess. (1991), Bush declared that "my signing this resolution does not constitute any change in the long-standing positions of the executive branch on either the President's constitutional authority to use the Armed Forces to defend vital U.S. interests or the constitutionality of the War Powers Resolution." Statement on Signing the Resolution Authorizing the Use of Military Force against Iraq, 27 Weekly Comp. Pres. Doc. 48 (Jan. 14, 1991). President Clinton

followed this example in Somalia, Haiti, Bosnia, and Kosovo. John C. Yoo, *Kosovo, War Powers, and the Multilateral Future,* 148 U. Pa. L. Rev. 1673, 1681 (2000).

30. Koh, *supra* note 14, at 117.

31. See Treaty of Amity, and Navigation, Nov. 19, 1794, U.S.-Gr. Brit., 8 U.S.T. 379; see generally discussion in Samuel Flagg Bemis, Jay's Treaty: A Study in Commerce and Diplomacy (rev. ed. 1962 [1923]).

32. See Jon Kyl, *Maintaining "Peace Through Strength": A Rejection of the Comprehensive Test Ban Treaty,* 37 Harv. J. on Legis. 325 (2000).

33. *Goldwater v. Carter,* 481 F. Supp. 949 (D.D.C.), *rev'd,* 617 F.2d 697, 716 (D.C. Cir. 1979), *vacated as moot,* 444 U.S. 996 (1979) (termination of treaty with Taiwan); George W. Bush, Remarks Announcing the United States Withdrawal from the Anti-Ballistic Missile Treaty, 37 Weekly Comp. Pres. Doc. 1783 (Dec. 13, 2001) (termination of ABM Treaty); Press Statement, U.S. Department of State, International Criminal Court: Letter to U.N. Secretary General Kofi Annan (May 6, 2002) (withdrawal from Treaty of Rome).

34. David Gray Adler, The Constitution and the Termination of Treaties 161 (1986) (nine out of eighteen treaties terminated by president); Executive *Goldwater v. Carter* Brief, at 21 (thirteen of twenty-six).

35. See *Clark v. Allen,* 331 U.S. 503, 509 (1947) (quoting *Techt v. Hughes,* 229 N.Y. 222, 242–43, *cert. denied,* 254 U.S. 643 [1920]) (termination of treaty by president and Senate). The Senate Foreign Relations Committee at one time claimed that "it is competent for the President and Senate, acting together, to terminate [a treaty] . . . without the aid or intervention of legislation by Congress." S. Rep. No. 97 at 3, 34th Cong., 1st Sess. (1856); *United States v. Stuart,* 489 U.S. 353, 375 (1989) (Scalia, J., concurring in the judgment) (congressional termination); see generally *Congressional Authority to Modify an Executive Agreement Settling Claims against Iran,* 4 A. Op. O.L.C. 289, 289 (1980) ("The authorities treat the power of Congress to enact statutes that supersede . . . treaties for purposes of domestic law as a plenary one, not subject to exceptions based on the President's broad powers concerning foreign affairs.").

36. When Senator Barry Goldwater challenged President Carter's unilateral termination of the Mutual Defense Treaty with Taiwan, the U.S. Court of Appeals for the District of Columbia Circuit held that the president enjoyed the constitutional authority to terminate international agreements. On appeal, the Supreme Court found the case nonjusticiable and dismissed the lawsuit. *Goldwater v. Carter,* 617 F.2d 697 (D.C. Cir. 1979), *vacated and dismissed,* 444 U.S. 996 (1979). Not surprisingly, the lower federal courts recently turned away a lawsuit by individual congressmen challenging President Bush's 2001 decision to withdraw the United States from the ABM Treaty as a case not subject to judicial review. *Kucinich v. Bush,* 236 F. Supp. 2d 1 (D.D.C. 2002).

37. See George Washington, Proclamation, reprinted in 1 Compilation of the Messages and Papers of the Presidents: 1789–1897, at 156 (James D. Richardson ed., 1900); Treaty of Alliance, Feb. 6, 1778, U.S.-Fr., Treaty Series 82, 7 Bevans 777; Treaty of Amity and Commerce, Feb. 6, 1778, U.S.-Fr., 8 Stat. 12.

38. In the first ABM controversy, senators claimed that the executive branch is bound by the understanding of a treaty held by both the Senate and president at the time a treaty is made, as reflected in contemporaneous statements and communications of both the Senate and the executive branch. See Yoo, *supra* note 11, at 858–64. For the differing points of view, see Abraham D. Sofaer, *The ABM Treaty and the Strategic Defense Initiative,* 99 Harv. L. Rev. 1972 (1986); Abram Chayes & Antonia Chayes, *Testing and Development of "Exotic" Systems under the ABM Treaty: The Great Reinterpretation Caper,* 99 Harv. L. Rev. 1956 (1986). In 1988, the Senate went

so far as to attach as a condition of ratification to the Intermediate Nuclear Forces Treaty that its meaning was fixed by the common understanding of the president and Senate at the time of ratification, and that any future reinterpretation of the treaty required Senate consent. See Joseph R. Biden Jr. & John B. Ritch III, *The Treaty Power: Upholding a Constitutional Partnership,* 137 U. Pa. L. Rev. 1529 (1989).

39. Even in domestic affairs, where the rights of Congress are more clearly established than is the case with foreign affairs, the courts recognize that the administrative agencies enjoy substantial deference in interpreting their statutes due to their superior expertise and democratic accountability. *Chevron, U.S.A. v. NRDC,* 467 U.S. 837, 865–66 (1984).

40. See Vázquez, *supra* note 8, at 706 (collecting cases).

41. See, e.g., *Goldstar (Panama) S.A. v. United States,* 967 F.2d 965, 969 (4th Cir. 1992); *More v. Intelcom Support Servs., Inc.,* 960 F.2d 466, 471 (5th Cir. 1992); *Frolova v. U.S.S.R.,* 761 F.2d 370, 374 (7th Cir. 1985); *Canadian Transp. Co. v. United States,* 663 F.2d 1081, 1092 (D.C. Cir. 1980); *Mannington Mills, Inc. v. Congoleum Corp.,* 595 F.2d 1287, 1299 (3d Cir. 1979); *United States v. Postal,* 589 F.2d 862 (5th Cir. 1979).

42. See generally Curtis A. Bradley & Jack L. Goldsmith, *Treaties, Human Rights, and Conditional Consent,* 149 U. Pa. L. Rev. 399 (2000) (detailing the U.S. treaty-making process and defending the role of proposed conditions in the ratification of treaties).

43. Once, the more pressing issue was whether treaties could extend beyond the limits of Article I, Section 8 and the general ambit of federal powers. With the vast expansion of federal power permitted by the Supreme Court's broad reading of the Commerce Clause, however, it is more likely that today's multilateral treaties will not extend beyond federal powers, but will adopt regulatory standards usually set by statutes or regulations pursuant to Congress's domestic legislative powers. Compare Curtis A. Bradley, *The Treaty Power and American Federalism,* 97 Mich. L. Rev. 390, 416–17 (1998) (arguing that the Framers assumed subject-matter limits on treaty powers); David Golove, *Treaty-Making and the Nation: The Historical Foundations of the Nationalist Conception of the Treaty Power,* 98 Mich. L. Rev. 1075 (2000) (treaties not subject to federalism limitations that apply to statutes).

44. G. Edward White, *The Transformation of the Constitutional Regime of Foreign Relations,* 85 Va. L. Rev. 1, 9–21 (1999).

45. John C. Yoo, *Laws as Treaties?: The Constitutionality of Congressional-Executive Agreements,* 99 Mich. L. Rev. 757, 766–67 (2001).

46. Laurence H. Tribe, *Taking Text and Structure Seriously: Reflections on Free-Form Method in Constitutional Interpretation,* 108 Harv. L. Rev. 1221, 1250, 1277–78 (1995).

47. Saikrishna B. Prakash & Michael D. Ramsey, *The Executive Power over Foreign Affairs,* 111 Yale L.J. 231 (2001).

48. Henkin, *supra* note 9, at 13–14.

49. Koh, *supra* note 14, at 67–68.

50. Henkin, *supra* note 9, at 31.

51. *Morrison v. Olson,* 487 U.S. 654, 705 (1988) (Scalia, J., dissenting).

52. Steven G. Calabresi & Kevin H. Rhodes, *The Structural Constitution: Unitary Executive, Plural Judiciary,* 105 Harv. L. Rev. 1153, 1176 (1992); Akhil R. Amar, *A Neo-Federalist View of Article III: Separating the Two Tiers of Federal Jurisdiction,* 65 B.U. L. Rev. 205, 229–30 (1985).

53. Thomas Jefferson, Opinion on the Powers of the Senate (1790), reprinted in 5 The Writings of Thomas Jefferson 161 (Paul L. Ford ed., 1895).

54. Alexander Hamilton, Pacificus No. 1 (1793), reprinted in 15 Papers of Alexan-

der Hamilton 33, 39 [hereinafter Papers of Hamilton]; Alexander Hamilton, Pacificus No. 7 (1793), reprinted in id. at 135.

55. 10 Annals of Congress 613–14 (1800).

56. Thomas Schelling, The Strategy of Conflict 18 (1960).

57. Edward S. Corwin, The President: Office and Powers 1787–1984 (1984).

58. The Federalist No. 70, at 423 (Alexander Hamilton) (Jacob E. Cooke ed., 1980).

59. The Federalist No. 74, id. at 447.

60. The Federalist No. 70, id. at 424.

61. United States v. Curtiss-Wright Export Corp., 299 U.S. 304, 319 (1936).

62. The Federalist No. 70, at 356 (Alexander Hamilton) (Clinton Rossiter ed., 1961).

63. Koh, *supra* note 14, at 119.

64. Id. at 118–23; see generally Schlesinger, *supra* note 27.

65. John C. Yoo, *War and Constitutional Text,* 69 U. Chi. L. Rev. 1639, 1677–78 (2002).

66. Henry Monaghan, *The Protective Power of the Presidency,* 93 Colum. L. Rev. 1, 4 (1993).

67. *Youngstown Sheet & Tube Co. v. Sawyer,* 343 U.S. 579 (1952).

68. Id. at 586.

69. Quoted in Bradford Perkins, The Creation of a Republican Empire, 1776–1865, at 55–59 (1993); see also Frederick W. Marks III, Independence on Trial: Foreign Affairs and the Making of the Constitution 3–51 (1986).

70. G. Edward White, *Observations on the Turning of Foreign Affairs Jurisprudence,* 70 U. Colo. L. Rev. 1109 (1999); White, *supra* note 44.

71. See, e.g., *Clinton v. City of New York,* 524 U.S. 417, 438–40 (1998) (describing the original intent of the Presentment Clause); *Plaut v. Spendthrift Farm,* 514 U.S. 211, 218–24 (1995) (describing the Framers' intention that the judicial and legislative powers be strictly separated); *Mistretta v. United States,* 488 U.S. 361, 380 (1989) (describing Madison's pragmatic view of the separation of powers); *Morrison v. Olson,* 487 U.S. 654, 674–75 (1988) (discussing the Framers' views on appointments); *Bowsher v. Synar,* 478 U.S. 714, 722 (1986) (describing the Framers' concern about maintaining separation of powers); *INS v. Chadha,* 462 U.S. 919, 946 (1983) (discussing the Framers' views of the Presentment Clause).

72. See, e.g., *Printz v. United States,* 521 U.S. 898, 910 (1997) (reviewing the Federalist Papers and other contemporary commentary); *Seminole Tribe v. Florida,* 517 U.S. 44, 71 (1996) (discussing areas of sovereignty that the Framers reserved to the states); *United States v. Lopez,* 514 U.S. 549, 552 (1995) (same); *New York v. United States,* 505 U.S. 144, 155 (1992) (same); *Gregory v. Ashcroft,* 501 U.S. 452, 458 (1991) (same). On this score, see John C. Yoo, *Judicial Safeguards of Federalism,* 70 S. Cal. L. Rev. 1311, 1357–58 (1997).

73. See, e.g., *Seminole Tribe,* 517 U.S. at 99–101 (Souter, J., dissenting); *United States Term Limits, Inc. v. Thornton,* 514 U.S. 779, 802–15 (1995).

74. See, e.g., *McIntyre v. Ohio Elections Comm'n,* 514 U.S. 334, 359 (1995) (Thomas, J., concurring); Antonin Scalia, *Originalism: The Lesser Evil,* 57 U. Cin. L. Rev. 849 (1989).

75. See, e.g., Steven G. Calabresi & Saikrishna B. Prakash, *The President's Power to Execute the Laws,* 104 Yale L.J. 541 (1994); Steven G. Calabresi & Kevin H. Rhodes, *The Structural Constitution: Unitary Executive, Plural Judiciary,* 105 Harv. L. Rev. 1153 (1992); Martin S. Flaherty, *The Most Dangerous Branch,* 105 Yale L.J. 1725

(1996); Lawrence Lessig & Cass R. Sunstein, *The President and the Administration,* 94 Colum. L. Rev. 1 (1994).

76. Randy Barnett, *The Original Understanding of the Commerce Clause,* 68 U. Chi. L. Rev. 101 (2001); Yoo, *supra* note 72, at 1311; Daniel A. Farber, *The Constitution's Forgotten Cover Letter: An Essay on the New Federalism and the Original Understanding,* 94 Mich. L. Rev. 615 (1995); H. Jefferson Powell, *Enumerated Means and Unlimited Ends,* 94 Mich. L. Rev. 651 (1995).

77. Ely, *supra* note 1, at 3.

78. Glennon, *supra* note 14, at 80–81, 84.

79. Koh, *supra* note 14, at 79.

80. Henkin, *supra* note 9, at 202 n.**.

81. Carlos Manuel Vázquez, *Treaty-Based Rights and Remedies of Individuals,* 92 Colum. L. Rev. 1082, 1110 (1992).

82. William M. Treanor, *Fame, the Founding, and the Power to Declare War,* 82 Cornell L. Rev. 695, 700 (1997); Martin S. Flaherty, *History Right?: Historical Scholarship, Original Understanding, and Treaties as "Supreme Law of the Land,"* 99 Colum. L. Rev. 2101 (1999).

83. See, e.g., Jesse H. Choper, Judicial Review and the National Political Process 242–43 (1980); Paul Brest, *The Misconceived Quest for the Original Understanding,* 60 B.U. L. Rev. 204 (1980).

84. See, e.g., Jack Rakove, Original Meanings: Politics and Ideas in the Making of the Constitution 94–130 (1996).

85. See Leonard Levy, Original Intent and the Framers' Constitution 1–29 (1988); Rakove, *supra* note 84, at 8–9; Charles A. Lofgren, *The Original Understanding of Original Intent?* 5 Const. Commentary 77, 111–13 (1988).

86. Rakove, *supra* note 84, at 8.

87. The Documentary History of the Ratification of the Constitution (Merrill Jensen, John P. Kaminski & Gaspare J. Saladino eds., 1976–).

88. Bernard Bailyn, The Ideological Origins of the American Revolution (1967); Gordon S. Wood, The Creation of the American Republic 1776–1787 (1969); Forrest McDonald, Novus Ordo Seclorum: The Intellectual Origins of the Constitution (1985); Jack N. Rakove, Original Meanings: Politics and Ideas in the Making of the Constitution (1996). Other important works that I have relied on include Bernard Bailyn, The Origins of American Politics (1968); Forrest McDonald, E Pluribus Unum: The Formation of the American Republic 1776–1790 (1965); Forrest McDonald, We the People: The Economic Origins of the Constitution (1958); Jack N. Rakove, The Beginnings of National Politics: An Interpretive History of the Continental Congress (1979); and the works of John Philip Reid, Jack Greene, Edmund S. Morgan, Richard B. Morris, Lance Banning, and Joyce Appleby.

89. See H. Jefferson Powell, *Rules for Originalists,* 73 Va. L. Rev. 659, 662–95 (1987) (setting out fourteen "rules" for the use of history by originalists); Martin S. Flaherty, *History "Lite" in Modern American Constitutionalism,* 95 Colum. L. Rev. 523, 552–55 (1995) (outlining "basic" historical standards, including taking account of a larger historical context, consideration of both primary and secondary sources, and some deference to settled historical scholarship).

90. See generally Wood, *supra* note 88, at 44653. See also Marc Kruman, Between Authority and Liberty: State Constitution Making in Revolutionary America 109–30 (1997) (recounting the experiences of various colonies in balancing power between the legislative and executive branches); Forrest McDonald, The American Presidency: An Intellectual History 98–153 (1995) (tracing the history of the presi-

dency through colonial and revolutionary times); Willi Paul Adams, The First American Constitutions: Republican Ideology and the Making of the State Constitution in the Revolutionary Era 271–75 (Rita and Robert Kimber trans., 1980); Charles C. Thach Jr., The Creation of the Presidency, 1775–1789: A Study in Constitutional History 34–35 (1923) (examining the weaknesses of executives in colonial constitutions during the revolutionary period).

CHAPTER TWO

1. As Forrest McDonald has observed, lawyers preparing for the bar in early America were required to learn the history of the British constitution and of the powers of the monarchy and Parliament; nearly two-thirds of the Philadelphia Convention delegates had received this education. See Forrest McDonald, The American Presidency 12–13 (1994).

2. See Arthur Nussbaum, A Concise History of the Law of Nations 126–33 (1947).

3. See 3 Hugo Grotius, De Jure Belli ac Pacis Libri Tres 804 (James B. Scott & Francis W. Kelsey trans., 1925 [1646]).

4. Id.

5. See 2 Albert de Lapradelle, *Introduction* to Emmerich de Vattel, The Law of Nations or the Principles of Natural Law Applied to the Conduct and to the Affairs of Nations and of Sovereigns xxvi–xxxi (James Brown Scott ed., Charles G. Fenwick trans., 1916 [1758]).

6. Id. at 21–22.

7. See 3 Grotius, *supra* note 3, ch. III, pt. VI.

8. Id. pt. XI.

9. 2 Vattel, *supra* note 5, at 22–23.

10. Id.

11. 3 Grotius, *supra* note 3, ch. IV, pt. III.

12. Id. at 805–6.

13. 2 Vattel, *supra* note 5, at 33.

14. Only if the leader has been given "full and absolute sovereignty," and has been exercising such power without dissent for some time, Vattel thought, could he then unilaterally alienate sovereign power to another nation. Id. at 101 (proclaiming that "[I]f the fundamental law forbids any such dismemberment by the sovereign he has no power without the concurrence of the Nation or of its representatives," before elaborating that "if the law is silent on that point, and if the Prince has been given full and absolute sovereignty, he is then the depositary of the rights of the Nation and the organ of its will.").

15. 3 Grotius, *supra* note 3, at 806.

16. The writers of *The Federalist Papers,* for example, sometimes quoted long passages from Montesquieu's *Spirit of the Laws.* See, e.g., *The Federalist* No. 9 at 16062 (Alexander Hamilton) (Clinton Rossiter ed., 1961). Blackstone's *Commentaries* had great appeal for the founding generation as the authoritative treatise on many areas of law. See Gordon S. Wood, The Creation of the American Republic 1776–1787 at 10 (1969).

17. See, e.g., Wood, *supra* note 16, at 10–18 (1972); Bernard Bailyn, Ideological Origins of the American Revolution 31 (1967).

18. See W. B. Gwyn, *The Meaning of the Separation of Powers,* 9 Tulane Stud. Pol. Sci. 37–40 (1965); M. J. C. Vile, Constitutionalism and the Separation of Powers 23–57 (2d ed. 1998).

19. John Locke, The Second Treatise of Government §§ 143–44 (1690).

20. Id. § 145.
21. Id. § 146.
22. Id. § 147.
23. Id. § 148.
24. Id.
25. Vile, *supra* note 18, at 60–61.
26. Locke, *supra* note 19, §§ 159, 160.
27. Id. § 168.
28. Id. § 135.
29. Id. § 141. According to Locke, the other two checks on legislative power are that it cannot exercise an arbitrary power that goes beyond what an individual possesses in the state of nature, and that it cannot take property without the owner's consent. See id. §§ 135, 138.
30. See generally Wood, *supra* note 16; Bailyn, *supra* note 17; J. G. A. Pocock, The Machiavellian Moment: Florentine Political Thought and the Atlantic Republican Tradition (1975).
31. See, e.g., Bailyn, *supra* note 17 , at 47–48; John Trenchard & Thomas Gordon, Cato's Letters (1995 [1755]).
32. See Donald S. Lutz, The Origins of American Constitutionalism 145 (1988) (table showing that Montesquieu's writings composed 29 percent of the cites by Federalists and 24 percent of the cites by Anti-Federalists). Montesquieu had a profound influence on the framing generation, and references to his *Spirit of the Laws* are sprinkled liberally throughout the records of the Philadelphia Convention, *The Federalist Papers,* and the state ratification debates. Putting to one side the debate over whether it accurately described reality, Montesquieu's chapter on the English constitution, and his discussion of the manner in which it enhanced liberty by separating power, served as a model for the framing generation. Montesquieu was perhaps the first major political thinker to accord the judiciary an equal status as a third branch of government, and he leavened Locke's stricter separation of powers theory with some of the balanced government arguments of English oppositionist thought. See Gwyn, *supra* note 18, at 109–13; Vile, *supra* note 18, at 83–106. His account of governmental power blended an emphasis on a functional allocation of authority with a measure of checks and balances to produce a system similar to the one adopted in Philadelphia in 1787.
33. Charles Louis de Secondat, Baron Montesquieu, Spirit of the Laws, bk. 11, ch. 6 (Thomas Nugent trans., 1949 [1748]).
34. Id.
35. Id. ¶ 62.
36. Id. ¶ 60.
37. Id. ¶ 61.
38. 1 William Blackstone, Commentaries on the Laws of England *252.
39. Id. at *245.
40. Id. at *249.
41. Id. at *254.
42. Id. at *249–50. The term "denunciation" had a meaning equivalent to what we understand as a "declaration."
43. Id. at *249–50.
44. Id.
45. Id. at *257.
46. Id. at *252.

47. Id. at *261.

48. Id. at *160.

49. Id. at *161.

50. Id. at *270.

51. Id.

52. Id. at *252.

53. Id. at *249.

54. One can see this, for example, in the Framers' discussion of war powers. See, e.g., Cato, IV (N.Y. J. 1787–88), reprinted in 2 The Complete Anti-Federalist 113, 115 (Herbert J. Storing ed., 1981) (comparing president's war powers to British king's prerogative); The Federalist No. 69, at 390–92 (Alexander Hamilton), reprinted in 16 Documentary History of the Ratification of the Constitution (John P. Kaminski & Gaspare J. Saladino eds., 1986) [hereinafter Documentary History] (arguing that president's war powers were weaker in operation than those enjoyed by British monarch); 2 The Records of the Federal Convention of 1787, at 541 (Max Farrand ed., 1911) (Pierce Butler comparing president's war powers to Duke of Marlborough's prolonged command of British army).

55. See, e.g., Bailyn, *supra* note 17, at 66–77, 94–117; 3 John Phillip Reid, Constitutional History of the American Revolution: The Authority to Legislate 68–74, 79–86, 126–41 (1991).

56. See generally John Brewer, The Sinews of Power: War, Money and the English State, 1688–1783 (1989). Uncited works that have been of assistance in this section include Francis R. Flournoy, Parliament and War: The Relations of the British Parliament to the Administration of Foreign Policy in Connection with the Initiation of War (1927); Henry Horwitz, Parliament, Policy and Politics in the Reign of William III (1977); Colin R. Lovell, English Constitutional and Legal History (1962); Richard Middleton, The Bells of Victory: The Pitt-Newcastle Ministry and the Conduct of the Seven Years' War, 1757–62 (1985); Marie Peters, Pitt and Popularity: The Patriot Minister and London Opinion during the Seven Years' War (1980); 4 Mark A. Thomson, A Constitutional History of England (1938); J. R. Western, The English Militia in the Eighteenth Century 1660–1802 (1965); Stephen B. Baxter, *The Conduct of the Seven Years War,* in England's Rise to Greatness, 1660–1763, at 323 (Stephen B. Baxter ed., 1983); Jeremy Black, *The Revolution and the Development of English Foreign Policy,* in By Force of By Default?: The Revolution of 1688–1689, at 135 (Eveline Cruickshanks ed., 1989); Jennifer Carter, *The Revolution and the Constitution,* in Britain after the Glorious Revolution 1689–1714, at 39 (Geoffrey Holmes ed., 1969); G. C. Gibbs, *Parliament and Foreign Policy in the Age of Stanhope and Walpole,* 77 Eng. Hist. Rev. 18 (1962); Edward R. Turner, *Parliament and Foreign Affairs,* 1603–1760, 34 Eng. Hist. Rev. 172 (1919).

57. See David Lindsay Keir, The Constitutional History of Modern Britain, 1485–1951, at 180–91 (5th ed. 1953); Frederick W. Maitland, The Constitutional History of England 306–11 (1961); J. R. Tanner, English Constitutional Conflicts of the Seventeenth Century 1603–1689, at 46–50 (1952); Thomas Pitt Taswell-Langmead, English Constitutional History from the Teutonic Conquest to the Present Time 481–90 (A. L. Poole ed., 9th ed. 1929).

58. 10 Sir William Holdsworth, A History of English Law 340–41 (1938).

59. See Keir, *supra* note 57, at 185–86.

60. King's Message to Commons (Dec. 3, 1621), reprinted in Tanner, *supra* note 57, at 48–49. He was responding to Commons Petition (Dec. 3, 1621), reprinted in The Stuart Constitution 1603–1688: Documents and Selected Commentary 43–47 (J. P.

Kenyon ed., 1st ed. 1966) [hereinafter Stuart Constitution]. Protesting James's theory of parliamentary authority, the Commons argued that it had the right to debate, and counsel the monarch on, any and all matters of state, including foreign policy and national defense, in addition to the power to make laws. See The Commons, Protestation (Dec. 18, 1621), reprinted in id. at 47–48. James became so enraged at this claim that he dissolved Parliament and even personally ripped the Commons's message out of the parliamentary journal. See Keir, *supra* note 57, at 187–88; Tanner, *supra* note 57, at 49.

61. See Subsidy Act of 1624, reprinted in Stuart Constitution, *supra* note 60, at 76–80.

62. King's Speech at the Opening of Parliament (Feb. 19, 1624), reprinted in Stuart Constitution, *supra* note 60, at 48–50.

63. See generally Keir, *supra* note 57, at 187–89; Stuart Constitution, *supra* note 60, at 58.

64. See Tanner, *supra* note 57, at 54–59; Keir, *supra* note 57, at 188–89.

65. See Tanner, *supra* note 57, at 59–82; Keir, *supra* note 57, at 190–212.

66. See Stuart Constitution, *supra* note 60, at 189–97.

67. See The Nineteen Propositions (June 1, 1642), reprinted in Stuart Constitution, *supra* note 60, at 244–47; King's Answer to the Nineteen Propositions (June 18, 1642), reprinted in Stuart Constitution, *supra* note 60 at 21–23; see generally id. at 294–95.

68. The Heads of the Proposals (Aug. 1, 1647), reprinted in Stuart Constitution, *supra* note 60, at 302–8; The First Agreement of the People (Oct. 28, 1647), reprinted in Stuart Constitution, *supra* note 60, at 308, 309; From a Remonstrance of Fairfax and the Council of Officers (Nov. 16, 1648), reprinted in Puritanism and Liberty, Being the Army Debates (1647–49), at 456, 457 (A. S. P. Woodhouse ed., 1938) (distinguishing between "the power of making laws, constitutions, and offices, for the preservation and government of the whole, and of altering or repealing and abolishing the same" and "the power of final judgment concerning war or peace"). Interestingly, several proposals discussed the idea of ending the war with the king by making a peace "treaty" with him, but then distinguished between such a treaty and the domestic scheme of government, which was addressed by legislation. See, e.g., The Humble Petition (Sept. 11, 1648), reprinted in Stuart Constitution, *supra* note 60, at 319–24.

69. The Instrument of Government (Dec. 16, 1653), reprinted in Stuart Constitution, *supra* note 60, at 342.

70. An Act Declaring the Sole Right of the Militia to be in the King, 1661, reprinted in Stuart Constitution, *supra* note 60, at 374.

71. G. C. Gibbs, *Laying Treaties before Parliament in the Eighteenth Century*, in Studies in Diplomatic History 116–37 (Ragnhild Hatton & M. S. Anderson eds., 1970).

72. See Keir, *supra* note 57, at 232–33. Parliament also began exercising its appropriations power during this period more effectively, as it began voting exact funds for specific budgetary items—"line-iteming," in modern legislative parlance. In 1677, for example, Parliament voted exactly 584,978 pounds, 2 shillings, and 2 pence for the construction of thirty warships, and in the next two years effectively ordered the demobilization of specific military units by cutting off funds unit by unit. See Stuart Constitution, *supra* note 60, at 363.

73. Jeremy Black, A System of Ambition?: British Foreign Policy 1660–1793, at 18–19 (1991).

74. Id. at 19. For a more critical view of Parliament, see Frederick Allen, The

Supreme Command in England, 1640–1780, at 127–43 (1966) (accusing Parliament of using its funding powers to usurp the "supreme command" over the military).

75. Commons Address (May 25, 1677), reprinted in Stuart Constitution, *supra* note 60, at 399; see John C. Yoo, *The Continuation of Politics by Other Means: The Original Understanding of War Powers*, 84 Cal. L. Rev. 167, 212 (1996).

76. See The King's Reply (May 28, 1677), reprinted in Stuart Constitution, *supra* note 60, at 400–1; id. at 397–98.

77. See Bill of Rights (1689), reprinted in The Eighteenth Century Constitution 1688–1815, at 28 (E. Neville Williams ed., 1960) [hereinafter Eighteenth Century Constitution]; see also Keir, *supra* note 57, at 268.

78. Act of Settlement (1701), reprinted in Eighteenth Century Constitution, *supra* note 77, at 59.

79. See Black, *supra* note 73, at 46–49.

80. Jeremy Black, British Foreign Policy in an Age of Revolutions, 1783–1793, at 491 (1994) [hereinafter Black, Age of Revolutions]; see also Jeremy Black, British Foreign Policy in the Age of Walpole 75–89 (1985) [hereinafter Black, Age of Walpole].

81. See Stuart Constitution, *supra* note 60, at 58 (Thirty Years' War); 1 James Kent, Commentaries on American Law 53–54 (2d ed. 1832) (Seven Years' War).

82. See 5 Cobbett's Parliamentary History of England 234–35 (1809) (declaration beginning King William's War of 1689).

83. See generally J. F. Maurice, Hostilities without Declaration of War (Her Majesty's Stationery Office 1883).

84. See Declaration against the French King (May 7, 1689), reprinted in British Royal Proclamations Relating to America, 1603–1783, at 147 (Clarence S. Brigham ed., 1911); Declaration against the French King (Mar. 29, 1744), reprinted in British Royal Proclamations Relating to America, 1603–1783, at 196; Declaration against the French King (May 17, 1756), reprinted in British Royal Proclamations Relating to America, 1603–1783, at 203–6.

85. See Douglas E. Leach, Arms for Empire: A Military History of the British Colonies in North America, 1607–1763, at 210 (1973). For the relevant declarations of war, see 6 Cobbett's Parliamentary History of England, *supra* note 82, at 1617 (1810) (War of Spanish Succession); 11 id. at 13 (1812) (George II's declaration of war against Spain); 13 id. at 688–91 (1812) (George II's declaration of war against France).

86. See 1 Kent, *supra* note 81, at 54. On the events and importance of the Seven Years' War, see Leach, *supra* note 85, at 340–41, 368, 380–81.

87. See, e.g., H. M. Scott, British Foreign Policy in the Age of the American Revolution 20 (1990). Jeremy Black's work emphasizes the manner in which Parliament's constitutional powers in foreign affairs, particularly in the treaty process, provided it with an important voice in the setting of foreign policy. Even the other significant line of work on British foreign relations during this period, which emphasizes the decisions and personalities of individual ministers and diplomats, acknowledges that Parliament and its constitutional powers were an important factor in the making of foreign policy. Id. at 19–22. Even as a formal matter, as the English legal historian Sir William Holdsworth has observed, the Crown's prerogative over treaties itself was no longer absolute by the eighteenth century. See 10 Holdsworth, *supra* note 58, at 374. By this time, according to Holdsworth, international agreements involving foreign trade had fallen outside the prerogative, as well as treaty provisions that involved revenues, such as tariff measures. See id. at 401.

88. J. L. De Lolme, The Constitution of England 72 (1821).

CHAPTER THREE

1. See Bernard Bailyn, Ideological Origins of the American Revolution 217–29 (1967); Jack P. Greene, Peripheries and Center: Constitutional Development in the Extended Polities of the British Empire and the United States, 1607–1788, at 19–43 (1986); 3 John P. Reid, Constitutional History of the American Revolution: Authority to Legislate 126–41 (1986–93).

2. Greene, *supra* note 1, at 55–78.

3. See, e.g., Jack P. Greene, The Quest for Power: The Lower Houses of Assembly in the Southern Royal Colonies 1689–1776, at 297–306 (1963) (showing how the lower houses influenced foreign affairs through sharing the exercise of military powers, enabled by the power of the purse); John C. Yoo, *The Continuation of Politics by Other Means: The Original Understanding of War Powers*, 84 Cal. L. Rev. 167, 219–21 (1996).

4. Bailyn, *supra* note 1, at 203.

5. Jack P. Greene, Negotiated Authorities: Essays in Colonial Political and Constitutional History 35 (1994).

6. See 3 Reid, *supra* note 1, at 63–86 (discussing theory and limits of parliamentary supremacy in context of the Declaratory Act).

7. See id. at 68–74, 113–25.

8. Greene, *supra* note 1, at 163.

9. Evarts B. Greene, The Provincial Governor in the English Colonies of North America 107–9 (1898); Yoo, *supra* note 3, at 219–21.

10. Forrest McDonald, The American Presidency: An Intellectual History 105–7 (1994).

11. See id. at 107–22. Works describing the struggles between the colonial governors and the assemblies include John F. Burns, Controversies between Royal Governors and their Assemblies in the North American Colonies (1923); Greene, *supra* note 1; Leonard Labaree, Royal Government in America 172–217 (1930). Jack P. Greene is the historian who most recently has attempted to synthesize these events into broader themes.

12. Greene, *supra* note 5, at 174–77.

13. See Bernard Bailyn, The Ideological Origins of the American Revolution 63 (1967).

14. Greene, *supra* note 9, at 98–99.

15. Charter of Massachusetts Bay (1691), reprinted in 3 Francis N. Thorpe, The Federal and State Constitutions, Colonial Charters, and Other Organic Laws of the States, Territories, and Colonies 1884 (1909) [hereinafter Thorpe]; see also Charter of Maryland (1632), reprinted in 3 id. at 1682; Charter of Georgia (1732), reprinted in 2 id. at 776; Charter of Connecticut (1662), reprinted in 1 id. at 534–35.

16. Greene, *supra* note 9, at 107–9. In fact, it appears that the colonies were almost constantly at war with one foe or another, whether it be the Indians or the French. See generally Douglas E. Leach, Arms for Empire: A Military History of the British Colonies of North America, 1607–1763 (1973). Some governors, however, exercised a limited power to declare war against the Indians. In 1722 and 1755, the governor of Massachusetts issued such a declaration with the advice of his council. New Hampshire's executive did likewise in 1745. Greene, *supra* note 9, at 107–8.

17. Bailyn, *supra* note 13, at 63–64.

18. Greene, *supra* note 9, at 101.

19. Greene, *supra* note 3, at 297–309.

20. Id. at 303. In addition to the spending power, the peculiar position of the

governor in the structure of the British imperial system blessed the colonists with an added check on executive power. Although the governor formally held the upper hand in the colonies, he, too, was subject to the higher authority of the Crown and its ministers in England. By the 1750s, the colonies had developed close communications with the political leadership in the mother country, links they used to appeal and overturn decisions by the colonial governors. Bailyn, *supra* note 13, at 90–91.

21. See Del. Const. art. VII (1776), reprinted in 1 Thorpe, *supra* note 15, at 563; Md. Const. art. XXV (1776), reprinted in 3 id. at 1695; N.J. Const. art. VII (1776), reprinted in 5 id. at 2596; N.C. Const. art. XV (1776), reprinted in 5 id. at 2791. New York provided for the direct election of the governor, an important exception that influenced the Framers of the federal Constitution.

22. Md. Declaration of Rights art. XXXI (1776), reprinted in 3 Thorpe, *supra* note 15, at 1689.

23. Pa. Const. § 19 (1776), reprinted in 5 Thorpe, *supra* note 15, at 3086–87.

24. Gordon S. Wood, The Creation of the American Republic, 1776–1787, at 138 (1969). See, e.g., Del. Const. art. VIII (1776), reprinted in 1 Thorpe, *supra* note 15, at 563–64; Ga. Const. art. XXV (1777), reprinted in 2 id. at 781–82; Md. Const. art. XXVI (1776), reprinted in 3 id. at 1695; N.C. Const. art. XIV (1776), reprinted in 5 id. at 2791; S.C. Const. art V (1776), reprinted in 6 id. at 3245; Vt. Const. art. XVII (1777), reprinted in 6 id. at 3744; Va. Const. ¶ 9 (1776), reprinted in 7 id. at 3816–17.

25. See, e.g., Abraham D. Sofaer, War, Foreign Affairs and Constitutional Power: The Origins 16–19 (1976).

26. Willi Paul Adams, The First American Constitutions: Republican Ideology and the Making of the State Constitutions in the Revolutionary Era 271 (Rita Kimber & Robert Kimber trans., 1980).

27. Charles C. Thatch Jr., The Creation of the Presidency, 1775–1789: A Study in Constitutional History 29 (1922).

28. Thomas Jefferson, First Draft of the Virginia Constitution, art. II (1776), reprinted in 1 The Papers of Thomas Jefferson 337, 341 (Julian P. Boyd ed., 1950) [hereinafter Papers of Jefferson].

29. The Mason Plan as Revised by the Committee art. IX (1776), reprinted in 1 id. at 369, 371.

30. The Constitution as Adopted by the Convention (1776), reprinted in 1 id. at 377, 380. The constitution forbade the executive from exercising "any power or prerogative by virtue of any Law, statute, or Custom, of England." Va. Const. ¶ 9 (1776), reprinted in 7 Thorpe, *supra* note 15, at 3816–17.

31. John Adams, Thoughts on Government (1776), reprinted in 4 Papers of John Adams 65, 89 (Robert J. Taylor ed., 1979) [hereinafter Papers of Adams]. Adams originally wrote the brief work in response to requests from representatives of North Carolina, Virginia, and New Jersey, who had come to him for advice on how to frame their new governments. See 4 id. at 65–73. Others then published the proposal as a pamphlet, in which form it reached many of the other states. Id.

32. Although some states such as Maryland initially introduced the innovation of prohibiting the raising of a standing army without the consent of the legislature, these provisions merely continued a principle first set out in the English Bill of Rights of 1689. As Alexander Hamilton noted, such provisions were redundant with the state legislatures' plenary power to raise and fund the armies: "It was superfluous, if not absurd, to declare that a matter should not be done without the consent of a body, which alone had the power of doing it." The Federalist No. 26, at 167 (Alexander Hamilton) (Clinton Rossiter ed., 1961).

33. Ga. Const. art. XXXIII (1777), reprinted in 2 Thorpe, *supra* note 15, at 782; see also N.J. Const. art. VIII (1776), reprinted in 5 id. at 2596; N.Y. Const. art. XVIII (1777), reprinted in id. at 2632.

34. Del. Const. art. IX (1776), reprinted in 1 Thorpe, *supra* note 15, at 564; see also Md. Const. art. XXXIII (1776), reprinted in 3 id. at 1696; N.C. Const. art. XVIII (1776), reprinted in 5 id. at 2791; Pa. Const. § 20 (1776), reprinted in id. at 3087–88; Vt. Const. art. XVIII (1777), reprinted in 6 id. at 3745; Va. Const. ¶ 14 (1776), reprinted in 7 id. at 3817.

35. Akhil R. Amar, *The Bill of Rights as a Constitution,* 100 Yale L.J. 1131, 1162–64 (1991); David C. Williams, *Civic Republicanism and the Citizen Militia: The Terrifying Second Amendment,* 101 Yale L.J. 551 (1991).

36. Va. Declaration of Rights § 13 (1776), reprinted in 7 Thorpe, *supra* note 15, at 3814; see also Md. Declaration of Rights art. XXVI (1776), reprinted in 3 id. at 1688; Mass. Declaration of Rights art. XVII (1780), reprinted in id. at 1892; N.H. Declaration of Rights art. XXV (1784), reprinted in 4 id. at 2456; N.C. Declaration of Rights art. XVII (1776), reprinted in 5 id. at 2788; Pa. Declaration of Rights art. XIII (1776), reprinted in id. at 3083; Vt. Declaration of Rights art. XV (1777), reprinted in 6 id. at 3741.

37. See, e.g., N.J. Const. art. X (1776), reprinted in 6 id. at 2596.

38. Mass. Const. art. VII (1780), reprinted in 3 id. at 1901; N.H. Const. (1784), reprinted in 4 id. at 2463–64. These provisions seemed to codify a similar ban on the king barring him from leading the militia outside of England.

39. See Charles C. Thach Jr., The Creation of the Presidency, 1775–1789: A Study in Constitutional History 34–35 (1922).

40. N.Y. Const. arts. VIII, XVII (1777), reprinted in 5 Thorpe, *supra* note 15, at 2632. Although it did not establish a privy council, the New York constitution created two more specialized councils: the Council of Revision, which exercised the veto power, and the Council of Appointment, which advised on appointments. N.Y. Const. arts. III, XXIII (1777), reprinted in id. at 2628, 2633–34.

41. See E. Wilder Spaulding, His Excellency George Clinton: Critic of the Constitution 95–98, 114–18 (1938); Thach, *supra* note 39, at 37–38.

42. See Clinton Rossiter, 1787: The Grand Convention 59, 65 (1966); Thach, *supra* note 39, at 34–38.

43. The Federalist No. 26, at 167 (Alexander Hamilton) (Clinton Rossiter ed., 1961).

44. Thach, *supra* note 39, at 43.

45. N.H. Const. (1784), reprinted in 4 Thorpe, *supra* note 15, at 2463–64; see also Mass. Const. art. VII (1780), reprinted in 3 id. at 1901.

46. The Rejected Constitution of 1778 (Mass.), reprinted in The Popular Sources of Political Authority: Documents on the Massachusetts Constitution of 1780, at 190, 197 (Oscar Handlin & Mary Handlin eds., 1966) [hereinafter Political Authority]. For another valuable documentary source for this period, see generally Massachusetts, Colony to Commonwealth: Documents on the Formation of Its Constitution, 1775–1780 (Robert J. Taylor ed., 1961).

47. See Thach, *supra* note 39, at 44–54; Jeff Rosen, Note, *Was the Flag Burning Amendment Unconstitutional?* 100 Yale L.J. 1073, 1076–77 (1991).

48. Adams, *supra* note 26, at 91.

49. The Essex Result (1778), reprinted in Theophilus Parsons, Memoirs 359 (1859).

50. Id. at 396.

51. Id.

52. Thach, *supra* note 39, at 44–54. As a prominent Massachusetts judge wrote of the Essex Result, it was an intellectual landmark that stood "beyond any other political document of that day, a clear exposition of the principles upon which the organic laws of a free state should be founded,—the very principles essentially adopted in forming the Constitution of Massachusetts." Harry A. Cushing, History of the Transition from Provincial to Commonwealth Government in Massachusetts 223 (1970 [1896]). For the history of the Massachusetts Constitution of 1780, see Adams, *supra* note 26, at 86–93; Samuel E. Morison, *The Struggle over the Adoption of the Constitution of Massachusetts, 1780,* 50 Proc. Mass. Hist. Soc'y 353 (1917).

53. Address of the Convention (Mar. 1780), reprinted in Political Authority, *supra* note 46, at 434, 437–38.

54. Wood, *supra* note 24, at 434.

55. S.C. Const. art. XXVI (1776), reprinted in 6 Thorpe, *supra* note 15, at 3247.

56. S.C. Const. art. XXXIII (1778), reprinted in id. at 3255.

57. It is arguable that the South Carolina constitution did not even represent the wishes of its own people. The first permanent constitution adopted after the Declaration of Independence, the constitution was drafted and approved by the sitting state legislature, rather than by a convention of the people. See Adams, *supra* note 26, at 70–72. In contrast, the New York constitution was drafted by a new legislative body specifically elected for the purpose, see id. at 83–86, while the Massachusetts constitution was ratified by "[t]he first true constitutional convention in Western history." Id. at 92.

58. Arthur Bestor, *Separation of Powers in the Domain of Foreign Affairs: The Intent of the Constitution Historically Examined,* 5 Seton Hall L. Rev. 527, 568 (1974); see also Raoul Berger, *War-Making by the President,* 121 U. Pa. L. Rev. 29, 33 (1972).

59. John Marshall, *A Friend of the Constitution Essays,* Alexandria Gazette, June 30–July 16, 1819, reprinted in John Marshall's Defense of *McCulloch v. Maryland* 155, 199 (Gerald Gunther ed., 1969); see also Akhil R. Amar, *The Consent of the Governed: Constitutional Amendment outside Article V,* 94 Colum. L. Rev. 457, 465 (1994) ("[The Continental Congress] was merely an international assembly of ambassadors, sent, recallable, and paid by state governments with each state casting a single vote as a state.").

60. See Jerrilyn Greene Marston, King and Congress: The Transfer of Political Legitimacy, 1774–1776, at 303–4 (1987); Eugene R. Sheridan & John M. Murrin, Introduction to Congress at Princeton: Being the Letters of Charles Thomson to Hannah Thomson (June–October 1783), at xxxiv–xxxviii (Eugene R. Sheridan & John M. Murrin eds., 1985)

61. Sheridan & Murrin, *supra* note 60, at xxxiv.

62. Arts. of Confederation, art. IX.

63. Arts. of Confederation, arts. II, VI, IX.

64. Marston, *supra* note 60, at 303.

65. The story is told in Forrest McDonald, E Pluribus Unum: The Formation of the American Republic 1776–1790, at 133–54 (1965); Richard B. Morris, The Forging of the Union 1781–1789, at 95–99 (1987); Jack N. Rakove, The Beginnings of National Politics: An Interpretive History of the Continental Congress 199–205 (1979). See also E. James Ferguson, The Power of the Purse: A History of American Public Finance, 1776–1790 (1961). Congress, which initially was dominated by a group of states-rights adherents, attempted to make and implement foreign policy by committee, which ended in dismal failure. By 1781, political leaders with a more nationalist bent decided to create independent executive departments under the control of in-

dividual secretaries for war, foreign affairs, finance, and the navy. See Rakove, *supra,* at 198–205. Even this more rational, unified control over executive functions did not produce success. Secretaries for foreign affairs failed to win the right to initiate policy, to control the activities of various envoys and commissioners, and to prevent Congress and its members from dealing independently with foreign diplomats. See, e.g., Lawrence S. Kaplan, Colonies into Nation: American Diplomacy 1763–1801, at 152 (1972). Because Congress was organized as an assembly, sectional divisions and commercial interests could arise that frustrated any unified action. Aside from the French-American alliance in 1778 and the peace treaty with Great Britain in 1783, Congress's ambassadors failed to conclude any significant commercial or strategic agreements under the Articles framework.

66. See Bestor, *supra* note 58, at 60–68; Rakove, *supra* note 65, at 349–50; 29 Journals of the Continental Congress 1774–1789, at 658 (1933) (instruction of August 25, 1785) [hereinafter Journals of Continental Congress]. The standard historical account of American relations with Spain, including the Jay-Gardoqui negotiations, remains Samuel Flagg Bemis, Pinckney's Treaty: America's Advantage from Europe's Distress, 1783–1800 (1960).

67. See 31 Journals of Continental Congress, *supra* note 66, at 595–96. These divisions prevented the United States from reaching an agreement with Spain until 1795, at which time, with American power dramatically increased, free navigation of the river was obtained. With the Louisiana Purchase in 1803, the United States would come into possession of the river itself and the port of New Orleans. See Bemis, *supra* note 66, at 281–82, 310–14.

68. See Lance Banning, The Sacred Fire of Liberty: James Madison and the Founding of the Federal Republic 66–71 (1995).

69. To enforce Article XI of the alliance with France, for example, Congress had to ask the states on January 14, 1780, to enact laws guaranteeing French subjects treaty-based privileges. See 2 Secret Journals of Congress 568–70 (1820) (recommending that state legislators "make provision, where not already made, for conferring like privileges and immunities on the subjects of his most Christian majesty"); Samuel B. Crandall, Treaties: Their Making and Enforcement 34–36 (1904) (collecting citations to state laws).

70. See generally Frederick W. Marks III, Independence on Trial: Foreign Affairs and the Making of the Constitution 52–95 (1973) (highlighting Congress's difficulty in eliminating foreign trade barriers due to state sovereignty and its effect on the ability to enter into commercial treaties); see also 1 Bradford Perkins, The Cambridge History of American Foreign Relations: The Creation of a Republican Empire, 1776–1865, at 57 (Warren I. Cohen ed., 1993).

71. Definitive Treaty of Peace between Great Britain and the United States, Sept. 3, 1783, U.S.-Gr. Brit., art. IV, 48 Consol. T.S. 487, 493.

72. 1 Perkins, *supra* note 70, at 42 (quoting James H. Hutson, John Adams and the Diplomacy of the American Revolution 128 [1980]). For discussions and evaluations of the Treaty of Paris, see Samuel F. Bemis, The Diplomacy of the American Revolution 243–56 (1957); Jonathan R. Dull, A Diplomatic History of the American Revolution 144–63 (1985); Richard B. Morris, The Peacemakers: The Great Powers and American Independence 173–90 (1965); Peace and the Peacemakers: The Treaty of 1783 (Ronald Hoffman & Peter J. Albert eds., 1986).

73. See Marks, *supra* note 70, at 11. On American violations, see Message from Mr. Hammond, Minister Plenipotentiary of Great Britain, to Mr. Jefferson, Secretary of State (Mar. 5, 1792), 1 American State Papers 226 (British report to the Conti-

nental Congress detailing the legislation and policies of each state that defied the recovery provision of the Treaty of Paris).

74. Descriptions of the case, and Hamilton's role in it, can be found in 1 Julius Goebel Jr., The Law Practice of Alexander Hamilton: Documents and Commentary 289 (1964). See Forrest McDonald, Alexander Hamilton: A Biography 64 (1979).

75. See Letter from Phocion to the Considerate Citizens of New York (Jan. 1–27 1784), reprinted in 3 Papers of Alexander Hamilton 483 (Harold C. Syrett ed., 1962) [hereinafter Papers of Hamilton]; Second Letter from Phocion (April 1784), reprinted in id., at 530. Phocion was an Athenian general well known in ancient times for his mercy toward the defeated enemy and his protection of prisoners of war. See Douglass Adair, A Note on Certain of Hamilton's Pseudonyms, in Fame and the Founding Fathers 272, 274–75 (Trevor Colbourn ed., 1974).

76. 3 Papers of Hamilton, supra note 75, at 489–91. Realizing that his arguments about national sovereignty were not widely shared, Hamilton devoted the majority of his "Phocion" papers to the economic and political benefits that would accrue to New York should it observe the 1783 treaty.

77. See 31 Journals of the Continental Congress, supra note 66, at 847.

78. See id. at 877–84. Congress adopted the three resolutions on March 21, 1787, but did not issue them to the states with an explanation until April 13.

79. The states voting to comply were New Hampshire, Massachusetts, Rhode Island, Connecticut, Delaware, Maryland, and North Carolina. See Edward S. Corwin, National Supremacy: Treaty Power vs. State Power 27–28 n.5 (1913). That state self-interest lay behind the impetus to pass these laws can be seen, for example, in the efforts of Alexander Hamilton on behalf of New York's legislation. See New York Assembly, Remarks on an Act Repealing Laws Inconsistent with the Treaty of Peace (Apr. 17, 1787), reprinted in 4 Papers of Hamilton, supra note 75, at 150–52.

Arguing that national sovereignty already existed in the Continental Congress, Edward Corwin believed that the request for repeal of the state statutes was necessary because judicial review was not yet commonly accepted. See Corwin, supra, at 28. Some treaty scholars of more recent vintage have taken Corwin's point farther and interpreted Jay's report as demonstrating that the Continental Congress already had the constitutional authority, under the Articles of Confederation, to directly enforce treaties against inconsistent state law. Jordan J. Paust, Self-Executing Treaties, 82 Am. J. Int'l L. 760, 760–61 (1988). Corwin and Paust seem to have misread the history. There was no widespread agreement that treaties were to have this effect; if anything, historical events and the Founders' reaction to them indicate a broader understanding that treaties did not have direct effect as law but instead required voluntary state compliance. Indeed, if their account were correct, there would have been little need for the Jay report in the first place, nor for the concern of the Framers such as Hamilton, Jay, and Madison about treaty enforcement.

80. See Jack Rakove, Original Meanings: Politics and Ideas in the Making of the Constitution 39–43 (1996).; see also Charles F. Hobson, The Negative on State Laws: James Madison, the Constitution, and the Crisis of Republican Government, 36 Wm. & Mary Q. 215, 223–25 (1979) (discussing Madison's disillusionment with "turbulent majorities who ruled the state legislatures"). In examining Madison's thought during the framing period, I also have relied on Banning, supra note 68; Drew R. McCoy, The Last of the Fathers: James Madison and the Republican Legacy (1989); and William Lee Miller, The Business of May Next: James Madison and the Founding (1992).

81. See Vices of the Political System of the United States (Apr. 1787), reprinted in 9 Papers of James Madison 349 (Robert A. Rutland et al. eds., 1975).

82. Id. at 351–52.
83. See Banning, *supra* note 68, at 5–6.

1. See 10 The Documentary History of the Ratification of the Constitution 1282 (John P. Kaminski & Gaspare J. Saladino eds., 1986) [hereinafter Documentary History] (Madison speech of June 14, 1788).

2. 1 The Records of the Federal Convention of 1787, at 19 (Max Farrand ed., 1911) [hereinafter Records].

3. See id. at 20–21.

4. Id. at 21.

5. Randolph was obviously influenced by Madison, who had authored the scheme for a negative over state laws. Madison shared a summary of his thoughts in his *Vices* memo with Randolph, George Washington, and Thomas Jefferson immediately before the Philadelphia Convention. See To Edmund Randolph (Apr. 8, 1787), reprinted in 9 Papers of Madison 368 (Robert A. Rutland & William M. E. Rachal eds., 1975); To George Washington, (Apr. 16, 1787), reprinted in id. at 383–84; To Thomas Jefferson (Mar. 19, 1787), reprinted in id. at 317–22. Madison's proposal for a federal negative on state laws is proposed in the same three letters. See Charles F. Hobson, *The Negative on State Laws: James Madison, the Constitution, and the Crisis of Republican Government,* 36 Wm. & Mary Q. 215, 219 (1979) (citing the same letters in which the negative is proposed); Jack N. Rakove, Original Meanings: Politics and Ideas in the Making of the Constitution 51-55 (1996) [hereinafter Rakove, Original Meanings] (same).

6. Rakove, Original Meanings, *supra* note 5, at 54.

7. 1 Records, *supra* note 2, at 64–65; see also id. at 65 (comments of John Rutledge); id. at 65–66 (comments of James Wilson).

8. Id. at 65–66. Oddly, the notes of Rufus King of New York show Madison, rather than Pinckney or Wilson, raising the issue. King records Madison as saying that "executive powers ex vi termini, do not include the Rights of war & peace &c. but the powers shd. be confined and defined." Id. at 70.

9. Id. at 67.

10. Id. at 242.

11. Id. at 244.

12. Id. at 292.

13. Charles A. Lofgren, "Government from Reflection and Choice": Constitutional Essays on War, Foreign Relations, and Federalism 13 (1986).

14. 2 Records, *supra* note 2, at 131–32.

15. 1 id. at 245.

16. Id. at 316.

17. Rakove, Original Meanings, *supra* note 5, at 173.

18. 2 Records, *supra* note 2, at 183.

19. As James Wilson declared on June 26, the "Senate will probably be the depositary of the powers concerning" relations "to foreign nations" because of senators' longer terms in office. 1 id. at 426. See also John C. Yoo, *The Judicial Safeguards of Federalism,* 70 S. Cal. L. Rev. 1311 at 1366–74 (discussing dual role of the Senate).

20. See 2 Records, *supra* note 2, at 15–16. The politics and consequences of the Great Compromise are retold in Rakove, Original Meanings, *supra* note 5, at 62–70.

21. 2 Records, *supra* note 2, at 27 (comments of Gouverneur Morris, Roger Sherman, and Luther Martin).

22. Id. at 27–29.

23. Id. at 318–19.

24. Id. at 314. Max Farrand, the editor of The Records of the Federal Convention of 1787, tells us that the printed version of the Journal was notoriously unreliable, especially in recording accurate vote tallies. Farrand concludes that in places where Madison's notes and the Journal disagree, Madison's notes are the more reliable source. Thus, it is likely that the Madison-Gerry amendment initially passed by a vote of 7 to 2, and later 8 to 1, after Ellsworth switched. Lofgren suggests an alternative view of the matter—that Madison's notes are incorrect and that the first vote was in the negative. King's explanation then becomes critical, because it convinces three states—Connecticut, Georgia, and South Carolina—instead of just one state, to switch their votes and approve the change. See Lofgren, *supra* note 13, at 8–9. This explanation is undermined by Madison's specific statement that King's speech changed only Ellsworth's vote. If other states had switched their votes in reaction to King on such a momentous question, Madison probably would have made note of them as well.

25. Cf. Henry P. Monaghan, *The Protective Power of the Presidency*, 93 Colum. L. Rev. 1, 67 (1993) (arguing that such protective power is limited to the protection of "personnel, property, and instrumentalities of the government that the President is supposed to administer").

26. 2 Records, *supra* note 2, at 318.

27. Id. at 319.

28. Id. at 392.

29. Jack N. Rakove, *Solving a Constitutional Puzzle: The Treatymaking Clause as a Case Study*, 1 Persp. Am. Hist. 233, 240–41 (1984) [hereinafter Rakove, Treatymaking].

30. 2 Records, *supra* note 2, at 392.

31. Id. at 393–94.

32. Id. at 498–99.

33. 4 The Debates in the Several State Conventions on the Adoption of the Federal Constitution 263 (Jonathan Elliott ed., 2d ed. 1881) [hereinafter Debates].

34. Id. at 264.

35. Rakove, Treatymaking, *supra* note 29, at 243.

36. When the convention took up the modified Treaty Clause on September 7, 1787, the supporters of majority rule made one more attempt to reduce the power of the states. Wilson immediately moved that the Constitution require that treaties receive the approval of both House and Senate, in order to render the procedures for statutes and treaties congruent. "As treaties . . . are to have the operation of laws," Wilson argued, "they ought to have the sanction of laws also." 2 Records, *supra* note 2, at 538. Wilson's amendment lost 10 to 1, and the convention approved the president and the Senate's shared control over treatymaking. One might see the vote simply as a decision that the House was not to be involved in treatymaking because of its structural inadequacies, rather than as a resolution of whether those treaties could supplant domestic lawmaking, in which the House was to play the dominant role.

37. Id. at 540.

38. Id. at 548.

39. Id. at 541.

40. Arthur Bestor, *Respective Roles of Senate and President in the Making and Abrogation of Treaties: The Original Intent of the Framers of the Constitution Historically Examined*, 55 Wash. L. Rev. 1, 88, 108–9 (1979).

41. See Carlos Vázquez, *Treaty-Based Rights and Remedies of Individuals,* 92 Colum. L. Rev. 1082, 1106–8 (1992); Jordan J. Paust, *Self-Executing Treaties,* 82 Am. J. Int'l L. 760, 761–62 (1988).

42. The Federalist No. 23 (Alexander Hamilton), reprinted in 16 Documentary History, *supra* note 1, at 147.

43. The Federalist No. 41 (James Madison), reprinted in id. at 270.

44. Brutus, The Dangers of a Standing Army (N.Y. J., Jan. 17, 1788), reprinted in 2 Bernard Bailyn, Debate on the Constitution 40, 43 (1993).

45. See, e.g., 3 Debates, *supra* note 33, at 378–81 (statement of George Mason at Virginia ratifying convention, arguing that state governments should retain the right to arm and discipline their own militias); Brutus, Essay X (N.Y. J., Jan. 24, 1788), reprinted in 2 The Complete Anti-Federalist 413, 416 (Herbert J. Storing ed., 1981) [hereinafter The Complete Anti-Federalist] (arguing that the Constitution should provide peacetime standing forces only to staff outposts and garrisons).

46. 2 The Complete Anti-Federalist at 414.

47. Letter from the "Federal Farmer" to "The Republican" I (Nov. 8, 1787), reprinted in 1 Bailyn, *supra* note 44 at 245, 252. The Federal Farmer, considered one of the most popular and influential of Anti-Federalist writers, was long thought to be Richard Henry Lee, but Gordon Wood has rebutted the case for his authorship. See Gordon S. Wood, *The Authorship of the Letters from the Federal Farmer,* 31 Wm. & Mary Q. 3d series 299 (1974). It may have been Melancton Smith of New York. See Robert H. Webking, *Melancton Smith and the Letters from the Federal Farmer,* 44 Wm. & Mary Q. 3d series 510 (1987).

48. Cato, Essay IV (N.Y. J. 1787–88), reprinted in 2 The Complete Anti-Federalist, *supra* note 45 at 113, 115. Although the identity of Cato is unknown, some have speculated that he may have been George Clinton, the governor of New York. Id. at 102 (preface to Cato's essays).

49. An Old Whig, Essay V (Phila. Indep. Gazetteer, Nov. 1, 1787), reprinted in 3 The Complete Anti-Federalist, *supra* note 45, at 34, 37–38.

50. Id. at 38; see also 3 Debates, *supra* note 33, at 496 (statement of George Mason at Virginia ratifying convention, warning that one as disinterested and amiable as George Washington might never command again).

51. Philadelphiensis, Essay IX (Phila. Freeman's J., Feb. 6, 1788), reprinted in 3 The Complete Anti-Federalist, *supra* note 45, at 127–28. Philadelphiensis is thought to be the pseudonym of Benjamin Workman, an Irish immigrant who became a tutor in mathematics at the University of Pennsylvania. 1 Bailyn, *supra* note 44, at 1054 (biographical notes). Luther Martin, a prominent Maryland delegate to the Philadelphia Convention who refused to sign the finished product, read the commander-in-chief power as vesting in the president the authority to appoint all military officers. As in classical Rome, an army so personally dependent on its commander would provide the president with an unstoppable weapon for imposing his wishes on the people. Martin warned in a widely circulated pamphlet that such an army and navy so "dependant [*sic*] on his will and pleasure, and commanded by him in person, will, of course, be subservient to his wishes, and ready to execute his commands." Luther Martin, Information to the General Assembly of the State of Maryland (1788), reprinted in 2 id. at 27, 67–68.

52. Tamony (Jan. 9, 1788), reprinted in 5 The Complete Anti-Federalist, *supra* note 45, at 145–46.

53. See, e.g., Poem, Jan. 28, 1788, reprinted in 15 Documentary History, *supra* note 1, at 486 (reprinted in New York, Boston, Philadelphia, New Jersey, and Vir-

ginia newspapers). Anti-Federalist writers throughout the states hammered home the theme that the president, with "his uncountroulable [*sic*] power over the army, navy, and militia" and the support of a "dependent" Congress, would be tempted to "give us law at the bayonets['] point." Republicus (Mar. 1, 1788), reprinted in 5 The Complete Anti-Federalist, *supra* note 45, at 165, 169; see also A Farmer (Feb. 29, 1788), reprinted in 5 The Complete Anti-Federalist, id. at 16, 25 (contrasting the proposed Constitution's arrangement with the institutional safeguards present in the British system of government, and noting that the protections against the danger of standing troops were greater in England).

54. George Mason, Objections to the Constitution (Oct. 7, 1787), reprinted in 13 Documentary History, *supra* note 1, at 349. Mason's objections were known to have been published in at least twenty-seven newspapers from Maine to South Carolina and served as a sounding board for numerous Federalist and Anti-Federalist essays. See id. at 348. As the influential Anti-Federalist "Federal Farmer" complained before the start of the Pennsylvania ratifying convention, "[I]n this senate are lodged legislative, executive and judicial powers. . . ." Letter III from the Federal Farmer (Oct. 10, 1787), reprinted in 14 id. at 32. The Letters from the Federal Farmer were published as forty-page pamphlets for sale, rather than as articles in newspapers. Apparently thousands of copies were sold throughout the states, and they appeared in Pennsylvania, New York, and Massachusetts before the ratifying conventions in these states concluded. See John P. Kaminski & Gaspare J. Saladino, *Editors' Note,* id. at 14–18. They are considered to be "one of the most significant publications of the ratification debate." Id. at 14.

55. Letter IV from the Federal Farmer (Oct. 12, 1787), reprinted in 14 Documentary History, *supra* note 1, at 43–44.

56. Brutus II (N.Y. J., Nov. 1, 1787), reprinted in 13 id. at 529.

57. Objections, reprinted in 13 id. at 350.

58. Widely circulated by October and November of 1787, both Mason's Objections and the Letters from the Federal Farmer reflected the views of other leading Anti-Federalists on the treaty question. Indeed, Mason's attack on the treaty power seems to have been repeated in each of the major states for which we have records, primarily in the press but also in the ratifying conventions themselves. See John P. Kaminski & Gaspare J. Saladino, *Editor's Note,* id. at 346–48 (describing circulation of Mason's objections in October, 1787); 14 id. 14–18 (describing distribution of Federal Farmer in October and November 1787).

59. George J. Graham Jr., Pennsylvania: Representation and the Meaning of Republicanism, in Ratifying the Constitution 52 (Michael A. Gillespie & Michael Lienesch eds., 1989).

60. See Convention Proceeding (Dec. 12, 1787), reprinted in 2 Documentary History, *supra* note 1, at 590–91. Delaware was the first state to ratify, on December 7, 1787, by a unanimous vote. See The Delaware Convention (Dec. 3–7, 1787), reprinted in 3 id. at 110.

61. Graham, *supra* note 59, at 53.

62. On this point, see, e.g., Thomas B. McAffee, *The Original Meaning of the Ninth Amendment,* 90 Colum. L. Rev. 1215, 1249–77 (1990) (discussing Federalist position on Bill of Rights); John C. Yoo, *Our Declaratory Ninth Amendment,* 42 Emory L.J. 967, 995–96 (1993).

63. James Wilson, Speech at Public Meeting in Philadelphia (Oct. 6, 1787), reprinted in 13 Documentary History, *supra* note 1, at 341. For the influence of Wilson's speech, which was widely published and referred to throughout the ratification, see John P. Kaminiski & Gaspare J. Saladino, *Editors' Note,* id. at 337–39.

64. An Old Whig III (Phila. Indep. Gazetteer, Oct. 20, 1787), 13 Documentary History, *supra* note 1, at 426.

65. Convention Debates (Dec. 3, 1787), reprinted in 2 id. at 459 (statement of William Findley). Notes from the Pennsylvania ratifying convention are sometimes difficult to decipher. Much of the day-to-day discussions were recorded by James Wilson, who took the notes in order to keep track of the objections to the Constitution. Aside from his own lengthy speeches, Wilson did not attempt to record speeches verbatim but only to capture the main thought of the speaker. See Merrill Jensen, *Note on Sources,* id. at 36, 40–43.

66. Convention Debates, reprinted in id. at 522.

67. Id. at 561–62.

68. Id. at 562–63.

69. Id. at 528.

70. Id.

71. John H. Ely, War and Responsibility: Constitutional Lessons of Vietnam and its Aftermath 3–5 (1993); Louis Fisher, Presidential War Power 7–8 (1995); Lofgren, *supra* note 13, at 19. See also Raoul Berger, *War-Making by the President,* 121 U. Pa. L. Rev. 29, 36 (1972).

72. Although this reading might explain Wilson's thoughts in a more cogent fashion, it is perhaps safer just to count Wilson as a dissenter from the prevailing Federalist view on war powers. But his statement on war powers does not square perfectly with his broad thoughts in favor of a strong executive expressed during the ratification debates. Nonetheless, even later in life, Wilson adhered to his belief that Congress should play the paramount role in war. In his lectures given as a professor of law at the University of Pennsylvania, Wilson contended that "[t]he power of declaring war, and the other powers naturally connected with it, are vested in congress." 2 James Wilson, Works 57 (James D. Andrews ed., 1896). He also suggested in his lectures that the Constitution had mimicked the Anglo-Saxon distribution of authority by giving all power over making war and peace in the legislature, just as the ancient "wittenagemote" had held the same power before the Norman Conquest. Id. at 57–58.

73. It is also the case that at this point in time, our records of the Pennsylvania and Virginia conventions are superior to that of New York's. The *Documentary History of the Ratification of the Constitution* provides complete documentation for Pennsylvania and Virginia, but it has yet to finish its volumes on New York, for which we must continue to rely on Jonathan Elliott's *Debates,* which are poorly edited and incomplete.

74. See The Dissent of the Minority of the Pennsylvania Convention (Pa. Packet, Dec. 18, 1787), reprinted in 15 Documentary History, *supra* note 1, at 7, 13–34. On the Dissent's wide distribution in New York, see John P. Kaminski & Gaspare J. Saladino, *Editor's Note,* id. at 10.

75. Id. at 29.

76. Cato VI (N.Y. J., Dec. 13, 1787), reprinted in 14 id. at 431–32. Cato warned that treaties could give away territory, send troops to Europe, pay out money, and "a thousand other obligations" without legislative participation. Id. at 432.

77. Id.; see also Brutus II, *supra* note 56, at 529.

78. The Federalist No. 69 (Alexander Hamilton), reprinted in 16 Documentary History, *supra* note 1, at 465.

79. Id. at 470.

80. The Federalist No. 25 (Alexander Hamilton), reprinted in id. at 161.

81. The Federalists continued to make these arguments until the very end of

the ratification process. Speaking before the last state convention, which took place in North Carolina, James Iredell overdrew the differences between president and Congress versus king and Parliament. Discussing the president's commander-in-chief powers, Iredell wrote:

> A very material difference may be observed between this power, and the authority of the king of Great Britain under similar circumstances. The king of Great Britain is not only the commander-in-chief of the land and naval forces, but has power, in time of war, to raise fleets and armies. He has also authority to declare war. The President has not the power of declaring war by his own authority, nor that of raising fleets and armies. These powers are vested in other hands. The power of declaring war is expressly given to Congress . . . . [Congress has] also expressly delegated to [it] the powers of raising and supporting armies, and of providing and maintaining a navy.

4 Debates, *supra* note 33, at 107–8.

82. The Federalist No. 69 (Alexander Hamilton), reprinted in 16 Documentary History, *supra* note 1, at 467–68.

83. Cato IV, reprinted in 2 The Complete Anti-Federalist, *supra* note 45, at 115–16.

84. See The Federalist No. 64 (John Jay), reprinted in 16 Documentary History, *supra* note 1, at 309.

85. The Federalist No. 69 (Alexander Hamilton), reprinted in id. at 467–68.

86. See The Federalist No. 53 (James Madison), reprinted in id. at 97, 100.

87. The Federalist No. 75 (Alexander Hamilton), reprinted in id. at 481–82.

88. Id.

89. Address to the Members of the New York and Virginia Conventions, Apr. 30, 1788, reprinted in 17 id. at 259.

90. Letter from the Federal Farmer XI (May 2, 1788), reprinted in 17 id. at 309. Although the date on Letter XI is January 10, 1788, it was not actually offered for sale until May 2. See id. at 265 (describing publication and distribution of additional letters).

91. Letter from Samuel Holden Parsons to William Cushing (Jan. 11, 1788), in 3 id. at 569–70. See also Richard H. Kohn, The Constitution and National Security: The Intent of the Framers, in The United States Military under the Constitution of the United States, 1789–1989, at 61, 83 (Richard H. Kohn ed., 1991) (discussing Federalist argument that Congress would hold sufficient power over the authorization of standing armies). Cushing was vice chairman of the Massachusetts ratifying convention and presided during John Hancock's absence until the final week of debate. He voted for ratification, served as a presidential elector for Washington in 1789, and served as an associate justice of the Supreme Court from 1789 until his death in 1810. Parsons, who had risen rapidly in the ranks of the Continental Army, saw only the early implementation of the Constitution for which he had voted; he died in November 1789 when his canoe overturned in the rapids of Big Beaver River. See 1 Bailyn, *supra* note 44, at 1001, 1031–32 (biographical notes).

92. See 2 Bailyn, *supra* note 44, at 1067.

93. Forrest McDonald, We the People: The Economic Origins of the Constitution 255–56 (1958).

94. Lance Banning, *Virginia: Sectionalism and the General Good,* in Gillespie & Lienesch, *supra* note 59, at 262.

95. See McDonald, *supra* note 93, at 259.

96. See 10 Documentary History, *supra* note 1, at 1538 (vote of June 25, 1788).

97. See Gordon S. Wood, *Ideology and the Origins of Liberal America,* 44 Wm. & Mary Q. 628, 632–33 (1987).

98. Initial counts appeared to show that as many as 200 of the 355 delegates to the Massachusetts convention were opposed to ratification. See McDonald, *supra* note 93, at 183. Governor John Hancock, who remained silent for much of the convention, was the key voice, and he could have thrown the final vote in either direction. See id. at 184–85. He apparently joined the Federalist camp after some had promised to support him for president or vice president. In announcing that he would support the Constitution, Hancock proposed several amendments, which helped mollify the opposition of some Anti-Federalists, such as Samuel Adams. See *Editor's Note,* in 16 Documentary History, *supra* note 1, at 63. Hancock's speech and his amendments, according to Federalists, turned the majority of the convention Federalist, and the convention soon ratified, 187 to 168, on February 6, 1788. See id. at 63–64. Massachusetts's amendments can be found in id. at 60.

99. See Letter from George Mason to John Lamb (June 9, 1788), in id. at 40–41; see also Letter from John Lamb to Richard Henry Lee (May 18, 1788), in id. at 36. Patrick Henry told New York Anti-Federalists in a separate letter that Mason's amendments would form the core of Anti-Federalist proposals for amendments during the Virginia convention. Letter from Patrick Henry to John Lamb (June 9, 1788), in id. at 39.

100. 10 id. at 1554 (proposed amendments reported out June 27, 1788).

101. See McDonald, *supra* note 93, at 259, 268, 366–67; Charles Warren, *The Mississippi River and the Treaty Clause of the Constitution,* 2 Geo. Wash. L. Rev. 271, 282–85, 296–97 (1934).

102. Speech by William Grayson to the Virginia Convention (June 12, 1788), reprinted in 10 Documentary History, *supra* note 1, at 1192.

103. See the excellent discussion of the politics of the Virginia convention in Banning, *supra* note 94, at 261–99.

104. Speech of June 5, 1788, reprinted in 9 Documentary History, *supra* note 1, at 964.

105. Id. at 965.

106. See McDonald, *supra* note 93, at 259; Banning, *supra* note 94, at 280–81.

107. Letter from James Madison to George Nicholas (May 17, 1788), printed in 9 Documentary History, *supra* note 1, at 804. Nicholas had received information that the delegates from the Kentucky region were focused wholly on the question of the Mississippi River, and he became so concerned that he asked Madison for the eighteenth-century version of talking points on the issue. See Letter from George Nicholas to James Madison (April 5, 1788), printed in id. at 704; Letter from George Nicholas to James Madison (May 9, 1788), printed in id. at 793.

108. Letter from James Madison to George Nicholas (May 17, 1788), printed in id. at 808.

109. Once the House's control over treaty implementation was acknowledged, Madison hoped, the delegates would recognize that the nature of the House and of popular democracy would prevent the new government from negotiating away its rights to the Mississippi. According to Madison, two elements of the House's structure would safeguard navigation rights to the river. First, members of the House would be more representative of all of a state's citizens, and would be chosen "more diffusively" from the state's population. In contrast, senators were chosen by state legislatures, and thus would be "considered as representatives of the States in their

political capacities." Further, Madison believed that most senators would come from "commercial and maritime situations which have generally presented the best choice of characters" for a body like the Senate. Here, Madison fully understood that the change in the Senate's selection process during the Constitutional Convention had altered the dynamic of the Senate from a council of state to a representative of state and sectional interests. Second, according to Madison, the more populous states had a strong interest in the Mississippi, and so their greater representation in the House would give them a greater voice than in the Senate. Members of the House themselves were more likely to be "a large majority of inland & Western members," than to be seaboard merchants, Madison predicted. "[T]he people of America being proportionally represented in [the House]," he concluded, "that part of America which is supposed to be most attached to the Mississippi, will have a greater share in the representation than they have in [the Continental] Congress, where the number of states only prevails." Id. Of course, this reasoning did not apply solely to the Mississippi; it would prevent the nation from entering into any treaty that did not receive the support of a majority of the people.

110. Statement of George Nicholas (June 10, 1788), reprinted in id. at 1130.

111. Statement of James Madison (June 13, 1788), reprinted in 10 id. at 1241.

112. Id. at 1251.

113. Speech of June 14, 1788, reprinted in id. at 1281.

114. Speech of June 9, 1788, reprinted in 9 id. at 964. For an analysis of Henry's odd statements on this point, see John C. Yoo, *The Continuation of Politics by Other Means: The Original Understanding of the War Powers,* 84 Cal. L. Rev. 167, 281–82 (1996).

115. 10 Documentary History, *supra* note 1, at 1282.

116. Id.

117. See, e.g., Banning, *supra* note 94, at 282.

118. The formal actions of the Virginia convention imply some agreement among Federalists and Anti-Federalists about the House's role, at least in the treaty process. By the end of June, Federalist arguments prevailed (and news arrived that the necessary ninth state, New Hampshire, had ratified), and the convention rejected, by a vote of 88 to 80, the Anti-Federalist proposal that Virginia condition its ratification on the acceptance of amendments. To mollify opposition, however, Federalists agreed to ratify the Constitution with recommendatory amendments clearly taken from Mason's draft. A draft of the amendments presented to the convention on June 27, 1788, undated but in Mason's handwriting, dropped the amendment calling for ratification of treaties by the House. See Draft Structural Amendments to the Constitution, ante-June 27, 1788, reprinted in 10 Documentary History, *supra* note 1, at 1547–50. Most of these amendments dealt with individual rights and some structural issues. One provision addressed the treaty power thus:

> That no commercial treaty shall be ratified without the concurrence of two-thirds of the whole number of the Members of the Senate; and no treaty, ceding, contracting, restraining or suspending the territorial rights or claims of the United States, or any of them, or their, or any of their rights or claims to fishing in the American Seas, or navigating the American rivers, shall be made, but in cases of the most urgent and extreme necessity, nor shall any such treaty be ratified without the concurrence of three fourths of the whole number of the Members of both Houses respectively.

Id. at 1554. The differences between Mason's original draft and this amendment are telling. Anti-Federalists dropped their general demand that the House be included in treaties, even those involving commerce. Mason's June 9 draft also required that all commercial and navigation laws, separate from treaties, receive a two-thirds vote in both houses. This change indicates some consensus among Anti-Federalists and Federalists, that the House generally would use its legislative power to participate in the treaty process. Federalists publicly conceded as much in the debates. Hence, an amendment creating a formal role for the House was unnecessary. For treaties involving territorial rights, however, even the House's power, exercised by majority vote, was not enough of a safeguard. On this issue, the Anti-Federalist amendments retained almost the exact language used by Mason's June 9 draft to require a three-quarters vote for such treaties. As several other sections of Mason's draft had undergone substantial revision between June 9 and June 27, it is safe to assume that the deletion of the demand that the House ratify all treaties was not stylistic, but was done for a reason. Since Federalists had assured Anti-Federalists that the House would play the same role that Parliament did in regard to treaties, Mason's proposal to formally include the House in the making of all treaties was no longer necessary.

CHAPTER FIVE

1. John Hart Ely, War and Responsibility 5 (1993).
2. Louis Fisher, Presidential War Power 11 (1995).
3. Michael D. Ramsey, *Textualism and War Powers*, 69 U. Chi. L. Rev. 1543 (2002); Jane E. Stromseth, *Rethinking War Powers: Congress, the President, and the United Nations*, 81 Geo. L.J. 597 (1993); William M. Treanor, *Fame, the Founding, and the Power to Declare War*, 82 Cornell L. Rev. 695, 700 (1997).
4. See, e.g., Edward S. Corwin, The President: Office and Powers, 1787–1984 (1984); Robert F. Turner, Repealing the War Powers Resolution: Restoring the Rule of Law in U.S. Foreign Policy (1991); Philip Bobbitt, *War Powers: An Essay on John Hart Ely's War and Responsibility: Constitutional Lessons of Vietnam and its Aftermath*, 92 Mich. L. Rev. 1364 (1994); Robert H. Bork, *Erosion of the President's Power in Foreign Affairs*, 68 Wash. U. L.Q. 693 (1990); Henry P. Monaghan, *Presidential War-Making*, 50 B.U. L. Rev. 19 (1970); W. Michael Reisman, *Some Lessons from Iraq: International Law and Democratic Politics*, 16 Yale J. Int'l L. 203 (1991); Eugene V. Rostow, *"Once More unto the Breach": The War Powers Resolution Revisited*, 21 Val. U. L. Rev. 1 (1986).
5. Ramsey, *supra* note 3, at 1590–1609.
6. Michael J. Glennon, Constitutional Diplomacy 17 (1990).
7. 1 Samuel Johnson, A Dictionary of the English Language (W. Strahan ed., 1755).
8. Adrian Vermeule and Ernest Young, *Hercules, Herbert, and Amar: The Trouble with Intratextualism*, 113 Harv. L. Rev. 730 (2000). But see Akhil Reed Amar, *Intratextualism*, 112 Harv. L. Rev. 747 (1999).
9. U.S. Const. art. I, § 10.
10. I have had the pleasure of engaging (not declaring) in several direct, published exchanges with pro-Congress scholars on war powers. See, e.g., Ramsey, *supra* note 3; Fisher, *supra* note 2. None of them has ever explained the difference in language between Article I, Section 8 and Article I, Section 10 other than to say that there is nothing wrong with using different language in different parts of the Constitution.
11. U.S. Const. art. I, § 8, cl. 11
12. Jane E. Stromseth, *Understanding Constitutional War Powers Today: Why Methodology Matters*, 106 Yale L.J. 845, 854 (1996) (quoting Jules Lobel, *Covert War*

and Congressional Authority: Hidden War and Forgotten Power, 134 U. Pa. L. Rev. 1035, 1045 [1986]). See also Charles A. Lofgren, *War-Making under the Constitution: The Original Understanding,* 81 Yale L.J. 672 (1972).

13. Privateers sought to capture enemy merchant vessels with the object of selling their cargoes back home. As individualistic commercial entrepreneurs, they failed miserably at actual fighting and did not coordinate their efforts with the American navy. See C. Kevin Marshall, Comment, *Putting Privateers in Their Place: The Applicability of the Marque and Reprisal Clause to Undeclared Wars,* 64 U. Chi. L. Rev. 953, 974–81 (1997); John C. Yoo, *The Continuation of Politics by Other Means: The Original Understanding of War Powers,* 84 Cal. L. Rev. 167, 250–52 (1996).

14. The Declare War Clause also comes immediately after another provision that is directly about legal effect and consequence. The immediate clause before gives Congress the authority "To define and punish Piracies and Felonies committed on the high Seas, and Offenses against the Law of Nations." Like the declare war power, this clause vests Congress with the authority to "define" the legal status of certain actions that, in its mind, constitute piracy, felonies, or violations of international law. It may then enact legislation criminalizing those actions. Similarly, the Declare War Clause gives Congress the power to "declare" whether the a certain state of affairs legally constitutes a war, which then gives it the authority to enact wartime regulations of individual persons and property both within and outside the United States.

15. Jerrilyn Greene Marston, King and Congress: The Transfer of Political Legitimacy, 1774–1776, at 303 (1987) (arguing that "the executive and administrative responsibilities that had been exercised by or under the aegis of the king's authority were confided to the successor to his authority, the Congress").

16. Articles of Confederation art. IX (1777).

17. Article IX also gave Congress the power to "establish[ ] rules for deciding, in all cases, what captures on land or water shall be legal," and "of granting letters of marque and reprisal in times of peace." Articles of Confederation art. IX. Both provisions remained substantially unchanged in the Constitution, and, in fact, they appear in the same clause as the power to declare war. The Framers' alteration of Congress's authority from determining on peace and war to declaring war, while leaving the other provisions unchanged, indicates an intention to alter Congress's war power.

18. See Yoo, *supra* note 13, at 222–23; Willi Paul Adams, The First American Constitutions: Republican Ideology and the Making of the State Constitution in the Revolutionary Era 271 (Rita and Robert Kimber trans., 1980).

19. S.C. Const. art XXVI (1776), reprinted in The Federal and State Constitutions, Colonial Charters, and Other Organic Laws 3247 (Francis N. Thorpe ed., 1909).

20. Johnson, *supra* note 7.

21. Nathan Bailey, An Universal Etymological English Dictionary (Neill ed., 24th ed. 1782).

22. Thomas Sheridan, A General Dictionary of the English Language (Dodsley ed., 1780).

23. See David Armitage, *The Declaration of Independence and International Law,* 59 Wm. & Mary Q. 39 (2002).

24. Id. at 39.

25. See Yoo, *supra* note 13, at 214–15.

26. See, e.g., 50 U.S.C. § 5(b)(1) (1994 & Supp. 1999) (seizure of foreign property); 50 U.S.C. § 1811 (1994) (electronic surveillance); 50 U.S.C . § 1829 (1994) (physical searches); 50 U.S.C. § 1844 (Supp. 1999) (trap and trace devices); 50 U.S.C. § 21 (1994)

(seizure of aliens); 10 U.S.C. § 2644 (1994 & Supp. 1996) (seizure of transportation systems).

27. *Korematsu v. United States,* 323 U.S. 214, 216 (1944) (upholding racial classifications during World War II and noting that "legal restrictions which curtail the civil rights of a single racial group" may be justified by "[p]ressing public necessity").

28. See generally Bradford R. Clark, *Separation of Powers as a Safeguard of Federalism,* 79 Tex. L. Rev. 1321 (2001); Bradford R. Clark, *Federal Common Law: A Structural Reinterpretation,* 144 U. Pa. L. Rev. 1245, 1271–99 (1996) (arguing that judicial federalism concerns do not apply to certain federal common law rules, including the Act of State Doctrine, allowing federal law in such instances to preempt state law).

29. Ramsey, *supra* note 3, 69 U. Chi. L. Rev. at 1600–1.

30. See, e.g., Harold H. Koh, The National Security Constitution: Sharing Power after the Iran-Contra Affair 79 (1990).

31. Joint Resolution to Authorize the Use of United States Armed Forces against Those Responsible for the Recent Attacks against the United States, Pub. L. No. 107-40, 115 Stat. 224 (2001).

32. Authorization for Use of Military Force against Iraq Resolution, Pub. L. No. 107-243, 116 Stat. 1498 (2003).

33. S. Con. Res. 21, 106th Cong., 1st Sess. (1999).

34. See Address to the Nation on Airstrikes against Serbian Targets in the Federal Republic of Yugoslavia (Serbia and Montenegro), 35 Weekly Comp. Pres. Doc. 516, 517 (Mar. 24, 1999).

35. See H.R. Res. 130, 106th Cong., 1st Sess. (1999) (supporting the American troops in the Balkans despite the "deep reservations" of some members of the House). After recognizing that President Clinton had sent American armed forces to operate against Serbia, the resolution merely declared that "the House of Representatives supports the members of the United States Armed Forces who are engaged in military operations against the Federal Republic of Yugoslavia and recognizes their professionalism, dedication, patriotism, and courage." Id.

36. See Letter to Congressional Leaders Reporting on Airstrikes against Serbian Targets in the Federal Republic of Yugoslavia (Serbia and Montenegro), 35 Weekly Comp. Pres. Doc. 527, 527–28 (Mar. 26, 1999).

37. In a follow-up letter on April 7, President Clinton refused to set an end date for American intervention and instead predicted that military operations would intensify until Milosevic ended his offensive against the Albanian Kosovars, stopped the repression, and agreed to a peace accord. See Letter to Congressional Leaders Reporting on Airstrikes against Serbian Targets in the Federal Republic of Yugoslavia (Serbia and Montenegro), 35 Weekly Comp. Pres. Doc. 602, 603 (Apr. 7, 1999). In addition to airstrikes, the president notified Congress that he had sent combat ground forces to Albania and Macedonia, ostensibly to engage in humanitarian relief operations. Id.

38. H.R. J. Res. 44, 106th Cong., 1st Sess. (1999).

39. John C. Yoo, *Point/Counterpoint: Kosovo, War Powers, and the Multilateral Future,* 148 U. Pa. L. Rev. 1673, 1681 (2000).

40. See 1999 Emergency Supplemental Appropriations Act, Pub. L. No. 106-31, tit. 11, ch. 3, 113 Stat. 57 (1999) (appropriating funding for operations "conducted against the Federal Republic of Yugoslavia (Serbia and Montenegro) during the period beginning on March 24, 1999, and ending on such date as NATO may designate, to resolve the conflict with respect to Kosovo").

41. See Address to the Nation on the Military Technical Agreement on Kosovo, 35 Weekly Comp. Pres. Doc. 1074, 1074 (June 10, 1999).

42. See generally Walter McDougall, Promised Land, Crusader State: The American Encounter in the World since 1776 (1998).

43. For a general discussion of the political and military background to the American and NATO intervention in Kosovo, see generally *Editorial Comments: NATO's Kosovo Intervention,* 93 Am. J. Int'l L. 824 (1999) (essays by Professors Henkin, Wedgwood, Charney, Chinkin, Falk, Franck, and Reisman on Kosovo).

44. See generally John C. Yoo, *International Law and the War in Iraq,* 97 Am. J. Int'l L. 563 (2003).

45. Id. See also William H. Taft IV & Todd F. Buchwald, *Preemption, Iraq, and International Law,* 97 Am. J. Int'l L. 557 (2003).

46. Thomas M. Franck & Faiza Patel, *UN Police Action in Lieu of War: "The Old Order Changeth,"* 85 Am. J. Int'l L. 63, 72 (1991).

47. See Michael J. Glennon & Allison R. Hayward, *Collective Security and the Constitution: Can the Commander in Chief Power Be Delegated to the United Nations?* 82 Geo. L.J. 1573, 1595–1601 (1994).

48. See Frank & Patel, *supra* note 46, at 74.

49. Louis Henkin, Foreign Affairs and the United States Constitution 252 (1996).

50. Alexander Hamilton, *The Defence No. 36,* Herald (New York) Jan. 2, 1796, reprinted in 20 Papers of Hamilton 4 (Harold C. Syrett ed., 1962) [hereinafter Papers of Hamilton]. Hamilton argued more fully that a treaty could legislate on any matter within Congress's Article I, Section 8 power, and that any effort to read the treaty power as limited by congressional authority would make it impossible for the nation to enter into treaties. See also Alexander Hamilton, *The Defence No. 37,* Herald (New York), Jan. 6, 1796, reprinted in id. at 16–22.

51. See, e.g., Ian Brownlie, International Law and the Use of Force by States 275–80 (1963); Louis Henkin, How Nations Behave: Law and Foreign Policy 141 (1979).

52. See Myres S. McDougal, *The Soviet-Cuban Quarantine and Self-Defense,* 57 Am. J. Int'l L. 597, 599 (1963) ("There is not the slightest evidence that the framers of the United Nations Charter, by inserting one provision which expressly reserves a right of self-defense, had the intent of imposing by this provision new limitations upon the traditional right of states."); Oscar Schachter, *The Right of States to Use Armed Force,* 82 Mich. L. Rev. 1620, 1634–35 (1984); Abraham D. Sofaer, *International Law and Kosovo,* 36 Stan. J. Int'l L. 1, 16 (2000); Thomas A. Franck, Recourse to Force: State Action against Threats and Armed Attacks 97–99 (2002); see generally Christine Gray, International Law and the Use of Force 84–119 (2000).

53. See Yoo, *supra* note 44, at 571–72.

54. Quoted in id. at 572.

55. Id. Many have argued, however, that the Security Council cannot require nations to intervene under Article 42 unless it has at its disposal national military forces, pursuant to special agreements under Article 43. See Michael J. Glennon, *Agora: The Gulf Crisis in International and Foreign Relations Law, UN Police Action in Lieu of War: The Constitution and Chapter VII of the United Nations Charter,* 85 Am. J. Int'l L. 74, 77–80 (1991) (collecting sources). No agreements between the U.N. and member nations under Article 43 ever took effect. This, however, only prevents the Security Council from requiring member nations to take military action, not from requesting that they do so voluntarily. The Charter also allows the Security Council to authorize police actions by regional organizations. See U.N. Charter art. 53 ("The Security Council shall, where appropriate, utilize such regional arrangements or agencies for enforcement action under its authority.").

56. Henkin, *supra* note 49, at 250.

57. See Statement of NATO Secretary General Lord Robertson (Oct. 2, 2001), available at www.nato.int/docu/speech/2001/s011002a.htm ("[I]t has now been determined that the attack against the United States on 11 September was directed from abroad and shall therefore be regarded as an action covered by Article 5 of the Washington Treaty"); *Terrorist Threat to the Americas,* Meeting of Consultation of Ministers of Foreign Affairs, Organization of American States, available at www.oas.org/OASpage/crisis/RC.24e.htm (resolving "[t]hat these terrorist attacks against the United States of America are attacks against all American states and that in accordance with all the relevant provisions of the Inter-American Treaty of Reciprocal Assistance (Rio Treaty) and the principle of continental solidarity, all States Parties to the Rio Treaty shall provide effective reciprocal assistance to address such attacks and the threat of any similar attacks against any American state, and to maintain the peace and security of the continent"); Fact Sheet, White House Office of Communications, *Campaign against Terrorism Results* (Oct. 1, 2001), available at 2001 WL 21898781, *1 (noting that "Australia offered combat military forces and invoked Article IV of the ANZUS Treaty, declaring September 11 an attack on Australia.").

58. See generally Yoo, *supra* note 44.

59. See, e.g., Michael J. Glennon, *Raising the Paquete Habana: Is Violation of Customary International Law by the Executive Unconstitutional?* 80 Nw. U. L. Rev. 321, 325 (1985); Louis Henkin, *International Law As Law in the United States,* 82 Mich. L. Rev. 1555, 1567 (1984). See also Jules Lobel, *The Limits of Constitutional Power: Conflicts between Foreign Policy and International Law,* 71 Va. L. Rev. 1071, 1179 (1985); *Agora: May the President Violate Customary International Law?* 80 Am. J. Int'l L. 913 (1986).

60. Henkin, *supra* note 59, at 1567. See also Louis Henkin, *The President and International Law,* 80 Am. J. Int'l L. 930, 937 (1986).

61. Compare Glennon, *supra* note 59, at 325; Henkin, *supra* note 60, at 936–37 (some exceptions), with Lobel, *supra* note 59, at 1075 (no exception).

62. For the arguments about the legitimacy of incorporating customary international law as federal common law, see Curtis A. Bradley & Jack L. Goldsmith, *Customary International Law As Federal Common Law: A Critique of the Modern Position,* 110 Harv. L. Rev. 815, 817 (1997); see also Alfred Rubin, Ethics and Authority in International Law 185–206 (1997); Philip R. Trimble, *A Revisionist View of Customary International Law,* 33 UCLA L. Rev. 665, 672–73 (1986); Arthur M. Weisburd, *The Executive Branch and International Law,* 41 Vand. L. Rev. 1205, 1269 (1988). For some of the responses to Professors Bradley and Goldsmith, see Harold H. Koh, *Is International Law Really State Law?* 111 Harv. L. Rev. 1824, 1827 (1998); Gerald L. Neuman, *Sense and Nonsense about Customary International Law: A Response to Professors Bradley and Goldsmith,* 66 Fordham L. Rev. 371, 371 (1997); Beth Stephens, *The Law of Our Land: Customary International Law As Federal Law after* Erie, 66 Fordham L. Rev. 393, 396–97 (1997). Bradley and Goldsmith have responded to their critics several times. See Curtis A. Bradley & Jack L. Goldsmith III, *Federal Courts and the Incorporation of International Law,* 111 Harv. L. Rev. 2260 (1998); Curtis A. Bradley & Jack L. Goldsmith, *The Current Illegitimacy of International Human Rights Litigation,* 66 Fordham L. Rev. 319, 330 (1997); cf. Bradford R. Clark, *Federal Common Law: A Structural Reinterpretation,* 144 U. Pa. L. Rev. 1245 (1996).

63. Professor Glennon, who has perhaps the most sensible view, applies the *Youngstown* framework to argue that presidents cannot act in this area of shared authority without congressional support. See Glennon, *supra* note 59, at 325.

64. See DOD News Briefings, available at www.defenselink.mil/news/Jun1999/to6111999_to611asd.html; www.defenselink.mil/news/Jun1999/990611-J-0000K-002.jpg; www.defenselink.mil/news/Jun1999 /990611-J-0000K-003.jpg (last visited Apr. 21, 2000).

65. See Edward Luttwak & Stuart Koehl, The Dictionary of Modern War 442, 466, 598 (1991); Joint Chiefs of Staff, Department of Defense Dictionary of Military and Associated Terms 262, 349–50, 363 (1987).

66. See David Kaye, *Are There Limits to Military Alliance? Presidential Power to Place American Troops under Non-American Commanders,* 5 Transnat'l L. & Contemp. Probs. 399, 425–28, 438–43 (1995); Michael J. Glennon & Allison R. Hayward, *Collective Security and the Constitution: Can the Commander in Chief Power Be Delegated to the United Nations?* 82 Geo. L.J. 1573, 1584–86 (1994) (discussing Americans serving under foreign command); Kaye, *supra,* at 420–25 (explaining that non-American officers sometimes shared strategic and operational command in World War I); see also David F. Trask, The United States in the Supreme War Council 23–24 (1961) (discussing the establishment of the Supreme War Council); Tasker H. Bliss, *The Evolution of the United Command,* Foreign Aff., Dec. 15, 1922, at 29–30 (discussing unified command under General Foch); Richard M. Leighton, *Allied Unity of Command in the Second World War: A Study in Regional Military Organization,* 67 Pol. Sci. Q. 399, 402, 425 (1952) (discussing the power to coerce).

67. See generally Dean Acheson, Present at the Creation: My Years in the State Department 402–13, 420–25, 445–55, 467–77 (1969) (Korea); George Bush & Brent Scowcroft, A World Transformed 302–492 (1998) (Persian Gulf).

68. See Memorandum from Alan J. Kreczko, Special Assistant to the President and Legal Adviser to the National Security Council, *Placing of United States Armed Forces under United Nations Operational or Tactical Control* (May 8, 1996), available at www.usdoj. gov/olc/mem_ops.htm.

69. The Appointments Clause declares that the President shall "nominate, and by and with the Advice and Consent of the Senate, shall appoint Ambassadors, other public Ministers and Consuls, Judges of the supreme Court, and all other Officers of the United States, whose Appointments are not herein otherwise provided for, and which shall be established by Law: but the Congress may by Law vest the Appointment of such inferior Officers, as they think proper, in the President alone, in the Courts of Law, or in the Heads of Departments." U.S. Const. art. II, § 2, cl. 2.

70. See John O. McGinnis, *The President, the Senate, the Constitution, and the Confirmation Process: A Reply to Professors Strauss and Sunstein,* 71 Tex. L. Rev. 633, 638–39 (1993); David A. Strauss & Cass R. Sunstein, *The Senate, the Constitution, and the Confirmation Process,* 101 Yale L.J. 1491, 1502–12 (1992); John C. Yoo, *Criticizing Judges,* 1 Green Bag 2d 277, 278 (1998).

71. See, e.g., *Edmond v. United States,* 520 U.S. 651, 663 (1997); *Ryder v. United States,* 515 U.S. 177, 180–84 (1995); *Weiss v. United States,* 510 U.S. 163, 169–76 (1994); *Freytag v. Commissioner,* 501 U.S. 868, 884 (1991); *Buckley v. Valeo,* 424 U.S. 1, 135 (1976).

72. See *Buckley v. Valeo,* 424 U.S. 1, 132 (1976).

73. There can be little doubt that if the president delegates command over American troops to foreign or international officers, those officers will exercise substantial authority under federal law. Under the Code of Military Justice, an American soldier who refuses to obey the orders of a superior officer is subject to potentially severe penalties, including death or long-term imprisonment. 10 U.S.C. § 890(2) (1994) (disobeying a superior commissioned officer, during time of war, is punishable by

death or other punishment as a court-martial may direct); 10 U.S.C. § 891(2) (1994) (disobeying a warrant, noncommissioned or petty officer can be punished as court-martial shall direct); 10 U.S.C. § 892(1) (1994) (disobeying a lawful general order or regulation shall be punished as a court-martial shall direct); 10 U.S.C. § 892(2) (1994) (disobeying any other lawful order shall be punishable as court-martial may direct).

74. *Ryder v. United States*, 515 U.S. 177, 182 (1995) (quoting *Freytag v. Commissioner*, 501 U.S. 868, 878 [1991]).

75. See, e.g., Steven G. Calabresi & Saikrishna B. Prakash, *The President's Power to Execute the Laws*, 104 Yale L.J. 541 (1994) (formalist); Martin S. Flaherty, *The Most Dangerous Branch*, 105 Yale L.J. 1725 (1996) (functionalist); Lawrence Lessig & Cass R. Sunstein, *The President and the Administration*, 94 Colum. L. Rev. 1 (1994) (functionalist).

76. See Calabresi & Prakash, *supra* note 75, at 593–99.

77. See, e.g., *Morrison v. Olson*, 487 U.S. 654, 691–92 (1988) (noting that "good cause" removal of the independent counsel still allows the president to retain authority over the counsel's duties); see also Lessig & Sunstein, *supra* note 75, at 106–16 (claiming that although there are numerous independent agencies, complete independence from the president would still raise constitutional problems).

78. One might respond to this argument by pointing out that if the president disapproves of the actions of the foreign commander, he may take back the power of command—in a sense, removing the foreign officer. This point, however, is not fully convincing. First, the question whether a delegation of power violates the nondelegation doctrine does not turn on whether Congress can terminate the delegation; Congress can always enact another statute to reverse an earlier delegation. Second, a presidential decision to undo a delegation of command may prove to be too little too late for an American military unit engaged in combat or in the midst of a dangerous situation as a result of a foreign commander's decisions.

79. See *Mistretta v. United States*, 488 U.S. 361, 371–79 (1989) (approving a congressional delegation of power where the goals were clearly set out, the purposes asserted, and the scope of the delegation was definitively confined).

80. For scholarly debate concerning the existence and scope of the nondelegation doctrine, compare Larry Alexander & Saikrishna Prakash, *Reports of the Non-Delegation Doctrine's Death Are Greatly Exaggerated*, 70 U. Chi. L. Rev. 1297 (2003), with Eric A. Posner and Adrian Vermeule, *Interring the Nondelegation Doctrine*, 69 U. Chi. L. Rev. 1721 (2002).

81. Quoted in Gordon S. Wood, The Creation of the American Republic, 1776–1787, at 78 (1969).

82. See John C. Yoo, *The New Sovereignty and the Old Constitution*, 15 Const. Comm. 87, 109 (1998). Forcing the president and Senate to share the appointments power opens up the selection and performance of public officials to public scrutiny, and thereby enhances responsibility and accountability in government. As Alexander Hamilton wrote in The Federalist No. 77, because the executive had to send nominees to the Senate, "the circumstances attending an appointment, from the mode of conducting it, would naturally become matters of notoriety; and the public would be at no loss to determine what part had been performed by the different actors." The Federalist No. 77, at 461 (Alexander Hamilton) (Clinton Rossiter ed., 1961). If the branches approved an unsuitable nominee, both would suffer at the hands of the public. "If an ill appointment should be made," Hamilton wrote, "the executive for nominating and the senate for approving would participate though in different degrees in the opprobrium and disgrace." Id. In contrast, for a state such as New York,

where secrecy prevailed over appointments, "all idea of responsibility is lost." Id. at 11. A shared appointment power allows the people to carefully evaluate their agents as they are appointed, and to hold their representatives responsible should the appointees abuse the public trust. See Yoo, *supra*, at 110–11. By forcing the government to conduct appointments in an open manner, the Constitution promotes government accountability and, ultimately, representative democracy.

83. NATO's military structure for the occupation of Kosovo attempted to minimize the likelihood that U.S. troops will have to serve on a regular basis under foreign or international command. Each nation that contributed troops to the NATO force—the United States, Great Britain, Germany, France, and Italy—bore primary control over a different geographic sector in Kosovo. The forces in each sector were commanded by a brigade commander from the same nation (thus, in the U.S. sector the troops are under the control of an American officer) who in turn reported to General Sir Michael Jackson, a British officer. General Jackson, who held operational command, reported to the theater commander, an American admiral, who in turn reported to General Wesley Clark, Supreme Allied Commander in Europe. See www.defenselink.mil/news/Jun1999/to6111999_to611asd.html. This arrangement did not preclude the forces of one nation from engaging in operations in a sector under the control of another NATO country, and thus serving under the tactical command of a foreign officer.

84. See John C. Yoo, *Globalism and the Constitution: Treaties, Non-Self-Execution, and the Original Understanding,* 99 Colum. L. Rev. 1955, 1968 & n.57 (1999).

CHAPTER SIX

1. Louis Henkin, Foreign Affairs and the United States Constitution 201 (1996).

2. *Harlow v. Fitzgerald,* 457 U.S. 800, 812 n.19 (1982).

3. *Nixon v. Fitzgerald,* 457 U.S. 731, 749–50 (1982).

4. *Department of the Navy v. Egan,* 484 U.S. 518, 529 (1988), quoting *Haig v. Agee,* 453 U.S. 280, 293–94 (1981).

5. *United States v. Curtiss-Wright Export Corp.,* 299 U.S. 304, 320 (1936).

6. See generally Saikrishna B. Prakash & Michael D. Ramsey, *The Executive Power over Foreign Affairs,* 111 Yale L.J. 231 (2001).

7. *Goldwater v. Carter,* 617 F.2d 697, 706–7 (D.C. Cir.) (en banc), *vacated and remanded with instructions to dismiss,* 444 U.S. 996 (1979).

8. Even in the cases in which the Supreme Court has limited executive authority, it has also emphasized that legislative prerogatives should not be construed to prevent the executive branch "from accomplishing its constitutionally assigned functions." *Nixon v. Administrator of General Services,* 433 U.S. 425, 443 (1977).

9. As the D.C. Circuit has recognized, "even after [the president] has obtained the consent of the Senate it is for him to decide whether to ratify a treaty and put it into effect. Senatorial confirmation of a treaty concededly does not obligate the President to go forward with a treaty if he concludes that it is not in the public interest to do so." *Goldwater,* 617 F.2d at 705; see also Henkin, *supra* note 1, at 184.

10. Laurence H. Tribe, *Taking Text and Structure Seriously: Reflections on Free-Form Method in Constitutional Interpretation,* 108 Harv. L. Rev. 1221 (1995).

11. 1 Annals of Congress 480 (Joseph Gales & William W. Seaton eds., 1834 [1789]).

12. Id. at 481–82.

13. Steven G. Calabresi & Saikrishna B. Prakash, *The President's Power to Execute the Laws,* 104 Yale L.J. 647 (1994).

14. *Bowsher v. Synar,* 478 U.S. 714 (1986). Even in *Morrison v. Olson,* 487 U.S. 654 (1988), in which the Court upheld the limitation on the president's authority to remove an independent counsel for "good cause," the justices emphasized that the restriction was constitutional because it did not "impede the President's ability to perform his constitutional duty" to exercise the executive power and to see that the laws are "faithfully executed." The president continued to enjoy the power to control and supervise the independent counsel, the Court found, because as an executive officer the independent counsel still remained subject to removal. "This is not a case in which the power to remove an executive official has been completely stripped from the President, thus providing no means for the President to ensure the 'faithful execution' of the laws." Because of this removal authority, even if diluted, the president still "retains ample authority to assure that the counsel is competently performing her statutory responsibilities."

15. 5 Green Hackworth, Digest of International Law § 509 (1943).

16. See 6 James D. Richardson, A Compilation of the Messages and Papers of the Presidents 246 (1897), announcing termination of Rush-Baggot Agreement regarding Naval Forces on the American Lakes with Great Britain, April, 1817, 12 Bevans 54. There is some contention over whether the Rush-Baggot Agreement was actually a treaty and whether President Lincoln terminated it alone. See David G. Adler, The Constitution and the Termination of Treaties 164 (1986). These concerns do not seem to be on the mark. Although the Rush-Baggot Convention originated as an executive agreement, it was submitted to the Senate for its advice and consent, which the Senate gave in 1818. Second, even if Congress maintained that termination could only be accomplished with its approval and purported to ratify the president's notice on that basis, it does not follow that the president acceded to Congress's view of the matter—*neither* branch may have acquiesced in the other's position. Third, the fact that the treaty was not actually terminated does not dispose of the question whether the president understood that he had the authority to terminate it.

17. See William Howard Taft, Our Chief Magistrate and His Powers 112–14 (1916). Adler argues, however, that this termination was an example of the president and Senate acting together. Adler, *supra* note 16, at 182.

18. *Goldwater v. Carter,* 481 F. Supp. 949, 954 (D.D.C. 1979).

19. *Goldwater v. Carter,* 617 F.2d 697 (D.C. Cir. 1979).

20. *Goldwater v. Carter,* 444 U.S. 996 (1979).

21. National Missile Defense Act of 1999, Pub. L. No. 106-138, 113 Stat. 205.

22. John C. Yoo, *Politics as Law? The Anti-Ballistic Missile Treaty, the Separation of Powers, and Treaty Interpretation,* 89 Cal. L. Rev. 865 (2001).

23. *ABM Treaty and the Constitution: Joint Hearings before the Senate Comm. on Foreign Relations and the Senate Comm. on the Judiciary,* 100th Cong., 1st Sess. 83 (1987).

24. *Chevron, U.S.A. v. Natural Resources Defense Council,* 467 U.S. 837, 865–66 (1984).

25. On the nature of the federal common law, see Bradford A. Clark, *Federal Common Law: A Structural Reinterpretation,* 144 U. Pa. L. Rev. 1245 (1996); Henry J. Friendly, *In Praise of Erie—And of the New Federal Common Law,* 39 N.Y.U. L. Rev. 383 (1964); Thomas W. Merrill, *The Common Law Powers of Federal Courts,* 52 U. Chi. L. Rev. 1 (1985).

26. Phillip R. Trimble & Jack S. Weiss, *The Role of the President, the Senate and Congress with Respect to Arms Control Treaties Concluded by the United States,* 67 Chi.-Kent L. Rev. 645, 661 (1991).

27. See, e.g., John F. Manning, *Textualism as a Nondelegation Doctrine,* 97 Colum. L. Rev. 673 (1997); Adrian Vermeule, *Interpretive Choice,* 75 N.Y.U. L. Rev. 74 (2000).

28. See William N. Eskridge Jr., *Textualism, the Unknown Ideal?* 96 Mich. L. Rev. 1509 (1998); William N. Eskridge Jr. & Philip P. Frickey, *Statutory Interpretation as Practical Reasoning,* 42 Stan. L. Rev. 321 (1990).

29. Antonin Scalia, A Matter of Interpretation 34–35 (1997).

30. For the relevant historical details, I have relied on Stanley M. Elkins & Eric L. McKitrick, The Age of Federalism 303–73 (1993); Forrest McDonald, The Presidency of George Washington 113–37 (1974); *Editorial Note,* Jefferson's Opinion on the Treaties with France, reprinted in 25 The Papers of Thomas Jefferson 597–602 (John Catanzariti et al. eds., 1992) [hereinafter Papers of Jefferson]; Letter from Alexander Hamilton to John Jay (Apr. 9, 1793), in 14 Papers of Alexander Hamilton 297, 298 n.4 (Harold C. Syrett et al. eds., 1969) [hereinafter Papers of Hamilton]. These events are also discussed in David P. Currie, *The Constitution in Congress: The Third Congress, 1793–1795,* 63 U. Chi. L. Rev. 1, 4–16 (1996).

31. Treaty of Alliance, Feb. 6, 1778, U.S.-Fr., Treaty Series 82, art. XI, 7 Bevans 777.

32. Treaty of Amity and Commerce, Feb. 6, 1778, U.S.-Fr., 8 Stat. 12., art. XVII.

33. Notes on Washington's Questions on Neutrality and the Alliance with France, May 6, 1793, reprinted in 25 Papers of Jefferson, *supra* note 30, at 665–66.

34. See Letter from Alexander Hamilton to John Jay (Apr. 9, 1793), in 14 Papers of Hamilton, *supra* note 30, at 297–98.

35. Letter from President George Washington to Alexander Hamilton, Thomas Jefferson, Henry Knox, and Edmund Randolph (Apr. 18, 1793), in id. at 326–27.

36. George Washington, Proclamation, reprinted in 1 Compilation of the Messages and Papers of the Presidents: 1789–1897, at 156 (James D. Richardson ed., 1900).

37. Elkins & McKitrick, *supra* note 30, at 338.

38. Opinion on the Treaties with France, Apr. 28, 1793, in 25 Papers of Jefferson, *supra* note 30, at 608–18.

39. Letter from Alexander Hamilton & Henry Knox to President George Washington (May 2, 1793), in 14 Papers of Hamilton, *supra* note 30, at 367–96.

40. Notes on Washington's Questions on Neutrality and the Alliance with France, reprinted in 25 Papers of Jefferson, *supra* note 30, at 666.

41. Neutrality Act, 1 Stat. 381 (June 5, 1794).

42. See Jack N. Rakove, The Beginnings of National Politics: An Interpretive History of the Continental Congress 113–18 (1979) (describing Congress's involvement in 1778 treaty); Samuel F. Bemis, The Diplomacy of the American Revolution 58–69 (1957) (describing treaty).

43. Prakash & Ramsey, *supra* note 6, at 325–27.

44. See Pacificus Nos. 1–7 (1793), reprinted in 15 Papers of Hamilton, *supra* note 30, at 33–35.

45. See Helvidius Nos. 1–5 (1793), reprinted in id. at 66–120.

46. See Elkins & McKitrick, *supra* note 37, at 362 (noting historians' judgment of Madison's weak performance).

47. Helvidius No. 2, reprinted in 15 Papers of Madison, *supra* note 30, at 82.

48. Treaty on the Further Reduction and Limitation of Strategic Offensive Arms, July 31, 1991, U.S.-Russ., S. Treaty Doc. No. 20, 102d Cong., 1st Sess. (1991); Treaty on Further Reduction and Limitation of Strategic Arms, Jan. 3, 1993, U.S.-U.S.S.R., S. Treaty Doc. No. 1, 103d Cong., 1st Sess. (1993).

49. See, e.g., *Ballistic Missiles: Threat and Response: Hearings before the Senate Comm. on Foreign Relations*, 106th Cong., 1st Sess. 409.

50. President George Bush, Address before a Joint Session of the Congress on the State of the Union, 27 Weekly Comp. Pres. Doc. 90 (Jan. 29, 1991).

51. Missile Defense Act of 1991, Pub. L. No. 102-190, § 232(a)(1), 105 Stat. 1321.

52. For general discussion, see Stephen Ratner, *Drawing a Better Line: Uti Possidetis and the Borders of New States*, 90 Am. J. Int'l L. 590 592–93 (1996).

53. See Edwin D. Williamson & John E. Osborn, *A U.S. Perspective on Treaty Succession and Related Issues in the Wake of the Breakup of the USSR and Yugoslavia*, 33 Va. J. Int'l L. 261, 267 (1993).

54. Memorandum of Understanding Relating to the Treaty between the United States of America and the Union of Soviet Socialist Republics on the Limitation of Anti-Ballistic Missile Systems of May 26, 1972, Sept. 26, 1997, available at www.state. gov/www/global/arms/factsheets/missdef/abm_mou.html.

55. Letter from President William J. Clinton to Benjamin A. Gilman, Chairman of the House Committee on International Relations (Nov. 21, 1997), reprinted in *Ballistic Missiles, supra* note 49, at 477–79 ("If, however, the Senate were to fail to act or to disagree and disapprove the agreements, succession arrangements will simply remain unsettled. The ABM Treaty itself would clearly remain in force."); Letter from President William J. Clinton to Sen. Jesse Helms, Chairman of the Senate Committee on Foreign Relations (May 21, 1998), reprinted in id. at 480–81 ("[T]here is no question that the ABM Treaty has continued in force and will continue in force even if the MOU is not ratified.").

56. See Letter from Senator Trent Lott et al. to President William J. Clinton (Oct. 5, 1998), reprinted in id. at 482–83 ("[I]t is our position that the ABM Treaty has lapsed and is of no force and effect unless the Senate approves the MOU, or some similar agreement, to revive the treaty."). See National Defense Authorization Act for Fiscal Year 1995, Pub. L. No. 103-337, § 232; Conventional Forces in Europe Flank Agreement, May 14, 1997, 36 I.L.M. 980, 984.

57. See, e.g., *Consumers Union v. Kissinger*, 506 F.2d 136 (D.C. Cir. 1974), *cert. denied*, 421 U.S. 1004 (1975).

58. Geneva Convention Relative to the Treatment of Prisoners of War, July 14, 1955, art. 2, 6 U.S.T. 3316, 3318, 75 U.N.T.S. 135, 136.

59. Press Briefing by Ari Fleischer (Feb. 7, 2002), available at www.whitehouse. gov/news/releases/2002/02/20020207-6.html; Katherine Q. Seelye, *In Shift, Bush Says Geneva Rules Fit Taliban Captives*, N.Y. Times, Feb. 8, 2002, at A1.

60. See generally John C. Yoo & James C. Ho, *The Status of Terrorists*, 44 Va. J. Int'l L. 207 (2003).

61. See, e.g., *Rasul v. Bush*, 124 S. Ct. 2686 (2004); *Hamdi v. Rumsfeld*, 124 S. Ct. 2633 (2004).

62. See, e.g., Michael Van Alstine, *The Judicial Power and Treaty Delegation*, 90 Cal. L. Rev. 1263 (2002); Carlos Vázquez, *Treaty-Based Rights and Remedies of Individuals*, 92 Colum. L. Rev. 1082 (1992).

63. See *Johnson v. Eisentrager*, 339 U.S. 763 (1950); but see *Rasul v. Bush*, 124 S. Ct. 2686 (2004).

CHAPTER SEVEN

1. The Federalist No. 63 (James Madison), reprinted in 16 The Documentary History of the Ratification of the Constitution 292 (John P. Kaminski & Gaspare J. Saladino eds., 1986) [hereinafter Documentary History]. Madison, for example, justified

the Senate's role in foreign affairs on the ground that, "[w]ithout a select and stable member of the government, the esteem of foreign powers will not only be forfeited by an unenlightened and variable policy . . . but the national councils will not possess that sensibility to the opinion of the world, which is perhaps not less necessary in order to merit, than it is to obtain, its respect and confidence." Id.

2. *Youngstown Sheet & Tube Co. v. Sawyer*, 343 U.S. 579, 587 (1952).

3. Lori F. Damrosch, *The Role of the United States Senate concerning "Self-Executing" and "Non-Self-Executing" Treaties*, 67 Chi.-Kent L. Rev. 515, 530 (1991) ("[O]ur constitutional law is clear: the treaty-makers may make supreme law binding on the states as to any subject, and notions of states' rights should not be asserted as impediments to the full implementation of treaty obligations."); see also Louis Henkin, Foreign Affairs and the United States Constitution 191 (1996) (on the attempt to limit treaties to matters of "international concern," observing "I know of no basis for reading into the Constitution such a limitation on the subject matter of treaties. Nor would I know any formula for determining which matters are and which are not our 'business' or the proper 'business' of other countries."); Gerald L. Neuman, *The Global Dimensions of RFRA*, 14 Const. Commentary 33, 34, 46–47 (1997).

4. Henkin, *supra* note 3, at 197.

5. David M. Golove, *Treaty-making and the Nation: The Historical Foundations of the Nationalist Conception of the Treaty Power*, 98 Mich. L. Rev 1075, 1090 (2000).

6. *City of Boerne v. Flores*, 521 U.S. 507 (1997).

7. Neuman, *supra* note 3, at 46.

8. Restatement (Third) of the Foreign Relations Law of the United States § 111(4) [hereinafter Restatement (Third)].

9. *See* Henkin, *supra* note 3, at 194–95.

10. Carlos Manuel Vázquez, *Laughing at Treaties*, 99 Colum. L. Rev. 2154 (1999).

11. U.S. Const. art. I, § 9, cl. 7.

12. See Restatement (Third), § 111 cmt. i; Henkin, *supra* note 3, at 203.

13. See, e.g., Restatement (Third), § 111 cmt. i & reporter's note 6; Henkin, *supra* note 3, at 203.

14. James Madison, Jay's Treaty (Mar. 10, 1796) in 16 Papers of James Madison 258 (Robert A. Rutland et al. eds., 1977) [hereinafter Madison Papers].

15. Id. at 259.

16. See *Reid v. Covert*, 354 U.S. 1 (1957) (plurality opinion).

17. Henkin, *supra* note 3, at 195.

18. See *Morrison v. Olson*, 487 U.S. 654 (1988) (upholding independent counsel law); *Bowsher v. Synar*, 478 U.S. 714 (1986) (invalidating deficit reduction act).

19. Henkin, *supra* note 3, at 191.

20. 252 U.S. 416, 433–35 (1920).

21. *Holmes v. Jennison*, 39 U.S. (14 Pet.) 540, 569 (1840); see also *New Orleans v. United States*, 35 U.S. (10 Pet.) 662, 736 (1836).

22. *United States v. Lopez*, 514 U.S. 549, 558–68 (1995); *United States v. Morrison*, 529 U.S. 598 (2000).

23. *United States v. Morrison*, 529 U.S. 598 (2000) (restricting Congress's Fourteenth Amendment enforcement power); *City of Boerne v. Flores*, 521 U.S. 507 (1997) (strictly tying Congress's Fourteenth Amendment enforcement power to a definitive pattern of unconstitutional behavior); *Alden v. Maine*, 527 U.S. 706, 710–60 (1999) (protecting states from suit in state court); *Printz v. United States*, 521 U.S. 898, 935 (1997) (prohibiting congressional action that compels state officers to execute fed-

eral law); *Seminole Tribe v. Florida,* 517 U.S. 44, 57–73 (1996) (limiting Congress's power to abrogate state sovereign immunity in federal court); *New York v. United States,* 505 U.S. 144, 161–66 (1992) (prohibiting Congress from commandeering states into the services of federal regulation).

24. Curtis A. Bradley, *The Treaty Power and American Federalism,* 97 Mich. L. Rev. 390 (1998).

25. Golove, *supra* note 5, at 1075.

26. Restatement (Third), § 302 cmts. c & d.

27. See, e.g., James M. Buchanan & Gordon Tullock, The Calculus of Consent: Logical Foundations of Constitutional Democracy 283–95 (1965) (discussing the important role of "pressure groups" in the promotion of economic interest); Mancur Olson, The Logic of Collective Action: Public Goods and the Theory of Groups 132–67 (1965) (discussing the theory of "special interests" and incentives to organize for the common benefit); William H. Riker, Liberalism against Populism: A Confrontation between the Theory of Democracy and the Theory of Social Choice 169–212 (1982) (discussing the theory of social choice and changes of the political agenda).

28. See, e.g., Theodore Lowi, The End of Liberalism 52–56 (1979) (noting that interest group liberalism is thought to settle conflicts in society).

29. See generally Keith Krehbiel, Information and Legislative Organization (1991) (proposing a link between distributive and informational theories of legislative organization); Arthur Maass, Congress and the Common Good (1980) (discussing the relationship between political institutions, public opinion, political actors, and elections); William N. Eskridge, *Overriding Supreme Court Statutory Interpretation Decisions,* 101 Yale L.J. 331, 356–57 (1991) (discussing information theory and the creation of public policy).

30. Cf. Cass Sunstein, *Interest Groups in American Public Law,* 38 Stan. L. Rev. 29, 33–35 (1985) (addressing the problem of factionalism in supplanting political discussion and debate).

31. Norman Ornstein et al., Vital Statistics on Congress 1998–1999, at 47–49, 64–65 (1998).

32. See Stanley Elkins & Eric McKitrick, Age of Federalism 55–58 (1993).

33. See *Whitney v. Robinson,* 124 U.S. 190, 194 (1888); see also *The Chinese Exclusion Case,* 130 U.S. 581, 600 (1889) ("the last expression of the sovereign will must control"); *Head Money Cases,* 112 U.S. 580, 599 (1884) (holding that a treaty does not have "superior sanctity" to a statute by nature); Henkin, *supra* note 3, at 209–11 ("At the end of the twentieth century, the power of Congress to enact laws that are inconsistent with U.S. treaty obligations, and the equality of treaties and statutes in domestic U.S. law, appear to be firmly established.").

34. 462 U.S. 919 (1983).

35. James Madison, Speech on Jay's Treaty (Mar. 10, 1796), in 16 Madison Papers, at 257. Although Madison admitted that the Roman constitution had operated similarly, he believed that it was only "a political phenomenon, which had been celebrated as a subject of curious speculation only, and not as a model for the institutions of any other Country." Id. In Madison's mind, vesting the legislative power in two separate authorities that could each "annul the proceedings of the other" would produce only an unstable and irrational government. Id.

36. See Richard H. Fallon et al., Hart & Wechsler's The Federal Courts and the Federal System 840–41 (1996).

37. See, e.g., *Central Bank of Denver v. First Interstate Bank of Denver,* 511 U.S. 164, 191 (1994) (refusing to find private cause of action for aiding and abetting under

§ 10(b) of Securities Exchange Act of 1934); Hart & Wechsler, *supra* note 36, at 840 n.5 & accompanying text (discussing the requirement of legislative intent).

38. See, e.g., Administrative Procedure Act, 5 U.S.C. § 701(a)(2) (1994) (decision committed to agency discretion); *Citizens to Preserve Overton Park v. Volpe,* 401 U.S. 402 (1971) (discussing reviewability of secretary of transportation's authorization of highway funds).

39. 726 F.2d 774 (D.C. Cir. 1984).

40. Id. at 801 (Bork, J., concurring).

41. See Jack L. Goldsmith, *The New Formalism in United States Foreign Relations Law,* 70 U. Colo. L. Rev. 1395, 1424–29 (1999) (reviewing cases).

42. See Hart & Wechsler, *supra* note 36, at 28. There is a strong debate, however, about whether certain classes of federal jurisdiction were considered mandatory and had to be vested by Congress in the federal courts. See, e.g., Akhil Reed Amar, *A Neo-Federalist View of Article III: Separating the Two Tiers of Federal Jurisdiction,* 65 B.U. L. Rev. 205, 260–62; Akhil Reed Amar, *The Two-Tiered Structure of the Judiciary Act of 1789,* 138 U. Pa. L. Rev. 1499 (1990); Robert N. Clinton, *A Mandatory View of Federal Court Jurisdiction: Early Implementation of and Departures from the Constitutional Plan,* 86 Colum. L. Rev. 1515, 1561–70 (1986).

43. Under the Madisonian compromise, Congress was given the discretion to establish lower federal courts or to rely on the state courts to enforce federal law. *See* Hart & Wechsler, *supra* note 36, at 7–9.

44. See Henry P. Monaghan, *Constitutional Adjudication: The Who and When,* 82 Yale L.J. 1363, 1379–86 (1973).

45. See, e.g., *Sanchez-Espinoza v. Reagan,* 770 F.2d 202, 210 (D.C. Cir. 1985) (dismissing a war powers claim as not ripe for judicial review); *Crockett v. Reagan,* 720 F.2d 1355, 1356 (D.C. Cir. 1983) (holding that the war powers issue presented a nonjusticiable political question); *Dellums v. Bush,* 752 F. Supp. 1141, 1146 (D.D.C. 1990) (holding that "the judicial Branch should not decide issues affecting the allocation of power between the President and Congress until the political branches reach a constitutional impasse"); *Ange v. Bush,* 752 F. Supp. 509, 512–15 (D.D.C. 1990); *Lowry v. Reagan,* 676 F. Supp. 333, 340 (D.D.C. 1987) (holding that the "judicial branch . . . is neither equipped or empowered to intrude into the realm of foreign affairs); *DaCosta v. Laird,* 405 U.S. 979, 979 (1972); *Massachusetts v. Laird,* 400 U.S. 886 (1970) (finding challenge to Vietnam War a nonjusticiable political question); *Mora v. McNamara,* 389 U.S. 934, 934 (1967); *Holtzman v. Schlesinger,* 484 F.2d 1307, 1310 (2d Cir. 1973).

46. *Baker v. Carr,* 369 U.S. 186, 211 (1962).

47. See, e.g., *Chicago & S. Air Lines v. Waterman S.S. Corp.,* 333 U.S. 103, 111 (1948); *Oetjen v. Central Leather Co.,* 246 U.S. 297, 302 (1918).

48. See, e.g., *Crockett v. Reagan,* 720 F.2d 1355 (D.C. Cir. 1983); *Lowry v. Reagan,* 676 F. Supp. 333 (D.D.C. 1987); Goldsmith, *supra* note 41, at 1414–18.

49. See, e.g., Charles A. Lofgren, *United States v. Curtiss-Wright Export Corporation: An Historical Reassessment,* 83 Yale L.J. 1 (1973); David M. Levitan, *The Foreign Relations Power: An Analysis of Mr. Justice Sutherland's Theory,* 55 Yale L.J. 467 (1946).

50. Carlos Manuel Vázquez, *Treaty-Based Rights and Remedies of Individuals,* 92 Colum. L. Rev. 1082, 1084–85 (1992).

51. Id. at 1108.

52. Henkin, *supra* note 3, at 198.

53. Jordan J. Paust, *Self-Executing Treaties,* 82 Am. J. Int'l L. 760, 760 (1988).

54. 16 Madison Papers, at 256.

55. See Vázquez, *supra* note 10, at 2174.

56. Bradley, *supra* note 24, at 424–25.

57. Curtis A. Bradley & Jack L. Goldsmith, *Treaties, Human Rights, and Conditional Consent*, 149 U. Pa. L. Rev. 399 (2000).

58. Alexander Hamilton, The Defence No. 37, Herald (New York), Jan. 6, 1796, reprinted in 20 Papers of Alexander Hamilton 13, 18 (Harold C. Syrett ed., 1962) [hereinafter Hamilton Papers].

59. 27 U.S. (2 Pet.) 253 (1829). Professor Vázquez's discussion of *Foster* is puzzling. He goes to great lengths to prove that Chief Justice Marshall recognized in *Foster* that the Supremacy Clause renders all treaties self-executing. Yet, it is quite clear that in *Foster* itself the Court found that the treaty at issue was not self-executing, and that it reached this conclusion because Marshall believed that the choice of treaty execution should be left primarily to the political branches. To say simply that Marshall found for self-execution, but then when he addressed the treaty at hand "he seemed to lose sight of this presumption," Vázquez, *supra* note 10, at 2198, fails to explain why the Court acted as it did in *Foster*. As I admit, the Court in *United States v. Percheman*, 32 U.S. (7 Pet.) 51 (1833), reversed *Foster's* interpretation of the treaty at hand. A remarkable case worth detailed historical study, *Percheman* did not reverse the doctrine expressed in *Foster*, although it rejected *Foster's* application of that doctrine.

60. Compare Bradley & Goldsmith, *supra* note 57, at 456–68, with Damrosch, *supra* note 3; Stefan A. Riesenfeld & Frederick M. Abbott, *The Scope of U.S. Senate Control over the Conclusion and Operation of Treaties*, in Parliamentary Participation in the Making and Operation of Treaties: A Comparative Study 205, 207–13 (Stefan A. Riesenfeld & Frederick M. Abbott eds., 1994) (describing practice of president and Senate).

61. See generally Elkins & McKitrick, *supra* note 32, at 52–54, 123–31, 209–56; Drew R. McCoy, The Elusive Republic: Political Economy in Jeffersonian America 76–104 (1996) (discussing a variety of U.S. attitudes to foreign powers and foreign trade at the end of the eighteenth century).

62. See Treaty of Amity, Commerce, and Navigation, Nov. 19, 1794, U.S.-Gr. Brit., 8 Stat. 116, T.S. No. 105 (signed at London, approved by Senate June 24, 1795, ratified by United States, Aug. 14, 1795). The policy and politics of the Jay Treaty are discussed in Samuel Flagg Bemis, Jay's Treaty: A Study in Commerce and Diplomacy (1962); Jerald A. Combs, The Jay Treaty: Political Battleground of the Founding Fathers (1970); Elkins & McKitrick, *supra* note 32, at 375–449. On the more specific question of the British debts, see Emory G. Evans, *Planter Indebtedness and the Coming of the Revolution in Virginia*, 19 Wm. & Mary Q. (3d ser.) 511 (1962); Emory G. Evans, *Private Indebtedness and the Revolution in Virginia, 1776 to 1796*, 28 Wm. & Mary Q. (3d ser.) 349, 359–67 (1971); Charles F. Hobson, *The Recovery of British Debts in the Federal Circuit Court of Virginia, 1790 to 1797*, 92 Va. Mag. Hist. & Biography 176 (1984); Wythe Holt, *"To Establish Justice": Politics, The Judiciary Act of 1789, and the Invention of the Federal Courts*, 1989 Duke L.J. 1421, 1430–58.

63. 2 U.S. (2 Dall.) 419 (1973). For the background and effect of *Chisholm*, see, e.g., 1 Charles Warren, The Supreme Court in United States History 96–102 (1922); 1 Julius Goebel Jr., History of the Supreme Court of the United States: Antecedents and Beginnings to 1801, at 734–41 (1971).

64. 3 U.S. (3 Dall.) 199 (1796). For useful information concerning the historical background of *Ware*, see, e.g., William R. Casto, The Supreme Court in the Early Republic: The Chief Justiceships of John Jay and Oliver Ellsworth 98–101 (1995); Richard B. Morris, John Jay, the Nation, and the Court 87–88 (1967); Goebel, *supra* note 63, at 748–56; 1 Warren, *supra* note 63, at 144–46.

65. See, e.g., Vázquez, *supra* note 10, at 1110–13 (explaining Justice Iredell's opin-

ion as the Supreme Court's first major treaty decision); Paust, *supra* note 53, at 765 & n.36 ("[T]reaty law was accepted as operating directly as supreme federal law in the face of inconsistent state law); Henkin, *supra* note 3, at 476 n.95.

66. Morris, *supra* note 64, at 97.

67. See David P. Currie, The Constitution in Congress: The Federalist Period 1789–1801, at 210–17 (1997).

68. See 4 Annals of Congress 863 (1795); see also Currie, *supra* note 67, at 210.

69. Alexander Hamilton, The Defence No. 36, Herald (New York) Jan. 2, 1796, reprinted in 20 Hamilton Papers, *supra* note 58, at 4. Hamilton argued more fully that a treaty could legislate on any matter within Congress's Article I, Section 8 power, and that any effort to read the treaty power as limited by congressional authority would make it impossible for the nation to enter into treaties. See also Alexander Hamilton, The Defence No. 37, Herald (New York), Jan. 6, 1796, reprinted in 20 Hamilton Papers, *supra* note 58, at 16–22.

70. 5 Annals of Congress 472.

71. Id. at 465.

72. Id. at 493.

73. Id. at 759.

74. See George Washington, *Message to the House of Representatives,* Mar. 30, 1796, reprinted in 35 Writings of George Washington 2, 2–5 (John C. Fitzpatrick ed., 1940).

75. 5 Annals of Congress 776.

76. Id. at 777.

77. 5 Annals of Congress 1291 (1849); Act of May 6, 1796, ch. 17, 1 Stat. 459.

78. Henkin, *supra* note 3, at 250.

79. See John C. Yoo, *Using Force,* 71 U. Chi. L. Rev. 729 (2004).

80. 555 F.2d 848 (D.C. Cir. 1976).

81. 859 F.2d 929 (D.C. Cir. 1988). See Military and Paramilitary Activities (*Nicaragua v. United States*), 1986 ICJ 14.

82. *Breard v. Greene,* 523 U.S. 371 (1998). The ICJ case was Vienna Convention on Consular Relations (*Paraguay v. United States*), 1998 ICJ 248.

83. *Federal Republic of Germany v. United States,* 526 U.S. 1111 (1999). The ICJ case was *LaGrande Case* (*Federal Republic of Germany v. United States*), 1999 ICJ 9.

84. *Case concerning Avena and other Mexican Nationals* (*Mexico v. United States*), 2004 ICJ.

85. Louis Henkin, *Provisional Measures, US Treaty Obligations, and the States,* 92 Am. J. Int'l L. 679 (1998); Carlos Manuel Vázquez, *Breard and the Federal Power to Require Compliance with ICJ Orders of Provisional Measures,* 92 Am. J. Int'l L. 683 (1998); Anne-Marie Slaughter, *Court to Court,* 92 Am. J. Int'l L. 708 (1998).

86. William N. Eskridge Jr. & Philip P. Frickey, *Quasi-Constitutional Law: Clear Statement Rules as Constitutional Lawmaking,* 45 Vand. L. Rev. 593, 597 (1992).

CHAPTER EIGHT

1. See Sen. Jon Kyl, *Maintaining "Peace through Strength": A Rejection of the Comprehensive Test Ban Treaty,* 37 Harv. J. on Legis. 325 (2000).

2. See Cong. Research Serv., 103d Cong., 1st Sess., Treaties and Other International Agreements: The Role of the United States Senate 15 (Comm. Print 1993) [hereinafter 1993 Senate Report]. While these nontreaty numbers include both congressional-executive agreements and sole executive agreements, most of them

appear to have undergone approval by both houses of Congress. See id. at 16.

3. Congressional Research Service, Treaties and Other International Agreements: The Role of the United States Senate, S. Prt. 106-71, 106th Cong., 2d Sess. 39 (2001).

4. Louis Henkin, Foreign Affairs and the United States Constitution 217 (1996).

5. Restatement (Third) of the Foreign Relations Law of the United States § 303 cmt. e [hereinafter Restatement (Third)].

6. Henkin, *supra* note 4, at 218.

7. Message of the President of the United States to Congress, H.R. Doc. No. 80-378, at 2 (1947).

8. See Myres S. McDougal & Asher Lans, *Treaties and Congressional-Executive or Presidential Agreements: Interchangeable Instruments of National Policy: I*, 54 Yale L.J. 181, 203–6 (1945).

9. Bruce Ackerman & David Golove, *Is NAFTA Constitutional?* 108 Harv. L. Rev. 799, 811. Professor Golove provides a more complete exegesis of this idea in his individual response to Professor Tribe. See David M. Golove, *Against Free-Form Formalism*, 73 N.Y.U. L. Rev. 1791 (1998).

10. 17 U.S. (4 Wheat.) 316 (1819).

11. See Andrew Jackson, Veto Message, July 10, 1832, in 3 Messages and Papers of the President 1139, 1145 (James D. Richardson ed., 1897).

12. *Printz v. United States,* 521 U.S. 898 (1997) (invalidating federal law that commandeered state executives to carry out federal regulatory scheme).

13. See, e.g., Edwin S. Corwin, The Constitution and World Organization (1944); Quincy Wright, *The United States and International Agreements,* 38 Am. J. Int'l L. 341 (1944); see generally McDougal & Lans, *supra* note 8.

14. *Field v. Clark,* 143 U.S. 649 (1892); *B. Altman & Co. v. United States,* 224 U.S. 583 (1912).

15. As Professor Henkin has suggested, "[o]ne way of rendering treaty making more democratic without constitutional amendment might be to have agreements made by the President if authorized or approved by both houses of Congress," which would serve "the cause of greater democracy." Louis Henkin, Constitutionalism, Democracy, and Foreign Affairs 60 (1990).

16. Henry P. Monaghan, *We the People[s], Original Understanding, and Constitutional Amendment,* 96 Colum. L. Rev. 121, 165–73 (1996) (criticizing recent theories of majoritarian amendments to the Constitution for ignoring antidemocratic features of the Constitution).

17. See Ackerman & Golove, *supra* note 9, at 861–73.

18. See generally Ackerman, We the People: Foundations (1991); Ackerman, We the People: Transformations (1998).

19. Ackerman & Golove, *supra* note 9, at 896.

20. See, e.g., Laurence H. Tribe, *Taking Text and Structure Seriously: Reflections on Free-Form Method in Constitutional Interpretation,* 108 Harv. L. Rev. 1221, 1228–49; Richard A. Posner, Overcoming Law (1995); Michael J. Gerhardt, *Ackermania: The Quest for a Common Law of Higher Lawmaking,* 40 Wm. & Mary L. Rev. 1731 (1999) (book review); Michael Klarman, *Constitutional Fact/Constitution Fiction: A Critique of Bruce Ackerman's Theory of Constitutional Moments,* 44 Stan. L. Rev. 759 (1992) (book review); Suzanna Sherry, *The Ghost of Liberalism Past,* 105 Harv. L. Rev. 918 (1992) (book review). To be sure, Ackerman's thesis has received praise from some, but not many, scholars. See, e.g., Sanford Levinson, *Accounting for Constitutional Change,* 8 Const. Comment. 409, 429 (1991); James Gray Pope, *Republican*

Moments: The Role of Direct Popular Power in the American Constitutional Order, 139 U. Pa. L. Rev. 287, 304 (1990); Mark Tushnet, *The Flag-Burning Episode: An Essay on the Constitution,* 61 U. Colo. L. Rev. 39, 48–53 (1990).

21. James MacGregor Burns, Roosevelt: The Soldier of Freedom 502 (1970).

22. Townsend Hoopes & Douglas Brinkley, FDR and the Creation of the U.N. 164 (1997).

23. To be sure, Ackerman and Golove raise several historical facts that they believe show this link between the 1944 elections and the alleged constitutional moment. They point, for example, to 1944 opinion polls, newspaper editorials, and proposed constitutional amendments in the House that all supported stripping the Senate of its exclusive power over international agreements. They then claim that the House withdrew proposals to achieve this result in exchange for approval of the Bretton Woods agreements by statute. Yet, Ackerman and Golove encounter severe difficulties in showing the necessary linkages that would indicate a constitutional moment: (1) that party leaders chose to make the 1944 elections a referendum on the Senate's treatymaking role; (2) that the electorate understood the 1944 elections to embody this choice; (3) that the president and the House intended to force the Senate to give up its role; and (4) that the Senate understood itself to be accepting interchangeability in allowing the Bretton Woods agreements.

In order to show that these events all occurred and were interlinked, Ackerman and Golove are forced to rest their argument on some very slim reeds indeed. One glaring example is that they make much hay out of small differences in the wordings of the platforms of the political parties (one mentions "treaty or agreement," the other only "agreements and arrangements") in order to claim a real difference between the parties concerning the interchangeability of congressional-executive agreements and treaties. Ackerman & Golove, *supra* note 9, at 884–85. Only by finding a difference between the parties can they claim that the 1944 elections demonstrated any choice of constitutional instruments. Yet they do not show that political leaders or the voters understood this difference in language to signify sharply divergent positions, if any, on interchangeability. Similarly, Ackerman and Golove believe that the timing of the passage of the Bretton Woods agreements by statute, coming as it did after the House considered a proposal to amend the treaty power, evidenced the Senate's acceptance of the "deal" for interchangeability. Yet they can show no historical evidence that any significant actor in the passage of Bretton Woods or of the U.N. Charter, which came shortly thereafter, understood these agreements to represent a constitutional settlement of any sort.

As an interpretive matter, none of these facts standing alone provides historical support for the notion that the voters in 1944 or their elected representatives undertook to engage the nation in a constitutional revolution on a par with the framing or the reconstruction. Newspapers editorialize and popular opinion polls register on any number of issues that never translate into constitutional amendments. Hundreds of proposed amendments are never added to the Constitution. One can never be sure whether these imperfect, and temporary, signals of popular preferences actually amount to the permanent support for a change in the written Constitution unless they actually meet the test for one: approval by two-thirds of the House and Senate and three-quarters of the states. Indeed, Ackerman and Golove cannot show that proposals to eliminate the Senate's monopoly over the treaty power ever had this support, because none ever came to a vote in both houses of Congress. While one amendment to strip the Senate of its exclusive treaty powers passed the House by 288 to 88, 91 Cong. Rec. 4367–68 (1945), these proposals never came to a vote in the

Senate. Ackerman and Golove present no explanation concerning the votes in the House. Was this part of a concerted campaign to strip the Senate of its authority? Or was this vote symbolic, meant only to show that the House was doing something about international agreements?

24. See Hoopes & Brinkley, *supra* note 22, at 162.

25. See, e.g., Franklin D. Roosevelt, Address at Dinner of International Brotherhood of Teamsters, Chauffeurs, Warehousemen and Helpers of America (Sept. 23, 1944), in The Public Papers and Addresses of Franklin D. Roosevelt, 1944–45 Volume: Victory and the Threshold of Peace 284 (Samuel I. Rosenman ed., 1950); Franklin D. Roosevelt, Radio Address at Dinner of Foreign Policy Association (Oct. 21, 1944), in id. at 342.

26. See Dean Acheson, Present at the Creation: My Years in the State Department 104–15 (1969). Secondary sources on Acheson's role likewise are silent about interchangeability and congressional-executive agreements. See, e.g., James Chace, Acheson: the Secretary of State Who Created the American World 97–109 (1998).

27. See, e.g., Burns, *supra* note 21, at 521–31; Frank Freidel, Franklin D. Roosevelt: A Rendezvous with Destiny 556–76 (1990). The definitive biography of FDR, by Kenneth S. Davis, has not reached the 1944 elections. See Kenneth S. Davis, FDR: The Beckoning of Destiny, 1882–1928 (1972); Davis, FDR: The New York Years, 1928–1933 (1985); Davis, FDR: The New Deal Years, 1933–1937 (1986); Davis, FDR: Into the Storm, 1937–1940 (1993).

28. Robert Dallek, Franklin D. Roosevelt and American Foreign Policy, 1932–1945 (1979); see also Robert A. Divine, Roosevelt and World War II (1969).

29. See, e.g., Warren F. Kimball, The Juggler: Franklin Roosevelt as Wartime Statesman (1991); Frederick W. Marks III, Wind over Sand: The Diplomacy of Franklin Roosevelt (1988). Specialized historical works on the home front and on wartime economic policy also show no evidence that interchangeability, the congressional-executive agreement, or the Senate's treaty role was an important part of the Roosevelt administration's thinking about the postwar world. See Alan S. Milward, War, Economy, and Society, 1939–1945 (1977).

30. See, e.g., Freidel, *supra* note 27, at 521–22 (describing Secretary of State Cordell Hull's activities with the senators of the Committee of Eight to develop a bipartisan policy on international organizations).

31. John Lewis Gaddis, Strategies of Containment: A Critical Appraisal of Postwar American National Security Policy (1982); Melvyn Leffler, A Preponderance of Power: National Security, the Truman Administration, and the Cold War (1992); Michael J. Hogan, A Cross of Iron: Harry S. Truman and the Origins of the National Security State, 1945–1954 (1998); see also Daniel Yergin, Shattered Peace: The Origins of the Cold War and the National Security State (1977).

32. Tribe, *supra* note 20, at 1239–45.

33. *INS v. Chadha*, 462 U.S. 919 (1983); *New York v. United States*, 505 U.S. 144 (1992).

34. Tribe, *supra* note 20, at 1272–75.

35. Id. at 1268. To support this proposition, Tribe relies solely on a letter written by his colleague, Anne-Marie Slaughter, to a senator during the Senate's consideration of the WTO. Id. at 1267 n.157. While I respect Professor Slaughter's work, to my knowledge she has never written a scholarly work about the nature of treaties under the American constitutional system, and I am sure that she herself would not hold out her letter as an authoritative examination of the question. While Peter Spiro does not scrutinize the merits of Tribe's distinctions, he likewise expresses surprise

that Tribe would rest a critical part of his argument on a letter from a colleague. See Peter J. Spiro, *Treaties, Executive Agreements, and Constitutional Methods,* 79 Tex. L. Rev. 961 (2001).

36. Henry P. Monaghan, *The Protective Power of the Presidency,* 93 Colum. L. Rev. 1, 4 (1993).

37. Henkin, *supra* note 4, at 195–96. Henkin even maintains that a treaty could "bargain away" Congress's authority to declare war by allowing war to be triggered automatically under certain events. See id. at 196.

38. See, e.g., Harold H. Bruff, *Can Buckley Clear Customs?* 49 Wash. & Lee L. Rev. 1309 (1992); William J. Davey, *The Appointments Clause and International Dispute Settlement Mechanisms: A False Conflict,* 49 Wash. & Lee L. Rev. 1315 (1992).

39. According to Professor Henkin, "[u]nlike the delegations to Congress which give it authority over enumerated substantive areas of national policy, the treaty power is authority to make national policy (regardless of substantive content) by international means and process for an international purpose." Henkin, *supra* note 4, at 191. He concludes that "[m]any matters, then, may appear to be 'reserved to the States' as regards domestic legislation if Congress does not have power to regulate them; but they are not reserved to the states so as to exclude their regulation by international agreement."

40. Restatement (Third), *supra* note 5, at § 301. This definition tracks Article 1 of the Vienna Convention on the Law of Treaties, which the United States has not ratified.

41. See Uruguay Round Agreements Act, 35 U.S.C. § 154 (1994), implementing Agreement on Trade-Related Aspects of Intellectual Property Rights, Apr. 15, 1994, art. 33, Marrakesh Agreement Establishing the World Trade Organization, Annex 1C, Legal Instruments—Results of the Uruguay Round vol. 31, 33 I.L.M. 81, 96 (1994) [hereinafter TRIPs Agreement].

42. See Jesse Choper, Judicial Review and the National Political Process 174–84 (1980). While I have criticized the political safeguards of federalism argument, it was on the ground that the theory erred in claiming that the safeguards excluded judicial review, not on the notion that the structure of the national political process itself protects federalism. See John C. Yoo, *The Judicial Safeguards of Federalism,* 70 S. Cal. L. Rev. 1311, 1380–81 (1997).

43. 469 U.S. 528 (1985).

44. *United States v. Curtiss-Wright,* 299 U.S. 304 (1936); *United States v. Belmont,* 301 U.S. 324 (1937); *United States v. Pink,* 315 U.S. 203 (1942).

45. *Belmont,* 301 U.S. at 330.

46. *American Ins. Assoc. v. Garamendi,* 539 U.S. 396 (2003); *Crosby v. National Foreign Trade Council,* 530 U.S. 363 (2000).

47. Gerald L. Neuman, *The Global Dimension of RFRA,* 14 Const. Commentary 33 (1997).

48. International Covenant on Civil and Political Rights art. 6(5), Dec. 19, 1966, 999 U.N.T.S. 171.

49. See *Stanford v. Kentucky,* 492 U.S. 321 (1978). This rule was recently reversed by the Supreme Court in *Roper v. Simmons,* 125 S. Ct. 1183 (2005).

50. Treaty between the United States of America and the U.S.S.R. on the Elimination of Their Intermediate-Range and Shorter-Range Missiles, Dec. 8, 1987, U.S.-U.S.S.R., 27 I.L.M. 90.

51. Speech by James Madison on Jay's Treaty (Mar. 10, 1796), in 16 Papers of James Madison 258 (J. C. A. Stagg et al. eds., 1989).

52. Id. at 258–59. To prevent a permanent military establishment, Madison argued, the Constitution had vested appropriations in Congress and subjected military

appropriations to a two-year limit, which intentionally coincided with the two-year cycle for House elections. "This is a most important check & security agst. the danger of standing armies, & against the prosecution of a war beyond its rational objects." Id. at 260.

53. According to the Bureau of the Census, in 1999 the sixteen most populous states were (in millions of people): California: 33.1; Texas 20.0; New York 18.2; Florida 15.1; Illinois 12.1; Pennsylvania 12.0; Ohio 11.3; Michigan 9.9; New Jersey 8.1; Georgia 7.8; North Carolina 7.7; Virginia 6.9; Massachusetts 6.2; Indiana 5.9; Washington 5.8; Missouri 5.5. These figures are taken from Census Bureau estimates, available at http://quickfacts.census.gov/qfd/ (last visited Mar. 7, 2001).

54. I conducted this survey by relying on the U.S. Dep't of State, Treaties in Force: A List of Treaties and Other International Agreements of the United States in Force on January 1, 2000 (2000), which groups agreements by subject matter and by party. I then used the Statutes at Large and the United States Treaty Series to verify whether an agreement had undergone the treaty process or the statutory process.

55. Mutual Defense Treaty, Oct. 1, 1953, U.S.-S. Korea, 5 U.S.T. 2368; Mutual Defense Treaty, Aug. 30, 1951, U.S.-Phil., 3 U.S.T. 3947; Treaty of Mutual Cooperation and Security, Jan. 19, 1960, U.S.-Japan, 11 U.S.T. 1632; Mutual Defense Treaty, U.S.-Taiwan (China), Dec. 2, 1954, 6 U.S.T. 433; Southeast Asia Collective Defense Treaty, Sept. 8, 1954, 6 U.S.T. 81, 209 U.N.T.S. 28; Security Treaty (ANZUS Pact), Sept. 1, 1951, 3 U.S.T. 3420, 131 U.N.T.S. 83; Inter-American Treaty of Reciprocal Assistance (Rio Treaty), Sept. 2, 1947, T.I.A.S. No. 1838, 21 U.N.T.S. 77. See also Spiro, *supra* note 35, at 999–1001.

56. See 1993 Senate Report, at 206–7.

57. Treaty on the Final Settlement with Respect to Germany, Sept. 12, 1990, S. Treaty Doc. No. 101-20 (1990), 29 I.L.M. 1186; Protocols to the North Atlantic Treaty of 1949 on the Accession of Poland, Hungary, and the Czech Republic, Dec. 16, 1997, S. Treaty Doc. No. 105-36 (1998).

58. The three significant exceptions appear to be the 1973 Paris agreement ending the Vietnam War, the 1988 agreement settling the Afghanistan conflict, and the 1991 agreement ending the Cambodian conflict. The latter two agreements did not involve use of American troops in combat. While the first did, it was not submitted for approval to Congress, but instead constituted a sole executive agreement that President Nixon appears to have undertaken pursuant to his sole executive powers. See Act of the International Conference on Viet-Nam, Mar. 2, 1973, 24 U.S.T. 485, 935 U.N.T.S. 405.

59. Treaty on Underground Nuclear Explosions for Peaceful Purposes, May 28, 1976, U.S.-U.S.S.R., 15 I.L.M. 891; Treaty Banning Nuclear Weapons Tests in the Atmosphere, in Outer Space, and under Water, Aug. 5, 1963, 14 U.S.T. 131, 480 U.N.T.S. 43; Treaty on the Limitation of Underground Nuclear Weapon Tests, July 3, 1974, U.S.-U.S.S.R., 13 I.L.M. 906; Treaty on the Limitations of Anti-Ballistic Missile Systems, May 26, 1972, U.S.-U.S.S.R., 23 U.S.T. 3435; Treaty on the Non-Proliferation of Nuclear Weapons, done July 1, 1968, 21 U.S.T. 483, 729 U.N.T.S. 161; Treaty between the United States of America and the U.S.S.R. on the Elimination of Their Intermediate-Range and Shorter-Range Missiles, Dec. 8, 1987, U.S.-U.S.S.R., 27 I.L.M. 90; Treaty on Conventional Armed Forces in Europe, done Nov. 19, 1990, S. Treaty Doc. No. 102-8 (1991), 30 I.L.M. 1; Treaty on the Prohibition of the Emplacement of Nuclear Weapons and Other Weapons of Mass Destruction on the Seabed and the Ocean Floor and in the Subsoil Thereof, done Feb. 11, 1971, 23 U.S.T. 701, 955 U.N.T.S. 155. See 1993 Senate Report, at 209–10 (observing that most arms control agreements have been submitted to the Senate as treaties); see also Spiro, *supra* note 35, at 971.

60. Strategic Arms Limitation I Agreement, Pub. L. No. 79-448, 86 Stat. 746.

61. See Phillip R. Trimble & Jack M. Weiss, *The Role of the President, the Senate and Congress with Respect to Arms Control Treaties Concluded by the United States,* 67 Chi.-Kent L. Rev. 645, 657–660 (1991); see also Henkin, *supra* note 4, at 179.

62. See Treaty on Further Reduction and Limitation of Strategic Offensive Arms, Jan. 3, 1993, U.S.-U.S.S.R., S. Treaty Doc. No. 103-1 (1993); Treaty on the Reduction and Limitation of Strategic Offensive Arms, July 31, 1991, U.S.-USSR, S. Treaty Doc. No. 102-20 (1991); Treaty on Armed Conventional Forces in Europe; Flank Document Agreement to the Conventional Armed Forces in Europe Treaty, adopted May 31, 1996, S. Treaty Doc. No. 105-5 (1997), 36 I.L.M. 866; Convention on the Prohibition of Development, Production, Stockpiling and Use of Chemical Weapons and on Their Destruction, Jan. 13, 1993, S. Treaty Doc. No. 103-21 (1993).

63. Convention on the Prohibition of the Use, Stockpiling, Production and Transfer of Anti-Personnel Mines and on Their Destruction, adopted Sept. 18, 1997, 36 I.L.M. 1507; Convention on the Prohibition of the Development, Production and Stockpiling of Bacteriological (Biological) and Toxin Weapons and on Their Destruction, opened for signature Apr. 10, 1972, 26 U.S.T. 583, 1015 U.N.T.S. 163.

64. See Phillip R. Trimble & Alexander W. Koff, *All Fall Down: The Treaty Power in the Clinton Administration,* 16 Berkeley J. Int'l L. 55, 56 (1998).

65. Convention Relative to the Protection of Civilian Persons in Time of War, done Aug. 12, 1949, 6 U.S.T. 3516, 75 U.N.T.S. 287; Geneva Convention Relative to the Treatment of Prisoners of War, done Aug. 12, 1949, 6 U.S.T. 3316, 75 U.N.T.S. 135; Geneva Convention for the Amelioration of the Condition of Wounded, Sick and Shipwrecked Members of Armed Forces at Sea, done Aug. 12, 1949, 6 U.S.T. 3217, 75 U.N.T.S. 85; Geneva Convention for the Amelioration of the Condition of the Wounded and Sick in Armed Forces in the Field, done Aug. 12, 1949, 6 U.S.T. 3114, 75 U.N.T.S. 31; Convention of July 27, 1929, Relative to the Treatment of Prisoners of War, July 27, 1929, 47 Stat. 2021; Convention Respecting the Rights and Duties of Neutral Powers and Persons in Case of War on Land, Oct. 18, 1907, 36 Stat. 2310; Convention Respecting the Laws and Customs of War on Land, Oct. 18, 1907, 36 Stat. 2277; Convention with Respect to the Laws and Customs of War on Land, July 29, 1899, 32 Stat. 1803; see also Spiro, *supra* note 35, at 999–1002.

66. International Covenant on Civil and Political Rights, *supra* note 48, at 171; Convention on the Prevention and Punishment of the Crime of Genocide, Dec. 9, 1948, S. Exec. Doc. O, 81-1, S. Exec. Doc. B, 91-2, 78 U.N.T.S. 277 (entered into force for U.S., Feb. 23, 1989); Convention against Torture and Other Cruel, Inhuman, or Degrading Treatment or Punishment, entered into force June 26, 1987 (for U.S., Nov. 20, 1994), S. Treaty Doc. No. 100-20 (1988), 1465 U.N.T.S. 113; International Convention on the Elimination of All Forms of Racial Discrimination, opened for signature Mar. 7, 1966, S. Exec. Doc. C, 95-2 (1978), 660 U.N.T.S. 195 (entered into force for U.S., Nov. 20, 1994); Convention on the Elimination of All Forms of Discrimination against Women, Dec. 18, 1979, 1249 U.N.T.S. 13; International Covenant on Economic, Social and Cultural Rights, adopted Dec. 16, 1966, 993 U.N.T.S. 3; American Convention on Human Rights, Aug. 27, 1979, 1144 U.N.T.S. 123; Convention on the Rights of the Child, adopted Nov. 20, 1989, 28 I.L.M. 1448.

67. See Duane Tananbaum, The Bricker Amendment Controversy: A Test of Eisenhower's Political Leadership 15 (1988). For a review of other examples of Senate refusal to approve human rights agreements, see Natalie Hevener Kaufman, Human Rights Treaties and the Senate: A History of Opposition (1990).

68. This information is all the more striking in light of the fact that several significant treaties have yet to be approved by the Senate decades after they were submitted. The International Labor Organization Convention No. 87, for example, has been awaiting Senate approval since 1949; the International Convention on Economic, Social and Cultural Rights, since 1978; the American Convention on Human Rights, since 1978; and the Convention on the Elimination of All Forms of Discrimination against Women, since 1980.

69. See, e.g., *Holmes v. Jennison*, 39 U.S. (14 Pet.) 540 (1840); *Terlinden v. Ames*, 184 U.S. 270 (1902); *Valentine v. United States*, 299 U.S. 5 (1936).

70. See Restatement (Third), *supra* note 5, at § 474.

71. For a discussion of the constitutional issues arising from this early extradition controversy, see Ruth Wedgwood, *The Revolutionary Martyrdom of Jonathan Robbins*, 100 Yale L.J. 229 (1990).

72. See 1993 Senate Report, at 227.

73. See *Ntakirutimana v. Reno*, 184 F.3d 419 (5th Cir. 1999). The executive agreements can be found as: Agreement between the United States of America and the International Tribunal for the Prosecution of Persons Responsible for Genocide and Other Serious Violations of International Humanitarian Law Committed in the Territory of Rwanda and Rwandan Citizens Responsible for Genocide and Other Such Violations Committed in the Territory of Neighbouring States, Jan. 24, 1995, T.I.A.S. No. 12601; Agreement between the United States of America and the International Tribunal for the Prosecution of Persons Responsible for Genocide and Other Serious Violations of International Humanitarian Law in the Territory of the Former Yugoslavia, Oct. 5, 1994, T.I.A.S. No. 12570. The statute allowing such agreements is the National Defense Authorization Act for Fiscal Year 1996, Pub. L. No. 104-106, § 1342, 110 Stat. 186, 486.

74. *Ntakirutimana*, 184 F.3d at 436 (DeMoss, J., dissenting). Judge DeMoss also pointed out that the expansion of the extradition statute to include the Rwanda and former Yugoslavia tribunals had occurred by way of a last-minute attachment to non-relevant legislation, without any hearings, committee consideration, or floor debate of the provisions. For scholarly discussion of *Ntakirutimana*, see Evan J. Wallach, *Extradition to the Rwandan War Crimes Tribunal: Is Another Treaty Required?* 3 UCLA J. Int'l L. & Foreign Aff. 59 (1998); Panayiota Alexandropoulos, Note, *Enforceability of Executive-Congressional Agreements in Lieu of an Article II Treaty for Purposes of Extradition: Elizaphan Ntakirutimana v. Janet Reno*, 45 Villa. L. Rev. 107 (2000).

75. See United Nations Framework Convention on Climate Change, done May 9, 1992, S. Treaty Doc. No. 102-38 (1992), 31 I.L.M. 849; The Antarctic Treaty, Dec. 1, 1959, 12 U.S.T. 794, 402 U.N.T.S. 71; Montreal Protocol on Substances that Deplete the Ozone Layer, adopted June 29, 1990, 30 I.L.M. 537; Vienna Convention for the Protection of the Ozone Layer, opened for signature Mar. 22, 1985, 26 I.L.M. 1516; Convention on Long-Range Transboundary Air Pollution, Nov. 13, 1979, 18 I.L.M. 1442; Treaty on Principles Governing the Activities of States in the Exploration and Use of Outer Space, Including the Moon and Other Celestial Bodies, done Jan. 27, 1967, 18 U.S.T. 2410, 610 U.N.T.S. 205; Agreement on the Conservation of Polar Bears, done Nov. 15, 1973, 27 U.S.T. 3918, 13 I.L.M. 13; Convention for the Conservation of Antarctic Seals, June 1, 1972, 29 U.S.T. 441, 11 I.L.M. 251; Benelux Convention concerning Hunting and the Protection of Birds, June 10, 1970, 847 U.N.T.S. 255; International Convention for the Protection of Birds, Oct. 18, 1950, 638 U.N.T.S. 185; International Convention for the Regulation of Whaling, Dec. 2, 1946, 62 Stat. 1716, 161 U.N.T.S. 72.

76. See Convention on Biological Diversity, done June 5, 1992, S. Treaty Doc. No. 103-20 (1993), 31 I.L.M. 818; United Nations Framework Convention on Climate Change.

77. President Reagan declined to sign the United Nations Convention on the Law of the Sea, Oct. 7, 1982, and hence prevented Congress from considering the agreement. Some more minor agreements involving the rules that apply at sea have been done as statutes, see, e.g., Convention for the Unification of Certain Rules with Respect to Assistance and Salvage at Sea, Sept. 23, 1910, 37 Stat. 1658, 1 Bevans 780, while others have been done as treaties, see, e.g., Convention on the High Seas, done Apr. 29, 1958, 13 U.S.T. 2312, 450 U.N.T.S. 82. President Clinton submitted the follow-on agreements to the Law of the Sea Convention to the Senate for approval as a treaty. See Bernard H. Oxman, *The Law of the Sea Convention,* ASIL Newsletter (Nov.-Dec. 1994).

78. Tax treaties might seem to be the exception that disproves this rule. Tax is certainly a matter of international economics and commerce, and yet our agreements with other nations on taxation usually assume the treaty form. It appears, however, that tax treaties do not apply domestically of their own force—in other words, they are non-self-executing. Rather, Congress has chosen to implement tax treaty obligations through provisions of the Internal Revenue Code. *See* I.R.C. §§ 894, 7852(d) (2000). Moreover, Congress regularly overrides tax treaty obligations through its normal tax statutes. See generally David Sachs, *Is the 19th Century Doctrine of Treaty Override Good Law for Modern Day Tax Treaties?* 47 Tax Law. 867 (1994) (examining the tax-treaty-override doctrine and arguing for its termination or modification). This practice indicates that the political branches have continued to use legislation, rather than treaties alone, to regulate international economics and commerce that would usually fall within Congress's Article I powers. For an examination of current international tax treaty issues, see, e.g., Reuven S. Avi-Yonah, *The Structure of International Taxation: A Proposal for Simplification,* 74 Tex. L. Rev. 1301 (1996); Julie Roin, *Rethinking Tax Treaties in a Strategic World with Disparate Tax Systems,* 81 Va. L. Rev. 1753 (1995).

CHAPTER NINE

1. 2 Documentary History of the Ratification of the Constitution 528 (John P. Kaminski & Gaspare J. Saladino eds., 1986).

2. John Hart Ely, War and Responsibility: Constitutional Lessons of Vietnam and Its Aftermath 3 (1993).

3. Michael J. Glennon, Constitutional Diplomacy 80–81, 84 (1990).

4. Abram Chayes & Antonia Handler Chayes, The New Sovereignty: Compliance with International Regulatory Agreements 15 (1995).

5. Ruth Wedgwood et al., *The United States and the Statute of Rome,* 95 Am. J. Int'l L. 124 (2001).

6. Madeline Morris, *High Crimes and Misconceptions: The ICC & Non-Party States,* 64 Law & Contemp. Probs. 13 (2001).

7. Ruth Wedgwood, *The Irresolution of Rome,* 64 Law & Contemp. Probs. 193, 194 (2001).

8. Jack Goldsmith, *The Self-Defeating International Criminal Court,* 70 U. Chi. L. Rev. 89 (2003).

9. American Servicemens' Protection Act, Pub. L. No. 107-206, 116 Stat. 899 (2002); Secretary Powell is quoted in Wedgwood, *supra* note 7, at 195–96.

10. John Bolton, *Should We Take Global Governance Seriously?* 1 Chi. J. Int'l L.

205, 221 (2000).

11. Joseph S. Nye Jr., The Paradox of American Power: Why the World's Only Superpower Can't Go it Alone 109 (2002).

12. Anne-Marie Slaughter, *Building Global Democracy*, 1 Chi. J. Int'l L. 223 (2000).

13. Bruce Ackerman, We the People: Transformations 281 (1998).

14. See *A. L. A. Schechter Poultry Co. v. United States*, 295 U.S. 495 (1935); *United States v. Butler*, 297 U.S. 1 (1936).

15. On the origins of the plan, see William E. Leuchtenburg, The Supreme Court Reborn: The Constitutional Revolution in the Age of Roosevelt 82–162 (1995).

16. Barry Cushman, Rethinking the New Deal Court: The Structure of a Constitutional Revolution 3 (1998).

17. Cass R. Sunstein, *Constitutionalism after the New Deal*, 101 Harv. L. Rev. 421, 447–48 (1987).

18. See, e.g., Gary Lawson, *The Rise and Rise of the Administrative State*, 107 Harv. L. Rev. 1231 (1994).

19. John O. McGinnis & Mark L. Movsesian, *The World Trade Constitution*, 114 Harv. L. Rev. 511 (2000).

20. *United States v. Lopez*, 514 U.S. 549 (1995) (invalidating Gun Free School Zones Act); *United States v. Morrison*, 529 U.S. 598 (2000) (invalidating Violence against Women Act).

21. See, e.g., Lawson, *supra* note 18; Steven Calabresi & Saikrishna Prakash, *The President's Power to Execute the Laws*, 104 Yale L.J. 541 (1994).

INDEX

Acheson, Dean, 263
Ackerman, Bruce: and Article V, 260; and
congressional-executive agreements,
284; and constitutional interpretation,
261–62, 265; and *Field v. Clark & B.
Altman*, 256; and "interchangeability,"
251, 259, 262–63; and *McCulloch v.
Maryland*, 255; and the Necessary and
Proper Clause, 254; and the New Deal
era, 260–61; and postwar construction,
264; and Roosevelt's third reelection,
262; and the Treaty Clause, 185, 265
Adams, John, 179, 288; *Thoughts on
Government*, 64–65
Adams, Willi Paul, Revolutionary War–era
state constitutions, 63
Afghanistan, vii, 12, 143, 155–57, 160–64,
169, 173, 246; and Taliban, 154, 163, 169,
205, 211–13
Agreement on Trade-Related Aspects of
International Property Rights, Article
33, 275
Agricultural Adjustment Act, 300
al Qaeda, x, 154, 156, 163, 169, 170, 205,
211–13
Anglo-Dutch wars: Second Anglo-Dutch
War (1665–67), 49; Third Anglo-Dutch
War (1672–74), 50
Annapolis Convention, 83
Anti-Ballistic Missile (ABM) Treaty, 205,
206, 209; and arms control, 285; Clinton
administration's interpretation of, 5,
15, 208, 210; and interpretation and
termination of, 188, 190, 210–11, 213,
295; and legislative history of, 197;

Reagan administration's interpretation
of, 191–94, 208, 210
Appointments Clause, 176–81, 184–86, 265,
267, 272
Appropriations Clause, 105, 219, 220
Armitage, David, 150
Articles of Confederation, viii, 27, 73, 78,
88, 133, 141, 153, 276, 295; Article II, 75;
Article VI, 75, 76–77; Article IX, 74–77,
108, 148; and Continental Congress (*see*
Continental Congress); and foreign
affairs powers, 24; and treaty power,
78–79; and *Ware v. Hylton*, 238
Australian–New Zealand–U.S. Agreement,
285

B. Altman & Co. v. United States, 256–57
Bailyn, Bernard, 38, 61; administration
of the English colonies, 57; and the
Framers' intellectual origins, 36;
*Ideological Origins of the American
Revolution*, 29
Baker v. Carr, *228*
Banning, Lance, 132
Belarus, and 1997 Memorandum of
Understanding with the United States,
207
Berger, Raoul, 264
Bestor, Arthur, and Continental Congress,
73
Bill of Rights, 115, 116–17, 248, 296;
Eighth Amendment, 278; Eleventh
Amendment, 235–36; Fifteenth
Amendment, 254; Fifth Amendment of,
151; Fourteenth Amendment, Section II,

357